A Guide to Garden Visits

About the Author

Judith Hitching's love of gardening, garden history, music, old houses, books and travel led her to write this book. The guide bounces with her enthusiasm and sense of fun as she describes gardens where the personality of the owner shines through. She is a hotelier and an award-winning cook and delights in finding places to stay where she feels relaxed and comfortable, and can spend the evening with companionable hosts, just as she enjoys pampering her own guests in her 17th-century Cotswold village house. As well as constantly developing her own garden, she has designed many gardens for others, and is currently helping her three daughters turn their London gardens into colourful havens.

A Guide to Garden Visits

with welcoming places to stay

Judith Hitching

MICHAEL JOSEPH
LONDON

MICHAEL JOSEPH LTD
ORDNANCE SURVEY

Published by the Penguin Group
27 Wrights Lane, London W8 5TZ
Viking Penguin Inc., 375 Hudson Street, New York, New York 10014, USA
Penguin Books Australia Ltd, Ringwood, Victoria, Australia
Penguin Books Canada Ltd, 10 Alcorn Avenue, Toronto, Ontario, Canada M4V 3B2
Penguin Books (NZ) Ltd, 182–190 Wairau Road, Auckland 10, New Zealand

Penguin Books Ltd, Registered Offices: Harmondsworth, Middlesex, England

First Published 1997
1 3 5 7 9 10 8 6 4 2

Copyright © Text by Judith Hitching 1997
Maps © Crown copyright, 1997

Ordnance Survey and Landranger are registered trade marks
and the OS symbol is a trade mark of Ordnance Survey
Ordnance Survey, Romsey Road, Maybush, Southampton, SO16 4GU

Typeset in Monotype Perpetua and Gill Sans
Printed in England by Clays Ltd, St Ives plc

A CIP catalogue record for this book is available from the British Library

ISBN 0 7181 4186 5

The moral right of the author has been asserted

Whilst every care has been taken to ensure the accuracy of the route directions and
mapping, the publishers cannot accept responsibility for errors or omissions.

Contents

About this Guide

Visiting gardens is my great pleasure. A perfect weekend break for me is strolling around a garden, admiring the ingenuity and flair of the owners, buying a rare plant in an interesting nursery, stopping at a pretty pub for lunch, poking about in a junk shop or second-hand bookshop and, at the end of a lovely day, staying somewhere small, friendly and comfortable where I am cosseted by kind hosts, and can enjoy a delicious meal.

All this can take a bit of arranging. Which gardens will be open? How do I find somewhere really nice to stay that isn't too far from the gardens? What other places nearby would be fun to visit? Are there any good specialist nurseries in the area? And what shall I do if it's bucketing down with rain?

To plan a short break like this, you usually have to consult a dozen or more maps, guides and directories (and, in my car at least, they tend to roll around with the picnic, newly acquired plants and the dog). So that's why I wrote this guide. Between two covers, I have described my favourite gardens, included marvellous B&Bs where you will be spoilt, and arranged each visit so that you don't have to spend too much time on the road, but for when you are driving, I have suggested some wonderful music you might like to listen to – something appropriate to the local landscape and gardens.

The Gardens

There are more than 3500 gardens in the UK open to the public, but often only for the occasional charity afternoon within the National Gardens Scheme (NGS), or for the Red Cross. Between them, splendidly, they raise more than £2 million a year, and some of these private gardens may well have open days to coincide with your visit.

I decided, however, that if you want to take a short break, you want to be certain that the gardens locally will be open when you're there. Virtually all the gardens described in this book are either open regularly or have owners who welcome visitors by appointment. Most of the latter are happy to arrange times over the telephone, but please be as flexible and considerate as you can to fit in with them. A few owners prefer to have an appointment made in writing, in which case a SAE would be appreciated. Remember that dogs are rarely welcome in the gardens themselves, although some owners allow them on leads in parkland or in woods. And please restrain yourself in the matter of snitching cuttings and seed pods – just don't do it, and don't let your mother-in-law do it either.

I have included about 500 gardens and nurseries in this book. They include many of the greatest gardens in England and Wales, together with many less well-known ones – little gems on which their owners have lavished time and tender loving care. Some of the nurseries are very small and special, and often a one-man band. It's best to telephone ahead to check that they are open.

Visits

England and Wales have been divided up into 50 separate visits, and each one has its own map especially prepared for the book by Ordnance Survey® (OS), which I'm sure you will find particularly helpful. If you want a more detailed map I have given the appropriate number of the OS Landranger® map, the main map for each visit being set in bold. The little arrows on the map edges point you towards an adjoining visit so that some gardens, B&Bs and other entertainments can be interchangeable. All care has been taken to ensure that most up-to-date information has been included in this guide, but inevitably some late amendments will have to wait for the next edition.

Where to Stay

During the summer I welcome paying guests to my Cotswold home so I have a pretty good idea of what most of you will be looking for – a comfortable bedroom and your own bathroom in an interesting house in pleasant surroundings, good food and nothing too expensive. In most of the homes and hotels I have chosen, the price per person per B&B night is from less than £20 to £35. Occasionally, if I think the place is special, it may be a little more. They are listed in the order of cost per night, from the most (A) to the least expensive, and these relate to the letters on the map. It may be a little more luxurious at the top, and a bit more modest lower down, but I can assure you that everyone who has stayed at any of these places, including myself, has had a lovely time. Most offer an evening meal, which might be a gourmet dinner costing perhaps £20, or a light supper for around £10. When you ring up, you will discover what is available, or if you should plan to eat out locally.

What Else to Enjoy

In each visit I have included a wide variety of other interesting things to look out for. There are stately homes and National Trust (NT) properties to go round if it's wet, craft centres, local museums, antique shops – anything that took my fancy, including some splendid old pubs. I also found some very special places where one can indulge in a meal to remember.

Lastly, don't forget that gardens are not just flower beds, lawns and trees; they are living works of art, created and much loved by the gardener. They change constantly through the seasons and suffer in bad weather so cannot always be at their best. We have a wealth of wonderful gardens in England and Wales (and I hope to write about the fabulous Scottish and Irish ones soon) so do get out and enjoy them. And when you find some undiscovered little gems, please write and tell me about them.

Judith Hitching
Gower's Close

Land's End

On the farthest south-west tip of England, where sub-tropical species flourish in the warming Gulf Stream, this visit has an almost embarrassing number of gardens worth visiting. Think luxuriant: palm trees and bamboos and, in spring, rhododendrons and azaleas which overwhelm the eye. The climate invites a plant-lover to see rare shrubs and other tender species thriving as nowhere else in Britain. When you get there, it is worth buying the *Gardens of Cornwall* coloured guide and map (£1), produced by Cornwall Gardens Society and the Cornwall Tourist Board with support from the National Trust. It points the way to even more gardens than I have chosen. Play something lush and lavish in your car during the long journey. Rachmaninov's Symphony No. 2, maybe. Make sure André Previn is the conductor.

OS maps: Landrangers 203, **204**

Gardens

Opening times: in larger gardens, and in NT properties, last admissions are usually 30–45 minutes before the garden closes. Admission charges are a guide to what one adult can expect to pay to go round the garden. It sometimes varies with the season or days of the week. When the house is also open to the public, there is usually an additional charge.

I TRENGWAINTON GARDEN (NT)

Penzance   Tel 01736 63021

Wed–Sat, March to Oct, 10.30–5.30 (5.00 Mar and Oct). £2.60
From Penzance go NW on A3071 for 1m; turn R where signed.

Lt. Col. Edward Bolitho, whose family have lived here since 1857, oversees this large shrub garden. Spectacular in spring, with its amazing collection of magnolias, rhododendrons and camellias, it is picturesque all the year, with lawns that look down to the sea, and a vista through the trees to St

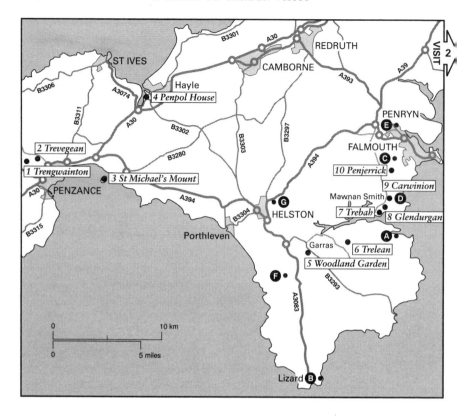

Michael's Mount. A unique series of five walled gardens contain tender plants that will fascinate any plant-lover. The stream and bog garden have their own charm.

2   **TREVEGEAN**   Penzance   Tel 01736 67407

By appointment, April to July. £1
From Penzance by-pass take minor road signed Treneere; garden at 9 Manor Way, Heamoor. Ask owner for final directions.

Unusually for gardens open in Cornwall, this is small – just one-third of an acre. It is an amazing discovery, completely hidden in the suburbs of Penzance by trees and hedges which surround a number of other concealed areas, some formal, some informal. Brick paths, edged with box, lead to a topiary garden, and shrub/perennial displays. Mr and Mrs Cousins's garden has won many awards, and plants are often for sale.

While you are in the area, you might like to find **Trewidden Nursery.**
It is signposted by name off the Penzance distributor road towards Land's
End; entrance is on R past crossroad to Newlyn (Tel 01736 67407). It
specialises in trees and shrubs. The adjoining woodland garden is best in
spring, particularly for camellias and magnolias (see *M. x veitchii*, thought to
be the largest in Britain).

A specialist nursery in the area is **Hardy Exotics Nursery**, Gilly Lane,
Whitecross, Penzance (Tel 01736 740660). It is excellent for unusual conservatory and patio plants.

3   ST MICHAEL'S MOUNT (NT)
nr Marazion   Tel 01736 710507

Garden at weekends, April to Oct, 10.30–5.30. £1.50
From Penzance go E on A30 for 1½m, turn R signed Marazion for 1m.
Garden ½m off-shore via causeway open for about 4 hours at low tide; other-
wise via passenger ferry except in unsuitable weather.

This is an unmissable site – a medieval castle on a granite outcrop with a
fine interior and a magical history. The gardens are still privately owned by
the St Aubyn family. First developed and planted in the 18th century, using
walls and terraces precipitously, sub-tropical species thrive despite gales and
sea spray. In spring, enjoy the wild narcissus, while in summer, yuccas,
geraniums, euryops, hebes, phormiums, and fuchsias abound. Around the
garden boundaries, native wild flowers are encouraged.

4   PENPOL HOUSE   Hayle   Tel 01736 753146

By appointment, May to July. £2
From St Ives go SE on A3074 for 4m. Garden in Penpol Avenue, Hayle. Ask
owner for final directions.

Major and Mrs Ellis's old-fashioned 3-acre garden is unusual in Cornwall,
having alkaline soil. Their 16th-century house is on a hill above the town
of Hayle, surrounded by sweeping lawns and herbaceous borders, and
self-contained gardens framed by stone walls, or hedges of box and yew.
Roses clamber everywhere. Granite troughs punctuate the garden. There
is an enchanting pond. Everywhere you can find something to spark the
imagination.

5 **WOODLAND GARDEN** Garras   Tel 01326 221295

Sats, April to Sept, 2–5, and by appointment. £1
From Helston go SE on A3083 for 2½m. Turn L on B3293 for 1½m.
Garden signed on R, ½m beyond Garras.

Mr and Mrs Froggatt have created this informal 2½-acre garden over the past 15 years, and continue with their planting and development, so that each year there is something new. Set in a woodland valley, the garden is at its peak in spring, with camellias, rhododendrons, magnolias, flowering trees and shrubs, primulas, and a succession of wild daffodils, primroses and bluebells. The garden is a sanctuary for the local fauna and more than 40 species of birds can be spotted here; wild flowers are encouraged (there are many unusual species to tempt the plant-lover), and are deliberately left to reproduce. No dogs in the garden, but you can have a fine walk nearby on Goonhilly Downs, especially beautiful in July to September when the heather is out.

6 **TRELEAN** St Martin-in-Meneage   Tel 01326 231255

By appointment May to Oct. £1.50
From Helston go SE on A3083 for 2½m. Turn L on B3293 for 2½ m. Turn
L on minor road signed Newtown for 1½m, and then turn L in village signed
St Martin for ½m. At St Martin P.O. turn R for 1½m. Garden signed on L.

George Witherwick started this garden in 1980, when it was a wilderness of trees and bracken on a steep hillside. Today it is a mature 3-acre informal garden within 18-acre surroundings designated an Area of Outstanding Natural Beauty, with new owners, Richard and Kristine Harper. Notable both for plant-lovers and for more casual garden visitors, it has been widely written about. Everyone can enjoy the winding walk along the Helford river, with two areas of wood, one of beech and one of oak, the marvellous foliage colour schemes (particularly in autumn) created by careful plantings, and the views. Specialists will note rare trees and shrubs: nothofagus, acers, conifers, eucalyptus, cistus, enkianthus and robinias. The Harpers have exciting new plans to develop the garden further.

7 **TREBAH** Mawnan Smith   Tel 01326 250448

Daily all year, 10–5.30. £2.90
From Falmouth go S on minor road for 5m. Garden signed 1m SW of Mawnan
Smith.

Listed as one of Cornwall's five great gardens, Major and Mrs J.A. Hibbert's spectacular ravine garden, now 150 years old, covers 25 acres and leads down a steep valley to the sea. From the lawns at the top of the garden you view a scene of sub-tropical jungle, with tall palms towering above rhododendrons, camellias and vast magnolia trees. Bananas and bamboo grow as in a rain forest, where glades of huge tree ferns are among a vast collection of rare sub-tropical trees and shrubs. A hydrangea collection covering more than 2 acres supplies colour when the spring shrubs have finished flowering. The paths drop down the valley to a little sheltered cove, where there is a poignant memorial to all the men from Trebah who left this magical haven and tiny jetty to take part in the Dunkirk landings and failed to return. If only more gardens had the same policy about dogs – they are welcomed, on leads of course, and their owners presented with a free pooper-scooper and tidy-up bag. Sit down to tea, coffee and refreshments.

8 GLENDURGAN GARDEN (NT)

Mawnan Smith   Tel 01326 250906

Tues–Sat and BHs, May to Oct, 10.30–5.30. £2.80
From Falmouth go S on minor road for 5m. Garden well signed ½ m SW of
Mawnan Smith.

This informal 28-acre garden leads steeply down to the enchanting waterside hamlet of Durgan, once famous for the many kinds of fish and shellfish landed here. Alfred and Sarah Fox lived in a thatched cottage at the top of the valley. In 1826, they began to clear the hillsides and plant trees and orchards, digging out ponds and setting out the original cherry laurel maze. Ten years later the cottage burned down (it was getting a bit small for them anyway; they had 12 children) and a far larger house was built, with a school. George Fox took over in 1890, adding more ornamental trees and shrubs. Future Fox generations continued to tend and plant the garden (they also created the garden at Penjerrick), which was given to the NT in 1962. It is absolutely best viewed in spring, when violets and primroses line the paths – beautifully cobbled along steepest bits and the steps, to stop you slipping. A majestic *Liriodendron tulipifera* extends its huge arms out over one of the paths, a wonderfully exciting picture when in flower. A bamboo bridge adds to the jungle-illusion in amongst the tree ferns. A nostalgic little family dogs' graveyard lies along the schoolroom walk. Visiting children will have fun on the Giant's Stride, a rope swing, and the maze. No dogs.

9 CARWINION

Mawnan Smith (*see also* Where to Stay)   Tel 01326 250258

Daily all year, 10–5.30. £2

From Falmouth go S on minor road for 5m. In Mawnan Smith take road past the Red Lion for 500 yds. Garden signed on R.

Anthony Rogers is the latest descendant of a family which has been living at Carwinion since the 18th century, and his 10-acre sub-tropical valley garden is deliberately left untended to encourage a profusion of wild flowers, grasses, and ferns. Justifiably designated a conservation area, the garden also contains one of England's largest collection of bamboos, with more than 100 varieties, all labelled. An immense forest of gunneras, their huge leaves creating a veiled grey gloom on a sunny day (and umbrellas during a shower), are dominated by the variety *G. manicata*, its crown as large as a human body. Plants are for sale, and there is an excellent garden map.

10 PENJERRICK nr Falmouth   Tel 01872 870105

Sun, Wed, Fri, March to Sept, 1.30–4.30, and by appointment. £1

From Falmouth go S on minor road for 2m. Garden signed in Penjerrick, opposite Penmorvah Hotel.

Best in spring, when the Barclayi and Penjerrick rhododendron hybrids are in bloom, Rachel Morin's 15-acre garden has considerable historical and botanical interest, and fine views to the sea. Created by the Fox family (*see* Glendurgan) 200 years ago from specimens collected abroad, camellias, magnolias, azaleas, bamboos and magnificent trees (including the second largest beech in England) abound in the upper garden. Lower down the valley is a wild woodland area with ponds, and tree ferns that date back almost to the original garden planting.

There are two good nurseries in the NW of this visit. **Church Town Nursery,** in Perranarworthal on the A39 (Tel 01872 863033), is a delightful, old-fashioned, inexpensive nursery that will tempt your wallet. Or you might want to drive a further 5m W to find **Burncoose Nurseries.** They are just off the A393 S of Gwennap (Tel 01290 86112). World famous and 1994 Gold Medallist winner at the Chelsea Flower Show, they offer more than 2,000 varieties of trees, shrubs and herbaceous plants. The gardens alongside the nursery were started about 1750 by the Williams family of Caerhays. The centre of the garden was devastated by the great storm in 1979, but the replanting is now maturing well. It's well worth walking around the garden in spring and autumn, and the plants are excellent value.

Where to Stay

All B&B prices are approximate per person, sharing a double/twin room usually with private or en suite facilities. It is a good idea to ask for any special requirements when booking.

A TREGILDRY HOTEL   Tel 01326 231378

Lynne & Huw Phillips, Gillan, Manaccan, Helston, Cornwall TR12 6HG.

This long-established family-run hotel, reached by a narrow country road, is set gloriously in 4-acre grounds overlooking Gillan Creek, Helford River, Falmouth Bay and beyond. Below is a private cove for swimming or dinghy sailing, or just watching the abundant bird life. Expect to meet lots of other garden lovers – almost everyone staying is on Cornwall's garden trail. All the 10 double bedrooms are well furnished (some are larger than others, ask), and most have marvellous views. Food is excellent, with a varied restaurant menu. Most guests eat in, as Tregildry is very much off the beaten track. Smoking in lounge and bar only. You should discuss dogs and children in advance. B&B £40–£45; D, B&B from £50.

B LANDEWEDNACK HOUSE   Tel 01326 290909

Peter & Marion Stanley, Church Cove, The Lizard, Cornwall TR12 7PQ.

This 17th-century former rectory has been recently restored to give exceptional comfort – a four-poster room, a stunning sea view room and 2 other bedrooms (1 twin, 1 single), all equally enticing with bathrooms that include jacuzzi. The peaceful tranquillity of the house and garden, with panoramic views over the Lizard Peninsula (an Area of Outstanding Natural Beauty), and the backcloth of the sea beyond the 1½-acre walled garden makes for an idyllic stay. Gourmet dinners (from £13.95) by arrangement. No smoking, no dogs, no children. B&B £30–£40.

C CRILL MANOR HOTEL   Tel 01326 211229

Peter & Jo Roberts, Budock Water, Falmouth, Cornwall TR11 5BL.

A highly rated, peaceful hotel and family home combined, with comfortably furnished lounges and bar, Crill Manor is a late 19th-century house set in a south-facing 1-acre garden featuring the many shrubs and plants that thrive in the famously mild Cornish climate. It is secluded and tranquil, and has its own heated swimming pool open from June to September. A freshly-prepared 5-course dinner, with good choice on the table d'hôte menu (£14.50, licensed), is served from 7 p.m. The 12 comfy bedrooms (including 2 single) have modern furnishings. No dogs, children should be over 10, smoking in the lounge only. B&B £30–£39.

D CARWINION   (*see* Garden 9)   Tel 01326 250258

Anthony Rogers, Mawnan Smith, Nr Falmouth, Cornwall TR11 5JA.

The atmosphere of this lovely house, set in its wonderful gardens, is entrancing in the slightly faded manner of any home lived in by many generations of the same family: portraits, objets d'art and collections of heirlooms are all there to be enjoyed. Three large en suite bedrooms have wonderful views and every comfort. Children and dogs welcome, and you can smoke. Evening meals £15, bring your own wine. A lift is provided for wheelchairs. B&B £25.

E PROSPECT HOUSE   Tel 01326 373198

Cliff Paul & Barry Sheppard, 1 Church Road, Penryn, Cornwall TR10 8DA.

Immaculately restored, packed with antiques, this comfortably furnished late Georgian "Gentleman's Residence" is listed Grade II. Cliff and Barry are keen gardeners as well as great hosts, and say that at least half their guests come to visit Cornwall's gardens. The Prospect House garden itself, alas, was recently devastated by the National Rivers Authority in a flood relief scheme. It has been newly landscaped and replanted, and is still very pleasant, but will take a couple of years to re-establish. There are 3 attractive bedrooms, and a drawing-room, well provided with books about the area. Restricted smoking. B&B only, but plenty of good places nearby to eat out in the evenings. Dogs and children over 12 welcome. B&B £24–£30.

F TREGADDRA FARM   Tel 01326 240235

June Lugg, Cury, Helston, Cornwall TR12 7BB.

Beautifully furnished and friendly 18th-century farmhouse set in a well-kept garden of winding flower beds. There is a heated outdoor pool for summer, log fires and candlelit dinners on chilly evenings. June makes sure she uses local produce for a traditional English supper (£9) served at 6.30. Four pretty bedrooms (2 with balconies, 1 a romantic four-poster, 1 single). No smoking, no dogs, children welcome. B&B £18.50–£21.50.

G CRASKEN FARMHOUSE   Tel 01326 572670

Jenny Ingram, Falmouth Road, Helston, Cornwall TR13 0PF.

Crasken is a gem. Almost every inch of wall of this 17th-century farmhouse and its outbuildings is covered with roses and climbers: vines, wisteria, honeysuckle, winter-flowering clematis. Guests entering the courtyard through the large oak gates have described it as like 'somewhere in France', 'stepping back in time', and 'an artist's paradise'. In the grounds is a pre-historic settlement. Flowers and shrubs in the garden are mostly cottage-garden, old-fashioned and often unusual. In one area, chickens, ducks, a goose and a goat roam. There are 4 very comfortable bedrooms in the farm-house, some sharing bathrooms, and 3 sensitively converted outbuildings for self-catering or B&B. Breakfasts are outstanding, and sometimes Jenny is able to cook evening meals (£16.50, bring your own wine). Smoking down-stairs. Children should be over 12. Dogs all right in the cottages, but must be very small to be allowed in the house. B&B £17–£24.

What Else to Enjoy

This is a short selection of the many good things recommended in the area by owners of places to stay. Your hosts will certainly be able to provide additional information.

Other Gardens

Massed bedding plants in municipal garden displays do not get much of a mention in this guide. But it so happens that, in this visit, two councils run gardens that far transcend the traditional image.

In **Penzance**, if you want to see a time capsule from 1888, go to **Morrab**

Sub-tropical Garden. Penzance Corporation bought it at that time, and its 3 acres have remained true to the original design by Reginald Upcher

In **Falmouth**, there are 3 municipal gardens, all near the seafront. **Gyllyngdune Gardens** and **Queen Mary Gardens** most nearly conform to what you would expect, being largely formal and ornamental. **Fox Rosehill Gardens**, spread over a 2-acre park, are more ambitious, with well-labelled exotic plants and shrubs that surround paths and lawns. Ask for the plant list – very helpful.

If It's Wet

Cornwall has a myriad of attractions, including no fewer than 14 museums (from tin mines to lighthouses) and art galleries. Everyone recommends a visit to **St Ives**, not just for the – now somewhat touristy – village itself, but for the Tate Gallery's display of modern art, the adjoining Barbara Hepworth Museum, and the gallery of the St Ives Society of Artists, founded in 1927 by artists working the the plein air tradition associated with the Newlyn School.

A little further west along the coast is **Zennor**, with its unique privately owned Wayside Museum. It explores life in the district from 3,000 BC to the 1930s. All the above have parking.

In **Penzance**, the Museum and Art Gallery has undergone a transformation, using the latest multimedia computer technology to recreate life from megalithic to modern times. The art collection is the largest in west Cornwall and includes examples, from 1750 to the present day, of the many painters who have lived in the area.

In **Falmouth**, the Cornwall Maritime Museum gives a fascinating insight into the town's rich maritime history. Pendennis Castle, a bit neat and tidy, is also worth a look.

Eating Out

In the S of the visit, you can't do better than **The Yard Bistro** on the **Trelowarren Estate**, 5m E of Helston, and just past Mawgan on the River Helford. Set in a flower-filled, vine-covered courtyard, with tables outside in good weather, chef Trevor Bayfield offers a blackboard menu with delicious local produce. Allow £20 per head, plus wine (Tel 01326 221595). To the N of the visit, The **Pig 'n' Fish** in Norway Lane, **St Ives**, is a seafood restaurant which has won many awards. Dinner will cost you upwards of £20, plus wine (Tel 01736 794204).

Around Falmouth Bay

Here is the quintessential Cornwall, much of it a listed Area of Outstanding Natural Beauty. Don't miss the Lost Gardens of Heligan, the largest garden reconstruction project in Europe, or the County demonstration gardens at Probus. Try to buy the *Gardens of Cornwall* coloured guide and map (£1), produced by Cornwall Gardens Society. Enjoy the sparkling sea views, and get yourself in a light-hearted mood by playing Jacques Ibert's Divertissement in the car (often coupled with the equally light and charming 'Les Biches' by Poulenc).

OS map: Landranger **204**

Gardens

Opening times: in larger gardens, and in NT properties, last admissions are usually 30–45 minutes before the garden closes. Admission charges are a guide to what one adult can expect to pay to go round the garden. It sometimes varies with the season or days of the week. When the house is also open to the public, there is usually an additional charge.

I   LANTERNS   Mylor   Tel 01326 372007

Daily all year, 11–dusk Collecting box
From Falmouth go NW on A39 for 1½m to Penryn. Turn R signed Mylor Bridge for 2½m and follow signs to Restronquet Passage/Pandora Inn; garden is on R before reaching the waterfront.

Mrs Chapman and her late husband planted this ½-acre estuary garden, now mature and with something of interest in all seasons. She is delighted to discuss the origin of their plants and the effects they have created. You will find an abundance: shrubs, bulbs, herbaceous perennials, climbers, and stock from their conservatory/greenhouse. In a smallish area they have managed to develop small streams and dry areas, and waterside walks. This makes for a wonderfully personal visit to what Mrs Chapman calls 'a natural working

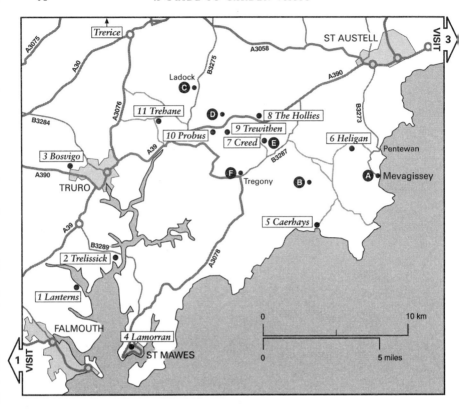

garden'. I think it is very special, and a change from the many classic sub-tropical gardens which Cornwall boasts.

2   TRELISSICK GARDENS (NT)   Feock   Tel 01872 862090

Mon–Sat, March to Oct, 10.30–5.30 (Suns 12.30–5.30). £3.40
From Truro go SW on A39 for 4m. Turn L on B3289 for 2m; garden signed
on R.

Cornish gardens are noted for their magnificent spring displays of camellias, rhododendrons, magnolias, cherries and bulbs. Trelissick has these in abundance, but the flowering interest continues through the year, with flower borders around the lawns, late-flowering shrubs, roses, fuchsias, hydrangeas, and a wide range of perennials and lilies. As you walk around the woodland paths the views out to sea over the Carrick Roads, and down to the River Fal, are stupendous. A well-stocked plant centre specializing in plants on show at NT properties, a restaurant, and a NT shop are here too.

3   BOSVIGO HOUSE   Truro   Tel 01872 75774

Wed–Sat, March to Sept, 11–6. £2
From Truro town centre go NW on A390 for ¾m. Turn R into Dobbs Lane just after Sainsbury's roundabout; garden signed 500 yds on L.

This is a very personal garden for plant-lovers which I found wonderfully refreshing to visit after all the large woodland gardens that are magnificent, impressive, yet somehow similar. Michael and Wendy Perry have developed, in 3 acres, an enchanting series of enclosed gardens around their charming house. A dazzling display of reds, yellows and hot colours sizzle in summer, contrasting with a slightly sinister and intriguing black and green garden tucked away at the back of the house. Hellebores are a speciality, and I found interesting pulmonarias here too. The pink and grey garden is unashamedly pretty. The whole garden is immaculately kept, and the nursery sells good and interesting perennial and herbaceous stock.

4   LAMORRAN HOUSE   St Mawes   Tel 01326 270800

Wed, Fri, April to Oct, 10–5, and by appointment. £2
From the centre of St Mawes turn R at garage, signed Castle; garden ½m on L in Upper Castle Road.

Mr and Mrs Dudley-Cooke have been working on this 4-acre garden since 1980, using Italian and other far-distant themes as their inspiration. Columns and statuary enhance spectacular views to St Anthony's Head; the many small gardens include one of Japanese design; extensive water gardens have a Mediterranean feel. The very mild climate allows a wide variety of plants from the southern hemisphere to thrive. Azaleas, rhododendrons, palms, eucalyptus, tree ferns, yuccas, agaves, and other exotic species have been carefully planted to express subtle colour and foliage combinations.

5   CAERHAYS CASTLE GARDEN
nr Mevagissey   Tel 01872 501310

Mon–Fri and some Suns, mid March to early May, 11–4. £2.50
From St Austell, go S on B3273 for 4m. In Megavissey, turn R on minor roads to the coast between Dodman Point and Nare Head; garden by Porthluney Cove.

Built by John Nash at the beginning of the 19th century, this large grey
Gothic castle has a fairy-tale setting in a gentle cleft in the hills, looking
straight out over the park and lake to the sparkling sea. All around the sides
and back of the castle, the hillside rises steeply, and is covered with pink
and white camellias, magnolias and rhododendrons. The Williams family
still live here. Their ancestors were noted Victorian plant hunters, who
scoured the Far East for the rare shrubs you can see flowering today. As
well as the famous Williams camellias, you can enjoy ferns, acers, oaks,
azaleas and nothofagus. Walks of varying lengths and steepness lead you up
the hillside. Recover with a delicious tea in the sheltered estate yard. The
castle itself is open for conducted tours most afternoons. You park down
by the lovely unspoiled sandy beach and walk up through the park. This is
a place for stout walkers.

6   LOST GARDENS OF HELIGAN

Pentewan   Tel 01726 844157

Daily all year, 10–6 (last visit starts 4.30). £2.90
From St Austell go S on B3273 for 5m. Turn R on minor road where signed.

Of all the gardens in Visit 2, this is a must. A large team of contractors and
massive voluntary labour is reclaiming a garden which has been here since
1603, was expanded in the early 18th century, and reached its present 57
acres in 1780. But from 1914 to 1991, the site hardly felt the touch of a
gardening hand. Since then, it has become the largest garden restoration
project in Europe. Fallen trees and massive brambles have been cleared, and
1,500 tons of timber removed. About 5,000 trees have been planted to provide shelter, and 2½ miles of intricate footpaths, unseen for fifty years, have
been uncovered and restored. They link a fern ravine, 4 walled gardens with
peach houses, a 150-yd long man-made rockery, vineries, a melon house, a
crystal grotto, summer-houses, a wishing well, an Italian garden with a
pool, a large Japanese valley garden, a 100-yd long herbaceous border, a
big vegetable garden, and much else. Such care was taken to conform to
original planting that metal detectors were used to find buried lead plant
labels. It is a stupendous project, and still in progress. Try to stop and look
at the before-and-after photographs, taken as Tim Smit and his team of
helpers hacked their way into the jungle here. You will be doubly impressed
by their efforts. Rumour has it that they have discovered another 'lost
garden' nearby. Garden archeology seems to be the coming thing.

7 CREED HOUSE

nr Grampound (*see also* Where to Stay)   Tel 01872 530372

Daily, May to Sept, 12–5.30. £2
From St Austell go SW on A390 for 5m to Grampound. Turn L on minor road
signed Creecd. After ½m turn L at Creed church; garden on L.

Mr and Mrs W.R. Croggon's fascinating 5-acre garden began restoration in
1974 when, like Heligan, it was a mess of brambles and fallen trees. Then
the magnolias lifted their heads out of the tangle and flowered, along with
ancient camellias and rhododendrons, and the owners realised they had taken
on a shrouded treasure. It is marvellous now, with colour and interest all
the year round. A great *Parrotia persica* flares into colour in October, and in
spring little red anemones poke through the grass surrounding the tennis
lawn. There is a sunken alpine garden and walled herbaceous gardens, and
a trickle-stream wanders through bogs and ponds. The Croggons are welcoming people and love to meet other gardeners. It is a delightful place to
stay.

8 THE HOLLIES Grampound   Tel 01726 882474

By appointment, April to Sept, 12–5. £1
From St Austell go SW for 5m; garden next to Grampound P.O.

Mr J.R. and Mrs N.B. Croggon have delightfully and informally planted this
garden which, despite covering nearly 2 acres, has a cottage feel. Wonderful in spring, with an underplanting of bulbs in island beds of trees and
shrubs, it keeps its appeal throughout the year, featuring alpines, herbaceous
borders, and many rare plants.

9 TREWITHEN nr Probus   Tel 01726 883647

Mon–Sat and some Suns, March to Sept, 10–4.30. £2.80
From St Austell go SW on A390 for 7m; garden signed on L, 1m before Probus.

Mr and Mrs Galsworthy's 30-acre garden is one of Cornwall's most renowned. Internationally famous – and justly so – it is featured in an NGS
video (and in an independent half-hour video describing its creation over
the years). There is much to see: rare climbers, a wisteria-clad pergola, a
lawn bordered with banks of flowering shrubs, island beds with heathers
and dwarf conifers, new beds of roses and mixed shrubs, fine beech trees
giving shelter and background shape – the list goes on and on. There is a
tea shop, plant shop, video theatre, and dogs are allowed on a lead. On

Monday and Tuesday afternoons from April to July the house is also open. This visit is an unmissable treat.

10 PROBUS GARDENS   nr St Austell   Tel 01726 882597

Daily, April to Oct (weekdays only in winter), 10–5 (10–4 in winter). £2.50
From St Austell go SW on A390 for 8m; garden signed on L.

Cornwall County Council is justifiably proud of its 7½-acre demonstration garden, packed with ideas, explanations and trials of new stock. Here you can look at different sorts of hedges for different situations; at various sorts of lawn grasses, and how they alter when fed with different fertilizers. Ground-cover plants, and ground-cover roses particularly interested me, as did the Historical Garden, showing how plants have been introduced over the years, from Roman times. The Herb Garden gives useful information on their use, and there are great herbaceous and shrub borders. Masses to see here and learn from – ideal for new gardeners, and so much on show that experts will find new things too. You can dive into greenhouses or the café if it starts to rain. A plant centre sells a range of plants particularly suited to different growing conditions.

11 TREHANE   nr Probus   Tel 01872 520270

2–3 days per month, March to July, 2–5, and by appointment. £1.50
From Truro go NE on A39 for 2m to Tressillian. Turn L on minor road for
1½m; garden signed on R.

David and Simon Trehane's 10-acre garden has something for the general visitor and plantsman alike. Half the garden is peaceful woodland, blanketed in spring by bluebells, claytonias and campions which make for a colourful and tranquil walk. Dogs are allowed on leads. The specialist gardener will revel in finding collections of geraniums, hemerocallis, romneyas, trilliums and camellias. Banks of rhododendrons, azaleas and magnolias give the background to splendid herbaceous borders, many of these plants are for sale. Teas are available.

Where to Stay

All B&B prices are approximate per person, sharing a double/twin room usually with private or en suite facilities. It is a good idea to ask for any special requirements when booking.

A   SHARKSFIN HOTEL   Tel 01726 843241

J.L. Goodhew, The Quay, Mevagissey, Cornwall PL26 6QU.

If you would like to stay by the sea on this visit, as a change from all those trees, shrubs, lawns and flowers, this small hotel is charming and well run. Set on the water's edge of the small busy fishing harbour in this pretty village, the 9 double/twin and 2 single bedrooms are mostly en suite with shower. They are on the small side, but carefully furnished, with good views. The restaurant food is universally acclaimed by guests (dinner about £18). Cooked to order, it uses fresh fish from the market, mussels and oysters from the Helford River, and lobsters and crabs directly from a local fishing boat. Non-seafood dishes are also locally based. Children are welcome, and dogs if you ask nicely (although there's nowhere much for dogs to go). B&B £32–£35.

B   KILBOL COUNTRY HOUSE   Tel 01726 842481

Tony & Jenny Woollam, Polmassick, Mevagissey, Cornwall PL26 6HA.

Total peace, tranquillity, extremely comfortable accommodation, good food from the Aga (half-board dinner works out at about £7, non-residents pay £15), old-fashioned service – entries in the visitors' book tell the story over and over again. Kilbol is a pretty, cottagey-feeling 16th-century hotel with 6 double/twin bedrooms (and 2 singles, sharing a bathroom), most of them looking out over secluded gardens (with a swimming pool) set in 7½ acres of leafy grounds going down to a trout stream. There is a newly refurbished self-contained cottage as well. If you want a rural retreat, you will find it here. Restricted smoking, no children, dogs welcome. There are ground floor bedrooms for wheelchair users. B&B £29–£35.

C BISSICK OLD MILL   Tel 01726 882557

Elizabeth & Keith Henderson, Ladock, Nr Truro, Cornwall TR2 4PG.

This charming 17th-century water mill has no garden, but is out of the ordinary because of the quality and range of food served by Liz in her slate-floored dining-room. Lunches, picnic baskets, teas, suppers and gourmet dinners (£12.50, licensed) with a large choice of menu (French-based) are all good value. The 3 double and 2 single pine-furnished bedrooms (with TV) are immaculate, and downstairs the walls are hung with pictures by local artists. Smoking in the guest lounge only, children should be 10 or over, dogs allowed by prior arrangement. B&B £25–£35.

D TREGOOSE   Tel 01726 882460

Anthony & Alison O'Connor, Grampound, Truro, Cornwall TR2 4BD.

If you want to know about gardening, Alison O'Connor is your person. A qualified lecturer in horticulture, she and her husband have created a stunning 2-acre garden around their mid 19th-century house. Surrounded by gentle countryside, it has sweeping lawns (one for croquet), mature trees, a fine landscaped overall design, many pots and urns, and colour from spring through to late autumn. Unusual plants include *Libertia* 'Amazing Grace'. There are 3 bedrooms, and dinner (£18, bring your own wine) is by arrangement. Guests have praised nice small touches. No smoking. Dogs not allowed upstairs and must be on a lead in the garden. B&B £25–£33.

E CREED HOUSE   *(see* Garden 7)   Tel 01872 530372

William & Lally Croggon, Creed, Grampound, Truro, Cornwall TR2 4SL.

The outstanding 5-acre setting and garden has already been described above, and I can't stress too strongly the warmth of welcome and the enjoyment you will have here. The house, a listed building dating from 1730, is elegant inside and out. The 3 bedrooms for guests have superking-sized beds (convertible to singles), and are comfortably furnished with antiques. B&B only, but there are plenty of good places to eat in the area. No smoking, no children. Dogs by arrangement. B&B £25–£32.

F   TREGONY HOUSE   Tel 01872 530671

Cathy & Andy Webb, Tregony, Truro, Cornwall TR2 5RN.

The long narrow walled garden at the back of Tregony House is charming, with trees, shrubs, colourful planting, a greenhouse with **a** mature vine, and fresh herbs for the excellent evening meals (£11 for 4 courses, including cheese and coffee; licensed). The house itself originally dates from the 17th century, with Georgian additions. Plenty of books and magazines give it a homely feel. There are 6 bedrooms, 2 sharing bathrooms. No dogs, children should be over 7, and smoking is in the sitting-room only. B&B £19–£22.

What Else to Enjoy

This is a short selection of the many good things recommended in the area by owners of places to stay. Your hosts will certainly be able to provide additional information.

Other Gardens

About 8m to the N of the last group of gardens is one of the NT's most charming properties, **Trerice.** Drive up the A39, and turn L at the major junction with the A3058 to Newquay. Trerice is signed on the L at **Kestle Mill.** It is a relatively small garden, set around an Elizabethan manor house (also open, with a fine interior and many antiques), kept immaculately by a single gardener. The gold and purple herbaceous planting scheme in the front court blends beautifully with the stone of the house. The back court has fuchsias, lonicera and roses. Many rare perennials, climbers and shrubs are to be found. The orchard, with old local varieties of apples, pears, quinces and plums, is planted in the 17th-century *quincunx* style – that is to say, one at each corner of a rectangle, and one in the middle. A collection of curious lawnmowers, old and new, is in a hayloft. It is open daily except Tuesday, April to Sept, 11–5.30, and costs £3.80. Tel 01637 875404.

Other Places to Stay

Wonderful woodland surroundings in the Royal Duchy of Cornwall Estate mark out **Arrallas, a** high-quality listed farmhouse only about 3m E of Trerice (its postal address, Ladock, is correct but geographically misleading). Wildlife luxuriates in the hedgerows and paths, with abundant wild flowers, and many kinds of birds and animals. There is true countryside peace here. One guest wrote: 'I thought the high spot was seeing the Barn Owl – until I had dinner! What a wonderful haven.' Arrallas has pretty bedrooms with tremendous views. Delicious dinners (by arrangement, from £11.50, bring your own wine) are served in a dining-room looking out over gardens, field and woodlands, with an elegant lounge where you take coffee. No dogs, smoking or children. B&B from £19. Address: Ian & Barbara Holt, Arrallas, **Ladock,** Truro, Cornwall TR2 4NP. Tel 01872 510379.

If It's Wet

The Royal Cornwall Museum in River Street, **Truro,** is excellent. It has superb displays of Cornish history and pre-history, paintings, ceramics, silver and gold. The shop and café are also good.

For a bit of shopping until the sun comes out, **Truro** has a good flea market. When you are near Gardens 9–11, Junk and Disorderly in **Probus** has bargains, and New Mills Pottery in **Ladock** is highly recommended. In the same area, there is a marvellous selection of take-home oak-smoked seafood and meat (and fresh seafood) from Atlantis Smoked Fish in **Grampound,** who also make great picnic sandwiches with locally-baked bread.

Eating Out

The first restaurant in Cornwall to achieve a Michelin star, **Pennypots Restaurant** in **Blackwater** is small, intimate and friendly. Owned by Kevin and Jane Viner (Kevin is the chef), its menu (from £24) uses the best of Cornish fish and game. It is about 6m off the visit map – but worth the detour, as they say. Drive W from Truro on the A390, and cross the A30 trunk rd. Turn L immediately where signposted for Blackwater. Open Tues–Sat. Book in advance. Tel 01209 820347.

Fowey to Bodmin Moor

The countryside and scenery in this visit has inspired two great writers. John Betjeman, in the north, wrote many poems describing his childhood in the small towns and villages and along the coast, and on Bodmin Moor. In the softer south, Daphne du Maurier lived and wrote. The Fowey Estuary, and Polruan on its southernmost tip, conjure up the romances of *Frenchman's Creek,* and you can find Bodmin Moor in *Jamaica Inn* and *Rebecca.* Driving there, enjoy that wonderful song 'Blow the Wind Southerly', a prayer that must have been on the lips of every fisherman's wife – so apt for this coastline. My version is on a cassette titled *The World of Kathleen Ferrier.*

OS map: Landranger **200**

Gardens

Opening times: in larger gardens, and in NT properties, last admissions are usually 30–45 minutes before the garden closes. Admission charges are a guide to what one adult can expect to pay to go round the garden. It sometimes varies with the season or days of the week. When the house is also open to the public, there is usually an additional charge.

1   **PORTHPEAN HOUSE**   nr St Austell   Tel 01726 72888

By written appointment, and some charity days March–May. £1.50
From St Austell go S on minor road, signed Porthpean, for 1½m; garden at white house on bottom of hill, on road leading to the beach.

Mrs Petherick is an expert on camellias (she wins prizes for them, including autumn-flowering ones, at the RHS), and although her 3-acre garden is open to the salty wind straight off St Austell Bay, her careful planting of wind barriers has allowed her to create a ravishing garden. I visited in spring when, tearing my eyes away from the sparkling views over the sea, I turned a corner behind the house to find what must be the world's sunniest, biggest

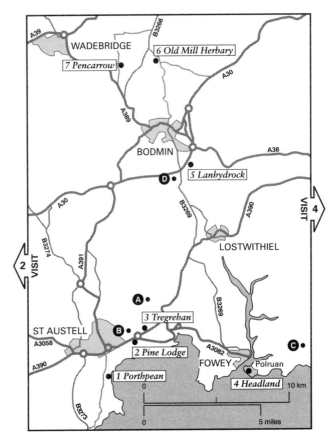

bank of primroses, under cherry trees, with rabbits hopping about. It made me gasp, it was so sensational. One little treasure I was proudly shown was a myrtle grown from a slip in Queen Victoria's wedding bouquet. Mrs Petherick welcomes visits from garden enthusiasts, but by prior written appointment, please. Good camellias for sale.

2   PINE LODGE   St Austell   Tel 01726 73500 (evenings)

By appointment, and charity days May and June. £3
From A39/A390 roundabout in St Austell go E on A390 for 1m; garden on R.

Mr and Mrs Clemo have more than 5 acres of gardens planted with over 5,000 well-labelled rare and tender plants – a pleasure for any plant-lover. The setting is 30 acres of parkland, lake and woodland, with a pinetum and arboretum. The herbaceous borders are sensitively laid out, with a masterly eye for colour combinations, and many climbers ramble over the pergola and walls. The abundant water provides a good marsh garden.

3 TREGREHAN nr St Austell Tel 01726 814389

Daily mid March to June (except Easter Sunday), 10.30–5. £2.50
From A39/A390 roundabout in St Austell go E on A390 for 2m; garden on L, opposite Brittania Inn.

Home of the Carlyon family since 1565, the 20-acre garden and park was developed from the 18th century onwards, but for much of this century was largely abandoned. In the 1970s, Miss Gillian Carlyon began a vigorous restoration, which since her death in 1987 has been continued by Mr T. Hudson. The splendid Victorian greenhouses, facing colourful borders and handsome stone terraces, alone make the garden worth a visit. They contain tender varieties of huge number of ericaceous plants, plus others of interest – Chatham Island forget-me-nots, clivias, and *Geranium maderense*. The garden is noted for its award-winning camellias, mostly bred here. An avenue of yews provides a Gothic tunnel to walk along to a statue of a much loved dog, and a doggie graveyard. The trees in the park are magnificent, and include a huge cork oak and a regal *Cupressus macrocarpa*. Many species are for sale in the nursery. An excellent coloured leaflet guides you through a memorable visit.

4 HEADLAND Polruan-by-Fowey Tel 01726 870243

Open Thurs, mid May to late Sept, 2–8. £1
From Fowey take the car ferry to Bodinnick and then follow minor roads for 3m to Polruan. Park in the public car park, walk down St Saviour's Hill and turn L at Coastguard office; garden on R.

Creating their cliff garden over the past 20 years, Jean and John Hill had to conquer a site which has spectacular views 100 ft above the sea, but can be buffeted on any of three sides by gales and salt spray. They have triumphed, using narrow paths, hedges and archways to hide and succour hidden areas where sub-tropical plants now thrive. Australian and New Zealand species are among their favourites, but everywhere you look you will find something interesting, and often rare, to enjoy. The garden is just over an acre in all, but seems larger. Visitors can swim off the beach in the cove 100 steps below.

5 LANHYDROCK (NT)   Bodmin   Tel 01208 73320

Daily all year during daylight hours. £2.50
From Bodmin town centre go S on B3268 for 2m; garden signed on L.

Part of this grandiose, but somehow impersonal, 30-acre garden is informal woodland (heavily damaged in the great gale), with paths meandering through specimen magnolias, rhododendrons and camellias, and a stream edged by water-loving plants; it's best in spring, of course. Below the house are formal terraces, and geometric self-contained gardens surrounded by yew and box. In summer these come into their own, with an unusual circular herbaceous border that provides colour through to September. The National Collection of crocosmias is here too. There are unusual rhododendrons on sale.

Within 2m of Lanhydrock is the **Duchy of Cornwall Nursery** (Tel 01208 872668), well worth a small detour. It has a huge variety of shrubs, trees, herbaceous perennials and half-hardy plants. If you are coming from the S, drive for about 2m past Lostwithiel on the A390, and turn L up Cott Rd, signposted to the Lostwithiel Golf and Country Club. The nursery is ¾ m past the club on the same road.

6 THE OLD MILL HERBARY
Hellandbridge   Tel 01208 841206

Daily, April to Oct, 10–5. £2
From Bodmin go NW on A389 for 2m. Turn R on B3266 for 2m, then R on minor road for ½m to Hellandbridge; garden beside river.

Mr and Mrs R. Drew Whurr's fascinating 5-acre garden is unique – a garden herbary of botanical and historical interest. The terraces are semi-wild and quite weedy, but extensively planted with displays of culinary, medicinal and aromatic herbs, as well as shrubs, climbing and herbaceous plants. There was a herb and hop garden here around 1775, based on a Greek fertility theme. Today this is still very much to the forefront as you walk around. It's hard to avoid really, when the magnificently erect statues thrust home the point. Gentlemen at all worried about their manhood might come away with a serious inferiority complex (though Mrs Whurr would surely have a herb to cure it). The water meadows beside the River Camel have been extensively planted with new trees, including liriodendra, sorbus, golden beech, *Betula nigra*, *Morus alba*, weeping elms, hornbeams and bamboos. Wild flowers are profuse, and the mill leat feeds a natural pond and water garden. Lots of interesting herbs for sale.

7 PENCARROW nr Wadebridge   Tel 01208 841369

Daily, Easter to mid Oct, dawn to dusk. £1.50
From Bodmin go NW on A389 for 2½m; turn R to garden where signed.

Pencarrow is stately and august – but not at all intimidating. Around the
Palladian mansion are formal gardens set out by Sir William Molesworth
from 1831. A large rock garden planted with shrubs was built with boulders
brought from Bodmin Moor. Geometry rules in the gardens on either side
of the house, with circular lawns and rectangular beds. Some 50 acres of
parkland and woodland boast more than 600 varieties of rhododendrons,
and many camellias. There are dozens of monkey puzzle trees, and the palm
trees rise 20 ft through the roof of the Palm House. Peacocks scream abuse
at you, but I loved Pencarrow for the charming friendliness of the notices,
urging you to enjoy the garden and woodlands, and inviting you to borrow
the croquet mallets for a game. There is a lovely tearoom, with plenty of
toys and a Wendy house outside for children to enjoy. The atmosphere at
this grand mansion was warm and gentle, and dogs are allowed off the lead
in the woodland.

Where to Stay

All B&B prices are approximate per person, sharing a double/twin room usually with private
or en suite facilities. It is a good idea to ask for any special requirements when booking.

A NANSCAWEN HOUSE   Tel 01726 824888

Janet & Keith Martin, Prideaux Road, St Blazey, nr Par, Cornwall PL24 2SR.

Nanscawen House, in 5 acres of grounds and gardens including a heated
swimming pool with spectacular views, and an outdoor whirlpool spa, is at
the luxury end of places to stay. The 3 bedrooms (1 a four-poster), sump-
tuously en suite, are spacious and richly furnished. Great breakfasts are
served in the conservatory. B&B only, but there are a number of good
restaurants locally. Janet and Keith say this is a family home where they
like to welcome a few guests, and everyone speaks of being cosseted. No
smoking, no dogs, and children should be over 12. B&B £34–£39.

B ANCHORAGE HOUSE   Tel 01726 814071

Steve & Jane Epperson, Nettles Corner, Tregehan, St Austell, Cornwall PL25 3RH.

Every attention has been paid to the smallest detail in this beautiful antique-filled house. It is newly built in a Georgian style, furnished to a very high standard, and makes the most of Cornwall's sunshine with a flower-filled garden. There are 3 good bedrooms with many special touches. Steve, a retired US Navy Special Forces Commander and avid golfer, will give you directions for everywhere you might want to go. Jane's candlelit 5-course evening meals (£19.50, bring your own wine) are prepared after talking to you. No smoking, no dogs, no children. B&B £22–£27.

C CARNEGGAN HOUSE   Tel 01726 870327

Sue Shakerley, Carneggan, Lanteglos-by-Fowey, Cornwall PL23 1NW.

This spacious Georgian farmhouse, surrounded by lawns and fields with panoramic sea views, is the relaxed home to a family-run farm, with piggies in the yard and lambs in the field. There are fabulous coastal walks, if you have the energy after garden visiting. Children are particularly well looked after here, and Sue cooks delicious food (supper £7–£9.50, dinner from £17; wine served). You sleep with happy dreams in any of the 3 double bedrooms; the main one, with a bay window, has fantastic sea views to wake up to. Smoking generally allowed (but ask other guests in the dining-room). Dogs welcome if you discuss it first. B&B £20–£27.

D TREFFRY FARM   Tel 01208 74405

Mrs Pat Smith, Lanhydrock, Bodmin, Cornwall PL30 5AF.

A 200-acre dairy farm is run from this listed 18th-century farmhouse, partly wood panelled, which has been beautifully decorated. The 3 pretty bedrooms have great views. Only 300 yds from Lanhydrock (*see* Garden 5), it is beautiful walking country. Eat out in the evenings (there are good local restaurants). Breakfasts are lavish. No smoking, children should be over 6, guide dogs only. B&B £19-£20.

What Else to Enjoy

This is a short selection of the many good things recommended in the area by owners of places to stay. Your hosts will certainly be able to provide additional information.

If It's Wet

Lanhydrock (*see* Garden 5) is thought by many to be the finest house in Cornwall, and will certainly keep a roof over your head for an hour or two. At the last count, 42 rooms were open, showing the upstairs downstairs contrast at the turn of the century. Originally built in the 17th century, a fire almost destroyed it in 1881. The gatehouse (1651) and the north wing (including a 116-ft gallery with a fine plaster ceiling showing Old Testament scenes) remain. The rest forms a spectacularly grand Victorian mansion, in which below stairs life can be seen in the great kitchen, the maids' bedrooms, and the nursery wing. It is open Tues–Sun, and BH Mons, from April to October, 11–5.30. A combined ticket with the gardens costs £5.90.

In the S of this visit, don't miss historic **Charlestown**, SE of St Austell. It is an 18th-century village and harbour frozen in time, and much in demand by film and TV crews.

If you want to go bargain-hunting while it rains, try the antiques centre in **St Austell**, which has good bric-à-brac.

On the NW tip of the map in **Wadebridge** is the John Betjeman Centre, packed with the poet's memorabilia.

Eating Out

Food for Thought in **Fowey** has been going for nearly 20 years, and still keeps up its standards. You don't have to be a fish-lover to eat here, because there are good meat dishes – but it's probably the sensitive way Martin Billingsley handles fresh local produce from the sea that you will remember. The restaurant is in a little cottage on the quay, and is not over-expensive. Set dinner is £15, and if you choose otherwise, and have wine, you will probably spend £25–£35 per person. Tel 01726 832221.

Around Plymouth

There are exceptionally good places to stay in this visit, which spans the county boundary on the River Tamar between Cornwall and Devon. Sarah Stone's wonderful old home, The Cider House, is shown on the cover of this book. The soft south Devon air brings a wealth of gardens and parks, enviable for the variety of half-hardy and sub-tropical plants that can be grown here. The lanes and backroads are easy to get lost in – but who cares? Enjoy some cheerful Mozart. The 3rd movement of his Piano Concerto No. 14, K.449, is the happiest piece of music I know.

OS map: Landranger **201**

Gardens

Opening times: in larger gardens, and in NT properties, last admissions are usually 30–45 minutes before the garden closes. Admission charges are a guide to what one adult can expect to pay to go round the garden. It sometimes varies with the season or days of the week. When the house is also open to the public, there is usually an additional charge.

I   CATCHFRENCH MANOR   St Germans   Tel 01503 240759

Mon–Sat, March to Oct, 10.30–4.30. £2.50
From Saltash go W on A38 for 6m; garden signed on L.

Humphry Repton landscaped this 25-acre garden to his famous *Red Book* design. The present owners, John and Judy Wilks, bought the house in a near-derelict state, and are restoring it and the gardens, including a vined courtyard, to their former glory. The many camellias, rhododendrons and azaleas already make it a fine spring garden, and the ruin, grotto and secret quarry garden have been re-established. Delicious home-made food in the tea room.

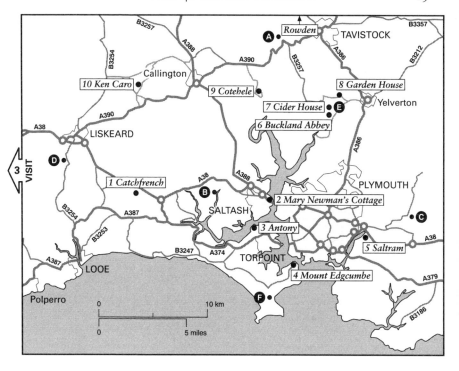

2   MARY NEWMAN'S COTTAGE   Saltash   Tel 01579 347993

Weekend afternoons, June to Sept. £1
From Saltash town centre, follow signs to the railway station; garden at
48 Culver Rd, off Station Rd.

Sir Francis Drake's first wife Mary Newman lived here, and the cottage has
recently been restored. Although only a quarter of a mile from the busy
town centre of Saltash, it is a peaceful cottage garden, with many herbs,
herbaceous borders, old-fashioned roses, shrubs and trees overlooking the
River Tamar and Brunel's famous bridge.

3   ANTONY (NT)   Torpoint   Tel 01752 812191

Tues–Thurs and BH Mons, April to Oct, 1.30–5.30. Also Suns, June to Aug.
£2.50
From Saltash go W on A38 for 5m. Turn L on A374 for 6m; garden signed
in St Germans village.

Sweeping lawns edged with clipped yew hedges give Repton-inspired vistas over the Tamar estuary from the terraces of this superb early 18th-century house. The formal garden has many attractive features: good topiary, a court-yard, a walled kitchen garden with espaliered fruit trees and magnolias, a knot garden planted with box and germander, a sheltered flower garden with continuous colour, and the National Collection of day lilies (more than 500 varieties).

Connected to it is **Antony Woodland Garden**, 100 acres designated an Area of Outstanding Natural Beauty. There are 300 varieties of camellias, and enchanting walks along the banks of the River Lynher. From April to October it is open daily 11–5.30 (Sundays 2–5.30).

4   MOUNT EDGCUMBE PARK   Torpoint   Tel 01752 822236

Park and formal gardens, daily all year, dawn to dusk. Free
From Plymouth, take the short car ferry ride to Torpoint, from where it is well signed. There is also a pedestrian ferry to Cremyll, a 10-minute walk from Mount Edgcumbe House. From the W, take the A374 and B3247, well signed.

Covering more than 800 acres, this was Cornwall's earliest landscaped park. It is a Grade I listed garden, with temples, follies, and a unique shell seat, all built eccentrically during the 18th century to impress friends and visitors. The park, almost surrounded by coastland, has two well-marked walks (about 3 miles each) with wonderful sea views. Within, surrounded by high hedges to keep out the salt wind, are 7 acres of formal gardens exotically planted in styles from all over the world: English, French, Italian, New Zealand and American. In the ampitheatre is the National Collection of camellias. Earl's Garden, surrounding the house, is Victorian in inspiration, with lawns, terraces and shrubberies that provide vivid year-round colour. Lunches, teas and refreshments available in the Orangery.

5   SALTRAM (NT)   nr Plymouth   Tel 01752 336546

Sun–Thurs, April to Oct, 10.30–5.30. £2.20
From Plymouth town centre go E on A379 for 2m. Turn L at second round-about after crossing River Plym on minor road signed Billacombe and Saltram; after 1m, garden on L.

Fanny Burney, the 18th-century novelist and diarist, visited in 1789 with the court of George III; and a classical garden house here is named Fanny's Bower. This wonderful mansion is surrounded by 20 acres of parkland and garden dating from 1770. In spring, there is a mass of narcissi, and later *Cyclamen hederifolium*, in the long Lime Walk which has fine trees in the background. To bridge the gap between spring and autumn, there have been fairly recent plantings of hypericum, hydrangeas, buddleias and fuchsias.

About 4m to the S (warning: it's a fiddly drive on minor roads) is a good nursery: **Pounsley Plants**, with many clematis, old roses and perennials. It is in Spriddlestone, which you find by taking the A379 Plymouth to Kingsbridge rd, and turning R 1m after leaving Plymouth in the village of Combe. Tel 01752 402873.

6   BUCKLAND ABBEY (NT)   nr Yelverton   Tel 01822 853607

Fri–Wed, April to Oct, 10.30–5.30. £2
From Plymouth go N on A386 for 4m. Turn L at Yelverton where signed on minor road for 2m.

Sir Francis Drake's home after he bought it in 1581, the Abbey was originally a 13th-century monastery. In the grounds are monastic farm buildings now used as active craft workshops, where you can watch (and buy) the results of basket-making, shoe-making, bellows-making, and wood-turning. The garden has mostly been made this century; there are two huge magnolias, and many climbers on the walls. The herb garden, with irregularly shaped dwarf box-hedged beds, contains more than 50 varieties (many on sale), planted after a visit by Vita Sackville-West.

7   THE CIDER HOUSE

nr Yelverton (*see also* Where to Stay)   Tel 01822 853285

2 charity Suns, and by appointment. £2
Next to Buckland Abbey (above)

The Cider House (both house and garden) is stunning. Entirely surrounded by NT land, and so quiet at night you can hear the owls breathe, it is a converted medieval building that was once part of a Cistercian monastery. The grounds extend to 16 acres overlooking a valley above the River Tavy. Around the house are luxuriant, mature gardens, abundantly and imaginatively planted around bones of old paths and walls. Among the treats are the walled kitchen garden, the herb garden, the terrace, and the wild garden with camellias and rhododendrons. Stay overnight and you can enjoy it on your own.

8 THE GARDEN HOUSE   nr Yelverton   Tel 01822 854769

Daily, March to Oct, 10.30–5. £3
From Plymouth go N on A386 for 4m. Turn L at Yelverton on minor road
signed Buckland Monachorum for 1½m; garden signed on R.

The Fortescue Garden Trust's spectacular garden has interest throughout
the year, and contains a 2-acre walled garden considered by many to be one
of the finest in the country. Within its surrounds are packed a vast array
of shrubs and herbaceous plants surrounding a 16th-century tower and
thatched barn. There is a new delight round every corner. Covering 10 acres
in all, the garden was created post-World War II by Lionel Fortescue, an
avid plant collector, purist and stickler for getting things right. It is now
run by Keith and Ros Wiley, and their new developments have taken
advantage of the wonderful views over the surrounding Cornish and Devon
hills. Plants – many unusual, all good value – are for sale, and refreshments,
including light lunches and cream teas, are served in the main house.

9   COTEHELE (NT)   Calstock   Tel 01579 50434

Daily all year, 11–5.30 (or dusk). April to Oct, £2.50. Nov to March, honesty
box.
From Tavistock go SW on A390 for 5m to St Anne's Chapel. Turn L on minor
road where signed for 1½m.

This fine house is almost unaltered since its original building in the late 15th
century. Terraces sweep down to a sheltered valley with a medieval stewpond now filled with waterlilies, a domed dovecot, exotic and tender
shrubs, azaleas and rhododendrons. The layout of the terraces, courtyards,
walled gardens and borders around the house is more formal, and planted
so that there is something to see when the main spring flowering season in
the valley is over: roses and many interesting climbers over the house, for
instance.

10 KEN CARO   Bicton   Tel 01579 62446

Sun–Wed, mid April to June; Tues and Wed, July and Aug; 2–6. £2
From Callington go SW on A390 for 4m. Turn R on minor road signed
Pensilva for ½m, then turn R at Gang for ½m; garden in village of Bicton.

Mr and Mrs Willcock's 4-acre garden in the village of Bicton, with its
panoramic views, is featured in the NGS video 2. Half the garden is
mature having been planted in 1970. A 2-acre extension was completed in

1993. The design consists of a series of small enclosed formal gardens, and plant-lovers will be delighted with the careful and comprehensive labelling of the many varieties of shrubs, conifers, rhododendrons and herbaceous specimens. The Willcocks are bird lovers, and have a collection of water-fowl and aviary birds.

Where to Stay

All B&B prices are approximate per person, sharing a double/twin room usually with private or en suite facilities. It is a good idea to ask for any special requirements when booking.

A   THE HORN OF PLENTY   Tel 01822 832528

Elaine & Ian Gatehouse, Gulworthy, Tavistock, Devon PL19 8JD.

It is hard to write too highly of this acclaimed restaurant with rooms, set in 4 acres of gardens and orchards in the foothills of Dartmoor overlooking the Tamar Valley – a marvellous setting, without doubt among the most beautiful described in this book. Inside, the 200-year-old house is supremely warm and comfortable. The 6 lovely bedrooms, including 1 single, all have balconies overlooking the walled garden below, with marvellous distant views. Elaine and Ian, since they took over five years ago, have carefully restored the pond, grotto and bog garden. Room and meal prices, naturally, are at the upper end – but worth every penny, both for the consistently inventive food, and the rich but unpretentious atmosphere. Dinner £19.50 on Mondays, £28.50 otherwise. No smoking in the restaurant, and 3 no-smoking bedrooms. Dogs and children over 13 welcome. Suitable for wheelchairs. B&B £44–£50.

B   ERTH BARTON   Tel 01752 842127

Guy Bentinck & Clio Smeeton, Saltash, Cornwall PL12 4QY.

On its own at the end of a mile-long drive, the manor house of Erth Barton has been inhabited since the days of Edward III. Massive oak doors, stone mullions and fireplaces abound, along with hundreds of books. It is an oasis of relaxation with a welcoming, peaceful atmosphere. Surrounded by water, it is a SSSI, and a wonderful place for birdwatching. Guy, who trained at some of the best hotels, does the cooking (dinner £18.50, bring your own wine). Clio is a writer. Among their wide-ranging interests are paintings, antiques, wildlife and sailing. Three lovely bedrooms. No dogs, no children, but you can smoke. B&B £32.

C   THE BARN   Tel 01752 347016

Bob & Frances Tagert, Windwhistle Farm, Hemerdon, Plymouth PL7 5BU.

The garden here, getting on for an acre, is fairly new – lawns surrounded by mixed borders, and established trees. It's interesting to look at the vegetable garden where produce is grown in raised boxes by the square-foot method, and then used in the excellent home cooking you will enjoy. On one side of the garden is a large field which goes up to Dartmoor and, just down the lane, Windwhistle Wood. The Barn has been meticulously converted and is extremely comfortable. Three bedrooms. Evening meals (£18, bring your own wine) should be arranged in advance. No smoking, or dogs, or children under 14. B&B £28.

D   THE OLD RECTORY   Tel 01822 853285

Pat & John Minifie, St Keyne, Liskeard, Cornwall PL14 4RL.

This is a peaceful and secluded family-run hotel, built in the early 1800s, set in 3 acres of pleasant gardens, and surrounded by its own farmland. The 8 bedrooms include 2 four-posters, and there is a ground floor room for wheel-chair users. 'Homely' and 'friendly' are words you find often in the visitors' book. Cooking ranges from traditional English to cordon-bleu adventurous (evening meals £16, bring your own wine); you discuss the menu in advance. Smoking allowed in the lounge and bar. Children should be 12 or older. Well-behaved dogs to be discussed while booking. B&B £25-£30.

E   THE CIDER HOUSE   *(see* Garden 7)   Tel 01822 853285

Sarah Stone, Buckland Abbey, Yelverton, Devon PL20 6EZ.

You saw how much I enjoyed Sarah's garden, so can I say the same about staying at her home? Definitely, yes. There's an old-fashioned country-house atmosphere, and if you like where you stay to have a history, as I do, you'll find it here. A tennis court, too. There are just 2 guest bedrooms with a shared bathroom. Meals (not all evenings, £15, bring your own wine), which you arrange in advance, are cooked by Sarah from organic produce in the garden. No smoking, and you have to be very persuasive about taking dogs. B&B £23.

F   CLIFF HOUSE   Tel 01752 823110

Ann Heasman, Devonport Hill, Kingsand, Cornwall PL10 1NJ.

Ann's listed 17th-century village house, at the top of a steep hill, has a balconied drawing room which wondrously overlooks Plymouth Sound and Cawsand Bay. For garden lovers, it is only a few yards from the South West Coast Path to Mount Edgcumbe (*see* Garden 4) and beyond. Her own small walled garden is profusely planted. There are 3 bedrooms, all en suite. For supper (£7) or dinner (£16–£20, inclusive of aperitif and wine), Ann is a home-cooking wholefood gourmet, with local produce where possible. She is also an enthusiastic guide to everything enjoyable in the area – picnic places, birdlife, gardens, other places to eat. No smoking. Dogs allowed, children by arrangement. B&B £17–£25.

What Else to Enjoy

This is a short selection of the many good things recommended in the area by owners of places to stay. Your hosts will certainly be able to provide additional information.

Other Gardens

About 5m N of the visit map you will discover (perhaps with some tricky route-finding) **Rowden Gardens**. Please try to go there. Find it by taking the B3362 Tavistock to Lawhitton rd. Turn R where signposted to Kelly, and then follow signposted minor roads to the tiny village of **Brentor**. Tel 01822 810275. You will meet John Carter, who changed his life 16 years ago in a most extreme way. A Cambridge-educated Arabist whose previous career was in the hot desert sands, he decided, in complete contrast, to create this damp 1-acre garden and nursery dedicated to bog-loving plants. The result is a delight – a succession of cool, canal-like ponds, with plants arranged to create colour schemes, as well as to make islands of plants of the same kind. The nursery has more than 3,000 varieties of aquatic, damp and shade-loving plants, and holds the National Collections of fallopias, persicarias and *Ranunculus ficaria*.

If It's Wet

There are 3 NT properties in this visit which will keep you happily occupied. **Saltram** (*see* Garden 5), just E of Plymouth, thought by many to be the most impressive house in Devon, is a remarkable survival of a George II mansion complete with its original contents. It is stunning, and takes at least an hour to appreciate properly. Open Sun–Thurs (and Good Friday), April to Oct, 12.30–5.30. Combined admission with garden £5.20.

Cotehele (*see* Garden 9), is a house notable for an exceptional display of tapestries and other textiles. Built 1485–1657, it was the home of the Edgcumbe family for centuries, and has much of the original furniture and armour on display. The restored mill is also open. On a rainy day early and late in the season, cross this one off your list – there is deliberately no electric light in the house, and things are hard to see. Open daily except Fris, April to Oct, 11–5.30. Combined admission with garden £5.60.

Don't miss **Mount Edgcumbe House** (*see* Garden 4) and its surrounding Earl's Garden. Dating from Tudor times, it was badly damaged during World War II, but has been completely restored by the sixth Earl and Countess of Mount Edgcumbe. Its magnificently furnished rooms show what grand life was like in the 18th century. A visit takes at least an hour. Open Wed–Sun (and BHs), April to Oct, 11–5. Admission £3.50.

Further N, near Buckland Monachorum is **Buckland Abbey** (*see* Garden 6), once a Cistercian monastery, and later the home of Sir Richard Grenville and Sir Francis Drake. It holds a 'voyage of discovery', with an introductory video presentation, exhibitions and furnished rooms. Open Fri–Wed, April to early Nov, 10.30–5.30; in winter months, Sat/Sun only, 2–5. Combined admission with grounds £4.20.

For some musical fun, try Paul Corin's Magnificent Music Machines, S of Liskeard. All manner of mechanical music is here, on programmed paper rolls and punched cards from the Edwardian era through to the 1930s, including performances from many composers and keyboard players including Rachmaninov – and ear-blowing live demonstrations of a 1929 Wurlitzer Theatre Pipe Organ. Find it from brown tourist signs at **St Keyne** on the B3254 Liskeard to Looe rd. Open daily May to Oct, 10.30–5; and Tues and Thurs evenings. July to Sept, 7.30–9. Tel 01579 343108. Admission £3.

Eating Out

A long-time favourite in this visit is **The Horn of Plenty** (*see* Where to Stay). Not unreasonably expensive (£28.50 for the table d'hôte menu), the last time I ate there I had noisettes of venison with caramelised apples, served with a black pepper and cider sauce – a perfectly balanced dish.

South Devon

When driving to the south coast of Cornwall, I have quite often broken the journey at Dartmouth just to enjoy the steep wooded estuary and another of Joyce Molyneux's wonderful meals at The Carved Angel. This is a part of England which has much to offer visitors, and it seems to do so gently, without ostentation. There are almost too many great gardens to be seen in a single visit – but definitely don't miss Coleton Fishacre or Hill House. For drive-along music on the way, I like a tape with a beautiful setting of John Ireland's 'Sea Fever', sung by Robert Lloyd, along with many other enjoyable sea shanties.

OS map: Landranger **202**

Gardens

Opening times: in larger gardens, and in NT properties, last admissions are usually 30–45 minutes before the garden closes. Admission charges are a guide to what one adult can expect to pay to go round the garden. It sometimes varies with the season or days of the week. When the house is also open to the public, there is usually an additional charge.

I   OVERBECKS (NT)   nr Salcombe   Tel 01548 842893
Daily all year, 10–8 (or sunset if earlier). £2.30
From Salcombe go SW on minor coast road for 1½m to Sharpitor, where garden is signed.

This 6-acre garden perched above the estuary has a Mediterranean feel – Devon's microclimate allows Chusan palms, daturas, mimosa, myrtles, olives and other tender exotic plants to flourish. Steep terraces and winding paths lead you down towards the sea. A magnificent *Magnolia campbellii*, planted at the turn of the century, invites you to visit in the spring.

2   THE PINES   Salcombe   Tel 01548 842198

By appointment, and some Sats/Suns March and April for charity. £1.50
On N outskirts of Salcombe at Devon Rd and Sandhills Rd X-roads. Ask owner
for final directions.

From the Bitmeads' sloping garden you can see Salcombe Bay and the NT's
sub-tropical garden at Overbecks. The owners terraced the garden and im-
ported 800 tons of topsoil before planting it. The result is glorious, with
camellias, azaleas and rhododendrons, with primulas and other little treasures
at their feet. You will find ground-cover plants in plenty, including
heathers, daphnes, cytisus, hebes, and varieties of *Euonymus fortunei*. Evergreens create a backdrop and wind barrier, and Mrs Bitmead is able to grow
many tender shrubs in this tranquil and informal garden.

3   COLETON FISHACRE GARDENS (NT)

nr Kingswear (*see also* Where to Stay)   Tel 01803 752466

Suns, March, 2–5; Wed–Fri, Suns and BH Mons, April to Oct, 10.30–5.30.
£3.10
From Dartmouth cross via car ferry to Kingswear, go NE on minor road for
1½ m and turn R where signed.

The mildest garden owned by the NT, profuse and luxuriant in all seasons.
Covering 25 acres in all, it has a formal pool garden close to the house,
and wooded areas with wild flowers sloping down to the sea. Like the
garden at Overbecks, a microclimate in a narrow sheltered valley enables
many rare and tender plants to grow exuberantly. Thickly planted magnolias,
camellias and rhododendrons are all quite stunning in the spring. Mimosas,
myrtles, bamboos and exotic moisture-loving plants fringe the pool and
streams. The garden was planted in 1926 by the D'Oyly Carte family, so
hum a bit of *The Mikado* to help you climb up to the gazebo for the view
of the sparkling sea below.

4   AVENUE COTTAGE   Ashprington   Tel 01803 732769

Tues–Sat, April to Sept, 11–5, and by appointment. £1.50
From Totnes go S on A381 for ½m. Turn L on minor road signed Ashprington
for 2m; garden 400 yds on R in no through road, past Ashprington church.

Mr Pitts and Mr Soans are always happy to show visitors their favourite –
and often unusual – plants in this enchanting 11-acre woodland valley
garden, replete with rhododendrons and azaleas. A magnificent driveway of

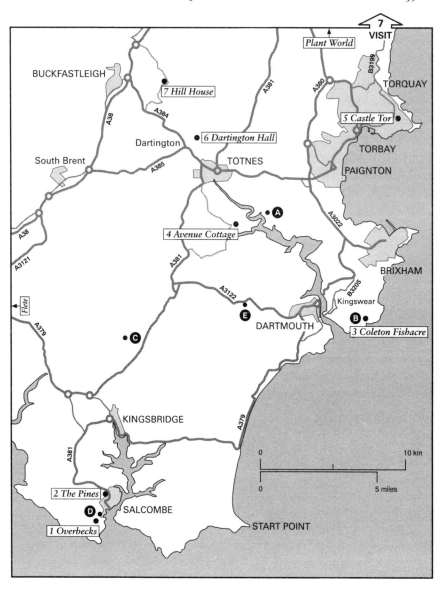

150-year-old turkey oaks leads to an 18th-century landscaped garden which is being carefully recreated, and much of which is already mature. You can stay here, too: an en suite twin room is £20 per person a night.

5   CASTLE TOR   Torquay   Tel 01803 214858

Throughout year, by appointment to keen gardeners. £1
Wellswood, Torquay. Ask owner for detailed directions.

The steep terraces of Mr Leonard Stocks's spectacular listed garden were
designed by Frederick Harrild around 1930. He was a pupil of Lutyens, and
this is reflected in the architectural style using flights of steps, pillars, a long
canal, a tower, an orangery and a gatehouse with a portcullis. The views
over Tor Bay, framed by shrubs and fine topiary, are stunning.

6   DARTINGTON HALL   nr Totnes   Tel 01803 862367

Daily all year, dawn to dusk. £2
*From Totnes go NW on A385 for 1m. Turn R on A384 for ½m, then turn R
at Dartington church on minor road for ½m; garden on R.*

This 28-acre garden surrounds a 14th-century hall and tiltyard. A succession
of garden designers since 1925 created a formal central design, with clipped
yews, sunken lawns and terraces. Look out for a fine Henry Moore carving.
Woodland walks have bay, yew and holly as a background. Camellias, rhododendrons and azaleas abound. There is usually a good plant stall. Around
the medieval courtyard, the historic buildings have been converted to provide a conference centre with numerous bedrooms. You can stay privately
in them (*see* Other Places To Stay).

7   HILL HOUSE   Landscove   Tel 01803 762273

Daily all year, 11–5. Free
*From Buckfastleigh go SE on A384 for ½m. Turn L on minor road for 1½m
where signed; garden in village of Landscove.*

How do you categorize this magnificent garden? For some, the enchantment
comes from its connection with the writer Edward Hyams, who wrote extensively about it in his book *An Englishman's Garden*. The present owners,
Mr and Mrs Raymond Hubbard, have been restoring it for the past 12 years,
continuing his love for exotic and unusual plants that provide colour at least
until Christmas. The conservatory has been rebuilt to his design, containing grapes, passion flowers and a lemon tree. A huge cedar towers over the
bulb display in the spring, and magnolias and other tender plants which
seem to thrive miraculously in what is sometimes a harsh climate. For other
visitors, it is the superb nursery which is integral to the garden. More than
18,000 sq ft of glasshouses are used. Featured many times on television,

Hill House is considered by many to hold one of the finest collections of plants anywhere.

Where to Stay

All B&B prices are approximate per person, sharing a double/twin room usually with private or en suite facilities. It is a good idea to ask for any special requirements when booking.

A GABRIEL COURT   Tel 01803 782206

Michael & Eryl Beacom, Gabriel Court, Stoke Gabriel, Nr Totnes, Devon TQ9 6SF.

You find wonderful surroundings and a good deal of luxury in this country hotel. The peaceful 2½-acre garden has two of the largest magnolia trees in the county, and is laid out with herbaceous borders, an Elizabethan terrace, unusual shrubs, carefully-tended vegetables, a swimming pool, croquet lawn, and tennis court. The house itself, with 19 bedrooms, is an attractive white-painted manor, which feels welcoming and traditionally old-fashioned. A 5-course dinner is £23. Dogs permitted (at a small charge). Smoking allowed, children welcome. B&B £37.

B COLETON FISHACRE   *(see* Garden 3)   Tel 01803 752683

Brian & Susan Howe, Coleton Fishacre, Kingswear, Dartmouth, Devon TQ6 0EQ.

Staying here is a unique privilege – the only NT-owned house and garden where you can stay overnight and have the garden to yourself. A guest wrote: 'It is a 1920s' time warp with 1990s' comfort, particularly when it comes to the beds! You feel as if you are staying in the Garden of Eden, but at the same time you are in a lavish house built for a millionaire theatre producer's son who owned the Savoy Hotel.' The house still has some furniture, fixtures and fittings belonging to the D'Oyly Carte family, and more is being added to the collection. There are 5 bedrooms (some bathrooms have original sunken baths), and a self-contained flat sleeping four. Evening meals on some nights (£20, £3 corkage on your own wine) but not all. No smoking in the bedrooms. Dogs accepted, but not allowed in the NT garden. B&B £30–£40.

C LOWER GRIMPSTONLEIGH   Tel 01548 521258

Joy Jones, Lower Grimpstonleigh, East Allington, nr Totnes, Devon TQ9 7QH.

This idyllically peaceful house is set at the end of a lane and surrounded by 12 acres of land that includes an old cider apple orchard, home to two Dexter cows, three horses, three donkeys, and myriad free-range hens. The stone-built house, part of the Grimpstonleigh estate mentioned in the Domesday book, has a pretty courtyard and two ancient barns. The three double bedrooms are special, with vaulted beamed ceilings and comfortable furnishings. No smoking. Dinners (£18, or £12 for supper, unlicensed) include locally-produced meat and fish. No smoking, dogs should be well-behaved and small, and children over 12. B&B £27–£32.

D THE WOOD   Tel 01548 842778

Pat & Malcolm Vaissiere, The Wood, De Courcy Road, South Sands, Salcombe, Devon TQ8 8LQ.

The ½-acre garden (created from 'an overgrown ivy-covered jungle', says Pat) has spectacular views down precipitous steps to a sandy cove below, and the distant winding coastline beyond. The garden, which won two 'Salcombe in Bloom' competitions, features terraces with a fish-filled pond and waterfalls, and the many trees shelter an abundance of birds. Most of the 6 bedrooms take advantage of the marvellous views, and all are luxuriously comfortable. Dinner is £10–£15, licensed. Smokers and dogs welcome. Children should be over 5. B&B £25–£39.

E WADSTRAY HOUSE   Tel 01803 712539

Philip & Merilyn Smith, Wadstray House, Blackawton, nr Dartmouth, Devon TQ9 7DE.

This superb Georgian country house with a double-bay frontage and an orangery alongside is notable for its mature and abundant garden, originally planted by Viscount Chaplin, a leading member of the Horticultural Society (before it became the RHS). Besides Devon's famed magnolias, camellias, azaleas and rhododendrons, there is much else of interest and all-year colour. B&B only, but plenty of restaurants nearby. Three double/twin bedrooms, and self-catering for two in the Orangery. No smoking or dogs, and children should be over 5. B&B £25.

What Else to Enjoy

This is a short selection of the many good things recommended in the area by owners of places to stay. Your hosts will certainly be able to provide additional information.

Other Gardens

About 7m W of the visit map is **Flete** – well worth a detour. It used to be very grand indeed. In the 1920s and '30s large-scale entertaining of royalty and nobility was usual, and the kitchen gardens were magnificent, usually with no less than a dozen gardeners working there. Now enjoy it for some remarkable trees and tranquil views. Russell Page designed the Water Garden, with helpful suggestions from Lawrence of Arabia. This is now being restored, largely through the splendid efforts of the residents of Flete. Interesting trees to watch out for are catalpas, *Parrotia persica,* wellingtonias, and on the upper lawn a Golden Rain tree, *Koelreuteria paniculata.* The garden is open Weds and Thurs, May to late Sept, 2–5, admission £2. You find it 2m W of **Modbury** on A379 Kingsbridge to Plymouth rd, the entrance on L nr Sequers Bridge. Tel 01752 830308.

    Plant World is something of an oddity, as the garden represents a map of the world, with native planting. The name and concept may sound a bit trippery, but the garden most certainly isn't. Ray and Lin Brown are fanatically keen gardeners, and hold three National Collections of primulas. The Himalayan and Japanese gardens are especially well planted. If you are an auricula fancier, this is the place for you. Their adjacent nursery has a choice variety of unusual plants. Find it just N of **Newton Abbot** 1m E of A380 Exeter rd, where you will find many brown tourist signs taking you there. Open daily, 9.30–5 (although the Browns are thinking of taking a day off each week in 1997, so phone to check). Tel 01803 872939.

Other Places to Stay

About 3m NW of the visit map is a superb place to stay: astonishingly good value, and set in outstanding countryside. The brochure photographs for **Oak Cottage** will show you more than I can tell in words – the cottage with its mullioned windows, the walls densely covered with climbers; a marvellously-designed and planted garden, constantly being developed, with pergolas, terraces, pools, stonework; the inside of the house packed with comfortable furniture, paintings, antiques and a collection of antiquarian books. Excellent 4-course evening meals (£14, bring your own wine) are based on imaginative home cooking. Two double/twin bedrooms, restricted smoking, dogs and children by arrangement. B&B £25. Address: Tony & Liz Williams, Oak Cottage, Luscombe Hill, **Dawlish**, Devon EX7 0PX. Tel 01626 863120.

You can make arrangements, too, to stay privately at **Dartington Hall** (*see* Garden 6; Tel 01803 866051). Some of the bedrooms have amazing beamed architecture – and if you like, you can dine with food cooked to order, and prepared in one of England's few surviving 14th-century kitchens. B&B £18–£25.

If It's Wet

Everyone recommends **Dartington Cider Press Centre**, just off the A384 to Buckfastleigh opposite the junction with the A385. Once the home of Dartington Cider, a series of old stone buildings now house a wonderful collection of Dartington crystal, jewellery and pottery, and many other tempting craft products. You can taste cider there, in the Farm Shop, and if you're lucky, you will find a variety of street entertainers performing.

For orchid lovers, **Orchid Paradise** is a must. Part of the adjoining Burnham Nurseries, and frequent exhibitors at the Chelsea Flower Show, it has been developed over the past 40 years, is entirely under glass, and has one of the finest orchid collections anywhere. Find it by going N from **Newton Abbot** on the A382 for 1½ m. Follow brown tourist signs and turn L at the cross-roads where you see a Toll House at the junction. Open daily all the year (except winter BHs), 10–4.

In **Dartmouth**, the Maritime Museum in Butterwalk is excellent – a fascinating record of sea-faring history off the Devon coast.

Eating Out

In the introduction to this visit, I mentioned Joyce Molyneux's **The Carved Angel**, 2 South Embankment, **Dartmouth**. Linger there over lunch, which will cost you about £30 per person plus wine. It is worth it, I promise. A quite small but airy dining room overlooks the River Dart. Open daily except Mons (lunches only on Suns), except for 6 weeks from early Jan. Advisable to book. Tel 01803 832465.

Around Barnstaple

You could decide to visit this area for Rosemoor alone. It is impossible to come away from the Royal Horticultural Society's masterpiece without being inspired to try new ideas in your garden – and probably find yourself with a lighter purse because of the temptations in their plant centre. Save some money, though, for your date at Glebe Cottage, where you will find Carol Klein, her face familiar from Channel 4, and her nursery's rare, special treasures. There is the north Devon coast, the pannier markets, Tarka the Otter's trail, Exmoor, and much else. While you're driving there: Arnold Bax knew this coastline well – listen to his 'Tintagel', and 'The Garden of Fand'.

OS map: Landranger **180**

Gardens

Opening times: in larger gardens, and in NT properties, last admissions are usually 30–45 minutes before the garden closes. Admission charges are a guide to what one adult can expect to pay to go round the garden. It sometimes varies with the season or days of the week. When the house is also open to the public, there is usually an additional charge.

I **ROSEMOOR** Great Torrington Tel 01805 624067

Daily all year, 10–6 (dusk in winter). £3
From Great Torrington go S on A386 for ½m. Turn L on B3220 for ½m, where garden is signed.

The original garden here was created by Lady Anne Berry in what became 8 acres of a beautifully planted hillside setting, full of roses, flowering trees and shrubs, bulbs and herbaceous plants. In 1988, Lady Anne generously gave Rosemoor to the RHS, together with an extra 32 acres where new gardens are now being created. Already established are two formal rose

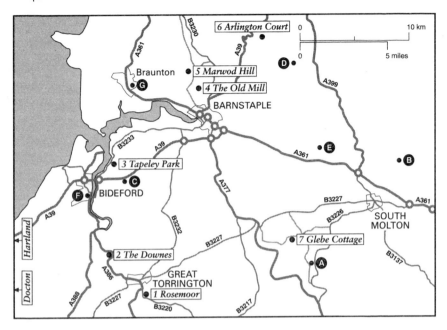

gardens (with 2,000 roses in 200 varieties), extensive herbaceous borders, a herb garden, a potager, and two colour theme gardens. In addition there is a cottage garden, a foliage and plantsman's garden, a fruit and vegetable garden, and a stream and bog garden leading to a lake. It's all here in marvellous profusion, plus a visitor centre, restaurant, and irresistible plant centre selling many rare and interesting species.

2   THE DOWNES   nr Great Torrington   Tel 01805 622244

*Daily, April to mid June, dawn to dusk. Other dates by appointment. £1
From Great Torrington go NW on A386 for 3m; garden signed on L.*

Mr and Mrs Stanley-Baker's 15-acre garden is noteworthy for its landscaped lawns and magnificent views overlooking fields and woodlands in the Torridge Valley, with different vistas opening between successive sections of the garden. There is a wide variety of unusual trees and shrubs in the garden, arboretum and woodland walks. These include davidia, embothrium, liquidambar, ailanthus, halesia, *Cornus kousa*, *Sorbus mitchellii*, *Thujopsis dolabrata*, small groves of sequoia and metasequoia, and many varieties of acer and silver birch. The garden's magnificent display of rhododendrons and azaleas was featured in *Homes and Gardens*.

3   TAPELEY PARK   Instow   Tel 01271 860528

Tues–Sun and BH Mons, Easter to early Oct, 10–5. £2 or more
From Bideford go N on A386 for 1m. Continue N on B3233 for 1m; garden
signed on R.

A delightful Italian fantasy in Devon, created in the last century by Sir John
Belcher, architect, under the direction of Lady Rosamund Christie. The
ground falls away from the handsome house in a series of ornamental
terraces, hedged with lavender and fuchsias. Now Kirsty Christie, aided by
Lady Mary Keen (who also helped redesign the new gardens at Glyndebourne), has been restoring the garden to its Arcadian splendour. There is
a dark ilex tunnel, imaginatively clipped yew, palms and exotic tender
plants, a grotto decorated with shells, an ice-house, and a walled kitchen
garden with a great lean-to greenhouse and old espaliered apples. Don't
miss the border on the Dairy Lawn, where renowned nurserywoman
Carol Klein has helped with the planting plan – glowing vivid colours of
agapanthus, salvias, lobelias and dark cannas.

4   THE OLD MILL   nr Barnstaple   Tel 01271 75002

Some charity days, and by appointment. £1
From Barnstaple go N on A39 for 1m. Turn L on B3230 for ½m, then turn
L at Blakewell Fisheries onto minor road for ½m; garden at end of road.

Les and Barbara Shapland learned that 3 acres of empty meadow went with
the Grade II listed mill house they bought in 1987. From this bare start,
they have gradually made an interesting garden, with water features, herbaceous borders, shrubs, vegetables, herbs, and a new lime avenue leading to
a folly Les built at the end. Les likes building things – look at his bridges,
pergolas, arches, and even a moon-gate. You can have good-value bed and
breakfast here too – 3 double rooms, one a four-poster, at £17.50 per
person.

5   MARWOOD HILL   Marwood, nr Barnstaple   Tel 01271 42528

Daily (except Dec 25) all year, morning to dusk. £2
From Barnstaple go NW on A361 for 1m. Turn R where signed on minor road
for 3m; garden opposite Marwood church.

Dr J.A. Smart's marvellous 20-acre garden holds the National Collection of
astilbes. Go and see them in the summer, flowering along the damp edges
of the lakes and streams. They are preceded by primulas and irises – the

National Collections of *Iris ensata* and tulbaghias are held here too. A very wide selection of plants thrive in this valley garden, including camellias and magnolias, eucalyptus, rhododendrons, eucryphias, hebes, willows, ferns, clematis, with 12 different species of wisteria cascading over a pergola. Although of supreme interest to any knowledgeable gardener, it is also delightful in the overall landscaping and effect, with three small lakes, a large bog garden, and a rock and alpine scree. Home-propagated plants are for sale, listed in a comprehensive catalogue, but not available by mail order. Dr Smart's clematis are particularly good.

6   ARLINGTON COURT (NT)

Arlington, nr Barnstaple   Tel 01271 850296

Daily except Sat, and BHs, late March to late Oct, 11–5.30. £2.40
From Barnstaple go NE on A39 for 7m. Garden signed on R.

The setting here is wonderful – rolling parkland, with woods and a lake, around a Regency house. The gardens consist of a terraced Victorian garden of herbaceous beds, with a conservatory. Shetland ponies are used instead of lawnmowers. If you go round the house (which has an additional entry price) you will find some fascinating collections of *objets d'art*, and a carriage collection in the stables (carriage rides, too, if you choose).

Nearby, if you have the time, is **Holywell** (Tel 01598 710213), which is open some charity afternoons from April to June, and by appointment. A woodland garden covers about 25 acres, with streams, ponds and borders (the woodland walk is best in spring). Mr Steele has green fingers when it comes to growing meconopsis, and has unusual plants for sale. It is in the village of Bratton Fleming. The garden is about ½ m W from the White Hart Inn. Look for a sign at the village hall. After 300 yds fork L for Rye Hall, and the drive-way for Holywell is ¼ m further on at a sharp L-hand bend. Admission £1.

7   GLEBE COTTAGE

Warkleigh, nr South Molton   Tel 01769 540554

Tues–Fri all year, and charity days June to Sept, 10–5. £1
From Barnstaple go S on A377 for 6m. Turn L on B3227 signed South Molton for 2m. Turn R at X-rds on minor road signed Chittlehamholt for 2m. Turn R at X-rds to Warkleigh; garden in Pixie Lane.

The 1-acre garden and nursery of Carol Klein, inspirational plantswoman, is on no account to be missed. The Gold Medal-winning exhibitor at

Chelsea grows all the plants you ever wanted in your own garden, including fine collections of hardy geraniums, pinks, campanulas, penstemons and primulas. Her colour and foliage combinations are stunning.

Where to Stay

All B&B prices are approximate per person, sharing a double/twin room usually with private or en suite facilities. It is a good idea to ask for any special requirements when booking.

A HIGHBULLEN   Tel 01769 540561

Hugh & Pam Neil, Highbullen, Chittlehamholt, nr Umberleigh, North Devon EX37 9HD.

With 35 bedrooms, this hotel is very different from most of the places to stay listed in this book. It is here because of the spectacular facilities it has to offer, because of its wondrous setting, because it is family-owned and informal, and because its half-board and short break prices keep it within our upper range. Originally a splendid Victorian Gothic mansion, the estate encompasses 135 acres, plus 85 acres of ancient semi-natural woodland with numerous deer and an endless list of birds. If you can spare the time and energy after garden visiting, these are some of the delights Highbullen offers (a few have a small extra charge): outdoor and indoor heated swimming pools, outdoor and indoor tennis courts, an 18-hole golf course free to residents, squash, croquet, billiards, table tennis, sauna, steam room, exercise room, sunbed. Oh, and massage, which you'll probably need. No dogs in hotel or restaurant, and no smoking where you eat. Fairly suitable for wheelchairs. D,B&B around £58.

B COURT HALL   Tel 01598 740224

Charles & Sally Worthington, Court Hall, North Molton, nr South Molton, North Devon EX36 3HP.

There are lovely surroundings for this house, set in its own park. It has a fine garden with sweeping lawns and mature trees, a walled garden started 11 years ago with a conservatory and swimming pool, and a productive vegetable garden used for the excellent *en famille* dinners (£20, licensed) which you can enjoy here. Charles and Sally are both keen cooks (and keen bridge players, too), and Sally, having lived in the area all her life, can point you to the right place for anywhere you might like to visit. Two double rooms, smoking allowed, dogs by arrangement, and children over 12. B&B £30.

C THE PINES   Tel 01271 860561

Barry & Jenny Jones, The Pines, Eastleigh, nr Bideford, North Devon, EX39 4PA.

Since taking over this country house hotel in 1994, Barry and Jenny (to use their words) 'have been working hard to restore the garden and surroundings to its former glory with shrubs, large water garden area and orchard'. There are fine views over rolling hills towards Bideford with Lundy island in the distance. Originally an 18th-century farmhouse, it is now an immaculately white-painted family home with 6 bedrooms (1 single), plus 2 self-catering cottages whose visitors can take advantage of the hotel, which is licensed. 2-course suppers are £11. No smoking. £2 charge if you bring dogs. Children welcome, and wheelchairs are manageable. B&B £25–£28.

D BRACKEN HOUSE   Tel 01598 710320

Prue & Lawrie Scott, Bracken House, Bratton Fleming, nr Barnstaple, North Devon EX31 4TG.

About 750 feet up on the western edge of Exmoor, this former rectory stands in 8 acres of garden, woodland and paddocks, including a small lake. Bird-life includes nuthatches, buzzards and nesting mallard in spring. The views are wonderful, over rolling hills and wooded valleys to the Taw estuary. A library of books, many of them devoted to natural history, tempt you to stay for weeks rather than days. The 8 bedrooms include 1 suitable for wheelchairs. Evening meals cost £15, licensed. Children over 8 and dogs are welcome, smoking restricted. B&B £22–£32.

E HUXTABLE FARM   Tel 01598 760254

Jackie & Antony Payne, Huxtable Farm, West Buckland, nr Barnstaple, North Devon EX32 0SR.

This attractive and secluded stone farm has been carefully restored or converted to provide 3 double rooms in the main farmhouse, and beds for 11 more people in the outbuildings. The house itself is early 16th-century and has many original features such as oak beams, screen panelling, open fireplaces with bread ovens, uneven floors and low doorways. Modern additions include a sauna, a games room with darts and table tennis, and a tennis court. The 4-course candle-lit dinner (£13, bring your own wine) is a treat, complete with a glass of home-made wine, and home-cooked food with local ingredients. Four twin/double bedrooms, and 2 family rooms. No dogs, smoking allowed, children welcome. B&B £22–£23.

F THE MOUNT HOTEL   Tel 01237 473748

Mike & Janet Taylor, Northdown Road, Bideford, North Devon EX39 3LP.

This is a rare find for those who like the bustle and activity of a market town, but also want an oasis of peace to stay in. The Mount, a 2-storey house of Georgian origin, is only 5 minutes' nearly-level walk from the centre of Bideford, yet the owners have managed to create in their sloping town garden a sense of enclosed tranquility. Dominated by a superb copper beech and a yew tree, a number of grassed and paved sun-traps have been cleverly placed. Best in spring and early summer, the garden has colour throughout the season. Janet does her best to pot-on types of plants which she has found guests most like. There are 8 bedrooms, 7 en suite. Furnishings are modern and comfortable. Smoking in the bar only, no dogs, children welcome. Suppers £6.50–£9. B&B £19–£22.

G ST MERRYN   Tel 01271 813805

Ros Bradford, Higher Park Road, Braunton, North Devon EX33 2LG.

Ros is an artist whose talent shows not just in her many paintings of local gardens, but in the imaginative charm of her secluded, south-facing garden, with winding paths through trees and shrubs leading to many peaceful sun-traps, a swimming pool, fishponds, hens, and a summerhouse. The 2 double and 2 twin rooms mostly share bathrooms and separate loos. Evening meals (£8, bring your own wine) are often served outside in the summer. Smoking, dogs and children are all fine by Ros. No wonder she has so many examples of guests who came for a night, and stayed a week. B&B £15–£17.

What Else to Enjoy

This is a short selection of the many good things recommended in the area by owners of places to stay. Your hosts will certainly be able to provide additional information.

Other Gardens

About 14m W of the visit map, and once a derelict watermill, **Docton Mill** is now one of Devon's most renowned and interesting gardens, a delight in all seasons. You will discover a fine blend of the cultivated merging with the wild. Ponds, leats and streams are lined with plants which like their toes to be damp – primulas, ligularias, ferns. In spring there are marvellous displays of narcissi, camellias, azaleas, magnolias and bluebells. In summer the shrub roses sway over perennial geraniums. And the great joy is, you can stay here too (*see* Other Places to Stay). It is open daily, March to Oct, 10–6. Admission £2. Find it by taking the A39 Bideford to Bude rd, turning off at the signpost to **Hartland**. Docton Mill is signed between Hartland and Elmscott, near the YHA.

When visiting Docton Mill, it would be a pity not to take in **Hartland Abbey** nearby. Founded in 1157, and tucked in the bottom of a narrow valley running down to the Atlantic, it is basically a shrub garden ablaze in spring with rhododendrons, azaleas and camellias, bluebells, daffodils and primroses. Peacocks screech and donkeys munch in the parkland. The Abbey has been passed down through generations and marriages since 1539, and has never been sold, so the interior and contents are fascinating. Great cream teas here. It is open Weds, May to Sept, 2–5.30; also Suns, July to Sept. Drive from Hartland towards Stoke and Hartland Quay; the Abbey is well signed to the R, about 1m. Admission £1. Tel 01237 441264.

Other Places to Stay

Enough to say that at Martin and Eva Bourcier's **Docton Mill**, the standard of accommodation in this converted 13th-century mill house is as high as its prize-winning garden. Martin is an experienced restaurateur and chef and uses the best local produce to create outstanding evening meals (£18.50, licensed). The ground floor rooms are inspirational, exploiting many original features. The 2 bedrooms are everything you could expect. You would be advised to book well in advance. A no smoking house, and no dogs allowed. The address is Spekes Valley, **Hartland**, North Devon EX39 6EA. Tel 01237 441369. B&B £35.

Eight miles N of the visit map is a homely B&B where, if you're a fuchsia lover, you will surely fill your car with take-home plants. Mary and Roger Gilbert at **Silverdale Nurseries**, Shute Lane, **Combe Martin**, Devon EX34 0HT (Tel 0127 882539) grow more than 600 varieties, and offer accommodation which had top rating in a national newspaper survey. The house has a breathtaking outlook over Combe Martin and there are 2 double and 1 single bedrooms (sharing bathrooms). Plenty of places to eat out in the evening, non-smokers preferred, no dogs. B&B £14.

If It's Wet

Top of the list is Dartington Crystal in **Great Torrington**. Open all the year and receiving more than 200,000 visitors, it is a large complex which includes exhibitions, a large kitchen and giftware shop, a restaurant and a factory alongside where you can watch skilled craftsmen blowing and shaping crystal glass. The factory is open Mon–Fri all the year, and weekends from April to end Sept, 9.30–4.30. It will cost you £2.50; a more detailed specialist tour costing £5 must be pre-booked (Tel 01805 624333).

In the main square of **Barnstaple** is the highly recommended Museum of North Devon, with seven centuries of wonderful local pottery on show. The town's pannier market, with dozens of stalls, is held on Wednesdays. Many of the same traders can be found in **Bideford**'s pannier market on Tuesdays and Saturdays.

The major NT property in the area to put a roof over your head for an hour or so while it's raining is **Arlington Court** (*see* Garden 6). It has fascinating exhibitions, and there is a good licensed retaurant. Admission is £4.80 which includes the garden.

Eating Out

Easily the most recommended place in this visit for a dinner to remember is **Lower Pitt Restaurant** in East Buckland (Tel 01598 760243). In this 16th-century farmhouse (sometimes you eat in the conservatory) you will find a menu with original ideas mostly based on local produce. Suzanne Lyons cooks the meals, her husband Jerome is an excellent host. You are surrounded by flowers – a friendly place, indeed. It is a restaurant-with-rooms (B&B from £30, set dinner £20). If you want to push the boat out, your meal with wine will cost about £35 per person.

The Exe Valley

There are ten lovely gardens to look at in this visit, some of them not at all well-known – hidden and personal, growing naturally out of the maze of lanes and back roads beneath the rolling hills in this part of Devon. Driving around, you should enjoy something lyrical and flowing: perhaps the amazing Brahms Clarinet Quintet, preferably in the version from the Amadeus String Quartet with Karl Leister's masterly, sensitive, warm clarinet playing.

OS maps: Landrangers 181, **192**

Gardens

Opening times: in larger gardens, and in NT properties, last admissions are usually 30–45 minutes before the garden closes. Admission charges are a guide to what one adult can expect to pay to go round the garden. It sometimes varies with the season or days of the week. When the house is also open to the public, there is usually an additional charge.

I **VICARS MEAD** nr Budleigh Salterton Tel 01395 442641

Some charity days in May/June, and by appointment. £1
From Exeter go E on A3052 for 8m. Turn R onto B3178 at Newton Popple-
ford for 3½m to East Budleigh. Garden in Hayes Lane opposite Sir Walter
Raleigh inn. Ask owner for final directions.

Here are 4 acres packed with interest to the specialist plantsman. On the steep terraced gardens, created by Mr and Mrs Read in the past 20 years around their 500-year-old former vicarage, are masses of rare and unusual shrubs, trees and border plants, planted informally on a sandstone escarpment. Specialists can dwell particularly on the many varieties of hostas, and the National Collections of dianellas (flax lilies), libertias, liriopes and ophiopogons (perennial grasses).

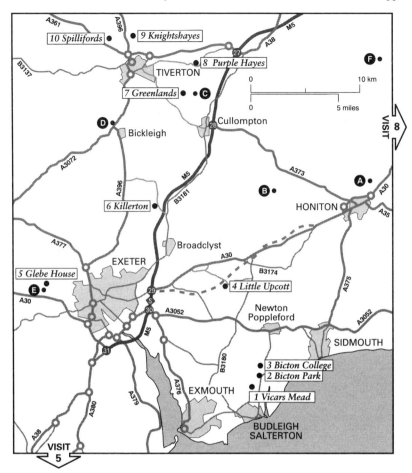

2 **BICTON PARK** nr Budleigh Salterton Tel 01395 568465

Daily, March to Oct, 10–5. £3.75
From Exeter go E on A3052 for 8m. Turn R onto B3178 at Newton Poppleford for 2½m; entrance signed on R just after Bicton College.

There is plenty for all the family in these 50-acre gardens, what with the woodland railway ride, children's play areas, a museum, a self-service restaurant and bar, and picnic areas where you can take your dog on a lead. Devoted garden lovers will enjoy more specialized treats: a very pretty formal Italian garden dating back to the early 18th century, an American garden from the early 19th century, a lake and water garden, and a pinetum. There are ranges of greenhouses and conservatories, and a glorious curved palm house, built in 1815.

3   BICTON COLLEGE   nr Budleigh Salterton   Tel 01395 568353

Daily all year, 10.30–5. £2
From Exeter go E on A3052 for 8m. Turn R onto B3178 at Newton Poppleford for 2m. Entrance signed on R at Sidmouth Lodge.

At this college of agriculture you will find display gardens with an extraordinarily large number of botanical collections, approached up a unique and much-photographed avenue of monkey puzzle trees. The many different species and varieties are partly laid out in beds for teaching and study purposes, but are also included in borders to show their effect in general planting. There is an old walled garden, many greenhouses and a ½-m long arboretum walk, brilliant to look at in spring. The National Collections of agapanthus and pittisporum are held here, and the plant centre contains rare treasures for sale.

4   LITTLE UPCOTT   Marsh Green, nr Exeter   Tel 01404 822797

3–6 afternoons monthly, May to Aug, and by appointment. £1.50
From Exeter go NE on A30 for 4m. Turn R onto minor road, signed Marsh Green, for 2m. Ask owner for final directions.

This is a 2-acre garden consisting of many small areas at different levels, each with its own style, colour and informal planting scheme. Unusual varieties of conifers, shrubs, alpines and perennials provide year round interest, and the original cottage garden is planted with soft colours, shrub roses, hebes, geraniums and variegated plants. A pond has recently been added in the old orchard, for the favourite ducks of Mike and Maureen Jones who also provide a home for hens, elderly sheep and cats so the garden is dog-free, apart from guide dogs. Mr and Mrs Jones have considered the comfort of people with disabilities, and while not all the garden is accessible for wheelchairs, there plenty of seats to rest on, and it is a very scented garden.

Four miles E from here is Ottery St Mary. **Otter Nurseries**, in Gosford Rd, is a large garden centre that has a wide variety of first-class stock, and is much used by good gardeners from all over the area because of the value and choice.Tel 01404 815815.

5   THE GLEBE HOUSE

Whitestone, nr Exeter   Tel 01392 811200

1 afternoon a week, end May to mid July, and by appointment. £1
From Exeter go NW on minor road for 4m to Whitestone; garden next to church.

A garden on three levels with lovely views from the Exe valley to Dartmoor. Of special interest are the climbers over the stonework: walls and buildings are covered with clematis, honeysuckle, jasmines, and roses (including a notably large *R. filipes* 'Kiftsgate' reaching along the walls of the tithe barn, as if to warn you what happens if you unwisely plant this viciously thorned and short-flowering variety in too small a garden; believe me, from personal experience, it's a nightmare). You will find more than 300 different roses, many fine acers, birches and eucalyptus, and a large heather garden, set among extensive lawns with fine mature trees.

6   KILLERTON (NT)   Broadclyst, nr Exeter   Tel 01392 881345

Park and garden all year, 10.30–dusk. £3.10
From Exeter go N on B3181 for 4m. Turn L where signed onto minor road for 1m.

Justly famous 15 acres of splendid hillside garden, created by John Veitch around 1770. Later, Sir William Robinson made his mark on the herbaceous borders. The trees and shrubs here are magnificent. There is a collection of nearly 100 different rhododendrons, a rock garden in an old quarry, follies and a new wild flower area. It doesn't matter what time of the year you visit, it is always good – well-maintained, wonderful views, with something new to catch your eye.

7   GREENLANDS   Ash Thomas, nr Tiverton   Tel 01884 821257

Charity Suns. March to Sept, and by appointment. £1.50
From Tiverton town centre take minor road E for 3m to Halberton. Turn R onto minor road to Ash Thomas for 1½m. Turn R at Crow Green X-roads. Garden immediately on L.

Lovely views to the Blackdown Hills can be enjoyed from Dr and Mrs Anderson's garden of one-third of an acre. The garden has been divided into several smaller rooms, with rustic poles supporting roses and clematis. The paths flow and curve around herbaceous borders, a large rock garden and a hot dry bed with Mediterranean plants. A telegraph pole has been cunningly disguised as the central support for netting in a circular fruit

garden. A pond, shaped like an apple, has its edges planted with interesting striped grasses. The veggies are immaculate, crammed into raised beds
in the approved RHS manner. Under an old oak tree, cyclamen and daffodils
delight in autumn and spring. At the back of the house, herbs and roses
make a lovely scented garden. Mrs Anderson is an expert on penstemons,
growing more than 90 different varieties. Dr Anderson sends the profits
from plant sales to a hospital he helps in Zambia, so spend lots of money
here in a good cause.

8   PURPLE HAYES   Halberton, nr Tiverton   Tel 01884 821295

3 charity Suns, and by appointment. 75p
From Tiverton town centre take minor road E for 3m to Halberton. Garden
½m further at Lake Farm.

This plantaholics' garden was begun nine years ago from two rough fields,
and already feels very mature, with exuberant planting. Parts of the garden
are south-facing, hot and dry, and here Mrs Thomas has planted a herb
garden and Mediterranean plants – beschorneria, cordylines, yuccas amongst
them. You will also find a rock garden, a bog garden, a white border and a
red border. Anyone who has an overgrown, uncultivated plot of land and
wants to turn it into a garden paradise couldn't do better than to browse
here and learn from this marvellous example. There are pigmy goats,
rabbits, ducks and guinea pigs too, to keep your children amused.

   Just to the E of here is the village of Sampford Peverell, where you can
find excellent value plants for sale. **Sampford Shrubs** has a wide range of
trees, shrubs, and many unusual fruit trees as well as some good herbaceous
stock. Tel 01884 821164.

9   KNIGHTSHAYES COURT (NT)
Bolham, nr Tiverton   Tel 01884 254665

Daily except Tues, end March to end Oct, 11–5.30. £3.10
From Tiverton go N on A396 for 2m. Turn R in Bolham where signed on minor
road for 2m.

One of the finest and most famous gardens in Devon, with formal terraces
and borders, and the well-known topiary of a fox and hounds racing across
a hedge. Features to look out for are the rare shrubs, and a woodland walk
with magnolias, acers, rhododendrons and tree peonies, beeches, oaks and
larches, under-planted with bulbs including cyclamen and trilliums. As a

contrast to the woodland, the tranquil pool garden is very formal, surrounded by a battlemented yew hedge. There are interesting plants for sale, too.

10 SPILLIFORDS

Lower Washfield, nr Tiverton   Tel 01884 252422

By appointment only – owner often acts as guide. £2
From Tiverton go N on A396 for 3m. Turn L onto minor road signed Wash-field for ½m; garden in village. Ask owner for final directions.

Not so much a garden, more a paradise for wildlife. Anyone with an interest in natural history will enjoy a personally-conducted tour by Dr Haig along his very steeply banked riverside (River Exe), to see the wild flowers, birds and butterflies that thrive here.

Where to Stay

All B&B prices are approximate per person, sharing a double/twin room usually with private or en suite facilities. It is a good idea to ask for any special requirements when booking.

A   WOODHAYES   Tel 01404 42011

Christy & Noel Page-Turner, Woodhayes, Honiton, Devon EX14 0TP.

Woodhayes is a classical listed Georgian house with stupendous views across the Otter Valley to Dartmoor. Its own 150 acres show a landscape of green fields interspersed with small blocks of deciduous woodland, declared an Area of Outstanding Natural Beauty and more recently designated an Environmentally Sensitive Area. The 1-acre garden consists of a series of rooms divided by box and beech hedges: herbaceous borders, a rock garden, roses and many lawns. In spring there is a mass of bulbs. The farm and vegetable garden provide provide much of the produce which Christy, a talented and imaginative cook, uses for delicious dinners (£20, bring your own wine) eaten in the 18th-century dining room hung with family portraits. Guests (2 double and 1 single bedroom) are treated to fine living with friendly hosts. Dogs by arrangement, no smoking in bedrooms. Children should be over 12. B&B £32.

B   COKESPUTT HOUSE   Tel 01404 841289

Caroline & Angus Forbes, Cokesputt House, Payhembury, nr Honiton, Devon EX14 0HD.

The garden and grounds here are worth a visit on their own. Since 1989, Caroline and Angus have planned, landscaped and planted from scratch, using the 'old bones' wherever they could. Around the house – spacious, elegant, and developed over four centuries – is a ½-acre of contrasting areas: a formal lawn edged with yew and 75 Margaret Merrill roses, an enclosed 'secret' herbaceous walled garden with climbing and shrub roses and a small potager with central gazebo. All are overflowing with well-loved plants. The grounds beyond include a wildflower meadow, a large natural pond, and a 2-acre cider orchard from which cider is made (and drunk and sold) on antique cider machinery. There is a well-stocked modern orangery/conservatory. Two double bedrooms and 1 single. No smoking, no dogs, and children should be 12 or over. Excellent evening meal for £18.50 (bring your own wine). You must book in advance. B&B £30.

C   LOWER BEERS   Tel 01884 32257

Anne & Gerald Nicholls, Lower Beers, Britten Bottom, nr Cullompton, Devon EX15 1NB.

For those of you with hungry taste buds, look forward to a visit here. What you find is for gourmets – house and food both. Anne runs a small, exclusive, upmarket cookery school and, as you might expect, her meals (£16–£22 for dinner, good choice of aperitifs, wines, etc.) are exceptional. So are the surroundings. The listed 16th-century Devon longhouse has a wonderfully eclectic range of furniture and furnishings, low ceilings, huge timbers and inglenook fireplaces. The 3 double bedrooms are extremely comfortable. Outside, the developing 3-acre 'hidden' garden includes an ornamental herb and vegetable garden, woodland dell, and a large open area being planted with trees, leading to a stream and a footbridge from which you can start a long walk. No dogs or children or smoking. B&B £28.

D   BICKLEIGH COTTAGE HOTEL   Tel 01884 855230

Stuart & Pauline Cochrane, Bickleigh Cottage Hotel, Bickleigh Bridge, nr Tiverton, Devon EX16 8RJ.

White-painted, thatched, built around 1640, this is everyone's dream of a Devon village cottage. Behind is a cottage garden, running the length of the property alongside the banks of the River Exe. Nearby is Bickleigh Bridge, a landmark famous for its scenic charm. Inside the house is a mixture of ancient and modern – good antiques alongside 20th-century furniture. The 8 bedrooms are mostly en suite, a little small, but comfortable. Ask for one which faces the river: the views are better, and a rather busy road runs along the other side of the hotel. No pets, or children under 12. No smoking in the dining-room or bedrooms. Evening meals (7 p.m., 3 courses and coffee, licensed) £11.50. B&B £23.

E   TRILLOW   Tel 01392 811282

John & Gill Schnadhorst, Trillow, Nadderwater, nr Exeter, Devon EX4 2LD.

This picturesque thatched medieval hall house has an abundantly stocked cottage garden with paths leading into a paddock with specimen trees and ancient woodland covering 7 acres. It is an early 15th-century house, one wing of which is given over to guests and their friends, who have their own dining- and drawing-room. There is a real feeling of antiquity, and the 2 guest bedrooms are large with comfortable armchairs. B&B only (substantial wholesome uncooked breakfasts), but good advice on where to eat nearby. No smoking. Dogs and children to be discussed. B&B £23.

F   PEAR TREE COTTAGE   Tel 01823 601224

Pam Parry, Stapley, Churchstanton, Taunton, Somerset TA3 7QA.

This enchanting thatched cottage, in an Area of Outstanding Natural Beauty, has almost an acre of abundantly flowering garden, with climber-clad walls, informal beds, and lawns leading to greenhouses and 2 vegetable gardens laid out in the raised bed system. In the 2½-acre meadow, many varieties of trees have established themselves as the basis for an arboretum. Two double bedrooms and 1 single. Evening meals should be requested at least a day in advance. No smoking in bedrooms. Pam has a sensible attitude about dogs and children: 'well-behaved smaller varieties by arrangement'. Evening meals £9, bring your own wine. B&B £13–£20.

What Else to Enjoy

This is a short selection of the many good things recommended in the area by owners of places to stay. Your hosts will certainly be able to provide additional information.

If It's Wet

You should think of exploring **Exeter**. The Royal Albert Memorial Museum in Queen St (10–5, admission free) is a treasure trove of intriguing items, many brought there during the great age of Victorian collecting. There are always visiting exhibitions of interest. Nearby, off Fore St, is St Nicholas Priory, a 900-year-old monastic building with a superb stone undercroft, and marvellous timbers on the upper floor. Open Mon–Sat, 1–5, admission £1.25. If the rain stops, many people find Exeter's main attraction the Maritime Museum, on the quay, with the world's largest musuem collection of boats. There are more than 100, on water and on land, to be explored and handled, together with special displays.

Honiton is good place to head for. Allhallows Museum, next to St Paul's Church in the town centre, has perhaps the best displays of lace in the country, made in the town since the middle of the 16th century. From June to August, Mon–Sat, there are daily demonstrations of lace-making by volunteers who want to keep this local craft alive. Honiton is also notable for its antique shops: more than 15, jostling next to each other, offering everything from bric-à-brac to choice collectables you would love but probably can't afford.

Close to Gardens 1–3, and easily found via brown tourist signs, is **Otterton Mill**, the last working mill on the River Otter. You can buy bread made from the various flours ground there, or eat it with with light meals in the restaurant. There is a museum, an exhibition of lace, craft shops and workshops, as well as occasional exhibitions of work from elsewhere. Fascinating and very wholesome, I thought.

Eating Out

Everyone locally recommends **The Drewe Arms** in **Broadhembury.** Me too. I first ate in this 13th-century pub more years ago than I shall admit. Today it is owned and run by Nigel and Kerstin Burge, who serve you fresh fish and seafood cooked to order. A 3-course meal in the restaurant costs about £20 per person plus wine (advisable to book: Tel 01404 841267), or you can eat bar food for £3–£10 per dish.

The Axe Valley

You are on the borders of three counties in this visit: Devon, Somerset and Dorset. There is a delightful variety of gardens, nearly all of them with a backcloth of a fine old house. These abound in this area, which always feels to me to be secret and private, its treasures hidden from public view. Forde Abbey must have heard many a Gregorian chant, but the music doesn't quite catch the mood of the place today. I settled for Samuel Barber's Adagio for Strings – quiet, sustaining, elegiac.

OS map: Landranger **193**

Gardens

Opening times: in larger gardens, and in NT properties, last admissions are usually 30–45 minutes before the garden closes. Admission charges are a guide to what one adult can expect to pay to go round the garden. It sometimes varies with the season or days of the week. When the house is also open to the public, there is usually an additional charge.

I BURROW FARM GARDENS

Dalwood, nr Axminster   Tel 01404 831285

Daily, April to Sept, 2–7, and mornings by appointment. £2
From Axminster go W on A35 for 3½m. Turn R signed to Stockland; garden ½m on R.

This 5-acre garden with magnificent views, created from farmland and still being developed and planted with great flair by Mary Benger and her family, has magnificent foliage effect. The woodland garden, with rhododendrons and azaleas, is at its best in spring, but later on the rose pergola and herbaceous borders are delightful. Plants are for sale in the nursery.

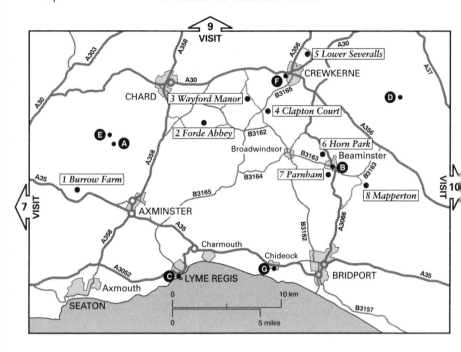

2   FORDE ABBEY   nr Chard   Tel 01460 220231

Daily all year, 10–4.30. £3.25
From Chard go SE on B3162 for 4m; garden well signed on R.

The Cistercian monks have left their mark on this wondrous 30-acre garden
not just with their fishponds, now lily-fringed, but in the peaceful and con-
templative atmosphere that you find. Fine mature trees and a more recent
arboretum surround the abbey. There are long, deep, colourful borders, an
impressive rock garden, calm lawns, yews, statuary, cascades and bog
gardens. In spring, a marvellous collection of magnolias and rhododendrons
blossom, and candelabra primulas and meconopsis revel in getting their toes
into the bog garden. There is a great deal to be seen here at all seasons.
Don't miss the walled kitchen garden, and the nursery selling fine rare
plants. Save a little energy to climb the Mount for the inspiring view, and
find the incense cedar *Calocedrus currens*; inhaling its fragrance will
revitalize you.

3   WAYFORD MANOR   nr Crewkerne   Tel 01460 73253

4 charity days, and private parties by appointment. £2
From Crewkerne go SW on B3165 for 3m. Turn R to Wayford; garden in
centre of village.

Mr and Mrs R.L. Goffe's fine Elizabethan manor house is surrounded by a
delightful garden, redesigned by Harold Peto in 1900. He made three fine
terraces close to the house, and a 3-arched loggia. Balustrades, stone steps
and a stone-edged pond give the garden strong bones, and within this formal framework is informal and exuberant planting. Some exceptional trees
have matured in the orchard, along with a collection of rhododendrons. Old
apple trees almost disappear under the snowy weight of rambling roses.
Magnificent magnolias and acers are around the pools, and the damp bottom
garden has luxuriant plantings of gunnera, rodgersias, skunk cabbage, and
primulas. There are three small 'secret gardens' to explore, and staggering
views to enjoy. An all-season garden, possibly at its best in April and May.

4   CLAPTON COURT   nr Crewkerne   Tel 01460 73220

3 charity days, and by appointment. £3
From Crewkerne go SW on B3165 for 2½m to Clapton; garden in centre of
village.

Mr and Mrs Giffin's 4-acre formal garden with many rare and unusual
plants, including the largest and oldest ash tree in Great Britain. Is this
perhaps the World Ash under which the three Norns sat and spun out the
destiny of the Gods in *Götterdammerung*. It's a great place to hum a lot of
Wagner anyway. The garden is on a south-west facing slope, with a series
of walls dividing it into terraces, all with different planting characteristics.

5   LOWER SEVERALLS   nr Crewkerne   Tel 01460 73234

Garden daily, April to Sept, 2–5. £1
Nursery daily except Thurs, March to Oct, 10–5 (Sun 2–5).
From Crewkerne go NE on A30 for 1½m. Signed L on first minor road.

A 1-acre plantswoman's cottage garden of special interest to lovers of hardy
geraniums, salvias and herbs. The nursery sells interesting herbaceous and
half-hardy plants, and many medicinal, culinary and scented herbs – Mary
Pring's speciality. A smallish garden, but packed with interest, and with
many tender and half-hardy perennials for sale. Splendid teas are served on
the lawn in front of the charming old farmhouse.

Only 1m away, on the W side of the A356 in the village of Merriott, is **Scott's Nursery**. It is large, and renowned for its extensive range of roses (more than 500 varieties), perennials, trees and shrubs. Tel 01460 72306.

6   HORN PARK   Beaminster   Tel 01308 862212

Tues, Thurs, Sun (and BH Mons), April to Oct, 2–5.30. £2.50
From Beaminster go NW on A3066 for 1½m. Garden on L, just before tunnel.

A large garden, with fine trees, in a splendid setting, looking out to terraces and lawns, then fields of buttercups, rolling hills, and at last the sparkling sea. The house is charmingly pretty, designed by a pupil of Lutyens, whose influence shows strongly. The formal terraces below the house have borders full of soft colours, and many butterflies. White roses flank the steps down to the bottom lawn; there, three formal beds use standard brooms and roses very attractively. Around the water garden are stronger colours. There are many seats from which you can enjoy the changing vistas. A wildflower meadow has mown grass paths leading to a bluebell wood. In the greenhouse are home-propagated plants for sale. Mr and Mrs John Kirkpatrick keep the garden in a marvellous state – not a weed or a deadhead to be seen.

7   PARNHAM HOUSE   Beaminster   Tel 01308 862204

Suns, Weds, and BHs, April to Oct, 10–5. £4.50
From Beaminster go S on A3066 for ½m. Garden signed on R.

The incredible ornamental 16th-century house now belongs to John Makepeace, the furniture maker (*see* If it's Wet). He and his wife have done much to restore the gardens. The huge lawn is dominated by clipped lanes of yew, with spring-fed water mills, plus all the treats one would hope to find in a garden such as this – old roses, gazebos, grand herbaceous borders, splendid old trees, a riverside walk, and woodlands including two majestic cedars of Lebanon.

8   MAPPERTON   nr Beaminster   Tel 01308 862645

Daily, March to Oct, 2–6. £2.50
From Beaminster go E on B3163 for 2m. Turn R for Mapperton where garden is signed.

A fine 17th-century manor house dominates this excellent garden, which is terraced through a coomb, down formal paths and steps, with an Italianate influence. Its two long pools are ornamented with many urns, statues and topiary. A shrubbery and woodland has been planted in the last 40 years. Fun to be had with the surprising statues.

On the S edge of **Bridport**, easily found in West Bay Rd, is an old, family-run nursery specialising in Victorian violets. **C.W. Groves and Son** also has a good range of other interesting plants and is well worth visiting. Tel 01308 22654.

Where to Stay

All B&B prices are approximate per person, sharing a double/twin room usually with private or en suite facilities. It is a good idea to ask for any special requirements when booking.

A   LEA HILL HOTEL   Tel 01404 881881

Hilary & Jim Reaney, Lea Hill Hotel, Membury, nr Axminster, Devon EX13 7AQ.

This superbly restored 14th-century thatched Devon longhouse is marvellous, inside and out. Approached through its own 8 rolling acres, it has fine views and comfortable places to sit in an immaculately kept garden. The house, which you enter through the original longhouse hall, luxuriously furnished, is heavily beamed and retains many of its historic architectural features – flagstone floors, wood panelling, stone interior walls, inglenook fires, bread oven, and so on. Including some converted outbuildings, there are now 11 bedrooms each with its own character, and luxuriously refurbished with matching furnishings and fabrics. The dinner menu (from £15) is imaginative, and the wine list captivating. No smoking. Dogs allowed only in certain rooms. Children welcome. B&B £32–£39

B   BRIDGE HOUSE   Tel 01308 862200

Peter Pinkster, Bridge House, 3 Prout Bridge, Beaminster, Dorset DT8 3AY.

Originally a 13th-century priest's house, this friendly hotel has more of a Georgian feel to it nowadays. At the back is a sizeable walled garden, landscaped a couple of years ago with lawns and borders, and wonderfully sheltered for sitting out. Inside, the house is beautifully decorated and furnished, and you are made to feel at home. The 14 bedrooms include 1 single. On fine evenings, you can eat in the conservatory. Set dinners, highly praised, cost £20, licensed. Children welcome, smoking and dogs restricted. B&B £29–£50.

C WILLOW COTTAGE   Tel 01297 443199

Elizabeth & Geoffrey Griffin, Willow Cottage, Ware Lane, Lyme Regis, Dorset DT7 3EL.

Here you have wonderful peace and quiet with amazing views over NT countryside and coast. Within 200 yds is an under-the-cliffs nature trail. A short walk along the cliff tops takes you to the Cobb, Lyme Regis's harbour. The double room in the studio is en suite, with an adjoining single bedroom. Guests usually eat out locally in the evenings, although you can arrange with Elizabeth to have tray suppers brought to you (from £8.50, bring your own wine). Smoking not encouraged, dogs by arrangement, children should be over 8. B&B £25.

D HALSTOCK MILL   Tel 01935 891278

Jane & Peter Spender, Halstock Mill, Halstock, nr Yeovil, Dorset BA22 9SJ.

Surrounded by 10 acres of its own gardens and paddocks, this tranquil setting forms part of Thomas Hardy's country – an Area of Outstanding Natural Beauty, bordered by hundreds of acres of undulating pastureland. Peacefully situated at the end of a private lane, the grounds host several varieties of wild orchid. Jane and Peter are experts in guiding guests to local nurseries with unusual plants. The mill, built in the 17th century, has been converted into a spacious country house of charm and character. There are 4 excellent bedrooms. Local ingredients form the basis of evening meals (£16, licensed). You can smoke, and bring dogs by arrangement. Children should be over 5. B&B £24–£30.

E GOODMANS HOUSE   Tel 01404 881690

Robert & Pat Spencer, Goodmans House, Furley, nr Axminster, Devon EX13 7TU.

Goodmans House is what everyone on a garden visit dreams of finding: a tranquil setting, glorious views, a garden planted by botanists, a welcoming family, supremely comfortable accommodation, sensationally good food – and all at prices that make you wonder how expensive (and much worse) hotels get away with it. The 12-acre grounds have the customary Devon spring display of bulbs and acid-loving shrubs. Later there are many unusual trees and shrubs to be enjoyed. Inside the mostly Georgian house is a superbly arched dining-room with an inglenook at each end, where Pat serves consistently excellent candlelit dinners (£15.95, including free aperitif). There is just 1 double/twin guest room in the house itself. Most guests stay in the 4 superbly equipped suites converted from an old stone barn, with fully equipped kitchen/dining/sitting areas in case you want to skip breakfast or make a snack. It is all very informal, flexible and luxurious, and is one of the very best recommendations in this guide. No smoking in the house. Dogs allowed if well behaved. Children can stay in the larger suites. B&B £24–£27.

F BROADVIEW GARDENS   Tel 01460 73424

Gillian & Robert Swann, Broadview Gardens, 43 East St, East Crewkerne, Somerset TA18 7AG.

This unusual colonial-style bungalow, built in an era of quality, has 3 en suite double/twin guest rooms, furnished in the Edwardian style, overlooking an acre of beautifully kept, terraced and landscaped grounds. Plenty of places to relax in this garden, with a good pergola, a koi pond, and abundant planting with many unusual herbaceous plants. Everything feels sunny, friendly and informal, and there is top quality traditional English home cooking (dinner £12.50, bring your own wine). The Swanns have won prestigious awards both from the English Tourist Board and the AA. Absolutely no smoking. Dogs by arrangement, and children welcome. B&B £23–£27.

G CHIMNEYS   Tel 01297 489368

Trevor & Jenny Yerworth, Chimneys, Main Street, Chideock, nr Bridport, Dorset DT6 6JH.

Chimneys lies in the heart of Dorset's finest countryside. Nearby Golden Cap is quoted by the National Trust as being 'the jewel in their crown'. As well as garden visiting, consider a stroll along the spectacular cliffs and beaches, famous for their fossils. The house itself, some 300 years old, was originally three merchants' cottages, converted in the late 1920s to its present form. There is a large sitting-room, and an oak panelled dining-room (dinner £12.50–£14.95, licensed). Upstairs are 5 guest bedrooms, one with a four-poster bed, and 1 sharing a bathroom. Rooms at the front are double-glazed because of a busy main road. At the back they are much quieter. No smoking, no dogs, no under-5s. B&B £17–£27.

What Else to Enjoy

This is a short selection of the many good things recommended in the area by owners of places to stay. Your hosts will certainly be able to provide additional information.

If It's Wet

All through this part of Britain there is a reassuring revival of craft activities. Pottery, jewellery, hand-made clothes, basketwork, furniture, paintings, prints, ironwork – name it, and you'll find it somewhere. The biggest selection under one roof is the Broadwindsor Craft and Design Centre, 3m W of **Beaminster** on the B3163. It has shops, workshops and studios, and a beautifully-designed, airy restaurant using local produce (and serving, of course, cream teas).

Of the Gardens above which can put a roof over your head, **Forde Abbey** (*see* Garden 2) is a must. It is open on Weds, Suns, and BH Mons, 1–4.30 (last admission). A combined adult ticket with the garden costs £5. The interior, much of it dating from the 16th and 17th centuries when the monastery was converted to a splendid house, is magnificent. You can eat in the 12th-century undercroft, now a licensed restaurant.

Another good house on a wet day is **Parnham House** (*see* Garden 7). The rooms in this enchanting Tudor manor house have been lovingly restored, and you can watch how the marvellous Makepeace furniture is made. There is a restaurant and craft shop. Open at the same times and with the same admission charge (£4.50) as the garden.

Eating Out

Meals in the places to stay which I have recommended are so good that I haven't been able to find anywhere in the area to better them. I have talked to owners about this, and in the unlikely event that you feel you absolutely have to get away for an evening out, their personal recommendations will certainly not let you down as they are such good cooks themselves. If you particularly want seafood (which may not be on the menu where you stay), try the **Riverside Restaurant** in West Bay, **Bridport** (Tel 01308 422011). Perched on a promontory in the harbour in this fishing village, with views from all the tables, you can find dishes and menus costing between £5 and £25.

Taunton to Yeovil

In this visit, grouped closely together, are some of England's greatest gardens. It is truly a 5-star area, set in the lanes and woods of deepest Somerset. Impossible to pick just one or two 'best' gardens – they should all be visited, and no other place in the world can boast such treasures. The music of Delius is rapturously English: 'First Cuckoo in Spring', 'A Song Before Sunrise', 'In a Summer Garden' – all these short pastoral pieces can usually be found in a collection on one tape.

OS maps: Landrangers 182, 183, **193**

Gardens

Opening times: in larger gardens, and in NT properties, last admissions are usually 30–45 minutes before the garden closes. Admission charges are a guide to what one adult can expect to pay to go round the garden. It sometimes varies with the season or days of the week. When the house is also open to the public, there is usually an additional charge.

I   **HESTERCOMBE HOUSE**
Cheddon Fitzpaine, nr Taunton   Tel 01823 337222

Mon–Fri all year, 9–5; also Sats and Suns, May to Sept, 2–5. £2
From Taunton go NE on A3259 for 2m. Turn L in Monkton Heathfield and follow garden signs through Cheddon Fitzpaine for about 2m.

Here is the classic Lutyens-Jekyll garden, perhaps the best remaining example in the whole country, designed by them in 1905. It has been restored sensitively by Somerset County Council. There are little rills, iris-fringed, fed by bearded stone gods spouting water. Miss Jekyll's bold planting includes a grey and silver border, and a pergola swagged with clematis and fragrant honeysuckles and roses. Lutyens's jewel in this garden is the stunning Orangery, and the circular garden with a round pool in the middle. As usual, his sure touch for detail makes every garden seat and flight of steps a pleasure to meet.

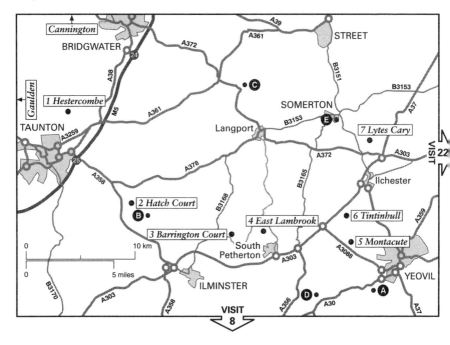

2   HATCH COURT

Hatch Beauchamp, nr Ilminster   Tel 01823 480120

Mon–Thurs, mid April to late Sept, 10–5.30. £1.50
From Taunton go SE on A358 for 5m. Turn L signed Hatch Beauchamp; turn
L at village X-roads for garden.

An exceptionally fine park, with magnificent trees and wonderful views
around a perfect Palladian mansion (which you can visit on Thursday afternoons). The great joy here is the huge walled kitchen garden which has been
restored most brilliantly by Robin and Janie Odgers since 1984; it won the
Taunton Deane Historic Garden Restoration Award in 1995. As you enter,
a magnificent palette of colours in pinks, purples, lavender, white and blue
glow out from roses and clematis, underplanted with blue hardy geraniums,
set against the rosy brick walls. The vegetable garden has clipped box edges,
espaliered fruit, with fig trees and kiwi fruit on the warmest wall. Unusual
vegetables and herbs are grown here to supply the prestigious kitchens at
the Castle Hotel, Taunton. It is amazing to think this ordered, fruitful
garden was a complete wilderness 8 years ago. I found Mrs Odgers cutting
a generous basket of asparagus for supper, and she guided me to the

photographs showing how the gardens were reclaimed; what energy and flair they show. An archway in a high wall takes you through to the rose garden, herbaceous borders, and immaculate lawns surrounded by mulberry trees, cedars, yews and copper beeches. Fallow deer graze the park and add to the beauty of Hatch Court.

About 1m to the E of Hatch Court, in the village of Curry Mallet, is an excellent nursery for trees and shrubs, particularly acers, oaks, birches, rowans and magnolias: **Mallet Court Nursery**. Tel 01823 480748.

3   BARRINGTON COURT (NT)

nr Ilminster   Tel 01460 241938

Daily except Fri, April to Sept, 11–5.30. £4 including house
From Ilminster go NE on B3168 for 5m; garden signed on R.

This is one of the last gardens Gertrude Jekyll had a hand in – a commission from Col. Arthur Lyle. She designed three of the garden rooms, and the NT is restoring them. Her iris garden is in soft pinks and blues; the lily pool garden is planted in golden shades – yellow lilies, azaleas and crinums; her roses are delicate old varieties. Note the old brick paths in intricate patterns. The cowsheds and stone cattle troughs indicate the farming origins of this bold garden. An immaculate, walled kitchen garden has pride of place, and you can refresh yourself with a glass of cider made from the apples in the orchard.

4   EAST LAMBROOK MANOR

nr South Petherton   Tel 01460 240328

Daily except Sun, March to Oct, 10–5. £2
From Ilminster go E on A303 for 6m to South Petherton. Turn L onto minor road for 2m; garden signed in East Lambrook.

The late Margery Fish created this abundantly planted garden, now carefully restored by the present owners, Mr and Mrs Norton, around the old stone manor house. The wobbly paths are half hidden by a glorious profusion of rare plants, and everything is charmingly informal, the gentle chaos and romantic atmosphere occasionally checked by tidily clipped evergreens lining a path. Mrs Fish wrote many books to popularise this style of cottage gardening, gathering many rare plants thought to have been extinct. These treasures have been propagated, and plant-lovers will have to restrain themselves in the plant shop. You will want to buy everything. The

National Collection of hardy geraniums (cranesbill) is here too, and rare primulas and euphorbias collected by Mrs Fish.

5 MONTACUTE HOUSE (NT)   nr Yeovil   Tel 01935 823289

Daily except Tues, all year, 11.30–5.30. £2.80 (£1.50 in winter)
From Yeovil go NW on A3088 for 4m; NT signs on R in Montacute village.

The late Tudor house dominates this formal garden, together with the fat yew hedges (they are reminiscent of somnolent old elephants). A raised walk gives a bird's-eye view of deep borders, with many shrub roses and herbaceous plants. There is a lake, and a gazebo of exceptional beauty. It's all on a very grand and imposing scale, though I daresay Elinor Glyn brought it to life when, living here with George Curzon, she wrote shocking potboilers (in the gazebo?) and probably sinned on a tiger skin (or erred on some other fur). The thought amused me as I strolled along the fig walk. Gardeners who helped develop the garden in the past included Vita Sackville-West, Phyllis Reiss (of nearby Tintinhull), and Graham Stuart Thomas.

6 TINTINHULL HOUSE GARDEN (NT)

nr Yeovil   Tel 01935 822545

Wed–Sun and BH Mons, April to Sept, 12–6. £3.50
From Ilchester go SW on A303 for 3m; garden signed on L and found on E edge of Tintinhull village.

This wonderful garden feels much larger than its 1½ acres, thanks to the inspired layout by Mrs Phyllis Reiss in the 1930s, when she created space and elegance in the different garden rooms. They include a cool fountain garden, and a walled kitchen garden with espaliered fruit trees edged with catmint. Interesting planting associations and unusual colour combinations make this one of the most satisfying and inspirational of gardens to visit. A plant list is available (and most helpful, as the plants are not labelled).

7 LYTES CARY MANOR (NT)   nr Somerton

Tel 01985 847777 (NT regional office) or 01458 223297 (garden)

Mon, Wed, Sat, April to Oct, 2–6. £3.70
From Ilchester go NE on A303 for 2½m. Turn L at large roundabout onto A372 for ½m. Turn R onto minor road and follow NT signs.

Once the home of the medieval herbalist Henry Lyte, there is a strong Elizabethan feel to this enchanting garden. The bones are yew hedges, alleys and topiary. Graham Stuart Thomas designed a deep mixed border of shrubs, roses, and herbaceous plants. In the orchard, find medlars, apples, pears and quinces, with naturalised bulbs in the spring, and a sundial where the mown paths meet.

Where to Stay

All B&B prices are approximate per person, sharing a double/twin room usually with private or en suite facilities. It is a good idea to ask for any special requirements when booking.

A HOLYWELL HOUSE   Tel 01935 862612

Jackie & Ronald Somerville, Holywell House, Holywell, nr Yeovil, Somerset BA22 9NQ.

Ron and Jackie have put in gargantuan efforts to develop their 'Garden in the Making' around this 200-year-old house. When they arrived at the property in 1991, it was a wilderness of bramble and thickets. It took a year just to clear the undergrowth. Now, after massive reconstruction and planting, and help from some of the best garden designers in the area, it is set to become one of the most interesting gardens in Somerset, its borders imperceptibly flowing into the fields beyond so that the abundant wildlife (including badgers) can thrive. Three luxurious double/twin bedrooms are let to guests. Eat out in the evening at an excellent pub two minutes away. Many guests have commented on how Jackie has cosseted them with extras not usually found at other places to stay. No dogs. Smoking and children OK. B&B £30–£33.

B FROG STREET FARM   Tel 01823 480430

Veronica Cole, Frog Street Farm, Beercrocombe, nr Taunton, Somerset TA3 6AF.

Frog Street derives its name from the Anglo-Saxon for 'meeting-place'. Today, you find this 15th-century listed farmhouse at the end of a lane deep in the Somerset countryside. On one side of the house is a large working farm; on the other, a colourful garden with a heated swimming pool hidden by a tall hedge. Veronica has run this country house hotel since 1981, and everyone comments on her warmth and sense of humour, and how she makes you feel part of the family. Her cooking has won many awards. Inside the house are beamed ceilings, fine Jacobean panelling and inglenook fireplaces. Three good double/twin bedrooms. Evening meals cost £16 (bring your own wine). No smoking, dogs, or children. B&B £25–£27.

C BEER FARM   Tel 01458 250285

Philip & Susan Morlock, Beer Farm, Bere Aller, nr Langport, Somerset TA10 0QX.

When Susan Morlock moved from Kent to Beer Farm early in 1994, she transferred some 800 plants in pots to start off her improvements to a run-down but potentially great 1-acre garden. Now, the results are showing – paths, hedges, borders, and vistas to distant views already look mature and settled, and there is a new pond area and vegetable garden. Susan loves discussing gardens, and the house contains a treasure trove of gardening and natural history books. Evening meals (£10 supper, £15 dinner, bring your own wine) are cooked to order. The 2 bedrooms are newly decorated and very comfortable. No smoking. Dogs if you discuss first. Babies or children over 10 welcome. B&B £25.

D CHINNOCK HOUSE   Tel 01935 881229

Guy & Charmian Smith, Chinnock House, Middle Chinnock, nr Yeovil, Somerset TA18 7PN.

This listed Georgian house is set in 2 acres of walled gardens with wonderful views over the countryside in the quiet hamlet of Middle Chinnock. You will find two large walled gardens, and a white garden with a heated swimming pool. Also in the grounds are an orchard and a productive vegetable garden providing ingredients for the kitchen and table. The house is furnished with style. There are 3 excellent bedrooms, and a fully equipped cottage in the grounds for 2 more people. Dinners should be booked in advance (£20 including wine, coffee and home-baked bread). Tea can be enjoyed in a large Victorian conservatory amid the fragrance of gardenia, jasmine and lilies. Guest dogs not allowed in the house, and no smoking in the bedrooms. Children welcome. B&B £25.

E LYNCH COUNTRY HOUSE   Tel 01458 272316

Roy Copeland, Lynch Country House, The Lynch, Somerton, Somerset TA11 7PD.

This supremely comfortable country house, lovingly restored and furnished with antiques, is set idyllically in a wildlife sanctuary. Thousands of trees have been planted to provide yet more shelter, and on the lake in the grounds of the house are black swans and exotic ducks. The 5 bedrooms are luxurious, and each has its own individual character, from a Victorian bedstead to a magnificent Georgian four-poster. B&B only, but there is a license, and good nearby places to eat. No smoking, and dogs not allowed in public rooms. B&B £23–£33.

What Else to Enjoy

This is a short selection of the many good things recommended in the area by owners of places to stay. Your hosts will certainly be able to provide additional information.

Other Gardens/Nurseries

Cannington College Gardens, 3m NW of Bridgwater just N of the A39, are set in the grounds of a Benedictine Priory, and are open in the afternoons daily from April to October. Seven old walled gardens protect many less hardy plants, and no fewer than 8 National Collections, including abutilons, ceanothus, argyranthemum and wisteria. There are 10 large greenhouses with ornamental plants; and all men obsessed with their lawns can look at trial plantings of lawn grass. Include ground cover plantings, and fine trees and shrubs, and this adds up to a very informative garden from which lots may be learned. Tel 01278 652226.

Gaulden Manor, at Tolland, is open on Sundays and Thursdays from May to the beginning of September, 2–5.30, (and Easter Sun/Mon, and all summer BHs). From Taunton, take A358 towards Williton. After 6m, turn L on B3188. Tolland is on L 4m further on. Driving to Mr and Mrs James Starkie's magical old house, through deep narrow lanes, with cow parsley and ox-eye daisies and pink campion coming through the car window, I began to feel as though time had stood still here. When I found the manor, with a dragon on its roof, I knew I was in a time warp. This ancient house, dating back to the 12th century, has a marvellous history, and if it is open, please go in to see the superb plasterwork and linenfold panelling. You enter the garden through ancient farm buildings, where swallows have their nests, and an old cider press sits among its empty barrels. Outside, roses climb up every wall and roof. A venerable fig tree leans on a hot south wall, and the rose beds are underplanted with lilies of the valley. Over a little stream is the herb garden, and in the old orchard is a butterfly garden. The stream runs the length of the garden, from the top pool to the bottom duck pond, and iris, ferns, primulas and ligurias are crammed along its bank. Near the pond is a secret garden, and Mr and Mrs Starkie are making a hidden, scented garden. There is great peace and tranquillity here, particularly in the Bishop's Garden by the house – a small courtyard with a vast stone trough planted with tulips, and the air heavy with fragrance from the roses and philadelphus. Throughout this garden, nature has been improved upon but not interfered with; the overall charm is that it isn't manicured, but blowsy and bosky and heavenly. Mind the Shetland pony. It bites, hard. Tel 01984 667213.

Less than 1m W of Lytes Cary (*see* Garden 7), **Patricia Marrow** is a specialist grower who offers more than 500 varieties of excellent, often rare plants. You find her in the middle of **Kingsdon**, just E of the B3151 from Somerton to Ilchester. Her nursery is open most days of the year, but you should phone to check. Tel 01935 840232.

Another good nursery is in **Langport**, on the A378. **Kelways Nurseries** here are famous for daylilies, irises and peonies. Tel 01458 250521.

Other Places to Stay

Just off the NW corner of the visit map is the village of **Spaxton**. Here you will find another old cottage similar to that which is offered at Beer Farm (*see* C above): a lovely setting, a memorable garden, a friendly welcome and good food. Rachel Harvey offers 2 bedrooms at **Gatesmoor**, Hawkridge, Spaxton, nr Bridgwater, Somerset TA5 1AL. Tel 01278 671353. B&B £25.

If It's Wet

There is a wealth of buildings and activities to explore. The most extensive NT property is **Montacute House** (*see* Garden 5), with a wonderful interior including many Renaissance features, fine furniture, and Elizabethan and Jacobean portraits from the National Portrait Gallery. House opening days and times as garden, but not until noon. Licensed restaurant for lunches and teas. A combined ticket for house, garden and park costs £5.

Somerset abounds with craft workshops. (There is a good free map, available at Tourist Information centres, which lists some 40 of them.) About 1m S of the A372 at Langport is the village of **Muchelney**, where you will find the family pottery now run by John Leach, grandson of Bernard Leach, perhaps the most famous potter England has known. The shop is open Mon–Fri all year, 9–5 (except 1–2), and Sat 9–1; if you want to go round the workshops and see the pottery being made, phone in advance for the best time to visit. Tel 01458 250324.

The 10th-century Muchelney Abbey, partly ruined, has an exhibition organised by English Heritage which contains many of John's pots, and medieval furniture re-created by Stuart Interiors. In the village is another NT property, **Priest's House**, a late-medieval hall house occupied by tenants and well worth seeing (£1.50), but only open Sun and Mon, 2–5, April–Sept.

Basket-making is a traditional craft industry in this area. **Stoke St Gregory** is a village midway between the A31 and A378, 6m E of Taunton. Here you can find two businesses with fascinating basket-work for sale: the English Basket and Hurdle Centre, and Willow Craft Industry. The latter, run by the Coate family for 150 years, has a visitor centre displaying how the craft has been practised through history, and runs guided tours every half-hour Mon–Fri, 10–4.

Somerset and cider-making – they go together. At **Dowlish Wake**, 1½ m SE of Ilminster, you will find **Perry's Cider Mills**. The 16th-century thatched barn where the cider is pressed houses an interesting collection of country bygones, including old cider-making equipment, and in a new thatched barn are many wagons and farm implements. You can taste the cider (and buy it, of course), and if you're driving, there is wonderful fresh apple juice.

Eating Out

Little Barwick House, in the village of **Barwick**, is a listed Georgian dower house which the owners, Veronica and Christopher Colley, call a 'restaurant-with-rooms'. She is the chef; he the host and wine-waiter. Dinner is served in a warm, spacious dining-room with French windows leading to a beautiful garden. There are two menus priced at either side of £20. Discuss other menu possibilities when you phone for a booking – you'll find an extraordinary level of helpful personal service. It is 5m to the S of Yeovil, just E of the A37. Tel 01935 23902.

Hardy Country

There is a fascinating variety of gardens in this visit, from the grandeur and splendour of Athelhampton House to the ¼-acre gem at Cartref cottage. Places to stay all have good gardens, two of them being open for the NGS, and one selling a range of delightful cottage garden plants. The fountains at Athelhampton, shimmering and sparkling, reminded me of Respighi's 'Fountains of Rome' (usually coupled with his 'Ancient Airs and Dances') – just what I wanted to hear on the car journey.

OS maps: Landrangers 183, **194**

Gardens

Opening times: in larger gardens, and in NT properties, last admissions are usually 30–45 minutes before the garden closes. Admission charges are a guide to what one adult can expect to pay to go round the garden. It sometimes varies with the season or days of the week. When the house is also open to the public, there is usually an additional charge.

1   KINGSTON MAURWARD GARDENS
    nr Dorchester   Tel 01305 264738

Daily, Easter to mid Oct, 1–5.30. £2.50
Signed off A35 roundabout at E end of Dorchester by-pass, 2m NE of Dorchester town centre.

This Edwardian garden, run by the Dorset College of Agriculture, is in the final stages of an entrancing restoration It surrounds a fine Georgian mansion. Hedges and stone balustrading divide up the garden into small intimate 'rooms', each full of interest, and providing lovely vistas, with statuary and steps, special architectural features, and an Elizabethan walled garden. A large display of roses, herbaceous plants, and the National Collections of penstemons and salvias are here. Walk to the lake for peaceful pastoral views of the water meadow.

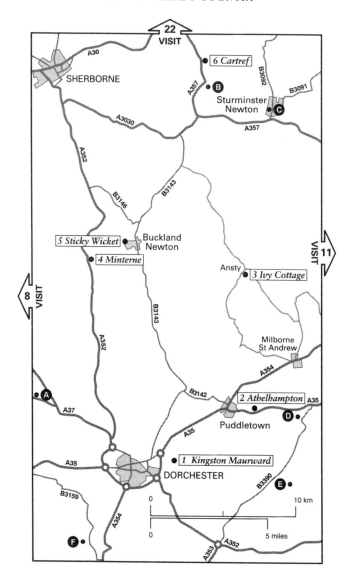

Almost next door, and worth a fleeting visit if you've ever fallen in love with the works of Thomas Hardy, is **Hardy's Cottage** (NT), where he was born in 1840, and later wrote *Under the Greeenwood Tree* and *Far From the Madding Crowd*. It is open daily, April to Oct, 11–5.30 (Tues 2–5.30), without charge. The garden doesn't take long to go round. It is small, and densely crowded with cottage plants and neatly trimmed yews and hedges – a photographer's dream of what a Dorset cottage garden should be. You get to it by walking 10 minutes from a well-signed NT car park through woods, images of Hardy in your mind. The cottage, built by his great grandfather, has been little altered. If you want to go inside (£2.50), make prior arrangements with the Custodian. Tel 01305 262366.

2   ATHELHAMPTON HOUSE

nr Dorchester   Tel 01305 848363

Daily except Sats, Easter to end Oct, 11–5. £2.50
From Dorchester, go NE on A35 for 4m to Puddletown; garden is 1m further on L.

This makes for a magnificent visit. The 15th-century mansion, perhaps the finest of its period in the country, is surrounded by one of England's great gardens that perfectly complement the house – 20 acres of beautiful grounds encircled by the River Piddle. Designed by Inigo Thomas in the early 1890s, it has eight walled gardens with fountains and pavilions. You will find a balustraded terrace, obelisks, statues, and vistas through stunning gate piers. Uniquely, there are twelve giant pyramids of immaculately clipped yew, set around the pool by the great terrace. On the south terrace, pots of tender shrubs are placed, backed by a huge *Magnolia grandiflora* and a Banksian rose. Old walls are covered with pear trees, themselves lending support to clematis and roses. Through each archway, there is a vista to a new garden over sparkling water from the many fountains. A statue of Queen Victoria looks down a long grassy walk to a stone Grecian female, topless, chained to her rock, and enjoying every minute of it. Let's hope the dear Queen was short-sighted.

3   IVY COTTAGE   Ansty, nr Dorchester   Tel 01258 880053

Thurs, April to Oct, 10–5, and some charity Suns. £1.50
From Dorchester, go NE on A35 for 4m. At Puddletown turn L on A354 for 4m. Turn L at Milborne St Andrew and follow signs for Ansty through Dewlish and Cheselbourne; garden is in Aller Lane, Ansty.

Gardeners who suffer from dryish soil will be green with envy at what can be achieved when you have a wet valley garden with natural springs and a stream running through it. Mr and Mrs Stevens have triumphed with their boggy patch, growing robust and healthy plants. Lushness rules here. Beside the stream, iris, primulas, skunk cabbage, azaleas, rhododendrons, astilbes, astrantias and giant hostas all revel in the dampness. The herbaceous borders are drier, on higher ground, and a constant blaze of colour is achieved. Oriental poppies, iris, aqualegias and camassias were out when I visited in early June, and would be followed by sedums, asters and alstroemerias. Under an old apple tree, on a damp and shady bank, grew primulas, ferns and *Corydalis flexuosa* whose blue was cleverly echoed by *Meconopsis betonici-folia*. The cottage is smothered with climbing roses. Through a honeysuckle and rose arch is an immaculate kitchen garden. Mr and Mrs Stevens are most knowledgeable, and love to give helpful gardening advice to their visitors.

Aller Green, nearby, is also a lovely garden and is sometimes open – worth asking the Stevens.

4   MINTERNE   Minterne Magna, nr Dorchester   Tel 01300 341370

Daily, April to Oct, 10–7 (or dusk). £2
From Dorchester, go N on A352 for 9m; garden on R in Minterne Magna.

Landscaped 18th-century gardens in the manner of Capability Brown, laid out in a horseshoe below Minterne House, with a chain of small lakes, waterfalls and streams. More than a mile of walks are best enjoyed in spring, with important collections of Himalayan rhododendrons, azaleas, acers and cherries, massively underplanted with bulbs; and in the autumn, for the foliage colours. The lakes and streams harbour good moisture-loving plants.

5   STICKY WICKET
Buckland Newton, nr Dorchester   Tel 01300 345476

Thurs, June to Sept, 10.30–8, and some charity Suns. £1.50
From Dorchester, go N on B3143 for 11m. Turn L to Buckland Newton; garden signed at T-junction nr church and school.

The garden here, which enfolds the house, has been designed by Peter and Pam Lewis to fulfil their ambition of creating an ecological haven which uses the land productively while keeping in balance with nature. They demon-strate their own 'Art of Planting', experimenting with different colours, forms, and textures of flowers and foliage. The Frog Garden is – naturally – watery, approached through a shady, wisteria-clad pergola, the pond edges planted with flag iris, water mint and marsh marigolds. In the Bird

Garden, food is provided by berries and hips and seed heads, while low-growing plants of thyme, thrift and acaena surround the bird bath. The Round Garden has paths radiating from a central camomile lawn, segmenting the floral ring of colour: pastel pinks, pale yellow and blue, violet, magenta and reds, with dusky pinks bringing the spectrum full circle – all beautifully maintained and with interesting varieties of perennials and annuals. The White Garden includes white-flowering trees, shrubs, perennials, grasses and bulbs, and a white dovecote with white fantail doves. I particularly liked the Ladybird House, made by Ian Whinfield of Snape Cottage; and the willow Mother Earth figure, who stands in the duck enclosure feeding her birds. This garden is delightful. It makes you realise that an ecological garden doesn't have to be a patch full of slugs and chickweed. It ranks with the best, and has very good plants are for sale.

6　CARTREF　Stalbridge　　　　　　　Tel 01963 363705

Tues (2–6), Fri (10–6), April to Oct, and by appointment. £1.50
From Sturminster Newton go W on A357 for 5m to Stalbridge P.O. Turn R into Station Road; garden 80 yds on R.

This little gem of a ¼-acre garden, hidden behind a village house is a collector's treasure-trove. Mrs Smith is a plantswoman with a great knowledge of flowers, and is delighted to share her skills with keen gardeners, stopping her gardening for a chat. There is a small woodland with choice shade-loving plants as well as an enchanting potager. Go there.

Not far away is another planting delight, inspiring for anyone with a small garden: **Hilltop Cottage**. There are many fascinating perennials to be seen, and some are for sale in a small nursery. Open occasionally in May, July and August. Phone 01258 880251 to find out if it's your lucky day – and also get directions.

Where to Stay

All B&B prices are approximate per person, sharing a double/twin room usually with private or en suite facilities. It is a good idea to ask for any special requirements when booking.

A　HYDE FARM HOUSE　　　　　　　Tel 01300 320272

John Saunders & Jan Faye-Scholl, Hyde Farm House, Dorchester Rd, Frampton, nr Dorchester, Dorset DT2 9NG.

John and Jan are gardening enthusiasts, and can list 50 gardens in the area they have personally visited – and they can certainly introduce you to good local gardens not normally open to the public. Their own grounds cover 7 acres, beautifully planted and maintained, with terraces, lawns, borders, woods and a wonderful 12-ft-high flint-faced wall covered with espaliered fruit trees, roses and other climbers. Inside their house are treasured collectables, good furniture and lavish furnishings. The 3 en suite double/ twin bedrooms have good-sized bathrooms, and – rare, this – cost the same per person whether you are on your own or sharing. You are served dinner (£15, bring your own wine) in the conservatory. No smoking, no dogs, no children under 12. B&B £28.

B THORNHILL PARK   Tel 01963 362746

Richard & Cary Goode, Thornhill Park, nr Stalbridge, Dorset DT10 2SH.

Here you can see the early fruits of a 5-acre garden being created by Cary, who is a professional garden designer. It already includes a formal and an informal pond, a nut walk, various garden buildings, mixed planting in different colour themes, a willow garden with a willow dome that is the inspiration of Clare Wilks, a living willow sculptress, a rose garden and a potager. A nursery is attached. The beautiful Georgian house, used in the film of *Far From The Madding Crowd*, has extensive views over the Blackmore Vale, and has 60 acres of park, pasture and woodland which provide good walks. Three guest bedrooms, B&B only, but there is a good choice of local places to eat out. No smoking. No dogs unless left in owner's car. B&B £25–£30.

C STOURCASTLE LODGE   Tel 01258 472320

Jill & Ken Hookham-Bassett, Stourcastle Lodge, Gough's Close, Sturminster Newton, Dorset DT10 1BU.

Although in the middle of this medieval market town, Stourcastle Lodge is peacefully tucked away down a quaint stone-walled lane, and has enough ground for an imaginative garden, partly walled, with an abundance of unusual shrubs and herbaceous plants, and sometimes open for the NGS. A family home from the beginning of the 18th century, it has been sensitively restored and extended. Good furnishing, and pictures by local artists downstairs, antique brass bedsteads and the fragrance of dried flowers and spices in the 5 bedrooms upstairs. Imaginative Aga-cooked food (dinner from

£16, bring your own wine), and Ken's collection of antique kitchenalia to enjoy. No smoking, dogs or children. B&B £20-£33.

D THE OLD VICARAGE   Tel 01305 848315

Michael & Anthea Hipwell, The Old Vicarage, Affpuddle, nr Dorchester, Dorset DT2 7HH.

Surrounding this fine Georgian house, its detailed architectural features still intact, are 1½ acres of well-tended gardens, featuring manicured lawns, mature yew hedges, and many roses. Anthea's gift for interior decoration has resulted in rooms which are light, colourful, graceful and supremely pleasing on the eye. Three excellent double/twin bedrooms have views of the garden and countryside. Suppers (£7–£9) are served from November to March. In summer months, there are good places to eat nearby. No dogs or children; smoking allowed. B&B £20–£23.

E VARTREES HOUSE   Tel 01305 852704

Doris Haggett, Vartrees House, Moreton, nr Dorchester, Dorset DT3 8BE.

Hermann Lea, a friend of Thomas Hardy, built this peaceful, turn-of-the-century country house. It is still undisturbed, set in a heathland garden and surrounded by woods, with spacious and comfortable rooms. It is a short walk to Moreton, a pretty village whose church has engraved windows by Lawrence Whistler, and is the burial place of Lawrence of Arabia. It also has good pubs where you can eat out in the evening. One very large bedroom has double and twin beds with an en suite shower. Two further double bedrooms share a bathroom. No smoking in bedrooms, no children under 10, dogs by arrangement. B&B £18–£25.

F FRIAR'S WAY   Tel 01305 813243

Christina & Les Scott, 190 Church Street, Upwey, Weymouth, Dorset DT3 5QE.

No wonder this pretty ¾-acre south-facing garden is packed with visitors on NGS open days – it is filled with interesting and unusual cottage perennial planting. It is still being developed, but when you see the crowded array of plants tumbling over the stone walls and paths, you would hardly think there was room for more. A large number of the varieties are potted on for guests to buy at exceptionally reasonable prices. The heavily beamed 17th-century thatched cottage is peaceful and secluded. It has 2 delightfully furnished bedrooms with hand basins, sharing a bathroom. There is an en

suite double in the barn cottage. Les and Chris (she is county organiser for
the Cottage Garden Society) spend so much time outdoors in the summer
that they offer evening meals only from October to March (£15, bring your
own wine), but there are plenty of good pubs nearby. Sorry, no dogs or
children or smoking. B&B £18–£22.

What Else to Enjoy

*This is a short selection of the many good things recommended in the area by owners
of places to stay. Your hosts will certainly be able to provide additional information.*

If It's Wet

Athelhampton (*see* Garden 2) is one of England's finest 15th-century
houses, built in 1485. It has a lived-in feel, with fine furniture and good
pictures which look as if they are there to be used, not just displayed. The
Tudor Great Hall is an outstanding example of domestic architecture.

In Dorchester, there are good museums including the Dorset County
Museum which has an excellent display from the archaeological digs in the
area. Thomas Hardy, of course, is not forgotten – there is a recreation of
his study. Open Mon–Sat, 9.30–5, with a small admission charge.

Sherborne is one of the most beautiful towns in Britain, famous for its
medieval buildings, and without doubt Dorset's showpiece. Its crowning
glory is the abbey, founded in 705, and taking its present late-Gothic form
from the 15th century.

Sherborne Castle was built by Sir Walter Raleigh in 1594 (the Old
Castle, dating back to the 12th century, is fascinating and worth seeing, but
largely a ruin). Its setting, laid out by Capability Brown in the late 18th
century, is lovely, with a lake, lawns and parkland.

Eating Out

Plumber Manor, nr **Sturminster Newton**, is a handsome Jacobean
house which has been the Prideaux-Brune family home since the early 17th
century. There are gracious gardens to wander round before dinner, and
you eat in style, with a largely traditional English menu (£20 and £25), and
a dessert trolley to die for. Tel 01258 472507.

Around Wimborne Minster

I spent many childhood holidays in Studland Bay, across the water from Poole Harbour. Today, the area still has a quiet gentility that reminds you of days gone by; there can be few places in England where people are generally so polite. The countryside is ravishing, and if you choose to take a short break here, Sunday to Wednesday would give you the best opportunity to visit all the gardens. My drive-along music was 'The Lark Ascending' and 'Fantasia on Greensleeves' by Vaughan Williams – pure rural bliss.

OS map: Landranger **195**

Gardens

Opening times: in larger gardens, and in NT properties, last admissions are usually 30–45 minutes before the garden closes. Admission charges are a guide to what one adult can expect to pay to go round the garden. It sometimes varies with the season or days of the week. When the house is also open to the public, there is usually an additional charge.

I   KINGSTON LACY (NT)

nr Wimborne Minster   Tel 01202 883402

Sat–Wed, April to Oct, 11.30–6. £2.20
From Wimborne Minster go NW on B3052 for 1½m; garden signed on L.

A very large, very grand National Trust property, with a once magnificent cedar avenue in the park. The formal gardens have a distinctly Victorian feel, with a recently restored fernery, a laurel walk, a Dutch parterre with bedding schemes, and lots of statues, urns, lions, vases – even an Egyptian obelisk.

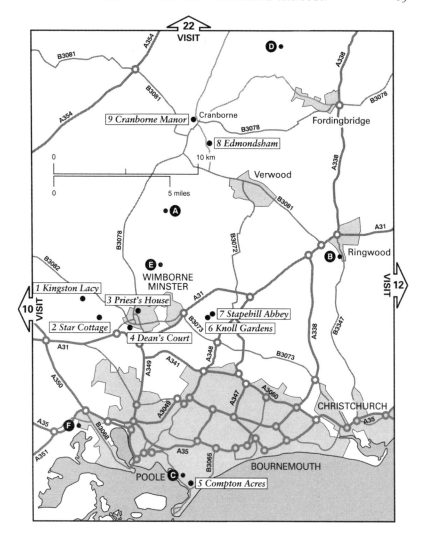

2   STAR COTTAGE

Cowgrove, nr Wimborne Minster   Tel 01202 885130

*Sat/Sun & BHs all year, 2–6 (2–4 in winter) and by apppoinment. 75p
From Wimborne Minster go NW on B3082. Immediately after leaving town,
turn L at hospital onto Cowgrove Rd for ½ m; garden is at 8, Roman Way.*

Gardeners who regularly visit the Royal Horticultural Society's shows in
Vincent Square will recognize the work of Lys de Bray, and may even

have bought one of her beautiful botanical paintings. She started creating her garden at Star Cottage from a field five years ago, and is still busy adding the finishing touches, and watching it mature. When you visit, her working studio is also open. Plans for this fascinating garden include an autumn garden for seasonal flowers and berries, and a winter garden which leads into a spring garden. It will be intriguing to watch it develop.

3   PRIEST'S HOUSE   Wimborne Minster   Tel 01202 882533

Most days throughout year (but not Suns, Jun to Sept). £1.50
23 High St, Wimborne Minster.

A peaceful small garden, behind the Museum and running down to the mill stream. There are unusual shrubs and trees, and it is perhaps best to visit when the wisteria is out all over the back of the house. But at any time, it is a delightful place to sit down and get away from the town and the traffic.

4   DEAN'S COURT   Wimborne Minster

First and last Sun in month, 2–6 (and BH Mons, 10–6), May to Oct. £1.50
Signed nr centre of Wimborne Minster, off B3073.

An oasis of peace in a busy market town, belonging to Sir Michael and Lady Hanham – 13 acres of partly wild, chemical-free gardens set around an old house, originally the Deanery to the Minster. Besides regular open days, there are a 'daffodil afternoons' (with teas) on the last two weekends in March. Many fine specimen trees, a splendid collection of herbs (and herbs for sale too), and a fascinating old walled kitchen garden where some of the oldest varieties of vegetable are grown. Part of the Henry Doubleday seed bank of endangered botanical species is held here.

5   COMPTON ACRES   Poole   Tel 01202 700778

Daily, March to Oct, 10.30–6.30 (or dusk). £4.20
On B3065 coast road from Bournemouth to Poole, signed E of Canford Cliffs.

This is a major tourist attraction, complete with coaches and a large car park. But resist the temptation to be a garden snob, and enjoy what Compton Acres offers: 9 acres of immaculately kept, exuberant, landscaped gardens overlooking Poole Harbour, with follies and statuary, formal borders, hedges and water gardens, and a perfect Japanese garden, authentically recreated by flown-in Japanese architects and workmen. The Palm Court always feels like the perfect setting for *Cosi Fan Tutte*, so I hummed a bit of Mozart here.

6   KNOLL GARDENS

Hampreston, nr Wimborne Minster   Tel 01202 873931

Daily, all year, Easter to Oct, 10–6 (earlier closing in winter). £4
From Wimborne Minster town centre, go E on B3073 for 2m. At A31 round-
about, take Stapehill road for ½m, then turn R on minor road for ½m; the
garden is signed on L.

Here is an award-winning garden that attracts thousands of tourists each year. It is beautifully maintained, well labelled, with lots of seating and level paths to walk on. It features almost every sort of garden you can imagine, and holds the National Collections of ceanothus and phygelius. It is perhaps a touch too much an improvement on nature for my personal gardening taste, but there is no doubt about its popularity.

Immediately next door is the renowned **Trehane Nursery**, well worth a wander with your cheque book. Tel 01202 873490.

7   STAPEHILL ABBEY

Ferndown, nr Wimborne Minster   Tel 01202 861686

Daily, all year (exc. Mon/Tues in winter), 10–5 (or dusk). £4.50
From Wimborne Minster town centre go E on B3073 for 2m. At A31 round-
about, take Stapehill exit; garden ½m on R.

The gardens around this old Cistercian Abbey have been sensitively re-stored, and visitors can now enjoy a splendid orchid house, a lake, a picnic area, a large rock garden with tumbling streams and pools, herbaceous borders and rose gardens, and a Victorian cottage garden. There is plenty to see here. There are fascinating craft workshops, a tour round the Abbey, and a 'Power to the Land' exhibition tracing the development of mecha-nised farming from medieval times until now.

8   EDMONDSHAM HOUSE   nr Cranborne   Tel 01725 517207

Suns and Weds, Apr to Oct, 2–5. £1
From Wimborne Minster go N on B3078 for 8½m. Turn R onto minor road
signed Edmondsham; garden in village centre.

A marvellously traditional walled kitchen garden, packed with delicious organically grown veggies, is at the heart of this peaceful, slumbering estate, where the house (sometimes open, check by telephone, admission £1.50) is offset by wide lawns and fine trees. An interesting feature is a circular grass hollow, said to have been a cockpit. A large collection of flowering shrubs and bulbs make it a delightful spring garden; the large herbaceous border, and the flowers in the adjoining Dower House garden, are a delight in summer. There is a recently restored sunken greenhouse – The Pit House – and another for growing peaches. My favourite place, in a fascinating garden, was the potting shed; it has the ghosts of tender loving care.

9 CRANBORNE MANOR   Cranborne   Tel 01725 517248

Weds, March to Sept, 9–5. £3
From Wimborne Minster go N on B3078 for 10m; garden in Cranborne village.

An exceptionally pretty garden, set around a ravishing ancient manor house, originally belonging to Robert Cecil, chief minister to Elizabeth I, and now lived in by his descendant Viscount Cranborne. The garden's basic lines were originally laid out by John Tradescant, who supplied many of the original plants. High yew hedges divide the garden into several rooms containing parterres, old roses, topiary and magnificent herbaceous borders. The gardens were enlarged in this century, and now include a white garden, a mount garden from which you can look down on the design below, and a water and wildlife garden. An excellent nursery garden next door, highly recommended locally, specializes in old-fashioned, climbing and shrub roses.

Where to Stay

All B&B prices are approximate per person, sharing a double/twin room usually with private or en suite facilities. It is a good idea to ask for any special requirements when booking.

A NORTHILL HOUSE   Tel 01258 840407

Courtney & Joy Gawsworthy, Northill House, nr Horton, Wimborne Minster, Dorset BH21 7HL.

This large country farmhouse, built in 1858 as part of Lord Shaftesbury's estate, has been modernised while keeping its period feel, with a striking dark-green lounge that has splendid book-cases. Many guests here are retired people who welcome the attention they are given, and the homely food (evening meal £14, licensed). Of the 9 bedrooms, 4 are on the ground floor, including 1 especially equipped for disabled people – Courtney and Joy have won awards for the way they look after disabled or handicapped guests. The lounge, bar and dining-room are all on one level so that they can be reached easily in a wheelchair. No dogs, restricted smoking, no children under 8. B&B £34-£38.

B MOORTOWN LODGE   Tel 01425 471404

Jilly & Bob Burrows-Jones, 244 Christchurch Rd, Ringwood, Hampshire RH24 3AS.

This small, family-run hotel has won many awards for its comfort, hospitality, and food. Facing a B-road 1½ m from Ringwood on the edge of the New Forest, it is a Georgian building dating back to the 1760s, and feels inviting from the moment you step through the front door. There are 5 double rooms (1 a four-poster) and 1 single. Jilly's evening meals (£16.95) are uncomplicated and much praised. Restricted smoking, children welcome, no dogs. B&B £25–£40.

C THE HERMITAGE   Tel 01202 707048

Susie Riaz, 52 Anthony's Avenue, Lilliput, Poole, Dorset BH14 8JH.

The garden around this seaside house is small but full of colour. A pergola, covered with a grape vine, rambling roses, clematis and hanging baskets, is lovely to sit under and eat breakfast – or dinner (£15, bring your own wine) on warm South Coast evenings. Susie has cooked half way round the world, on board a large yacht, picking up culinary tips as she went. At her home, she is fond of serving locally caught fish. There are 2 comfortable bedrooms. No smoking, no dogs. B&B £25.

D HENDLEY HOUSE   Tel 01725 518303

Pat Ratcliffe, Hendley House, Rockbourne, nr Fordingbridge, Hampshire SP6 3NA.

On the edge of an exceptionally pretty village, this wisteria-clad, timber-hung house faces south over lawns, borders and espaliered apples towards views of water meadows and farmland. There is a heated swimming pool and a tennis court. Inside the house are beams, antiques, and comfy chairs to relax in after a hard day's garden visiting. The 2 double/twin bedrooms are well furnished. It is a short walk to a pub with a restaurant where you can eat in the evenings. Smokers welcome, no dogs, no children under 10. B&B £24.

E THORNHILL   Tel 01202 889434

John & Sara Turnbull, Thornhill, Holt, nr Wimborne Minster, Dorset BH21 7DJ.

Sara fights a constant battle with rabbits and deer to keep her garden colourful. Island beds set in lawns lead to quiet rural views from this attractive and very comfortable modern thatched house. There is a tennis court. The 3 guest bedrooms, including 1 single, mostly have private bathrooms. There are good nearby pubs where you can eat out in the evenings. No smoking, no children, no dogs. B&B £20–£22.

F LYTCHETT HARD   Tel 01202 622297

Liz & David Collinson, Lytchett Hard, Beach Road, Upton, nr Poole, Dorset BH16 5NA.

An acre of gardens with lawns and large trees, themed borders with unusual plants, a kitchen garden, and broad terrace, surround this spacious, sunny, friendly house. There are plenty of places to sit and enjoy the views across Poole Harbour to the Purbeck Hills, and if you fancy a stroll, there are tracks below the garden across the heathland (SSSI) towards the reedbeds overlooking Lytchett Bay. Dinner (£10–£15, English country cooking) is by arrangement, and in good weather can be eaten on the terrace or in the conservatory (bring your own wine). The 3 bedrooms are south-facing, with views over the water. Downstairs there is a lounge with an open log fire and a separate dining-room, all with antique furniture. No smoking in the house, children by arrangement, well-mannered dogs welcome. B&B £18–£28.

What Else to Enjoy

This is a short selection of the many good things recommended in the area by owners of places to stay. Your hosts will certainly be able to provide additional information.

If It's Wet

The NT's **Kingston Lacy** (*see* Garden 1) is a 17th-century house, altered in the 19th century, with one of the finest collections of paintings anywhere, including works by Rubens, Titian, Van Dyck and Lely. Open Sat–Wed, April to Oct, 12–5.30. Combined admission with park and garden costs £5.50.

Priest's House Museum (*see* Garden 3) is packed with bygones, from toys and dolls to a working Victorian kitchen. It's open Mon–Sat, April to Oct, 10.30–6. Admission £1.50.

Wimborne Minster has much to oser besides the above museum. The Minster itself, dating from c. 1120 AD, has a quite extraordinary feeling of serenity. Guides will take you to the wonderful chained library, a must for any book-lover.

Also from Cranborne, you can go E for 2m on a minor road signed **Alderholt**, where you will find outstanding terracotta garden pots and urns made by Jonathan Garratt at Hare Lane Pottery.

There has been a tradition of pottery-making in **Poole** since Roman times, continued today at Poole Pottery, on the quay. This large concern is well worth visiting, whatever the weather. The pottery is colourful, and good value with factory shopping and low-priced 'seconds'. You can watch the pottery being made, have a go yourself, and spend time in the museum. There is a bar and brasserie open 8 a.m. to ll p.m., with great views over the harbour, and a good menu.

Eating Out

At **Tarrant Monkton**, S of A354, is a pretty thatched pub, **The Langton Arms**, (Tel 01258 830225), with a skittle alley and a cosy inglenook fire. They serve robust food, and in summer you may eat in the garden.

Around the New Forest

Local tourist literature calls the Test Valley 'Hampshire's best-kept secret'. I love the variety of countryside you find here, from the water meadows of the valleys with their charming villages, through woodland to downland with wonderful views and an abundance of prehistoric sites. The gardens in this visit are special, and Mottisfont Abbey is among my favourites anywhere. For music in the car, I chose John Ireland's Piano Concerto in E flat – romantic, lyrical and hauntingly nostalgic.

OS maps: Landrangers 184, **185**, 195, 196

Gardens

Opening times: in larger gardens, and in NT properties, last admissions are usually 30–45 minutes before the garden closes. Admission charges are a guide to what one adult can expect to pay to go round the garden. It sometimes varies with the season or days of the week. When the house is also open to the public, there is usually an additional charge.

I **APPLE COURT GARDEN** nr Lymington Tel 01590 642130

*Thurs–Mon, Feb to Oct (daily July/Aug), 9.30–5.30 (closed 1–2). £1.50
From Lymington go W on A337 for 4m. Turn R at Downton X-roads for ½m; garden adjoins Yeatton House.*

You will find it almost impossible to believe that this 1½-acre garden has been created in just nine years from a derelict builder's yard. In a wasteland, full of glass from annihalated greenhouses, lay what had once been a splendid Victorian kitchen garden. Now it has been transformed. Arrangements of clipped yew, topiary and a lime walk provide superbly-designed backcloths for abundant planting displays. The formal white garden can only be described as theatrical: approached through an arch, you find pleached hornbeams encased by yew – a stunning example of garden architecture. Diana Grenfell started the British Hosta and Hemerocallis Society in 1981 and has written extensively on both subjects. She has a pillared hosta walk

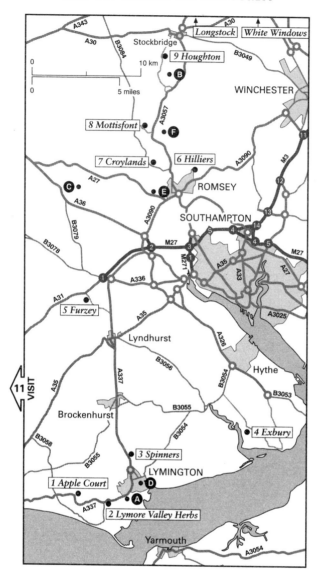

in this garden and grows more than 500 varieties. Her husband Roger Grounds is equally expert on ornamental grasses and ferns, both of which abound in the garden. They hold 3 National Collections: the small-leafed hosta, *Rohea japonica,* a rare Japanese woodlander, and woodwardia (the chain fern). Their specialist nursery, visited by buyers from all over Europe, reflects their gardening passions, and sells what must be the biggest choice of hostas and daylilies in the country.

If you time your visit here to be in Lymington on a Tuesday between June and September, try to visit **The Little Cottage.** Take the A337 Lyndhurst road going N, and look out for the Toll House Inn. The garden is opposite, and is charming. Divided up into little rooms by hedges or fences wreathed with ivy, each garden has a different colour theme. A potager has bold planting of rich, dark purples, crimsons and violets. Other little compartments have softer colour combinations. There is a wealth of interesting planting ideas here – all quite amazing, and beautifully maintained, with carefully clipped box hedges, and rows of standard variegated euonymous and holly. Please phone Wing Commander or Mrs Prior before you visit (Tel 01590 679395).

2   LYMORE VALLEY HERBS   Lymington   Tel 01590 642008

Daily, March to Dec, 9–5. Donations requested for NGS.
From Lymington go W on A337 for 3m. At Everton turn L on B3058; garden signed immediately on L.

Tucked away behind the shelter of old walls and a courtyard is a charming herb garden – the pride of Nicholas Aldridge. A knot garden, with a design taken from an old manuscript, is planted with germander and santolina. Beautiful roses add colour, including the ancient Apothecary's Rose, which no herb garden should be without. There is a lily pool, a dovecote and lovely lawns. The Herb Shop is in a barn and is full of good presents to take home. The plant centre is well stocked with unusual herbs, alpines and shrubs. Future developments will include a viewing mound, as used in medieval times to look down on the patterns and shapes below, a pool garden and a hornbeam stilt hedge.

Another garden in the southern part of this visit is worth noting. **Macpenny Woodland Garden and Nurseries** is open daily except Christmas and New Year's Day, in the village of Bransgore. No wonder the nursery is so well known – it has a huge collection of good stock, which spills over into the surrounding garden. Garden visit by donation.

3   SPINNERS   nr Lymington   Tel 01590 673347

Wed–Sat, mid April to mid Sept, 10–5, and by appointment. £1.50
From Lymington go N on A337 for 1½m. Turn R onto minor road for ¼m to Boldre; garden in School Lane.

A delightful garden on sloping acid soil, so enjoy choice woodland trees and shrubs – camellias, magnolias, exochordas, with cyclamen, erythroniums and trilliums nestling at their feet. There are rare dogwoods, as well as hazels and oaks; and masses of hardy geraniums, hostas, primulas and ferns. Mr Chappell has these pleasurable rare plants for sale in his splendid nursery, open all year.

4   EXBURY GARDENS   nr Beaulieu   Tel 01703 891203

Daily, March to early Nov, 10.30–5.30. £4.80
From Lyndhurst, go SE on B3056 for 7m to Beaulieu. Turn L and almost immediately turn R on minor road for 2m to garden, well signed on R.

Easily the most popular garden in Hampshire: 120,000 people a year come here to enjoy not just the 200 spectacular acres of river-side rhododendrons, azaleas, maples and camellias in spring, but also the rockeries, screes and valleys, the roses and the general ambience. You can take your dog on a lead, refresh yourself in the restaurant, and shop for plants, books and memorabilia.

5   FURZEY GARDENS   Minstead   Tel 01703 812464

Daily, all year, 10–5 or dusk. £3
From Lyndhurst go N on A337 for 1m. Turn L on minor road to Minstead for 1m; garden signed in village.

An 8-acre garden in the New Forest, with acid soil on a sloping site, which has magnificent herbaceous planting giving interest in the summer, but really shows its strength in the spring when a dazzling selection of bulbs are out, followed by azaleas, rhododendrons, and the brilliant Chilean Fire trees. Autumn again provides a vivid foliage colour from parrotias to *Liquidambar styrax*. There are some spectacular trees here, including many different varieties of oaks. Also see the craft gallery, and a cottage built in the 16th century with timbers from the Tudor boatyards at Lymington. Plants for sale.

6   SIR HAROLD HILLIER GARDENS

Romsey   Tel 01794 368787

Daily throughout year (except Christmas Day, New Year's Day) 10.30–6 (or dusk). £3
From Romsey go NE on A31 for 1m. Turn L for 1m where signed.

The sheer size of this collection is mind-boggling – 160 acres containing 12,000 different species, and a grand total of more than 40,000 plants. But don't let this put you off. The late Sir Harold Hillier began his collection in 1953 around his own house and garden, and it grew and grew. It is superbly laid out – marvellous for spring and autumn colour – and contains 9 National Collections. There are scree beds, peat beds and bog gardens, magnificent azaleas, rhododendrons and magnolias, a heather garden, and a valley full of acers.

7 CROYLANDS   Awbridge, nr Romsey   Tel 01794 513056

Charity afternoons most Weds and Suns, late May and June, 2–6. £1.50
From Romsey go N on A3057 for 1m. Turn L at Duke's Head pub onto B3084; garden on R in Awbridge village.

A charming 2-acre garden; time your visit to coincide with the weeks when Mrs Kitchener's marvellous collection of peonies are in flower. Basically, this is a particularly elegant cottage garden, with winding paths and romantic arbours. Note the clever way she has combined ornamental grasses into a white border; other useful planting ideas come from the shady border. Without doubt, a garden to linger in.

8 MOTTISFONT ABBEY (NT)
nr Romsey   Tel 01794 340757

Sat–Wed, April to Oct, 12–6 (last admission 5.00). £3
From Romsey go N on A3057 for 4m; garden signed on L.

Graham Stuart Thomas is the name most people will associate with Mottisfont – the walled rose garden, established in the 1970s, was his inspiration, and his great love and knowledge of old roses makes it an an exciting visit in late May and June (when the garden is open until 8.30, and costs £1 more). There are plenty of other things to see too – generous herbaceous borders, early flowering aubretias and pinks. Geoffrey Jellicoe designed a pleached lime walk, and Norah Lindsay laid out a parterre of box, santolina and lavender. Rolling lawns and magnificent and dignified old trees (planes, oaks and chestnuts) run down to the River Test, which borders the Abbey grounds.

9   HOUGHTON LODGE   Tel 01264 810177

Sat/Sun and BHs, 10–5, Mon/Tues/Fri 2–5, and by appointment, March to Sept. £3

From Stockbridge go S on minor rd for 1m. Garden signed on L before the village of Houghton.

This is a sensational house in wonderful surroundings. To call it 'an 18th-century cottage orné' (the accurate architectural description) hardly does justice to this white-painted Gothic beauty, its lawns sweeping down to the River Test. The beauty is more in its setting than in the gardens themselves, but of specialist interest is the Hydroponic Greenhouse, demonstrating what can be grown (on your window-sill, or in a spaceship if you have one) without soil. It is fascinating.

Where to Stay

All B&B prices are approximate per person, sharing a double/twin room usually with private or en suite facilities. It is a good idea to ask for any special requirements when booking.

A   CHEQUERS GREEN   Tel 01590 674660

Jamie & Caroline Heron, Chequers Green, Lymington, Hampshire SO41 8AH.

A croquet lawn backed by old walls and well-stocked shrub and herbaceous beds form the main garden of this fascinating 18th-century house once occupied by various salt barons, and linked to local smuggling. You can sit out with a cup of tea by the old wisteria, and then take a 3-minute stroll to the creek and sea wall. In the house, you ramble through panelled rooms, a comfortable sitting-room, and upstairs to find 2 lovely bedrooms. No smoking, no dogs, no children under 12. B&B £29.

B   HOW PARK FARM   Tel 01794 388716

Caroline Halse, How Park Farm, King's Somborne, nr Stockbridge, Hampshire SO20 6QG.

John of Gaunt lived here – or rather, he had a hunting lodge on this site, where you will now find a substantial and restful white-painted farmhouse with 2 double bedrooms and 1 single, with a piano in the drawing-room that is yours to play. There are 7 acres of land which Caroline is hoping to turn back into a deer park. Around the lawns close to the house, she has planted David Austin roses, clematis and lavender. A trained cook, she serves evening meals (unlicensed, and not on Sundays) at £20. No dogs, children, or smoking. B&B £27–£35.

C LANDSBROOK FARM   Tel 01794 390220

Penelope O'Brien, Landsbrook Farm, Landford Wood, nr Salisbury, Wiltshire SP5 2ES.

Down a quiet cul-de-sac on the edge of the New Forest, the 1-acre garden around this attractive house has been created over the years by the present owners, with interesting trees and unusual shrubs. Clematis are a summer feature, with more than 20 varieties. Penelope loves discussing gardens and plants, and can arrange visits to local private cottage gardens. She uses homegrown vegetables where possible for her evening meals (by request, £13 and £16, bring your own wine). Two good bedrooms. No smoking, no dogs, children should be teenage. B&B £22.

D MULBERRIES   Tel 01590 679549

Jan Messenger, Mulberries, 6 West Hayes, Lymington, Hampshire SO41 3RL

A handsome detached house which is only five minutes walk from the High Street and quay. It is situated in a quiet cul-de-sac. The walled garden, about one-third of an acre, is south facing and secluded. There is a heated swimming pool in the sunken garden. Two double bedrooms and 1 single. Two-course suppers (bring your own wine) cost £10, and there are many pubs and restaurants in Lymington if you want something more elaborate. No dogs, no smoking, no children under 12. B&B £20–£30.

E SPURSHOLT HOUSE   01794.512229

Anthea Hughes, Spursholt House, Salisbury Road, Romsey, Hampshire SO51 6DJ.

Magnificent gardens surround this ancient country house. There are paved terraces with geranium-filled urns, sweeping lawns, impressive topiary, and a view of Romsey Abbey in the distance. Gardens lead one into another, a parterre followed by apple trees, and a lily pool. One of the 3 bedrooms is oak-panelled, and all have antiques, king-size beds, sofas and garden views. Light suppers (£12.50) can be ordered in advance, though not at weekends; bring your own wine. Most guests eat out locally. Dogs and children welcome. No smoking. B&B £20–£25.

F   MICHELMERSH HOUSE   Tel 01794 368644

Jennifer Lalonde, Michelmersh House, Michelmersh, nr Romsey, Hampshire SO51 0NS.

You leave this spacious late Georgian farmhouse with memories of its mellow old red brick incorporated beautifully into the 4 acres of gardens and grounds: winding brick paths around the house take you to 3 walled gardens, festooned with climbers, lined with deep herbaceous borders, leading into one another, one of them a walled wild flower garden made 5 years ago. Guests love the peace and quiet (it is next to a church and a private estate of 6,000 acres) and the wonderful views. They also like the large bedrooms with good-sized bathrooms (2 doubles, 1 single), prettily furnished and wallpapered, with antique furniture. Jennifer serves evening meals from Monday to Thursday (£15, bring your own wine). No smoking and no children. No dogs unless kept in the car. B&B £20–£22.

What Else to Enjoy

This is a short selection of the many good things recommended in the area by owners of places to stay. Your hosts will certainly be able to provide additional information.

Other Gardens/Nurseries

To the N of the visit map are two gardens well worth the extra journey. **Longstock Park Gardens** (Tel 01264 810894) is a justly famous water garden, regrettably not often open (first and third Sun of each month, April to Sept, 2–5, £2.50). Many little islands, linked by bridges, grow delicate water irises, primulas, kingcups, astilbes (all the plants that love to get their toes into water), and dazzling blue *Meconopsis betonicifolia*. You can take a woodland walk through the park to **Longstock Park Nursery**, which has a great herbaceous border, climbing plants and roses, and a comprehensive clematis collection. It is signed L off the A3057, 1m N of **Stockbridge**.

About 6m further N, branching R off the A3057 on the B3048 towards Whitchurch, is the little village of **Longparish**, where you will find a very special garden: **White Windows** (Tel 01264 720222). Jane Sterndale-Bennett is a highly knowledgeable plantswoman who took on the challenge of gardening on chalk and made a flourishing garden of great interest throughout the year. She is particularly good at finding foliage contrasts of colour and form, using gold, silver and variegated leaves throughout the garden. Pulmonarias, hellebores, euphorbias, erysimums and brunneras are used widely. *Exochorda x macrantha* 'The Bride' is a splendid sight in April/May, and more blossoms are provided by *Malus transitoria*. Many of the more unusual perennials are to be found here. The garden is open by appointment on Wed afternoons, April to Sept.

Other Places to Stay

A great place to stay, and well worth the 4 or 5 miles motoring E from the Romsey edge of the visit map, is Belinda and Will Martin's home at **Hill Farm**. Originally an open hall house built in the 1560s, it is fascinating, quiet, comfortable, pretty, with great views, and at the centre of a 50-acre farm where guests can wander. The 1-acre garden is out of the ordinary, too, divided by mellow brick walls and tall yew hedges into rooms – like a mini-Hidcote or Sissinghurst without the visitors. Belinda and Will are generous with their time, always willing to discuss places to visit nearby. Give 24 hours' notice for supper (£15) or gourmet dinner (£25). Guests may bring their own wine, but Belinda generously gives wine along with the meals in more than reasonable quantities. Two double bedrooms, 1 single. Dogs and children welcome, no smoking upstairs. B&B £30. Address: Hill Farm, **Morestead**, Winchester, Hampshire SO21 1LZ. Tel 01962 777692.

If It's Wet

The most-visited stately home in the area is **Broadlands**, where Lord Mountbatten lived. An elegant 18th-century Palladian house with a fine collection of furniture and pictures, Capability Brown designed the wonderful grounds that drift down to the River Test. It is signed from Romsey, 1 m S on the A3057. Admission £5.

In Church St, **Romsey**, almost opposite Romsey Abbey, is King John's House, a 13th-century building with many of its original features, including medieval plaster, timbers, and carved stone window and door surrounds.

Eating Out

La Parisienne, 21 Bell St, **Romsey** (Tel 01794 512067), run by Fabrice and Tanya Berthonneau, is highly recommended. Expect to spend about £25 per head including wine.

The Isle of Wight

I have loved the Isle of Wight ever since I started coming to Seaview for bucket-and-spade holidays. It is a place in which to dawdle, where everything seems to happen at a slower pace. It was a favourite retreat for Queen Victoria, and you can still capture memories of those times when you see the little thatched cottages and the occasional grand house. Of course, much of the shore has been given over to tourism, but you can still see brilliant butterflies on the chalk downs and take bracing walks along the headland at St Catherine's Point where nothing seems to have changed. Fitting music here is the breezy nautical ballet score of Pineapple Poll, arranged by Sir Charles Mackerras, from the music to *HMS Pinafore*.

OS map: Landranger **196**

Gardens

Opening times: in larger gardens, and in NT properties, last admissions are usually 30–45 minutes before the garden closes. Admission charges are a guide to what one adult can expect to pay to go round the garden. It sometimes varies with the season or days of the week. When the house is also open to the public, there is usually an additional charge.

I   **BARTON MANOR**   nr Cowes   Tel 01983 292835

Mon–Fri, early June to end Aug, 10.30–5.30. £3.75
From East Cowes go SE on A3021 for 1m. At Whippingham turn L where signed.

A garden with royal connections – Edward VII built the terraces to enhance the views out to sea. Prince Albert laid out much of the estate and was responsible for planting the fine trees, including an avenue of cork trees. The National Collection (better called National Abomination, in my view) of kniphofias is here, and there are dazzling herbaceous borders, a secret garden and a maze. In spring, thousands of daffodils are a joyous sight around the lake. You may revive your flagging spirits after looking at all those red hot pokers with a glass of wine from the vineyard.

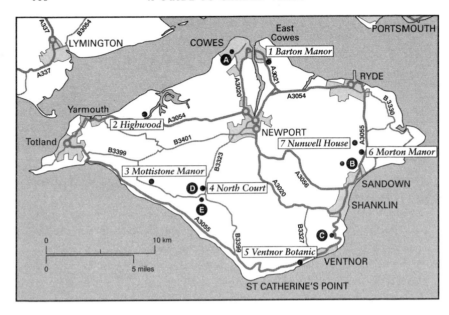

2   HIGHWOOD   Cranmore, nr Yarmouth   Tel 01983 760550

March to October, by appointment. £1.50
From Yarmouth go E on A3054 for 2m. Garden is down a bumpy track in the
village of Cranmore. Ask owner for final directions.

Mrs Cooper is an extremely knowledgeable gardener, and shows brilliantly what can be achieved on a heavy clay soil. Four acres of a 10-acre site are under cultivation, and very well cared for. This is a plantsman's garden, with many unusual varieties, and a spectacular display of hellebores in the spring.

Not far away from Highwood, Kitty Fisher at **Westport Cottage**, Tennyson Lane, Yarmouth (Tel 01983 526206) loves showing visitors round her Victorian walled garden, where vegetables, fruits and herbs are grown alongside borders of flowers and shrubs. Admission £1.

3   MOTTISTONE MANOR (NT)

nr Newport   Tel 01983 526445

Weds and BH Mons, end March to early Oct, 2–5.30. £1.80
From Newport go SW on B3323 for 4m. Turn R at Shorwell on B3399 for
3½ m; garden signed on R.

A terraced garden on a steep slope with sparkling views out to sea. There are herbaceous borders and a rose garden, but to me the most fascinating part is the way fruit trees have been trained to make avenues – under-carpeted in spring with bulbs, and veggies around them. If these fruit trees inspire you, **Deacons Nursery**, Godshill, sells more than 250 different varieties of apples, as well as other fruit. Tel 01983 840750.

Near Mottistone Manor is the 16th-century **Owl Cottage**, at Hoxall Lane, Mottistone (Tel 01983 740433 in the evenings). Mrs Hutchinson is a plantswoman with great flair, who has created this vibrant cottage garden, planned so as to give colour all the year round. It is a delight, with marvellous sea views. More than 50 varieties of honeysuckle are among the treasures. Mrs Hutchinson prefers parties of 10 or more for afternoon visits, so gather your friends for a combined visit – or ask if you can tag along with a party that has already been pre-arranged. £1.50.

4   NORTH COURT

Shorwell (*see also* Where to Stay)   Tel 01983 740415

Charity days May/June, and parties of 10-plus by appointment. £1.50
From Newport go SW on B3323 for 4m; turn R where signed in Shorwell.

There are three different gardens here, belonging to different members of the Harrison family. The main features are sub-tropical plants, and lots of tender salvias, diascias and abutilons in a garden with a Mediterranean feel. You will also find lots of old and modern roses, fine herbaceous borders and a lake. There are particularly interesting specimens for plantlovers, and many fine trees.

5   VENTNOR BOTANIC GARDEN

Ventnor   Tel 01983 855397

Daily, April to Oct, 10–5; other months times differ. Free admission.
From Ventnor town centre go W on A3055 for 1m; garden signed on L.

A fascinating botanic garden to visit at any time of the year. If it's a rainy day you can dodge into the temperate house, keep dry, and admire the col-lections of species from Australia, New Zealand, South Africa and Mexico, including citrus and banana plants. Outside there are herbaceous borders, and a fascinating herb garden which contains medicinal plants used world-wide. In all, an extremely fascinating and informative garden.

6 MORTON MANOR   nr Sandown   Tel 01983 406168

Daily except Sats, April to Oct, 10–5.30. £3.50 (includes tour of house)
From Sandown go N on A3055 for 1m; garden signed on L at traffic lights in
Brading.

The origins of this fascinating old manor go back to the 13th century. In its
6-acre award-winning garden, one of the oldest box hedges I've seen encloses a sunken garden prettily planted with old roses and a huge *Magnolia*
grandiflora. In spring, masses of bulbs are joined by the brilliant colour of
the splendid acers, azaleas and rhododendrons. There is a pagoda, and a
maze for the children. The Trzebski family have been gardening here for
40 years, and the result just gets better and better. I loved the delightful
bee boles. You can lunch here, and enjoy wine from the vineyard.

7 NUNWELL HOUSE   nr Sandown   Tel 01983 407240

Sun–Wed, July to Sept, 10–5 (Suns 1–5). £3
From Sandown go N on A3055 for 1m. Signed on L in Coach Lane, Brading.

Col. and Mrs Aylmer are busy restoring this splendid garden to its former
glory. Designer Vernon Russell-Smith replanted the garden in the late
1950s and added an arboretum. There are some splendid old trees framing
the wonderful views, and features include a rose garden, herb garden,
interesting garden plants, and stunning garden ornaments and obelisks.

Where to Stay

All B&B prices are approximate per person, sharing a double/twin room usually with private
or en suite facilities. It is a good idea to ask for any special requirements when booking.

A NORTHLANDS   Tel 01983 293764

Ian & Christine Kelly, Northlands, 52 Baring Road, Cowes, Isle of Wight
PO31 8DJ.

This substantial Victorian house, mock-Tudor on the outside, has spectacular sea views across the Solent. The Kellys make no claim to be great
gardeners, but even so, their pleasant ½ acre has plenty of roses and shrubs,
and the lawn at the back of the house opens up on to the green fairways of
Cowes Golf Course. Ian, a R.Y.A. yachtmaster, is a native of the Isle of

Wight, and knows all the back-road treasures there are. Evening meals (£12.50 and £18.50) are *en famille*, with local sea food when possible. Bring your own wine. Three double/twin bedrooms (2 with own bath). Smoking welcomed. So are children, if the parents are well behaved. B&B £25–£35.

B   THE GRANGE COUNTRY HOUSE   Tel 01983 403729

Geraldine & David Watling, The Grange Country House, Alverstone,
nr Sandown, Isle of Wight PO36 0EZ.

Big lawns with cedars and hydrangeas surround this grand country house, built in 1877 as the island home of Lord Alverstone. The peaceful ¾-acre gardens lead to a nature reserve where barn owls hoot at night. There are large reception and sitting-rooms here, with 7 big bedrooms (1 single), all en suite. There is excellent food in the dining-room at night (from £13.50, bring your own wine). No smoking, no dogs, children welcome. B&B £19–£24.

C   HILLSIDE   Tel 01983 852271

Brenda Hart, Hillside, Mitchell Avenue, Ventnor, Isle of Wight PO38 1DR.

Sit in the conservatory after dinner at this small family-run hotel, and you can often see badgers on their nocturnal strolls. It is peaceful here, set below St Boniface Down and looking over the roof-tops of Ventnor to the sea. The thatched house is one of the oldest in Ventnor, and generally has good-sized rooms downstairs and upstairs, where there are 11 bedrooms, all with bath or shower en suite. Brenda is a vegetarian, and while this is reflected on her menus, carnivores are catered for as well. Choice of menus, varied every day, are £8.50, licensed. Dogs welcome, restricted smoking, no children under 5. B&B £19–£22.

D   NORTH COURT   (*see* Garden 4)   Tel 01983 740415

Christine Harrison, North Court, Shorwell, nr Newport, Isle of Wight PO30 3JG.

Much the best way to enjoy this 14-acre landscaped garden is to stay in the lovely large manor house it belongs to. Christine is local organiser for the NGS, and can help you plan your garden visiting. There are marvellous walks from the doorstep. Three double/twin bedrooms. Unlicensed. You can arrange light snacks (£5–£8) with Christine, but mostly you eat at an excellent pub within walking distance. No smoking, no dogs, children by arrangement. B&B £18–£20.

E   WESTCOURT FARM   Tel 01983 740233

Joy Russell, Westcourt Farm, Shorwell, nr Newport, Isle of Wight PO30 3LA.

This historic Elizabethan manor, smothered with Virginia creeper and with outstanding views over the countryside, gives you a feel for the island as it was long ago. There is a lovely old lounge, and 3 en suite double rooms with TV. Excellent village pub meals in the evening. No smoking, dogs by arrangement, children welcome. B&B £16–£19.

What Else to Enjoy

This is a short selection of the many good things recommended in the area by owners of places to stay. Your hosts will certainly be able to provide additional information.

If It's Wet

Rain never seems to be too much of a problem during the summer on the Isle of Wight (at least, not in my memory), but if you want to be inside for an hour or two, **Osborne House** is certainly the first choice. English Heritage look after it, together with **Appuldurcombe House**, a romantic ruined 18th-century Baroque mansion near Ventnor, and **Carisbrooke Castle**, on the hills in the centre of the island, where inside there is a Wheel House with donkeys walking round and to show what their forebears (foredonkeys?) used to do day in, day out. £3.80.

For a glimpse of rural domestic life in Victorian times and earlier, call in on **Calbourne Water Mill**, on the B3401 from Newport to Freshwater, which is now a fascinating small museum and café which bakes cakes and bread from flour still ground here (Tel 01983 531227).

Eating Out

A boat hangs from the rafters in the dining-room at **Salty's**, a busy, friendly restaurant with exposed brick walls and many beams in Quay St, **Yarmouth**. This is by far the most recommended place to eat on the Isle of Wight, and is run by Jo Green with her daughter Nicky. The hand-written menu changes every couple of days, and always includes local fish, shellfish and a dish for meat-lovers. Inexpensive – even with wine, you will spend only about £20 per person. Tel 01983 761550.

Around Petersfield

Soft chalk downs shield the inland valleys here from sea breezes, and the Meon Valley has great charm, with its lush water meadows and gentle wooded slopes. Jane Austen both lived in the area, and loved its natural beauty. So did Gilbert White, the great naturalist. Reading his famous *Natural History of Selborne* brought Respighi's 'The Birds' to mind, so I put it on the car tape deck as I drove there.

OS maps: Landrangers **185, 186**, 196, 197

Gardens

Opening times: in larger gardens, and in NT properties, last admissions are usually 30–45 minutes before the garden closes. Admission charges are a guide to what one adult can expect to pay to go round the garden. It sometimes varies with the season or days of the week. When the house is also open to the public, there is usually an additional charge.

I   **FAIRFIELD HOUSE**   Hambledon   Tel 01705 632431

3 charity afternoons between April and June, and by appointment any time for garden lovers. £2
From Petersfield, go W on A272 for 7m. Turn L on A32 for 5½m, then L onto B2150 for 3m to Hambledon. Ask owner for final directions.

Lanning Roper helped to redesign Mrs Susan Wake's beautifully-maintained garden more than 20 years ago, and I wish he could see it now. It has the most glorious collection of roses of every sort, billowing and climbing up walls, over pergolas and arches, with fat bushes of shrub roses in rough grass in the more informal parts, and a huge display of bulbs and flowering trees and shrubs. A meadow garden has recently been planted with wild flowers, and there are interesting perennials – but I urge you to try to visit when the roses are at their best; they are sensational.

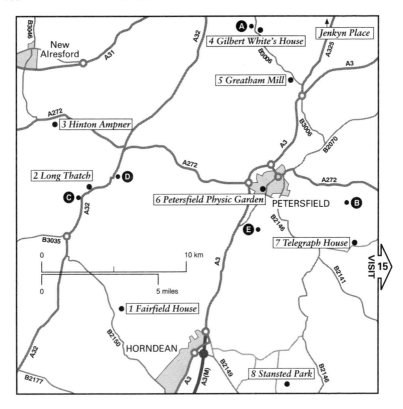

Before you go to Hambledon, try to make an appointment to see **Ferdy's Garden**, one of the most inspiring and extraordinary I have ever seen. On a tiny, very steep slope at White Cottage on Speltham Hill, with a wonderful view from the highest point, 'Ferdy' (actually Mr Ferdinando, Tel 01705 632373) has used every inch of ground to create minute gardens within gardens, built a made-to-measure greenhouse that exactly fits a tiny bit of spare space and constructed paths and steps that teem with much-loved plants. It is entrancing (no wonder it has been seen on TV), and shows all of us what can be achieved if you are a plant-lover and garden designer with hardly enough room to step sideways. The steps and paths are precipitous, and definitely not for people with shaky legs. Admission £2.

2 LONG THATCH   Warnford, nr Petersfield   Tel 01730 829285

Weds, March to Aug, 10–6, many charity days, and any time by appointment.
£1.50
From Petersfield, go W on A272 for 7m. Turn L on A32 for 2½m to Warnford.
Turn R by George and Falcon pub, then R at T-junction; garden ½m on R.

This 2-acre plantsman's garden is set in the lovely Meon valley. From the 17th-century thatched cottage the lawns roll down to the River Meon. Colour all the year round here, starting off with a magnificent collection of hellebores, bulbs, pulmonarias and primulas, plus bog and alpine plants; and in the summer, colourful herbaceous borders, and a fine collection of trees and shrubs. A wide variety of plants are for sale, grown from their own stock by Peter and Vera Short.

3 HINTON AMPNER (NT)   Bramdean   Tel 01962 771305

Sat/Sun, Tues/Wed, BH Mons, April to Sept, 1.30–5.30. £2.50
From Petersfield, go W on A272 for 7m; garden signed on L.

A lovely garden on a hillside, created by Ralph Dutton (later Lord Sherborne) in the 1930s, with a strong feeling for the gardens at Hidcote – firm architectural bones and exuberant planting. He created vistas and walks with delightful surprises at the end: stone figures, a temple, an obelisk, and a lovely statue of Diana. There is an avenue of philadelphus – bliss to sniff if you don't get hayfever – massed daffodils planted in the orchard, with wild flowers and shrub roses everywhere. Bold effects and stunning views make this a garden not to be missed.

4 GILBERT WHITE'S HOUSE   Selborne   Tel 01420 511275

Daily, end March to Christmas, Sat/Sun Jan to March, 11–5. £3
From Petersfield, go NE on A3 for 3m, then L at roundabout onto A325 for
½m. Turn L onto B3006 for 3m to Selborne; car park behind Selborne Arms.

Anyone who has read and been enthralled by Gilbert White's *Natural History of Selborne* will want to explore the house and garden where he lived for most of his life. Many of the plants he loved are still grown (and sold) here, and it is being gradually restored to being as close as possible to his own original garden. Already established are his 'quincunx', wooden ha-ha, and 'six quarters' (beds to display many of the fascinating plants he described). Later additions include a spectacular laburnum arch, topiary and fragrant herb garden. The beech-clad Selborne Hanger, on which he used to stride for his exercise, still looms over the countryside, dominating the scenery. Nice to go in June when the foxgloves are out.

5   GREATHAM MILL   nr Liss   Tel 01420 538245

Daily, end Feb to end Sept, 10–6. £2
From Petersfield go NE on A3 for 3m. Turn L at roundabout onto A325 for ½m, and then L onto B3006 for 600 yds. Turn L into no through lane to find garden.

Fifty years ago, Mrs Pumphrey came to this mill house and made a cottage garden of great exuberance and charm. Her grand-daughter, Mrs Groves and her husband Ed now continue to love and care for it. Well-chosen plants and shrubs, a bog garden (with wonderful irises) and bosky shrub roses all add to its lush and flamboyant whole. Cross the little bridge and you will find some interesting plants for sale.

6   PETERSFIELD PHYSIC GARDEN   Petersfield

Daily, all year, 9–5. Admission free.
In the centre of Petersfield, behind 16 High St.

A restful oasis this charming – although sometimes a bit weedy – garden is laid out in the style of other 17th-century physic gardens (such as Chelsea and Oxford Botanical), which were founded as teaching institutions with medicinal plants are grown in defined geometric shapes. Here, apart from formal herb beds, there are roses, trees, shrubs and herbaceous plants which were all known in the 17th century. Entrance is through a knot garden, followed by a topiary walk to an informal orchard that shelters endangered species of wild flowers and bulbs. This is a delightful and highly informative garden.

7   TELEGRAPH HOUSE   North Marden   Tel 01730 825206

By appointment, May to Aug, 2–5, and 4 charity afternoons June/July. £1.50
From Petersfield go SE on B2146 and later B2141 for 6½m. Garden signed on L before North Marden.

An old semaphore keeper's cottage was here originally, sending news from Portsmouth to London. Now the house, belonging to Mr and Mrs David Gault, has a grand and imposing avenue of copper beeches, surrounded by parkland, with lovely views. The garden is enclosed by yew and beech hedges, is on chalky soil, and is both intimate and inviting. Lots of shrub roses and chalk-tolerant shrubs, herbaceous plants with interesting combinations in form and colour, hydrangeas, cistus and clematis all thrive here.

8   STANSTED PARK   nr Horndean   Tel 01705 412833

Sun/Mon, July to mid Sept, 2–5.30. £2
From Horndean, go SE on B2149 for 2m and turn L to Rowlands Castle. Cross
railway line. Garden is 2m further via minor roads.

There is a gracious park and a fine arboretum around this stunning 18th-century house, home of the Countess of Bessborough. There are three walled gardens to look at. The first, Victorian in inspiration, has box-edged paths and many tender plants. The beautiful old greenhouses still produce magnificent crops of Muscat grapes and figs, but are too dangerous to open to the public until further structural repairs have taken place. The second, smaller, is Dutch in style – formal, very pretty and with a rose garden.

The third garden is unusual and fascinating – a surreal **Garden in Mind** created by landscape gardener Ivan Hicks in 1991 for a TV series about dream gardens. Salvador Dali would have been at home here. Amongst the foliage and flowers you find strange monsters, bits of furniture, an odd pair of legs and other quirky jokes. A huge range of plants grows here, with the emphasis on bold architectural shapes – acanthus, bamboos, paulownias and hostas. The whole garden has a magical dream-like voluptuousness to it. You pay a separate surreal price of £2.01 for admission to this garden. Open Suns, June to Sept, 2–6 and by appointment. Tel 01705 413149.

Where to Stay

All B&B prices are approximate per person, sharing a double/twin room usually with private
or en suite facilities. It is a good idea to ask for any special requirements when booking.

A   CONEYCROFT HOUSE   Tel 01420 511296

Julie & Derek Edwards, Coneycroft House, Selborne, nr Alton, Hampshire
GU34 3JF.

The garden at this large, comfortable, cream-painted house leads across a wide lawn to a marvellous lake, where on still days at any time of the year the foliage of the surrounding trees is reflected wondrously towards you.

There are 30 acres of grounds in which to wander, a swimming pool and tennis court to enjoy, and Selborne, where Gilbert White wrote his *Natural History*, is only minutes away. Julie is an interior designer, Derek a stockbroker and banker. Two double bedrooms. Dinner £20, bring your own wine. No smoking in bedrooms, no small children, and you have to be persuasive about dogs. B&B £30–£35.

B MIZZARDS FARM   Tel 01730 821656

Harriet & Julian Francis, Mizzards Farm, Rogate, nr Petersfield, Hampshire GU31 5HS.

Beauty is all around when you stay here. The 16th-century farmhouse is a treasure, and the 2 acres of gardens that stretch in all directions a delight. There is a cottagey feel to them – masses of colourful mixed planting next to stone terraces, and lawns that sweep away to a stream, a bluebell wood, and a small lake with bog plants and water lilies. Elsewhere are a rose garden with a weeping silver pear, a croquet lawn with a summer house built from old oak beams, and a covered swimming pool. Inside the house is an elegant drawing-room and a vaulted dining-room. The 3 guest bedrooms have won awards for their high standard. Eat out in the evening at one of the many pubs and restaurants nearby. No smoking, no children under 8, and dogs must stay in the car. B&B £24–£29.

C PAPER MILL COTTAGE   Tel 01730 829387

John & Diana Larrett, Paper Mill Cottage, Warnford, nr Petersfield, Hampshire SO3 1LA.

If you want to be lulled to sleep by the sound of water lapping under your bedroom, this is the place for you. It's a beautifully furnished, comfortable conversion of a 17th-century paper mill. There is just one enchanting double bedroom which looks out through a leaded window straight down the River Meon and its wildlife. There are good pubs in nearby West Meon to eat out in the evenings. No dogs, no smoking, no children. B&B £23.

D HOME PADDOCKS   Tel 01730 829241

Simon & Ray Ward, Home Paddocks, West Meon, nr Petersfield, Hampshire GU32 1NA.

Here you will find a garden that is worth visiting in its own right (although it is not open to the public, so it's a good reason for staying overnight). Packed with flowers and architectural features, with a box-edged parterre, a croquet lawn, a tennis court and, above all, a sense of spaciousness, several generations of owners have loved and tended the large garden. The white-painted house is a rambling family home. There are 2 excellent bedrooms for guests who can use and enjoy the living-room, dining-room, live-in kitchen, and the Victorian conservatory (where meals on warm days are taken). Dinner, by arrangement, is £13 (bring your own wine). Dogs welcome, smoking restricted, and children should be over 7. B&B £20–£21.

E   PILLMEAD HOUSE   Tel 01730 266795

Sarah Moss, Pillmead House, North Lane, Buriton, nr Petersfield, Hampshire GU31 5RS.

Sarah's large garden tumbles steeply down from a rock garden near the house to terraces flanked with beds of roses and lavender, with superb views. In the house are 2 pretty double bedrooms. What all the guests praise, are Sarah's delicious suppers (£12.50, not on Sunday), served at 7 p.m. because most people's appetite can't wait any longer. Much of the fresh produce comes from her own kitchen garden. Bring your own wine. No smoking. Dogs and children welcome. B&B £19.

What Else to Enjoy

This is a short selection of the many good things recommended in the area by owners of places to stay. Your hosts will certainly be able to provide additional information.

Other Gardens

Six miles to the north of the visit map, and absolutely worth the journey, is **Jenkyn Place** (Tel 01420 23118). This lovely garden, justly famous, is laid out in the Hidcote style with garden rooms and vistas along corridors lined with beech or yew, sheltering some rare and interesting plants. Magnificent borders, herbs, a rock garden, old roses and climbers, a woodland garden with noble trees and fine garden sculptures make this an example of

English gardening style at its best. It is open Thurs–Sun and BH Mons, early April to early Sept, 2–6. Admission £2. You will find it signed 400 yds N of **Bentley** on the A31 midway between Alton and Farnham.

Other Places to Stay

To the E of the visit map is **The Old Rectory**, run by Peter and Anna Blencowe. It is a substantial and spacious house, quietly set down a country lane and the landscaped garden is now well established. There is a tempting swimming pool. The 3 double bedrooms (plus 1 single) are large and well furnished. Eat out at the nearby pub. Restricted smoking. You can arrange for dogs, and children welcome. B&B £20–24. Address: The Old Rectory, **Chidham**, West Sussex PO18 8TA. Tel 01243 527088.

If It's Wet

Jane Austen being so much in vogue, it would be a shame to miss out on the modest red-brick house where she wrote (or re-wrote) most of her best-known books. You can visit the parlour where she wrote and there is plenty of memorabilia and letters which give a lovely feel of her and her times. The pretty garden is stocked with herbs and flowers she would certainly recognise. It is super-nostalgic. Open 11–4.30, March to Sept, you will find it in **Chawton** village, 1m SW of Alton, signed off the roundabout junction of the A31 and A32. Admission charges vary (Tel 01420 83262).

For something grander, go and see the amazing reconstruction job which the NT has achieved after the disastrous fire at **Uppark**. The army of craftspeople and builders have done such a wonderful job that you would never guess the extent of devastation they inherited. The interior, together with its furnishing and paintings, is stunning. There is a timed ticket system operating here, so you may have to queue before getting inside. Find it just off the B2146, 5m SE of **Petersfield**. Admission £5.50.

Eating Out

If your man isn't as keen on garden visiting as you are, but loves cricket, treat him to lunch in **West Meon** at **The Thomas Lord** – a lovely local pub with a definite cricket flavour. Here you can indulge in steak and kidney pie and spotted dick, or bread and butter pudding, generously served at reasonable prices. Tel 01730 829244. Another good cricketing pub is the **Bat and Ball** which overlooks the famous ground at **Hambledon**.

The South Downs

It all feels very prosperous around here. The weather-boarded houses in the pretty villages are beautifully maintained, and beyond the wooded hill-tops and chalk downs are the south coast resorts with their restaurants and glitzy shopping. As a break from visiting some of the wonderful gardens in the area, don't miss out on lunch at the Spread Eagle in Midhurst — it's a real treat. A mood-setting piece of music might be Leonard Bernstein's 'Chichester Psalms', which he wrote for the cathedral there; or, if you want a tranquil piece of sacred music more familiar and hummable, Fauré's Requiem.

OS map: Landranger **197**

Gardens

Opening times: in larger gardens, and in NT properties, last admissions are usually 30–45 minutes before the garden closes. Admission charges are a guide to what one adult can expect to pay to go round the garden. It sometimes varies with the season or days of the week. When the house is also open to the public, there is usually an additional charge.

1 DENMANS Fontwell Tel 01243 542808

Daily except Christmas, 9–5 (or dusk). £2.50
From Chichester, go NE on A27 for 5m; turn R into Denmans Lane before racecourse.

John Brookes has been running his School of Garden Design from his renowned garden since 1980. It is immaculate, a shop window for his work. He has splendid ideas for paths and for contrasts of forms and foliage. His herbaceous borders, old roses and climbers, and an impeccable herb garden, will all spark your imagination. Especially tender plants are housed in a huge greenhouse, and more are planted out in gravel near the circular pond. A fascinating garden at any time of the year.

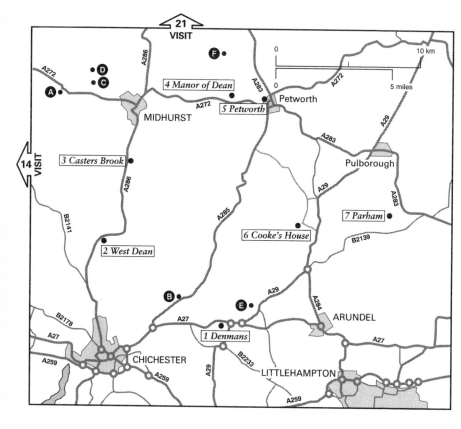

2   **WEST DEAN GARDENS**   nr Chichester   Tel 01243 811303

Daily, March to Oct, 11–5. £3.50
From Chichester, go N on A286 for 5m; garden signed on R.

The early 18th-century West Dean House was designed by James Wyatt, and is now a college of arts and crafts. The gardens, grand and Edwardian, are undergoing an energetic burst of restoration. Magnificent ancient cedars hold sway over the lawns, and tall conifers, oaks and horse chestnuts all lend dignity. Perhaps the most impressive feature is the 100 yds long pergola, designed by Harold Peto, which leads to a pavilion liberally draped with roses, clematis and honeysuckle. The walled kitchen garden has recently been restored, and is sheer heaven – Edwardian greenhouses, now back to their former beauty, shelter peaches, figs, melons, ferns and tender plants. Perfectly trained espaliered fruit trees climb round the warm walls.

3   CASTERS BROOK   Cocking, nr Midhurst   Tel 01730 813537

3 charity openings June/July; garden lovers welcome by appointment. £1.50
From Midhurst go S on A286 for 2m. Turn L before Post Office in Cocking
village; garden next to church.

As you might guess, water features largely in Mr and Mrs Whitehorn's
2-acre garden, the brook running down to a mill pond, with a small bridge
leading to two smaller ponds under a truly giant plane tree. In the flower
garden, old roses predominate, with santolina, lavender, iris and and ferns;
I loved the fig court and the herb garden. There are surprises too – I won't
give them away!

4   THE MANOR OF DEAN   nr Petworth   Tel 01798 861247

Sat–Mon for charity, middle of each month, March to Sept, 2–6, and by ap-
pointment. £1
From Petworth go W on A272 for 2m. Turn R where signed on minor road for
¼m.

The present garden was started by Captain William Mitford in 1943, and
his daughter, Miss Mitford, now cares for it. A delightful air of nostalgia
abounds on the lawns, with fine old trees and borders. Antique copper containers and troughs from the house and farm are planted up, while barn
owls and kestrels have kept their homes over the centuries in the outbuildings. One of the most charming touches was finding an orange tree in
the greenhouse, grown from a cutting from a family wedding bouquet
in 1920, which in turn was taken from wedding bouquets dating three
generations back. Now the fruit is made into marmalade (you might be able
to buy a pot). Plenty of year-round interest – spring bulbs, azaleas, bluebells, a kitchen garden, and summer colour from hanging baskets and
containers in the courtyards.

5   PETWORTH PARK (NT)   Petworth   Tel 01798 342207

Daily, all year, 8–sunset. Admission free.
Signed in centre of Petworth on A283.

The grounds surrounding the 17th-century house consist of two distinct
areas: the deer park, and the pleasure grounds, designed by George London
and Capability Brown which inspired Turner to paint his famous landscape.
There are noble trees and a lake, and fallow deer. The pleasure grounds
have marvellous bulbs and wild flowers in spring, and herbaceous borders

from June to August. Also splendid autumn colour in October. It's not so much a garden, more a beautiful setting for a magnificent house.

6 COOKE'S HOUSE

West Burton, nr Pulborough   Tel 01798 831353

April/May charity days, and by appointment. £1
From Pulborough, go SW on A29 for 4½m. Turn R at Bury on minor road for ½m; garden in West Burton village.

A charming small garden set around Miss Courtauld's Elizabethan house, with small perfect rooms, chic topiary, and fine shrubs which are under-planted with snake's-head fritillaries and bluebells. The meadow is fragrant with cowslips. It makes a late April visit particularly enticing – but there is a riot of colour later from roses, and then herbaceous plants.

7 PARHAM HOUSE   nr Pulborough   Tel 01903 744888

Wed/Thurs, Sun and BHs, Easter to early Oct, 1–6. £3
From Pulborough, go SE on A283 for 4m; garden signed on R.

An ancient deer park, with venerable oak trees, surrounds this Elizabethan house; there is also a grand walled garden of nearly 4 acres. The historic character of the gardens remains, but it was imaginatively replanted in 1982, giving year-round interest, with shrubs, a potager, an orchard with unusual fruit trees, herbaceous borders, and specialist plants of interest to plant-lovers. In the park you can lose your children in the maze, and sit down to enjoy the peaceful lake and views.

Where to Stay

All B&B prices are approximate per person, sharing a double/twin room usually with private or en suite facilities. It is a good idea to ask for any special requirements when booking.

A TROTTON OLD RECTORY   Tel 01730 813831

Caroline & John Pilley, Trotton Old Rectory, Trotton, nr Petersfield, Hampshire GU31 5EN.

It is gorgeous here. The beautifully proportioned Georgian house, with curled slate roof and shutters, is smothered with climbers and creepers. The garden, on two levels running down to a lake and the River Rother, is brilliantly planned and planted, with subtle changes of colour and foliage in the formal beds of roses framed in box and yew, and in the rich herbaceous borders. You will find wonderful trees, shrubs and hostas. Caroline Pilley loves gardens, cooking (evening meal £20, bring your own wine), and entertaining, and saves 2 lovely double/twin bedrooms for guests. No dogs or children or smoking. B&B £35.

B OLD STORE GUEST HOUSE   Tel 01243 531977

Robert Grocott, The Old Store Guest House, Stane Street, Halnaker, nr Chichester, West Sussex PO18 0QL.

Views over a large garden and farmland to Chichester Cathedral can be enjoyed from this impressive 18th-century house on the edge of the Goodwood Estate. The guest lounge is comfortably furnished, and the 7 bedrooms (including 1 single) all have en suite shower rooms. In the evening, it is a short walk to the Anglesey Arms, an excellent pub/restaurant. In the morning, there is a charming breakfast room where you are set up lavishly for your garden visiting. Children welcome, dogs by arrangement, restricted smoking. B&B £28.

C FISHERS HILL   Tel 01730 813474

Michael & Jenny Gordon Lennox, Fishers Hill, Iping, nr Midhurst, West Sussex GU29 0PF.

This handsome and welcoming Sussex stone-built house has 2½ acres of garden. In spring you will find masses of crocuses, daffodils and other bulbs, and all the year round a typical Sussex outlook of fine trees and shrubs set in well-mown lawns. There's a swimming pool and tennis court. Michael and Jenny are great entertainers (Michael was with the Royal Navy) and guests are full of praise for their friendly hospitality. Two good double/twin bedrooms. Evening meals £18. Unlicensed, but ask about wine. No dogs, no smoking, children welcome. B&B £25.

D FITZHALL   Tel 01730 813634

Mrs Bridger, Fitzhall, Iping, nr Midhurst, West Sussex GU27 0JP.

Within 110 acres of lovely grounds, with panoramic views of the South Downs, is this 9-acre garden, with extensive shrubberies, a rockery, herbaceous borders, wild places and an exciting enclosed herb garden. Mrs Bridger (nobody ever uses her Christian name) serves teas for pre-booked parties of more than 10, sells home-made cakes and jams, and opens up a small farm for children to enjoy cows, calves and sheep — so you may have some daytime company here. Seven double bedrooms and 1 single share 3 bathrooms. You eat out at local pubs in the evening. No dogs, no smoking, children welcome. B&B £20–£22.

E MILL LANE HOUSE   Tel 01243 814440

Sarah & Peter Fuente, Mill Lane House, Slindon, nr Arundel, West Sussex BN18 0RP.

Three acres of garden and woodland surround this handsome 17th-century house. There are superb views to the coast, you can walk directly on to the South Downs, and there is excellent bird-watching to be enjoyed locally. The pretty village of Slindon is within walking distance and has a number of pubs, but you can also arrange evening meals with Sarah (£10, bring your own wine). The 7 bedrooms, all en suite, include 1 single. Children and dogs welcome, no smoking in the dining-room. B&B £19.

F RIVER PARK FARM   Tel 01798 861362

Pat & Nick Moss, River Park Farm, Lodsworth, nr Petworth, West Sussex GU28 9DS.

This pretty 17th-century farmhouse is typically Sussex: tile-hung, and smothered with wisteria and a Kiftsgate rose. The garden is simple (lawns and roses wonderfully set in the surrounding trees), giving peace and quiet while you watch the abundant bird life. It is a friendly house, full of character, where you will find 3 double/twin bedrooms sharing 2 bathrooms. Simple evening meals cost £6–£7 (bring your own wine), and more adventurous cooking is easily found at good pubs and restaurants locally. No smoking, no dogs, children welcome. B&B £18.

What Else to Enjoy

This is a short selection of the many good things recommended in the area by owners of places to stay. Your hosts will certainly be able to provide additional information.

Other Gardens/Nurseries

Apuldram Roses has a marvellous specialist display, mostly in island beds and in fields where the roses are cultivated, but also planted more as your garden might like them, cottage-garden style. The shop stocks a good selection of arches and trellis to fire your imagination. Open daily except 24 Dec to 6 Jan, 9–5 (Suns and BHs 10.30–4.30). Go W of **Chichester** on A259 for 1m and turn L down Apuldram Lane. Tel 01243 785769.

If It's Wet

Chichester must be your first port of call because there is so much to do here. It has what are probably Britain's best Roman remains at Fishbourne Palace. The 900-year cathedral starts with Romanesque stone carvings and continues to 20th-century works of art. Pallant House, built in 1712, is a perfect example of a Queen Anne town house; as you see it today, each room reflects a particular period in the history of the house. The art collection includes works by Moore, Sutherland, Piper, Klee and Cézanne. It is open Tues–Sat all year, 10–5, admission £2.50.

To keep out of the rain in a stately home, **Arundel Castle** would be my first choice. It is so impressive, inside and out, that it takes your breath away, with fine furniture, classic paintings by Gainsborough, Reynolds et al, and personal possessions of Mary, Queen of Scots. It is open daily except Sats, April to Oct, 11–5. **Goodwood House**, N of Chichester off the A285, ancestral home of the Dukes of Richmond, is set in wonderful parkland with modern sculptures. Fine paintings by Canaletto, Stubbs and Reynolds hang above exquisite Sèvres porcelain and French furniture. It is open most Suns and Mons from Easter to Sept, and some other days, 2–5, but you should telephone to check: 01243 774107. **Petworth House** (see Garden 5) contains one of the NT's best collections of pictures (don't miss the famous Turner), fine furniture and carvings by Grinling Gibbons.

Eating Out

Midhurst is great for antiques, or just pottering about. The **Spread Eagle**, a 15th-century coaching inn which has many of its original features, offers a outstanding set lunch for £16.50 and dinner for £25 in wonderful beamed surroundings. Tel 01730 816911. For eating, this market town is spoiled for riches, because just down the road is the Georgian **Angel Hotel**, much written about since it was refurbished four years ago. Set lunch is £13.50, dinner £17.50. Tel 01730 812421.

East Sussex

Two gardens in this visit – Charleston Farmhouse and Monk's House – are associated with the Bloomsbury Group, and might encourage you to read some Virginia Woolf when you rest your legs in the evening. Glyndebourne, with its wonderful new garden and opera house, is in this area too. I have been lucky enough to go often to Glyndebourne, and it always seems to me that Mozart is the fulfilment of a wonderful night out. So on your car tape deck, Mozart it has to be: *The Marriage of Figaro*, of course.

OS maps: Landrangers **198, 199**

Gardens

Opening times: in larger gardens, and in NT properties, last admissions are usually 30–45 minutes before the garden closes. Admission charges are a guide to what one adult can expect to pay to go round the garden. It sometimes varies with the season or days of the week. When the house is also open to the public, there is usually an additional charge.

1 PRIESTHAWES Polegate   Tel 01323 763228

2 charity days in June, and by appointment for garden lovers. £2
From Hailsham town centre go SE on B2104 for 2½m; garden signed on L.

This is a charming 15th-century house with a 2½-acre garden around it. Mr and Mrs Wadham have a tremendous collection of clematis which scramble up walls and shrubs and cover the pergola. In front is a wide border whose colours echo those behind – pinks, purples and a touch of lemon, from acanthus, phlox, aconitums and many annuals. Two fat yew hedges have been trimmed into an arch. They were planted by Mr Wadham's grandmother, and the monkey puzzle tree and weeping ash are reminders of the original Victorian planting. They are strong on ornamental trees here. I particularly admired a *Robinia hillieri* and a *Halesia carolina* – the snowdrop tree.

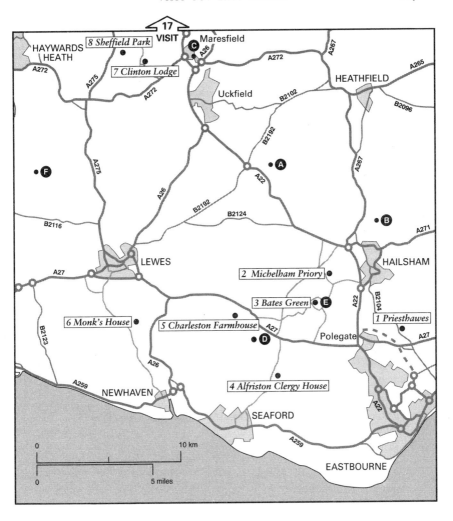

2   MICHELHAM PRIORY

Upper Dicker, nr Hailsham   Tel 01323 844224

Daily, end March to Oct, 11–5.30

From Lewes go E on A27 for 6m. Turn L on minor road for 1m, then turn L at X-roads for 2m to Upper Dicker; garden signed on R.

A soothing place to visit, with water lilies and reflections constantly near since the 14th-century moat encircles the garden. This includes an orchard, a kitchen garden, some very fine old trees, and a most intriguing physic garden. Here you can amble between fragrant plants, and read the fascinating labels. The poor old monks must have suffered with their knees, because there are lots of herbs for gout and sciatica. There are herbs for animal husbandry, cures for wounds and broken bones, and – most fascinatingly – herbs for depression, insomnia and nightmares. Some things don't change. If you get a bit tired walking round all the gardens in this book, perhaps try wild thyme infused with rose water, which we are told 'will cure them that hv the long phrensie and lethargie'.

3   BATES GREEN

Arlington, nr Hailsham (*see also* Where to Stay)   Tel 01323 482039

Thurs, April to Oct, 10.30–6, and by appointment. £2
From Lewes go E on A27 for 6m. Turn L on minor road for 2½m to Arlington village; 350 yds past Old Oak Inn, turn R up lane where signed.

Anyone wishing to create a tranquil garden with colour and interest all the year round could learn how to do it by walking around Mrs McCutchan's artistically designed garden. It has several different areas – a pond fringed by bog-loving plants, a large rock garden, and marvellous mixed borders. There are excellent ideas for shady areas as well. You can stay here overnight and enjoy the garden in the pearly dawn light, when gardens like this look so magical.

4   ALFRISTON CLERGY HOUSE (NT)

nr Polegate   Tel 01323 870001

Daily, April to Oct, 10.30–5 (or dusk). £2.20
From Lewes go E on A27 for 7½m. Turn R, signed Alfriston, for 1½m; garden in village centre.

The Clergy House was the first property bought (for £10) by the National Trust in 1896, and is now lovingly restored. Around the house there is in essence a small cottage garden, its tranquil feel generated by the soft colours used in the planting scheme. Four clipped box trees are under-planted with pinks; old scented roses sway across well-worn brick paths. A remarkable Judas tree is at the entrance to a small orchard, with a nicely new walnut and mulberry planted amongst the apples and plums. The herb garden, edged with neat santolina, and a productive kitchen garden, where bantams were having a good peck and a scratch, added to the overall charm.

5 CHARLESTON FARMHOUSE

nr Lewes   Tel 01323 811265

Wed–Sun and BH Mons, April to Oct, 2–6 (11–6 mid July to Sept). £2
From Lewes go SE on A27 for 5m; garden entrance on R.

Virginia Woolf's sister, Vanessa Bell, lived here with Duncan Grant, so it's fun to compare it with Monk's House. It is very personal and eccentric, full of follies and jokes, and not a plantsman's garden. If you are a literary person you'll love it (or turn your nose up at it) for its associations with the Bloomsbury Group. Is that Carrington laughing behind the hedge?

6 MONK'S HOUSE (NT)

Rodmell, nr Lewes   Tel 01892 890651 (NT regional office)

Weds and Sats, April to Oct, 2–5.30. £2.20
From centre of Lewes go S on minor road, signed Rodmell, for 4m; garden signed in village.

The garden has not changed much since Leonard and Virginia Woolf lived here. She worked in the garden house, and her writing desk is still here, together with photos and extracts from her letters and diaries. Leonard spent a great deal of his time growing prize-winning veggies. There are three ponds, and an orchard under-planted with different species of daffodils and autumn crocuses. Near the house, yew hedges, paths and flint-stone walls shelter a herbaceous area, and there are some fine old trees.

7 CLINTON LODGE   Fletching, nr Uckfield   Tel 01825 722952

4 charity afternoons in June, and for garden lovers by appointment. £2.50
From Haywards Heath go E on A272 for 7m. Turn L on minor road for 1m to Fletching; garden in centre of village.

A vast yew hedge and great oak gates hide this elegant Carolean house from the village street. Behind it is a magical garden which overlooks parkland with far-reaching views across Sussex. A broad terrace, with a coy statue of a maiden pouring water, is above a wide lawn bordered by a hornbeam avenue. Clipped yew and beech hedges divide the 6-acre garden into several smaller rooms, all romantic and perfect. A magnificent double herbaceous border of yellows, creams and blues, with more than 100 lemon hollyhocks, simply bowled me over. The pear walk, with hooped fruit trees, is planted with lilies, hellebores, alliums and aquilegias. The potager has arches of apples, box-edged, with standard gooseberries, a sun-dial and decorative arbours where blue beans and gourds climb. The little orchard is full of wildflowers, and alpine strawberries are planted at the base of the trees. The herb garden has a pleached lime walk on two sides, and is crossed by a camomile path. And what joy – I found medieval-style turf seats and a therapeutic camomile seat. The swimming-pool area is walled, with roses, vines and *Campsis radicans* ramping up the rosy bricks. Four paulownias and a silver pear, plus arches of old apple varieties are here too. In the rose garden, Portland roses are planted with foxgloves, *Alchemilla mollis* and hardy geraniums, a dovecote standing in the centre. This is a wildly romantic and beautifully maintained garden. I urge you to go there on NGS open days, or – better still – if you can put together a small group of friends and interested gardeners.

8   SHEFFIELD PARK (NT)   nr Uckfield   Tel 01825 790231

Daily except Mons, and BH Mons, April to mid Nov, 11–6 (or dusk). £4 From Haywards Heath go E on A272 for 4m. Turn L on A275 for 2m; garden signed on R.

A vast, famous and grand landscaped garden, with a string of lakes, laid out by Capability Brown in the 18th century, and added to in the 20th. The lakes reflect the colours of fine trees and shrubs, so on a calm day you get double the amazing beauty of this woodland garden. Spring bulbs and blue-bells are abundant in spring, and gentians and crocuses add to the explosion of colour in the autumn.

Where to Stay

All B&B prices are approximate per person, sharing a double/twin room usually with private or en suite facilities. It is a good idea to ask for any special requirements when booking.

A   OLD WHYLY   Tel 01825 840216

Sarah Burgoyne, Old Whyly, East Hoathly, nr Uckfield, East Sussex BN8 6EL.

This 17th-century manor house has a sweeping drive which leads to its porticoed front door through marvellously well kept grounds and gardens. From this house, you can take walks through an unspoiled area of Sussex, visit gardens and go to the opera at Glyndebourne – a wonderful combination. The house has a fascinating history through the Civil War, and is full of antiques and pictures. Sarah trained as a cook in Paris, and her outstanding food (dinner £20, bring your own wine) is based on her time there. Two lovely double bedrooms. No smoking, no dogs, discuss children. B&B £38.

B   HOLMBUSH HOUSE   Tel 01435 813078

Jeffrey & Lorraine King, Holmbush House, North St, Hellingly, nr Hailsham, East Sussex BN27 4EE.

It is peaceful here in this Georgian farmhouse, with 3 acres of gardens leading to a golf course. Jeffrey and Lorraine refurbished their house splendidly to launch their B&B operation in 1995. You eat out in the evenings, with a good choice of nearby pubs and restaurants. There are 2 en suite twin rooms for guests, and you can have breakfast in your bedroom or in the dining-room. No smoking, no dogs, children welcome. B&B £28.

C   SOUTH PADDOCK   Tel 01825 762335

Major & Mrs Graham Allt, South Paddock, Maresfield Park, nr Uckfield, East Sussex TN22 2HA.

South Paddock still has the feel of the time it was built – 1929, when architects were given the opportunity to design a spacious family home facing the right way (south), and landscape a garden of 3½ acres. Nowadays, guests praise the comfort, and the help given about local places of interest. They also enjoy the 1930's character of the garden, including a croquet lawn. The 3 bedrooms (1 with private bathroom, the others sharing) all have good south views. No evening meals and unlicensed, but you can eat well at several nearby pubs and restaurants. Children should be over 10. Be persuasive about your dog. Smoking allowed. B&B £25–£36.

D   DAWES HOUSE   Tel 01323 871276

Catherine & Michael Wardroper, Dawes House, Berwick, nr Polegate, East Sussex BN26 5QS.

This attractive tile-hung, white-painted thatched house has wonderful views, a pretty garden and a vineyard. Attached to the house is a luxurious converted barn set aside for guests. Inside is a double bedroom and a single, and if there are 5 of you in a party Catherine can occasionally put up the extra in the main house. Here is where you can arrange evening meals (£12.50, bring your own wine), or just sit in the lounge and relax. No smoking, but children over 10 and dogs welcome. B&B £23.

E BATES GREEN   (*see* Garden 3)   Tel 01323 482039

Carolyn McCutchan, Bates Green, Arlington, nr Polegate, East Sussex BN26 6SH.

Carolyn's stunning garden should be seen at all costs; staying at her house makes it a double treat. Originally an 18th-century gamekeeper's cottage, it became a tile-hung family farmhouse now restored and enlarged; it is completely surrounded by fields and woodland, and arrived at via a leafy lane. Round the house are 2 acres using colour and foliage to create marvellous atmosphere and effect. The profuse and abundant planting, and the design, are superb. Three cottagey double bedrooms. Tea and cake when you arrive, marvellous fresh ingredients for breakfast – Carolyn knows what her guests like. Early supper from £7.50 (take your own wine). No dogs, or children, or smoking. B&B £21–£27.

F ELM GROVE FARM   Tel 01273 890368

Ann & Bryan Nicholls, Elm Grove Farm, Streat Lane, Streat, nr Hassocks, East Sussex BN6 8RY.

What a find – what bliss! Here is somewhere to stay with a garden to drool over, but is not open to the public. Off a quiet country lane and completely secluded, it is surrounded by farmland with good views to the South Downs. Lawns, shrubs, rose garden, spring bulbs, flowering trees, rose garden, winding paths, five water features – yes, it has all those, but just listing them doesn't do justice to the vistas created by the pergolas, the sound of the water trickling down the fountains, the old apple tree bursting with blossom . . . I could go on. Three good bedrooms in a listed 14th-century house, relaxing and friendly hosts, 4-course dinner £15 if you ask beforehand (take your own wine). No smoking, no dogs, children should be over 14. B&B £20–£25.

What Else to Enjoy

This is a short selection of the many good things recommended in the area by owners of places to stay. Your hosts will certainly be able to provide additional information.

Other Gardens/Nurseries

On minor roads 2m to the SW of Heathfield is the little village of **Waldron**. Here you find **St George's Vineyard**, which calls itself the prettiest in England. Its claim may be justified because the fields of vine are attached to an enchanting old house, with colourful and well-kept gardens, and a 300-year-old barn converted to a shop where there is local produce and many tempting gifts. There is a self-service snack bar if you want to eat in the gardens, and a more elaborate Winery Restaurant. The 11th-century tithe barn has exhibitions and events during many weeks from May to Sept. Unconducted tours of the vineyard cost £1.50, including a glass of wine. Conducted tours cost from £3.

If It's Wet

The 14th-century **Alfriston Clergy House** (*see* Garden 4), nr Polegate, was the first property bought by the NT, in 1896. Thatched, half-timbered, the interior rooms open to the public include a medieval hall and exhibition hall. Opening hours as for garden.

Michelham Priory (*see* Garden 2) in Upper Dicker, has 13th-century origins, and an imposing 14th-century gatehouse still stands. After the dissolution, the monastic buildings were incorporated into two Tudor houses which in due course became a splendid country house. This, now open to the public, stages many events. The Elizabethan Great Barn is spectacular. Opening hours are approximately the same as for the garden.

On the SW edge of the visit, at the junction of the A259 and B2123, is **Rottingdean**. The Grange here was built as a vicarage in the mid-18th century, and remodelled by Lutyens in 1919. It contains a museum of historic toys, and a collection of letters, books and pictures connected with Rudyard Kipling.

For shopping, both **Lewes** and **Hailsham** are brilliant – plenty of antique and gift shops set in charming old-world surroundings. If you want a whole day out with more to look at, **Brighton** is just off the visit map to the W.

Eating Out

Still popular and still serving wonderful meals after twenty years, the **Hungry Monk** in **Jevington**, is one of my long-time favourites – and their recipe books are well-thumbed in my kitchen. The dishes, both traditional and new, are constantly inventive. The set meals at lunch and dinner cost about £22 plus service and wine. Find it on a minor road W of the A22 from Polegate to Eastbourne. Tel 01323 482178.

The Sussex Weald

Acid soil and sheltered valleys here, not far from London, have made it possible to create some of Britain's best-known gardens. Nymans, Leonardslee and Wakehurst are all enormously popular, and are now recovering well from the awful losses in the great gales. Ashdown Forest, where the game of Poohsticks was invented, is still heavily wooded and a stunning place for country walks. If all this lovely countryside makes you feel proudly English, I suggest you listen to highlights from Purcell's opera *King Arthur*, which includes 'Fairest Isle', the most patriotic song you will ever find.

OS maps: Landrangers **187**, 188, 198, 199

Gardens

Opening times: in larger gardens, and in NT properties, last admissions are usually 30–45 minutes before the garden closes. Admission charges are a guide to what one adult can expect to pay to go round the garden. It sometimes varies with the season or days of the week. When the house is also open to the public, there is usually an additional charge.

I   LEONARDSLEE GARDENS

Lower Beeding, nr Horsham   Tel 01403 891212

Daily, May to Oct, 10–6 (May 10–8). £3.50 (£4.50 in May)
From Haywards Heath go W on A272 for 7m. At Cowfold turn R on A281 for 2m; garden signed on R.

This is Sir Leonard Loder's great woodland garden, famous for acid-loving ornamental trees and shrubs. Choice collections of rhododendrons and azaleas, camellias and magnolias, under-planted with bluebells and spring bulbs, dazzle with colour in May, and again in autumn for foliage colour. You can also find a magnificent collection of alpines in the Alpine House, and a bonsai collection as well. Crowded with visitors in the high season. And no, you didn't lunch too well – those really are wallabies nibbling the grass.

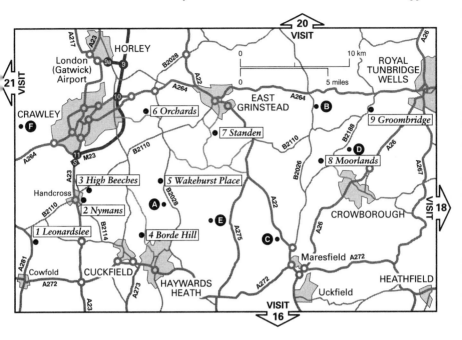

Near Leonardslee, you can turn S off the A281 down minor roads for about 1m to find the village of **Nuthurst**. At Cooks Farm, **Architectural Plants** is a unique concept in what is both a nursery and a garden. Angus White stocks and sells only plants, mostly exotic evergreens, that will liven up your garden in winter. His excellent descriptive catalogue (free), truly inspirational, contains many plants and shrubs that you will never have heard of, but will surely want. The postal address is Nuthurst, Horsham, RH13 6LH. The nursery is open daily except Suns all year, 9–5. Tel 01403 891772.

2   NYMANS (NT)   Handcross   Tel 01444 400321

Wed–Sun and BH Mons, March to Oct, 11–6 (Sat/Sun 11–7). £4.20
From Crawley go S on A23 for 5½m. At Handcross take B2114 for ½m; garden signed on L.

Romantic and theatrical, the ruined walls of a great old house stand out as a superb dramatic background to some wonderful planting. It is the creation of several generations of the Messel family, who gave the gardens to the National Trust in 1954. Great losses were suffered in the gales of 1987, but there are still many magnificent trees, and an abundance of magnolias, camellias, eucryphias and rhododendrons. The rose garden has been restored, and in late summer the herbaceous borders, influenced by William Robinson's ideas, are magnificent. The garden and wild garden cover more than 30 acres, so there is plenty of variety to please florists, botanists, plant-lovers, and artists. Give yourself plenty of time to enjoy it all.

3   HIGH BEECHES GARDENS

Handcross   Tel 01444 400589

Daily except Weds, April to Oct (closed July), 1–5. £3
From Crawley go S on A23 for 5½m. Turn L on B2110 for 1m; garden signed on R.

An ecologically fascinating garden, with a front meadow of wild flowers, home to cowslips and many different varieties of orchids. The gardens were laid out by the Loder family, of Leonardslee fame, and have since been beautifully looked after by the Boscawen family. Magnificent magnolias, camellias, maples and rhododendrons, with colour washes of iris, primulas and willow gentians underneath them. The National Collections of styrax, stuartias and pieris are here, and in autumn the massed foliage colour of acers, parrotias and nyssas rivals the spring explosion of blossom.

4   BORDE HILL GARDEN

nr Haywards Heath   Tel 01444 450326 (weekends 412151)

Daily, all year, 10–6. £2
From centre of Haywards Heath go N on minor road, signed Balcombe, for 1½m; garden signed on L.

A large informal garden of great botanical interest, as many of the great plant hunters from the Himalayas brought back seeds and plants that are flourishing here – so there is a marvellous collection of rhododendrons and magnolias. Around the house are more formal gardens, where a warm walled garden shelters rare Chinese and Japanese plants. Colonel Stephenson Clarke, who subscribed to many of these plant-hunting expeditions, raised the famous camellia 'Donation' at Borde Hill: see if you can spot it. Andrewjohn Clarke, his great-grandson, now lives at Borde Hill with his family, and is committed to restoring the garden to its former glory. He has introduced many events and features to help fund the garden. Catering in the Victorian stable block is admirably varied, from bar meals, snacks and teas to a brasserie restaurant with a good international menu.

5 WAKEHURST PLACE (NT)

Ardingly, nr Haywards Heath   Tel 01444 892701

Daily, all year (except Christmas Day, New Year's Day), 10–7 (or dusk). £4
From Haywards Heath go N on B2028 for 6½m; garden signed on L.

The Royal Botanical Gardens have their home at Kew. Wakehurst is their place in the country, very large, and packed with interest both for plant-lovers and those who just appreciate the beauty of the landscape planted with an amazing collection of trees and shrubs. There is a Himalayan Glade sizzling with colour from azaleas, rhododendrons and magnolias in late spring, and again in autumn when the leaves turn. There are 4 National collections here: hypericum, nothofagus, skimmia and betula. Near the house are walled gardens, more intimately planted with fragrant herbs and herbaceous flowers. There are clipped yews, formal flower beds, roses, and a pool and fountain. So much to see here – it really needs visiting in every season to grasp the full magnificence of the place.

6 ORCHARDS Rowfant, nr Crawley   Tel 01342 718280

Some charity Suns, and by appointment, 11–4. £2
From Crawley go E on A264 for 4m. Turn R on B2028, then R on minor road
for 1½m to Rowfont; garden in Wallage Lane.

Orchards was the home of Arthur Hellyer, renowned among the gardening community as a horticulturalist, columnist and author of 30 books. The main garden, on the site of a market garden, was created from the 1950s onwards. Arthur's daughter, Penelope, has now restored the garden, extending and developing the design while maintaining its original spirit, one of great beauty and tranquillity. Sited on a warm, south-facing slope, it has fine mature trees and shrubs, herbaceous and shrub borders, camellias and rhododendrons, daffodils and snowdrops in early spring, followed by bluebells in the wood. Apple orchards and a vegetable garden are entrancing. Penelope also runs an excellent nursery, specialising in hardy geraniums.

7 STANDEN (NT) nr East Grinstead   Tel 01342 323029

Last 2 weekends March, then Wed–Sun and BHs, April to Oct, 2.30–6. £3
From centre of East Grinstead go S on minor road, signed Saint Hill, for 2m;
garden signed on L.

The house (*see* If it's Wet) was designed by Philip Webb, a friend of William Morris, in the 1890s. The garden is on a steep, south-facing slope, on several levels linked by flights of steps, with marvellous views across the valley. It all feels very Edwardian, very English, very Elgar. Hum a bit of 'Nimrod' as you go around. The formal garden, enclosed by yew and beech hedges, is blowsy with catmint and rugosa roses. Azaleas, rhododendrons and acers stretch in drifts along the paths, and there is a magnificent tulip tree. The charming fernery is in an old quarry.

8 MOORLANDS

Friars Gate, nr Crowborough   Tel 01892 652474

Weds, April to June, 11–6, 4 charity Suns, and by appointment. £2
From Crowborough go NW on minor road for 1½m to Friars Gate. Ask owner for final directions.

Dr Smith's parents started the garden here 50 years ago, and he took it over and began restoring it in the 1970s. Constructed on 3 levels, the top one near the house has tender shrubs, including *Grevillea rosmarinifolia*, *Leonotis leonurus* and *Colletia armata*. Then comes a heather bed. The yew hedges are swathed with sparkling red *Tropaeolum speciosum* in summer, and there is a long herbaceous border. On the lower levels it can be very damp – take your wellies, and enjoy bog-loving primulas, gunneras, lysichitons and wonderful acers around the lake.

9 GROOMBRIDGE PLACE

Groombridge, nr Tunbridge Wells   Tel 01892 863999

Daily, April to mid Dec, 10–6 rest of year weekends and BHs. £4
From Tunbridge Wells go W on A264 for 2m. Turn L on B2110 for 1m; garden signed on L.

I first fell in love with Groombridge when I saw Peter Greenaway's film *The Draughtsman's Contract*. The classically romantic 17th-century walled gardens have survived virtually unaltered to this day. They are set at the bottom of a valley, bordered by the River Groom, with the woods behind the house making a perfect backdrop. You may think an area called 'The Enchanting Forest' sounds a bit Disneyland, but it turns out to be a charming woodland garden where themed gardens are under construction. Formal gardens lie behind the house, and include a splendid walk of tall clipped yews, a 'drunken' garden where the misshapen old topiary appears to lean unsteadily, a parterre beside the moat on which black swans lazily paddle. A very charming oriental garden has old *Acer palmatum* trees, with gnarled trunks; the colours in the borders are used to echo the vibrancy of the Orient; standing guard are two granite Chinese dogs. There is a nut walk, a secret garden, a rose garden, statues and peacocks. Masses to enjoy. Children will love it too

Perryhill Nursery, in Hartfield, is only 3m W of Groombridge Place on the B2110. All knowledgeable gardeners in this visit recommend it unhesitatingly. Tel 01892 770377.

Where to Stay

All B&B prices are approximate per person, sharing a double/twin room usually with private or en suite facilities. It is a good idea to ask for any special requirements when booking.

A LYWOOD HOUSE   Tel 01555 892369

Max & Cleone Pengelley, Lywood House, Ardingly, nr Haywards Heath, West Sussex RH17 6SW.

This substantial 17th-century yeoman's house is peacefully set in rolling countryside with large, mature gardens that have fine old lawns and trees. There is an attractive swimming pool. Inside, the house is beautifully decorated, and guests have a luxurious drawing-room to themselves. Evening meals (by arrangement, £15–£20, bring your own wine) are a particular treat here – Cleone is a professional cook who delights in trying new recipes. There are 2 luxurious double/twin bedrooms. No dogs, no children under 10, and no smoking in bedrooms. B&B £30.

B BOLEBROKE MILL   Tel 01892 770425

David & Christine Cooper, Bolebroke Mill, Edenbridge Road, Hartfield, nr East Grinstead, East Sussex TN7 4JP.

This is perhaps the most unusual accommodation you will find in this guide. Recorded in the Domesday Book, there was a working mill here until 1948, enchantedly tucked away at the end of a winding track, surrounded by woodland, mill streams and pasture. Three buildings were rescued from disuse by David and Christine, who retained the original machinery and grindstones, fitted 2 double/twin bedrooms and a lounge around them in the mill, and managed to make en suite bathrooms where there were corn bins. There are 3 further rooms in the barn, including the Honeymooners'

Hayloft with a four-poster bed. Bolebroke was a main location for the film *Carrington*. It has won many tourist awards, including a 'Best Breakfast in Britain' competition. Unlicensed. Eat out in the evenings. No smoking, or dogs or children under 7 – and you have to be agile enough to climb narrow stairs and duck low doorways. B&B £28.

C DOWN HOUSE   Tel 01825 712328

Mick & Gilly Hudson, Down House, Down Street, Nutley, nr Uckfield,
East Sussex TN22 3LG.

About half the guests here go garden visiting, the other half enjoy opera at Glyndebourne (of course, you can combine both, now that tickets at the enlarged opera house are easier to come by). Mick and Gilly have created their 1-acre garden since 1991 – but the great trees, the 12-acre bluebell wood and the wonderful views over a large duckpond to the Downs beyond make it seem more mature, with richly planted borders, interesting roses and large lawns. Down House was originally two Georgian cottages, and is now beautifully converted and furnished with antiques. Two double/twin bedrooms. Excellent dinners (£17.50, bring your own wine). Restricted smoking, dogs by arrangement, children should be over 9. B&B £28.

D LYE GREEN HOUSE   Tel 01892 652018

Ann Hynes, Lye Green House, Lye Green, nr Crowborough,
East Sussex TN6 1UU.

What a pleasure this place is (one guest described it as 'a stately home on a smaller scale – fantastic!'). A large comfortable country house in 6 acres of gardens, its 3 double/twin bedrooms are luxurious, and Ann's welcome and attention to guests' needs is commented on by everyone who stays. The garden rivals (some say is better than) those more generally known in the area. Recently restored, but now fully mature it is based on a series of ponds with bridges and a boathouse in a woodland setting. The 8 formal gardens, divided by clipped yew hedges, include a potager/kitchen garden, a rose garden, a croquet lawn and large herbaceous borders. Everywhere you walk, there is a new dimension and a new outlook. Wonderful. Eat out in the evenings. No smoking, dogs or children. B&B £28.

E RIXONS   Tel 01825 790453

Jean & Geoffrey Pink, Rixons, Horsted Keynes, nr Haywards Heath, East Sussex RH17 7DP.

A mature and pretty garden with cottage plants, herbs, roses of many kinds, shrubs and trees, is tucked away at the back of this listed Elizabethan house. Jean and Geoffrey both enjoy gardening, and are keen cooks (there are many congratulatory comments in the visitors' book for the evening meals: £17.50, bring your own wine). Two good double/twin guest bedrooms are furnished with antiques. No smoking or dogs, and children should be over 12. B&B £28.

F BLACKFRIARS   Tel 01293 871263

Peggy Cooper, Blackfriars, Friday Street, Rusper, nr Crawley, East Sussex RH12 4QA.

This part-Jacobean house has a lot to offer – peaceful views over the countryside surrounding its own 4 acres of grounds, with 1½ acres of gardens, a swimming pool and tennis court. Inside, the house is architecturally fascinating, and full of antiques. The 3 guest bedrooms (including 1 single), with their own sitting areas, are in a well-converted cottage and granary alongside. In the evening, you can arrange to eat with Peggy in the main house, with menus at £10 and £15 (bring your own wine). No dogs, restricted smoking, children welcome. B&B £24.

What Else to Enjoy

This is a short selection of the many good things recommended in the area by owners of places to stay. Your hosts will certainly be able to provide additional information.

If It's Wet

Strangely, there are few stately homes open to the public in this area. If you go to **Wakehurst Place** (*see* Garden 5), it will put a roof over your head during a shower – but half an hour is all you will need to see the five rooms, some of them with good furniture, the rest with audio-visual displays, an exhibition and a shop.

A better bet is the NT's **Standen** (*see* Garden 7) where the house is entrancing – a showpiece of the 19th-century Arts and Crafts Movement. Decorated throughout with William Morris carpets, fabric and wallpaper, it also has pre-Raphaelite paintings and tapestries. There is a conservatory to die for. It is open on the same days as the garden, but for fewer hours: 1.30–4.30. Admission £4.50, includes garden.

Otherwise, you might like to consider the **Bluebell Railway** which the indomitable Miss Bessemer kept alive in the 1950s, and is now run by the 7,000 members of the Bluebell Railway Preservation Society. It has a nostalgic and thriving museum of locomotives, coaches and memorabilia. There are so many possibilities for travelling, dining and even sleeping overnight (in the *Queen of Scots*) in these hugely entertaining surroundings that you are advised to ask for up-to-date information at the Bessemer Arms in **Sheffield Park** (Tel 01825 722008), or on the enquiry line 01825 723777.

For a bit of light-hearted shopping and delicious cream teas, think about **Pooh Corner**. Not far away from the famed Poohsticks Bridge in Ashdown Forest, this 17th-century cottage is now a gift shop and tea-room. You find it in High Street, **Hartfield**, at the junction of the B2110 and B2026, not far from Moorlands (*see* Garden 8).

Eating Out

If you want to push the boat out (and enjoy a wonderful garden before you dine), there is no doubt that **Gravetye Manor** is the place to choose in this visit. This superb, creeper-clad Elizabethan mansion, heavily panelled, has a true country-house feel to it. To enjoy the superlative cooking to its full, you need a deep pocket. Reckon £40 per person as a minimum – but it could easily be double that if you shut your eyes and think of Epicurus. From **East Grinstead**, go SW on B2110 for 2m. At sharp R/H bend, take minor rd S to West Hoathly. Ask hotel for final directions when making your booking. Tel 01342 810567.

The Weald of Kent

Surely nowhere in the world has such a concentration of great houses and gardens as you find here. The castles at Lamberhurst and Bodiam are outstanding, and Sissinghurst's garden is the greatest of them all. For any garden enthusiast, Great Dixter is a must. Brush up on a verse or two of Kipling before you visit Bateman's. There is a musical tradition at Finchcocks. John Williams playing his guitar has always been a favourite of mine. He has recorded two Vivaldi concerti, and Rodrigo's Concierto de Aranjuez, with Sir Charles Groves conducting.

OS maps: Landrangers **188**, 189, 199

Gardens

Opening times: in larger gardens, and in NT properties, last admissions are usually 30–45 minutes before the garden closes. Admission charges are a guide to what one adult can expect to pay to go round the garden. It sometimes varies with the season or days of the week. When the house is also open to the public, there is usually an additional charge.

1 **MERRIMENTS GARDENS**   Hurst Green   Tel 01580 860666

Daily, April to Oct, 10–5. £1
From Cranbrook go S on A229 for 10m. Turn L on minor road where garden signed for ½m.

This is a 4-acre garden attached to the splendid nursery garden of the Buchele family. Here you can see many of the plants for sale attractively laid out in beds, including the perennials they specialize in: euphorbias, geraniums, lobelias, violas, sages, penstemons and many others – plus trees and shrubs. From spring to autumn the richly planted borders create a display of careful colour combinations.

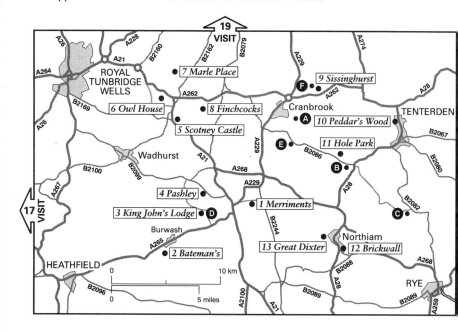

2   BATEMAN'S (NT)   Burwash   Tel 01435 882302

Sat–Wed, April to Oct, 11–5.30. £4
From near Tunbridge Wells go SE on A21 for 17m. Turn R on A265 for 7m;
garden signed on L outside Burwash.

An Edwardian air of nostalgia hovers over this garden where Rudyard
Kipling lived for 30 years or so at the beginning of this century. He clipped
the hedges and pruned the roses, while in his head stories grew and poems
brewed. The garden hasn't changed much since then; it is still peaceful and
tranquil, with fat old yew hedges, a pond, an arbour, a rose garden, a wild
garden and a fine herb garden. A little bridge will take you to a working
watermill (also NT), which grinds up local corn into flour – but it only
seems to grind on Saturday afternoons.

3   KING JOHN'S LODGE

nr Hurst Green (*see also* Where to Stay)   Tel 01435 882302

Several charity days, and by appointment. £1.50
From near Tunbridge Wells go SE on A21 for 17m. Turn R on A265 for
1½m, then R on minor road just after Etchingham church for 1m; garden
signed on L.

Richard and Jill Cunningham bought this property in 1987, immediately after the great gale had left dozens of huge trees lying flat on the ground. Today the garden is better than it ever was. The addition of a lily pond and ha-ha lets the 3 acres stretch seamlessly from the old house through wide lawns, trees and shrubs to the meadow beyond where sheep graze. It has a distinctly romantic feel. There is a beautifully-designed formal garden with a fountain, while vistas lead away to the many linked areas: a large wild garden at its best in April/May, featuring a rose walk and a pond; large herbaceous borders and a multitude of shrub roses; a 'secret garden' with its pond which is magical throughout the year; a 17th-century barn covered in roses and honeysuckle; a garden house with a greenhouse section. There is well-placed statuary (and also statuary for sale).

4   PASHLEY MANOR   Ticehurst, nr Hurst Green

Tel 01580 200692

Tues–Thurs and Sats, mid April to end Sept, 11–5. £3
From near Tunbridge Wells go SE on A21 for 16m. Turn R on B2099 for
1½m; garden signed on L.

A garden of great age and beauty, full of romance, and orchestrated by bird-song and splashing water. In the last 15 years Mr and Mrs James Sellick have, with help of garden designer Antony du Gard Pasley, greatly improved what was basically a Victorian garden. Five new beds sweep across the manor's south front, with its delightful Queen Anne façade, filled with shrub roses, peonies, viburnums, caryopteris and ceratostigmas – soft pinks and blues, all gentle colourings. In contrast is a stunning new golden garden, which leads down to the woods and streams, where rhododendrons, azaleas, and maples reflect their colours in the water. Pashley Manor holds regular flower festivals: a Tulip Festival in May, a Rose Festival in June and a summer Plant Fair in August. Pashley prides itself on delicious plough-man's lunches, and has very good plants for sale.

5   SCOTNEY CASTLE (NT)   Lamberhurst   Tel 01892 891081

Wed–Sun and BHs, April to Oct, 11–6 (Sat/Sun 2–6), or dusk. £3.50
From near Tunbridge Wells go SE on A21 for 9m; garden signed on L.

This famous landscaped garden was created by the Hussey family around their fairytale moated 14th-century castle. Edward Hussey built a new house on the hill in 1843, which looks down onto the now ruined castle. Rhododendrons and azaleas cover the steep hillside. Inside the castle walls is an enchanting herb garden designed by Lanning Roper, and a cottage garden. Wisteria trails over old stone, water lilies shine out from moat and lake – you will want to take your camera with you.

6 OWL HOUSE GARDENS
nr Lamberhurst   Tel 01892 890230

Daily except Christmas and New Year's Day, 11–6. £3
From near Tunbridge Wells go SE on A21 for 5m. Turn R on minor road for 1m and then R towards Lamberhurst for ½m; garden signed on L.

Owl House Gardens were created from a cabbage patch in 1952 by Maureen, Marchioness of Dufferin and Ava, in the hope that visitors would love and appreciate them as much as she has done. The 'cabbage patch' is now 16 acres of sheer beauty, part of which is woodland under-planted with azaleas, rhododendrons and bulbs. Wisterias, clematis and roses are encouraged to scramble up as many trees as possible: wisterias climb willows by the pool, and droop down to form perfect reflections; rose 'Bobby James' adds a cream cascade to a group of silver birches. A big stone owl, guardian of the garden, stands in a circle of standard rhododendrons, and in autumn a grove of brilliant *Parrotia persica* is not to be missed. There are some lovely touches here – pink standard roses in formal beds over blue iris, an apple and cherry blossom walk, a 'river' of grape hyacinths cascading down a hill in the woodland, while a recycled heating vent, long since chucked out from Buckingham Palace, makes a splendid column for a rather debauched looking fat cherub holding a glass of bubbly.

7 MARLE PLACE
Brenchley, nr Tunbridge Wells   Tel 01892 722304

Daily, April to Oct, 10–5.30, and by appointment. £2.50
From near Tunbridge Wells go SE on A21 for 8m. Turn L on B2162 for 1½m, then turn L where garden signed.

After all the grand castle gardens of Kent, this very personal 'family' garden, with bantams strutting about, is one I greatly enjoyed. Mrs Lindel Williams likes growing herbs and fragrant plants – culinary and medical, or just plain beautiful. The National Collections of santolina (cotton lavender) and calamintha are here, and the borders contain unusual plants and shrubs. Plans are afoot for a wild flower garden, and there is a nursery specializing in herbs and fragrant treasures. The Old Potting Shed shop sells home-grown produce, including tiny fresh bantam eggs. Mrs Williams is an artist as well as a fine plantswoman, and admits to a slight fondness for kitsch: witness the waves painted round the swimming pool, flowers painted on a wheelbarrow, a weeping willow with its fronds tied back like curtains to reveal an intriguing wattle sculpture of a serpentine hedge – or was it a question mark? Her daughter Lucy makes garden sculptures and seats out of wood. A particularly covetable one had speckled wooden hens along the back rest; a craft exhibition is held here in early September. I particularly admired the immaculate topiary, velvet lawns, and a gothic pleached lime tunnel which led me to an enchanted scented garden, and impeccably trained shrub roses. Don't miss Marle Place.

8 FINCHCOCKS Goudhurst, nr Cranbrook   Tel 01580 211702

Suns and BH Mons, Easter to Sept (Wed–Sun in August), 2–6. £1.50
From near Tunbridge Wells go SE on A21 for 7m. Turn L on A262 for 2m; garden signed on R.

You may know of this manor house because of its splendid collection of historical musical instruments. They are fascinating; and the garden is too. The 13 acres of grounds include parkland with fine old trees, mature shrub borders, an autumn garden, an orchard garden planted with spring bulbs, and a recently restored walled garden with a circle of whitebeams. Sit down and enjoy the extensive views over the Kent hop-yards. Listen carefully: apart from the birds you may hear glorious music wafting out of the house. There is a series of summer concerts organised here which you might like to attend, with afternoon and evening recitals.

9 SISSINGHURST GARDEN (NT)

nr Cranbrook   Tel 01580 715330

Daily except Mons, April to mid Oct, 1–6.30 (Sat/Sun 10–5.30). £5
From near Tunbridge Wells go SE on A21 for 7m. Turn L on A262 for 8m; garden signed on L.

Perhaps the most famous of English gardens, made by Vita Sackville-West and Harold Nicolson from 1930 onwards. The bones of the gardens are of firm lines of clipped yew, walls, paths and vistas, everywhere exuberantly planted, plants spilling out of their restraining boundaries. The Rose Garden, with a great collection of old roses, is truly bosky. The Cottage Garden is a riot of hot orange, yellow and red plants. The White Garden floats ethereally, and should really be seen by moonlight. Visiting is restricted, and timed tickets are now in operation: go really early, or buy your ticket, then have a picnic or lunch in the restaurant until your turn comes. Don't be annoyed by this system – the garden is just too popular, and cannot properly be seen if it is swamped by people who threaten to wear out the lawns and paths. It is still the best garden of all.

10 PEDDAR'S WOOD   Tenterden   Tel 01580 63994

Once a month for charity May to Aug, and by appointment. £1
From Tenterden go N on A28 for 1m to St Michaels; garden at 14 Orchard Rd. Ask owner for final directions.

A great treat for plantsmen is in store when they visit this smallish town garden. Mr and Mrs Honeysett are amazingly knowledgeable gardeners, and this little plot is packed with interesting plants, including more than 100 different clematis, 40 varieties of lilies, 50 varieties of climbing roses, plus ferns, vines, solanums and wisterias. It is quite remarkable.

11 HOLE PARK   Rolvenden, nr Cranbrook   Tel 01580 241251

Suns, April to early June, and early Oct, 2–6, and parties by appointment. £2
From Tenterden go SW on A28 for 3m. Turn R at Rolvenden on B2086 for 1m; garden entrance on R.

The structure of this garden was laid down by the grandfather of the present owner, Mr Barham. The great yew hedges and topiary are an especial feature, and shelter the fine borders and lawns. Splendid climbing plants scramble up the walls, and there are terrific views over the park and across the Kentish Weald. In the woodland garden, bluebells and daffodils are planted under rhododendrons and azaleas, and the autumn colouring is as exciting as the spring show.

12 BRICKWALL   Northiam   Tel 01797 223329

Sats and BH Mons, mid April to Sept, 2–5. £2
From Tenterden go SW on A28 for 9m. Turn L on B2088; garden signed immediately after junction.

An early lady gardener, Jane Frewen, chose the plants for this interesting Stuart garden around 1680, and as far as possible the same varieties are here now, looked after by the Frewen Educational Trust. There are bergamots, pinks and columbines, as well as lavender beds, clipped yews and mulberries. A new addition is the chess garden, with chessmen made of green and yellow yew. I loved the pleached beech walk, the herb displays and the sumptuous herbaceous borders.

13 GREAT DIXTER Northiam Tel 01797 253107

Daily except Mons (but BH Mons), April to early Oct, 2–5. £2.50
From Tenterden go SW on A28 for 8m. Turn R at Northiam Post Office; garden signed in Dixter Road.

For garden lovers this is one of the most inspiring places to visit – but go often, not just once, in all seasons. It is constantly changing and developing as Christopher Lloyd, garden writer supremo, uses his flair and plantsman's knowledge to experiment with strong shapes, bold colours, and plant settings which complement each other. The gardens are set around a magnificent 15th-century house, restored by Lutyens, whose recognisable stamp of design is on the stone arches, buttressing, and the way stone paths and steps are laid. The topiary garden has yew trees sculpted into charming plump birds, and in spring the wild garden is embroidered with cowslips, cuckoo-pint, tiny tulips and orchids. The sunken garden is walled and sheltered by old farm buildings, with fig trees, ceanothus and some of the many clematis Mr Lloyd grows, scrambling energetically and gloriously up the walls. The old formal rose garden has been most excitingly replaced by a subtropical garden (including a banana tree) which is a riot of strong jungly colours and shapes at the end of summer. The renowned Long Border has no equal. Many rare plants are for sale in the excellent nursery, where you can also ask staff to identify plants that baffle you. Mr Lloyd does not like to see too many labels in his garden – and he knows what they all are anyway!

Where to Stay

All B&B prices are approximate per person, sharing a double/twin room usually with private or en suite facilities. It is a good idea to ask for any special requirements when booking.

A THE OLD CLOTH HALL Tel 01580 712220

Katherine Morgan, The Old Cloth Hall, nr Cranbrook, Kent TN17 3NR.

Superlatives aren't enough to describe this marvellous family property. It is an exquisite Tudor manor house: Queen Elizabeth I really did lunch here, and the panelling, fireplaces and beamed ceilings are still exactly as she saw them. The Old Cloth Hall is set in 13 acres of gardens laid out 100 years ago, and was open for the NGS and other charities for many years until Mrs Morgan found the additional catering too much to handle. So now guests can have its wonders to themselves: fine yew hedges, a glorious old oak pergola smothered with climbers, a croquet lawn, sunken rose garden, swimming pool peacefully situated, banks of rhododendrons and azaleas in the spring, a tennis court and even an oasthouse. Three historic double/ twin bedrooms, 1 a four-poster. Much-praised dinners (£16–£20, bring your own wine). No dogs, and no smoking in the bedrooms. Discuss if you want to bring children. B&B £33–£45.

B BRATTLE HOUSE   Tel 01580 763565

Maureen & Alan Rawlinson, Brattle House, Watermill Bridges, nr Tenterden, Kent TN30 6UL.

This mellow orange-tiled and weather-boarded Georgian house was reputedly once the home of Horatia, illegitimate but much-loved daughter of Admiral Nelson and Lady Hamilton. It is set in 10 acres of meadow, including a 1½-acre ancient wood. Around the house is an acre of delightful and skilfully-planted garden, with a pond, pergola, rockery, and some interesting plants (if the rabbits and moles leave them alone, says Maureen), and wonderful views of the countryside. Dinners (£17.50, bring your own wine) are delicious, using fresh local fish and organic produce, and are served *en famille*. Breakfast and tea are served in the conservatory, leading off from a cosy low-beamed sitting-room. Three extremely comfortable double/twin bedrooms. Visitors return and return. One wrote in the guest book: 'comfort 10/10; food 10/10; hosts 12/10'. No smoking, no dogs or children. B&B £28–£30.

C WITTERSHAM COURT   Tel 01797 270425

Mim & Ian Watson, Wittersham Court, Wittersham, nr Tenterden, Kent TN30 7EA.

A feeling of spaciousness surrounds you when you stay at this handsome 300-year-old house in a quiet Kent village. Mim is an expert flower arranger and has made a lovely garden around her home, with wide lawns sweeping away from the house, rich herbaceous borders, many climbers and roses, and well-established shrubs. If your partner fancies a game of golf as a change from garden visiting, Ian, keen on the game himself, will fix it. The house has many antiques, and dinner (£18, licensed) is served by candlelight in an elegant dining-room. Breakfast is often served outside in the summer. Three excellent double/twin bedrooms with good views. Restricted smoking, no dogs, no children under 14. B&B £28.

D KING JOHN'S LODGE   (see Garden 3)   Tel 01580 819232

Jill & Richard Cunningham, King John's Lodge, Sheepstreet Lane, Etchingham, nr Hurst Green, East Sussex TN19 7AZ.

This is a spectacularly good place to stay. The garden (*see* Garden 3) seems almost an extension of the mainly Jacobean house, whose extensions in Victorian times, and later in the 1930s, blend in unobtrusively. There are exceptionally interesting rooms, and fine furniture. The 3 double/twin bedrooms are furnished in keeping with their particular period: Elizabethan, Jacobean and Victorian. Jill is an exceedingly good cook, and dinners (£17.50, by arrangement, bring your own wine) in the Jacobean dining room are a special experience. Pashley Manor (*see* Garden 4) is within walking distance on footpaths through marvellous countryside. Restricted smoking, no dogs, children welcome. B&B £25–£28.

E CRIT HALL   Tel 01580 241743

Sue & John Bruder, Crit Hall, Cranbrook Rd, Benenden, Kent TN17 4EU.

As you turn into the driveway, a large evergreen oak dominates the 1-acre garden around this gracious Georgian house. Lawns, rose beds, borders – the garden is informal and well tended, and the views magnificent in every direction. 'A secret hideaway transformed by excellent company and exquisite food', wrote one guest. There are 4-course dinners (£17.50, bring your own wine). Three lovely double/twin bedrooms. No dogs, no smoking, and children should be over 10. 'Our aim is that from the moment you pull our front door bell, you will feel a warm welcome,' says Sue. B&B £25–£26.

F SISSINGHURST CASTLE FARM   Tel 01580 712885

Pat & James Stearns, Sissinghurst Castle Farm, Sissinghurst, nr Cranbrook, Kent TN17 2AB.

What a location! Set alongside the grounds of England's most famous garden, you can sit under a cedar tree with a cup of tea and look at

Sissinghurst's castle tower, where Vita wrote, and imagine yourself back in her time. The farmhouse is a redbrick former Victorian mansion, with long corridors and large rooms. Pat Stearns is rightly unashamed of her own garden, even though it is so close to the masterpiece next door. It is large, with pretty borders and an amazing display of rhododendrons in May. There is a delightful lakeside/woodland walk in what is still a working farm, with a good farm shop where you can buy local fruit, veg and cheese to take home. There are 5 guest bedrooms (including 1 single), 1 en suite, the remainder sharing bathrooms. Light suppers (bring your own wine) can be arranged. No smoking, no dogs, children welcome. B&B £20–£24.

What Else to Enjoy

This is a short selection of the many good things recommended in the area by owners of places to stay. Your hosts will certainly be able to provide additional information.

Other Gardens/Nurseries

The climate, soil and the abundance of gardens in this area are serviced by many excellent specialist nurseries. At **Peasmarsh**, W of Rye on the B2089, you will find **Axletree Nursery**, charming, addictive and holding a wide range of many rare herbaceous plants, plus a vast stock of hardy geraniums. Open Wed–Sat, mid March to Sept, 10–5. Tel 01797 230470. **Just Roses**, in Beals Lane, **Northiam**, is a nationally-known business. Tel 01797 252355. **Washfield Nursery**, 1m SW of **Hawkhurst** at the junction of the A268 and A229, has great collections of hellebores bred by Elizabeth Strangman, as well as many other treasures. Tel 01580 752522. Nearby, up minor roads to the NE, in the little village of **Iden Green**, is **Tile Barn Nursery** (Tel 01580 240221). This is the place to buy every sort of cyclamen you could wish for.

If It's Wet

Smallhythe Place (NT) is a 16th-century half-timbered house famous because actress Ellen Terry lived here for nearly thirty years, and still containing many items reminding you of her theatrical career. There is a charming cottage garden, and Miss Terry's rose garden. It is open Sat–Wed, April to Oct, 2–6 or dusk, and costs about £3. You find it well signed S of **Tenterden** just off the B2082.

Other NT properties in this visit have already been mentioned in Gardens above, and each has a house which you can visit during a shower: **Bateman's**, Rudyard Kiping's home, **Scotney Castle**, with a fascinating priest hole, and **Sissinghurst** where you can see Vita Sackville-West's study and the Long Library.

Tenterden is worth a visit if you're near – a charming little town with good shopping for books and antiques. **Peggoty's** tea shop, with fattening cakes, is renowned. The Kent and East Sussex Railway steams along from here to **Great Dixter** (*see* Garden 13), where you can enjoy the interior of the house as well as its garden.

Tunbridge Wells still retains much of the Georgian architecture particularly around the Pantiles, where young ladies in search of a husband used to wander. Today, this is a traffic-free area with pubs, hotels, cafés and interesting shops. You may have to compete for space with tourists and costumed guides.

Eating Out

Pashley Manor (*see* Garden 4) does one of Kent's best lunches on the days when it is open. It's worth going down to **Rye**, a lovely little town in its own right, to have dinner at **Landgate Bistro**. Despite its name, it serves decidedly un-bistro food, being far more adventurous and tasty, but at a reasonable price. Nick Parkin and Toni Ferguson-Lee serve dinners only, with a set 3-course menu at £15.50, but many other dishes as well. You will probably spend £25–£35 per head. Tel 01797 222829.

The Garden of England

Orchards and hop fields fill the valleys of the wonderful, intimate country-side here. Along the Weald, the Pilgrim's Way leads eastwards towards Canterbury and its 11th-century cathedral, with the tomb of the Black Prince, and the shrine of Thomas à Becket. Some sacred music seemed appropriate, but I wanted it lyrical and tender, to match the scenery. Duruflé's Requiem was perfect.

OS maps: Landrangers **178, 188**

Gardens

Opening times: in larger gardens, and in NT properties, last admissions are usually 30–45 minutes before the garden closes. Admission charges are a guide to what one adult can ex-pect to pay to go round the garden. It sometimes varies with the season or days of the week. When the house is also open to the public, there is usually an additional charge.

1 THE OLD PARSONAGE
Sutton Valence, nr Maidstone   Tel 01622 842286

4 charity days in June, 2–6, and by appointment. £1.50
From outskirts of Maidstone go SE on A274 for 3m. Turn R on minor road in Sutton Valence at King's Head pub; garden 1m on R, at top of Tumblers Hill.

Dr and Mrs Perks set out to develop a labour-saving garden here in 1959, and now it is gloriously mature. Perched high on the Weald, with aston-ishing views as far as Hastings, your eye is constantly drawn to the distance over the tops of huge shrub roses and tree peonies. The shrubs have their feet clothed in ground-cover plants – numerous cranesbills, hellebores, bulbs, and lathyrus are allowed to scramble through the shrubs. An old Norman keep guards a corner of the garden, and dropping down the steep hillside is a nut grove. Ornamental trees around the garden give extra colour, and there are massed bulbs in spring.

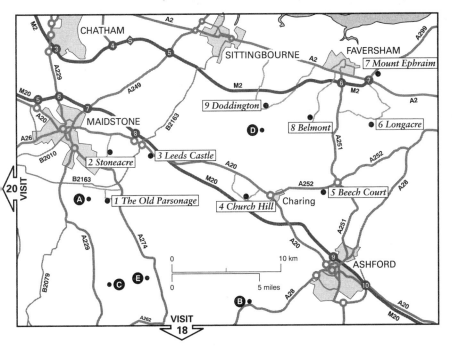

2 STONEACRE (NT)   Otham, nr Maidstone   Tel 01622 862871

Weds and Sats, April to Oct, 2–6, and parties by appointment. £2.20
From outskirts of Maidstone go SE on A274 for 1m. Turn L on minor road for
1m to Otham; garden in village.

The garden here has evolved over centuries, and radiates its old world character. Much of the recent planting and restoring has been done by the tenant, Rosemary Alexander of the English Gardening School, whose students have helped. In her choice of cottage garden plants, she has created a perfect setting for this beautiful timber-framed hall house, built around 1480. A rare gingko tree is at the entrance, and the stone path leading to the front door is edged with *Alchemilla mollis* and grape hyacinths. Hotter colours are in the summer border, but the best times are spring and autumn. A rare tree, *Staphylea colchica*, has scented blossom like a hawthorn. A lovely small herb garden has low box hedging. The terraced courtyard at the back of the house is a perfect place to sit and enjoy the pastoral views over the apple orchard. Try to visit on weekdays; weekends can be crowded.

3   LEEDS CASTLE

(and Culpeper Garden), Maidstone   Tel 01622 765400

Daily (rare exceptions), March to Oct, 10–5 (winter 10–3). £6
From outskirts of Maidstone go E on A20 for 3m. Turn R on B2163 for 1m;
garden signed on L.

This romantic moated castle is a huge tourist attraction, and in the summer
holds many musical events, firework displays, and so on. The 50-acre park
is grandiose, and the castle setting spectacular. For me, the interesting part
is the Culpeper Garden, surrounded by old brick walls, designed by Russell
Page in 1980. Here old roses flourish with a nostalgic charm, and catmint
billows underneath. Trim box edges keep the exuberant planting under con-
trol. There is also a maze of yew hedges, with a strange shell-lined grotto
at the centre.

4   CHURCH HILL COTTAGE   *Been twice*

Charing Heath, nr Ashford   *Good*   Tel 01233 712522

Daily except Mons (but BH Mons), March to Sept, 10–5. Nursery all year ex-
cept Dec. £1.50
From Ashford go NW on A20 for 9½m. 1m past Charing, turn L on minor
road, signed Charing Heath, for 1m. Turn R at Red Lion pub, then R again;
garden 250 yds on R.

I have never much liked island beds until I came here, where they are perfect – packed with low alpine treasures that would have been lost in a large
border. Seen in a cold April, the garden was full of colour: tulips, daffodils,
primulas, pansies, crown imperials, hellebores, dicentras, fritillarias,
erythroniums, blue and white anemones – a feast of spring delights under
cherry blossom. Pots of sedums and sink gardens were sheltered against a
south wall by the conservatory. You won't be able to resist the magnificent
stock in the nursery: unusual hardy plants, hostas, dianthus, alpines, and
shrubs that Mr and Mrs Metianu are famous for raising.

5   BEECH COURT   Challock, nr Ashford   Tel 01233 740641

Daily except Mons (but BH Mons), April to Oct, 10–5 (Suns 12–5). £1.50
From Ashford go NW on A20 for 8½m. Turn R at Charing on A252 for 5m;
garden signed on R.

A woodland garden of 8 acres around a medieval farmhouse. Marvellous
spring colour from azaleas and rhododendrons, acers, conifers and spring

bulbs. There are plants and local crafts for sale, and you may picnic in the paddock.

6 LONGACRE Selling, nr Faversham   Tel 01227 752254

Daily, April to Oct, 2–5, and by appointment. £1
From Faversham go S on A251 for 3m. Turn L on minor road for 2m to Selling,
then turn R to Perrywood; garden signed in village.

Thirty years ago Dr and Mrs Thomas – they are both horticulturalists and met at Wye College – bought this house with an acre of old cherry orchard around it. Gradually they turned it into one of the most interesting small gardens in Kent. Initially they planted trees and shrubs: purple plum, snakebark, maple, tulip trees, a dawn redwood, a *Cedrus deodora*. The largest tree heather I have ever seen is by the gate. A variegated holly was well and truly swagged with the boisterous Kiftsgate rose, and silver birches helped the garden to merge into the surrounding woodland. Under the trees grow rare ferns, hellebores, anemones, erythroniums. Out in the sunny borders are flowering shrubs and a vast selection of different herbaceous plants, in which these two knowledgeable gardeners specialize. In their nursery you will see what their awesome skill as propagators can bring you: more than 700 varieties of rare and interesting plants. You wander through hop fields to find it, but little notices point the way. Don't give up – the short journey is well worth what you find at the end.

7 MOUNT EPHRAIM nr Faversham   Tel 01227 751496

Daily except Tues, April to Sept, 1–6. £2
From Faversham go E on A2 for 1m. Turn L on A299 for 2m. At Duke of Kent
pub turn R to Hernhill; garden well signed.

This wonderful garden is magically set to give fine views of sloping orchards and a vineyard to the Thames estuary. There is plenty of interest here – a Japanese garden, rock and water gardens, herbaceous borders, and rose terraces leading to a lake. The daffodils and rhododendrons start off the season with a flourish of colour. You may taste the wine from the Dawes family vineyard.

8   BELMONT PARK   Throwley, nr Faversham   Tel 01795 890202

Sat/Sun and BH Mons, mid April to Sept, 2–5. £2
From Faversham go S on A251 for 4m. Turn R on minor road for 1½m where
signed at Badlesmere.

A tranquil park of old and dignified trees surrounds an 18th-century house designed by Samuel Wyatt. Here you will find a yew walk, a pinetum and handsome follies including a shell grotto. A walled garden contains a pool and some very good flower borders. Cast a tearful eye over the tombstones of many beloved pets buried in their own graveyard.

9   DODDINGTON PLACE   nr Sittingbourne   Tel 01795 886101

Weds and BHs (and Suns in May), mid April to Sept, 1–6. £2
From Faversham go W on A2 for 1m. Turn L, signed Doddington, for 6m;
garden signed on R.

A large garden landscaped by William Nesfield (1793–1881), who worked on more than 200 gardens and estates in England and Scotland. Among his triumphs that can still be seen are Kensington Gardens, Harewood House, Castle Howard gardens, the parterre at Holkam Hall in Norfolk, and some of the fine vistas at Kew Gardens. Here at Doddington his design incorporated marvellous views, an Edwardian rock garden and superb yew hedges. The formal garden is a blaze of colour in late summer, and the woodland garden is full of spring interest, with azaleas, rhododendrons and bulbs.

Where to Stay

All B&B prices are approximate per person, sharing a double/twin room usually with private or en suite facilities. It is a good idea to ask for any special requirements when booking.

A   TANYARD HOTEL   Tel 01622 744705

Jan Davies, Tanyard Hotel, Wierton Hill, Boughton Monchelsea, nr Maidstone, Kent ME17 4JT.

This small medieval country house hotel is full of character – heavily beamed, beautifully converted, luxuriously furnished with antiques, and with a friendly atmosphere. It is set in 10 acres of garden and woodland, with a stream running through, and two ponds that attract wildlife. A book of local walks has been compiled for guests. The 5 double bedrooms and 1 single, each with its own character, are exceptionally comfortable. The restaurant, in the oldest part of the building (c.1350), has lunch at £20, and a 4-course dinner at £25. No smoking in the restaurant, no dogs, and children should be over 6. B&B £45–£62.

B LITTLE HODGEHAM   Tel 01233 850323

Erica Wallace, Little Hodgeham, Bull Lane, Bethersden, nr Ashford, Kent TN26 3HE.

So popular has the award-winning Little Hodgeham become that you would be advised to make a booking well in advance during the months Erica takes guests (mid March to the beginning of September). The garden, the 500-year-old beamed cottage, the comfort, the furnishings, the food, the personal attention – everything about this place is given superlatives by guests. 'Why did we bother to go to Sissinghurst? We have it all here in miniature', wrote one. A densely-planted ½ acre, the garden is dominated by a large pond close to the house, floodlit at night, with a sunken patio at one end where coffee and cognac is served after dinner amid the scent of lilies and roses, and the sound of tinkling fountains. The flowers are grown in colours to complement the decoration in the house – bright red, gold and white to match the Crown Derby china on the polished dinner table, and blue, pink and apricot for the 3 double/twin bedrooms (one a four-poster). Staying here has a house-party feel to it, and you won't want to miss the Cordon Bleu dinner (£17.50, licensed) with Erica and other guests on the evenings she serves it. Smoking allowed, no dogs in house (but a place for them in a barn), and children should be discussed. B&B £29–£35.

C MAPLEHURST MILL   Tel 01580 852203

Heather & Kenneth Parker, Maplehurst Mill, Frittenden, nr Staplehurst, Kent TN17 2DT.

This house is exceptional – and staying here is something to remember. In a village 3m from Sissinghurst, the Parkers found a derelict 18th-century watermill, a perfect example of its kind, attached to a medieval mill house. They carefully restored the mill, and made the machinery a feature of the house: the hopper area is now a huge plant-filled landing, a bedroom looks directly onto the mill wheel, and the large, comfortable, antique-filled drawing-room straddles the mill stream. Around are 11 acres of tranquil gardens, meadows and water courses, with a heated outdoor swimming pool. Candle-lit dinners cost £19, licensed, served in the beamed dining-room. Organically grown vegetables come from the garden – Heather is passionate about both gardening and cooking. Three beautifully furnished double/twin bedrooms, 1 on the ground floor for those who find stairs difficult. No smoking, no dogs, and children should be over 12. B&B £29–£35.

D   FRITH FARM HOUSE   Tel 01795 890701

Susan & Markham Chesterfield, Frith Farm House, Otterden, nr Faversham, Kent ME13 0DD.

A stay in this fine late-Georgian farmhouse is widely recommended. Set high on the North Downs in an area of outstanding natural beauty, there are 2 acres of colourful, well-kept and imaginative gardens with a formal pool, and a further 4 acres of cherry orchard – wonderful when the blossom is out. Susan is a great cook (dinner £19.50, bring your own wine), and Markham is passionately fond of music. They make marvellous hosts. The 3 large double/twin bedrooms include 1 with a four-poster. Strictly no smoking, no dogs, and children should be over 12. B&B £24–£26.

E   VINE FARM   Tel 01622 890203

Jane Harman, Vine Farm, Waterman Quarter, nr Headcorn, Kent TN27 9JJ.

You will get a great deal of help with your garden visiting here. Because of her knowledge of local gardens, Jane, with a friend, set up Kent Garden Tours, and can offer tailor-made itineraries. Her own garden is continually being developed from meadowland around the house, and because it is on clay, she has been able to create interesting ponds. Part of the 50 acres of the surrounding sheep farm is set aside as a conservation area with a lake, which guests are encouraged to discover. The long, typically-timbered yeoman's farmhouse is charming, and dates from the early 16th century. Guests have their own sitting-room, and evening meals (£16, bring your own wine) are provided if arranged in advance. Large beds in 3 excellent double/twin bedrooms (1 downstairs suitable for wheelchairs), and additional accommodation in a converted barn. No smoking, or dogs, or children. B&B £20–£25.

What Else to Enjoy

This is a short selection of the many good things recommended in the area by owners of places to stay. Your hosts will certainly be able to provide additional information.

Other Gardens/Nurseries

Five minutes' drive from **Maidstone** is the **Museum of Kent Life**, one of Britain's finest rural museums and winner of countless awards. The 50-acre site by the River Medway has the country's last traditional working oast house and last hand-harvested hop garden. There is plenty to do inside if the weather turns cold or wet – there are barns and granaries where exhibitions are held, plus wagons, a forge and much more – but ideally you should go on a fine day when you can enjoy the lovely gardens. It is a unique look at life as it was in this part of the country in times gone by. You find it via brown tourist signs on the A229 between Maidstone and junction 6 of the M25. It is open daily, April to Sept, 10–5.30, and most weekends in winter. Admission £3.50.

Just SE of Maidstone, on the B2010, is **East Farleigh**. In Dean St, you will find **Hazeldene Nurseries**, which specialise in violas, pansies and violets, including old and rare varieties. You may have seen their stunning exhibits at Chelsea Flower Show. Tel 01622 726248.

Apple-lovers should make a point of going to **Brogdale**, just S of **Faversham**. It holds the National Collections of apples, plums, pears and bush fruits, with more than 2,500 distinct varieties of apples alone which you can taste freshly-picked from the trees from July onwards. It is open Wed–Sun and BHs, April to Dec, 11–5. Tel 01795 535286.

Other Places to Stay

Being N of the M25, **Hartlip Place** is distanced somewhat from most of the gardens in this visit, but you should consider it. Lovely 4½-acre gardens sit on a south-facing slope surrounding this fine Georgian house, clad with creepers and roses. There are mature trees and lawns, a large lily pond, a 'wilderness' full of snowdrops and aconites in early spring, rhododendrons, and a 'secret garden' planted with old roses. Gill Yerburgh is a fount of knowledge about gardens locally – she is chairman of the Kent Gardens Trust. You will find lavish hospitality, with dinners by arrangement (£20, including wine) in an elegant dining-room. The 3 double/twin bedrooms have beautiful views. No smoking, no dogs, and children over 12 preferred. B&B costs £35. Address: **Hartlip**, nr Sittingbourne, Kent ME9 7TR. Tel 01795 842583.

To the E of the visit map, towards Canterbury, is **Little Mystole**. This is Patricia and Hugh Tennent's enchanting small Georgian house, where climbers ramp up mellow old brick walls that frame an abundantly planted, mature, colourful garden with a lovely old mulberry tree. Inside, the house is warm and comfortable, and full of Patricia's flowers. Her dinners (£20, bring your own wine) are much praised. Two double bedrooms. No smoking in bedrooms, dogs by arrangement, and children should be over 12. B&B £29. Address: **Lower Mystole**, nr Canterbury, Kent CT4 7DB. Tel 01227 738210.

If It's Wet

About 3m off the E edge of our map is **Canterbury**, which you should surely visit if you are staying in this area. Besides the essential visit to the cathedral, the Heritage Museum is superb.

On the NW edge of the map you come to **Rochester**, where the Charles Dickens Centre has had £500,000 spent on refurbishment, and will give you a new outlook on his life and works.

For a stately home, you will never find better than **Leeds Castle** (*see* Garden 3). The interior, each room with a guide to talk you through its treasures, lives up to its spectacular setting. It advertises itself as 'the best day out in history' – not an idle boast. It will be crowded, of course, but it is still an experience not to be missed.

Eating Out

If you think that B&B at **Tanyard Hotel** ('A' in Where to Stay) is beyond your budget, you should still consider having lunch or dinner in their great restaurant. Phone for directions – it is quite tricky to find. Tel 01622 744705. Everyone says that a big gastronomic treat in the area is **Reid's**, at **Painter's Forstal**, 2m SW of Faversham. The chef and owner David Pitchford uses only the very best basic ingredients, and with imagination and a dash of flair turns classic dishes into memorable meals. Set dinners in the evening are from £25, plus wine. Tel 01795 535344.

West Kent

This visit is abundant with stately homes and castles of the great and wealthy. Hever Castle and Penshurst Place, with extravagant and very old gardens, will each take up many enjoyable hours. Driving to find these mostly formal and orderly gardens, I wanted some music to match, and chose Bach's English Suite, and his Italian concerto, played by Glenn Gould.

OS map: Landranger **188**

Gardens

Opening times: in larger gardens, and in NT properties, last admissions are usually 30–45 minutes before the garden closes. Admission charges are a guide to what one adult can expect to pay to go round the garden. It sometimes varies with the season or days of the week. When the house is also open to the public, there is usually an additional charge.

I   PENSHURST PLACE   nr Tonbridge   Tel 01892 870307

Daily, April to Sept, 11–6; also weekends in March and Oct. £5
From Tonbridge go S on A26 for 1m. Turn R onto B2176 for 4m. Garden signed on R in Penshurst village.

The garden (and house) dates back to the 14th century, and although 10 acres in size, the fact that it is divided up into many garden 'rooms' (more than a mile of clipped yew hedge) gives it an intimate and personal feel. The Italian parterre is on the south side of the house. Try to visit when the magnificent bed of peonies near the orchard is flowering. Lanning Roper was responsible for one of the splendid borders, and there is a new garden for the blind – lovely idea. There is a nut garden, old crab apple trees under-planted with bulbs, a formal rose garden and a lake. The view from the top terrace down to the Italian garden, which peeps through all the other garden rooms, is worth lingering over. The ancient apple and pear

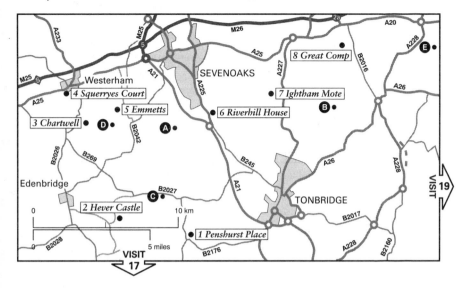

trees are pruned to perfection, and the yew hedges are so impeccably cut I think they must be the *haute couture* of hedges. There is a nostalgic Doll Museum to browse around as well.

2   HEVER CASTLE   nr Edenbridge   Tel 01732 865224

Daily, mid March to early Nov, 11–6. £4.90
From Tonbridge go NW on B245 for 2m. Turn L on B2027 for 6m, then turn L on minor road for 1½m where signed.

William Waldorf Astor, when he was ambassador to Rome at the turn of the century, went looting and rummaging in Italy – and then decided he had to make a marvellous Italian garden in England to house the treasures. It is magnificently large and opulent, with the longest rose- and wisteria-covered pergola I've ever seen. Statues, busts, urns, pillars and sarcophagi all look at home here, set amid playing fountains. At the end of the Italian garden is a colonnade and a piazza, and then the great 30-acre lake (dug out by hand) is waiting to make you gasp with delight. It feels totally Italian, particularly on a sunny day. However, around the enchanted moated castle everything is English. There is a yew-hedge maze, topiary clipped into chessmen, Anne Boleyn's garden, old roses and a herb garden. On the surrounding hillsides are woods with rhododendrons, azaleas and bluebells. You will walk miles, but try to find the rock garden and the rose garden.

There is a map to help you, and so much to see that I suggest you take a substantial picnic.

3 CHARTWELL (NT)   nr Westerham   Tel 01732 866368

Wed–Sun and BH Mons, April to Oct 11–5.30. £2
From Westerham go S on B2026 for 2m; garden signed on L.

Chartwell's historical associations are more interesting than the garden alone. However, there are large lakes, five lawns and a rose garden, and glorious views over the Weald of Kent. There is a golden rose garden, given to Sir Winston and Lady Churchill by their family as a golden wedding anniversary present.

4 SQUERRYES COURT   Westerham   Tel 01959 563118

Suns in March; Wed, Sat/Sun and BH Mons, April to Oct, 2–6. £2
From Westerham go W on A25 for ½m; garden signed on L.

There are woodlands and a lake in this 15-acre garden, and the formal areas are being restored as closely as possible to a well-documented 1700 plan, and a 1719 print. Box-edged beds hold fragrant lavenders, sages and to-bacco flowers, penstemons and verbenas. A charming old dovecote, yew hedges and topiary, rose gardens, borders and a pleached lime walk all add to pleasures in this garden. Magnolias, azaleas, rhododendrons, heathers and spring bulbs extend the season – it's delightful all the year round.

5 EMMETTS GARDEN (NT)

Ide Hill, nr Sevenoaks   Tel 01732 750429

Sat/Sun in March, 2–5; Wed–Sun and BH Mons, April to Oct, 1–6. £2
From Westerham go E on A25 for 2m. Turn R at Sundridge on minor road, signed Ide Hill, for 2m; garden on R.

This landscape high above the Weald is a truly impressive site. The views are stunning, and so is the collection of rare trees. Watch out for *Cercidiphyllum japonicum*, a great beauty, with little delicate heart-shaped leaves; and an *Acer palmatum* 'Ruflescens' with bright pink leaves in spring; there's a great Dawycks beech too. The shrubs, notably rhododendrons and azaleas, are splendid in spring against drifts of bluebells, but it is equally good for autumn foliage. Recently an Italianate rose garden and a rock garden have been added.

6   RIVERHILL HOUSE   Sevenoaks   Tel 01732 458802

Suns and BH weekends, April to June, 12–6. £2.50
From Sevenoaks go S on A225 for 2m; garden signed on L.

A keen plant collector, John Rogers planted many of the oustanding trees
and shrubs here more than 150 years ago. Today his family continue to keep
up the estate. Huge cedars of Lebanon tower above it all. Rhododendrons
and azaleàs, with bulbs beneath, look marvellous in spring and again in the
autumn. The views are breathtaking, and there is a rose walk for summer
interest.

7   IGHTHAM MOTE (NT)
nr Borough Green   Tel 01732 810378

Daily except Tues and Sats, April to Oct, 12–5.30. £4
*From Tonbridge go N on A227 for 4m. Turn L on minor road for 1m where
garden signed.*

This manor house is so popular that you may find a timed ticket system in
operation. Try and visit at quiet times – avoid weekends and Bank Holidays. The beautiful house, moated and medieval, is set in a wooded valley.
The ancient stewpond is now a lawn; the garden feels old, and in character with the house, and includes herbs for cooking and medicines. The Long
Border near the house is full of old English roses, sweet williams, aquilegias and pinks. There is a lily pool and fountain, and a woodland walk.

8   GREAT COMP   nr Borough Green   Tel 01732 882669

Daily, April to Oct, 11–6. £3
*From Sevenoaks go E on A25 for 9m to Wrotham Heath. Turn R on B2016
for 1m then turn R on minor road where garden signed.*

A 7-acre garden with year-round interest, made by Mr Cameron nearly 40
years ago. If you like island beds and heather and conifer gardens, you'll
find plenty to interest you here. There are also roses, borders, a new
Italianate garden, and a woodland garden with grand specimen trees. Good
hellebores in early spring. Excellent nursery plants for sale.

Where to Stay

All B&B prices are approximate per person, sharing a double/twin room usually with private or en suite facilities. It is a good idea to ask for any special requirements when booking.

A WICKHURST MANOR   Tel 01732 463226

Barbara Rawlings, Wickhurst Manor, Sevenoaks Weald, nr Sevenoaks, Kent TN14 6LY.

Five acres of lovingly tended gardens, with a large pond and views to open countryside, surround this ancient house which has a 13th-century Great Hall and a beautiful oak-panelled drawing-room. The large kitchen garden supplies the house with fresh produce for traditional English meals (dinner £20, bring your own wine). You can eat either in the dining-room, or – in good weather – in the summer-house next to the swimming pool. The 3 double/twin bedrooms are large and handsomely furnished. You feel cosseted at Wickhurst Manor, enjoying a sense of history and of luxury. Yes to smoking and children, but no to dogs. B&B £35.

B EGYPT FARM   Tel 01732 810584

Helen & Francis Bullock, Egypt Farm, Hamptons, nr Tonbridge, Kent TN11 9SR.

Four acres of undulating garden with interesting shrubs, all-season colour, and wonderful views surround this loving conversion of three oast houses and a 300-year-old barn. Helen and Francis came here 30 years ago, and they have created a marvellous place to stay and enjoy. Set in a conservation area, there is a pond and water garden, a sculpted swimming pool, hard tennis court, interesting outbuildings – all very enviable, and often open for charity. Great evening meals in a candlelit dining-room full of antiques (£20, bring your own wine). Perfectly furnished bedrooms (2 double, 1 single). No smoking, no dogs, and usually no children. B&B £30.

C JESSOPS   Tel 01892 870428

Judith & Frank Stark, Jessops, Tonbridge Road, Bough Beech, nr Edenbridge, Kent TN8 7AU.

Jessops is fascinating. A 15th-century cottage, its garden with clematis and roses rambling everywhere leads to a large natural pond with geese and Muscovy ducks. Frank is an artist whose landscapes cover the walls inside the house, where antiques and memorabilia abound. The rooms are beamed and flowery. Judith makes her own bread, croissants and marmalade for your breakfast. Eat out nearby in the evenings. Two cosy double bedrooms (one downstairs is all right for wheelchairs) and 1 single. No smoking, no children under 15, no dogs in the house. B&B £20–£22.

D   HEATH HOUSE   Tel 01732 750631

Patricia Murkin, Heath House, Scords Lane, Toy's Hill, nr Westerham, Kent TN16 1QE.

On fine mornings you can sit and enjoy breakfast with french windows open on to the terrace and stunning views across National Trust land to the Kentish Weald beyond. This is a rare site: 800 ft above sea level, with tempting local walks directly from a garden that is colourful and interesting in its own right. The house, once just a cottage, has been sympathetically extended, and is clad with Virginia creeper and honeysuckle. Here you are in deep countryside: one visitor was entranced when she followed the badgers home on a footpath from a nearby hill. Two double/twin bedrooms, each with a lovely outlook, sharing a bathroom. Eat out locally in the evenings. No smoking, no dogs, children welcome. B&B £19–£20.

E   BLACKLANDS HOUSE   Tel 01732 844274

Ann & Vernon Leonard, Blacklands House, Blacklands, East Malling, Kent ME19 6DS.

A stream runs enchantingly through the large, informal garden around this elegant house. Built in 1830 for Robert Tassell, a local mill-owner and farmer, it is a wonderful example of a Georgian gentleman's residence: secluded, quiet, beautifully proportioned with fine sash windows, high-ceilinged rooms generously furnished. Ann and Vernon have travelled widely, and have a gift for making their guests feel at home. Eat out in the evenings at any of the many local restaurants or pubs. One of the 5 double/twin bedrooms is en suite; the others share bathrooms. No smoking in bedrooms. Dogs OK if well behaved. The same with children. B&B £18–£23.

What Else to Enjoy

This is a short selection of the many good things recommended in the area by owners of places to stay. Your hosts will certainly be able to provide additional information.

Other Gardens/Nurseries

Starborough Nursery is a perfect place to buy your camellias, azaleas and any other kind of acid-loving plant or shrub – they are the speciality here. You will find it at **Marsh Green**, 1m SW of Edenbridge on the B2028. Open Thurs–Mon for 10 months of the year (closed Jan and Jul), 10–4. Tel 01732 865614.

About 6m SE of here, on the B2188 at Grove Rd, **Penshurst**, you can have fun at **Penshurst Vineyards** – not just the free wine tastings, but making friends with the many wallabies that lope about. There are wonderful views here, rare breed sheep, exotic wildfowl and home-made apple juice if you're driving.

Other Places to Stay

Heavers, just off our map to the N of the M26/M20, is a homely sort of place – a 17th-century cottage on a hill, surrounded with good walks immediately from its large garden. Jean Edwards bakes her own bread (and teaches you how), grows her own vegetables, provides free range eggs and local honey. She travels as often as possible to France, bringing back new recipes for her 4-course dinners (£14, bring your own wine). It is cosy and comfortable inside the house. The 3 prettily decorated double/twin bedrooms share a bathroom. No smoking. Dogs by arrangement, restricted where they are allowed in the house. Children welcome. B&B £17–£18. Address: Chapel Street, **Ryarsh**, nr West Malling, Kent ME19 5JU. Tel 01732 842074.

If It's Wet

You are spoiled for choice in this visit. Going roughly from E to W, you might start at **Tonbridge Castle**, perhaps with a few too many waxworks for some tastes, but nevertheless a clever and vivid re-creation of the sights and sounds of 13th-century life. Mon–Sat all year, 9–5. £3.

Penshurst Place (*see* Garden 1) is the magnificent castellated home of

Viscount De L'Isle. Its medieval Barons Hall has a 60-ft high beamed room. State rooms contain fine collections of furniture, tapestries, portraits and armour. House open as for Garden dates, but times 12–5.30.

Hever Castle (*see* Garden 2) is as magical inside as outside. Dates and times of opening as for Garden.

Chartwell (*see* Garden 3) has many of Churchill's memorabilia and documents, together with a major exhibition devoted to him. The house is open as for the Garden, but also on Weds and Sat/Sun in March and Nov. £4.50 includes garden.

Squerryes Court (*see* Garden 4) is a 17th-century manor house lived in by the same family since 1731. The rooms contain paintings, furniture, tapestries and porcelain collected before 1780.

Knole is one of England's great houses, where you can easily spend a whole day. The childhood home of Vita Sackville-West, and the setting for Virginia Woolf's novel *Orlando*, it dates from 1456 and has wonderful collections of tapestries, silver and furniture and paintings by Van Dyck and Reynolds. Find it at the S outskirts of Sevenoaks, just E of the A225. Open Wed–Sun and BH Mons, April to Oct, 11–5 (Thurs 2–5). Admission £4.50. Tel 01732 450628.

Eating Out

Honours Mill is excellent. A converted mill house at 87 High St, **Edenbridge** (near Gardens 1 and 2) dating from 1750, you walk in to find the original mill machinery on an old brick floor, where the Goodhew family have built a bar for pre-dinner drinks. Upstairs the dining-room is more luxurious and heavily beamed. Set 3-course lunches are £15.50. In the evenings these cost £26 and include wine, and there is a gourmet menu for £33. Expect to spend £25–£50 per head. Tel 01732 866757.

The Surrey Hills

Most garden enthusiasts in this visit will home in on the Royal Horticultural Society's gardens at Wisley. Its huge range of plants, trees and shrubs, plus its restaurant, shop and plant sales, make it easy to spend a whole day there. The hills and ridges around here are famous for their views. It is said that from Leith Hill, on a clear day, you can see twelve counties. Ralph Vaughan Williams lived around here, and his Pastoral Symphony (No. 3) has an elegance and poignancy that suits the countryside.

OS maps: Landrangers **186**, 187

Gardens

Opening times: in larger gardens, and in NT properties, last admissions are usually 30–45 minutes before the garden closes. Admission charges are a guide to what one adult can expect to pay to go round the garden. It sometimes varies with the season or days of the week. When the house is also open to the public, there is usually an additional charge.

I **RAMSTER**   nr Chiddingfold   Tel 01428 644422

Daily, mid April to mid July, 11–5.30. £2
From Godalming go S on A283 for 7½m. 1½m S of Chiddingfold; garden entrance on R via large iron gate.

This well-established and interesting garden, owned by the same family for the last 70 years, was laid out at the beginning of the century by a local nursery, Gauntletts of Chiddingfold. Today, Mr and Mrs Gunn have a woodland garden with mature camellias and magnolias, rhododendrons and azaleas, and many fine shrubs, beside lakes and ponds – all looking breathtaking in the spring with bluebells at their feet.

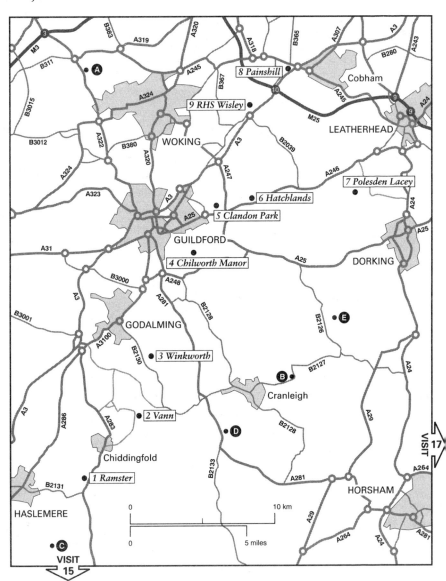

2   VANN   Hambledon, nr Godalming   Tel 01428 683413

4 separate weeks between Easter and early July, 10–6, and by appointment. £2.50
From Godalming go SW on A3100 for 2m to Milford. Turn L on A283 for
6m then turn L into Hambledon; garden signed in village.

One of those natural-looking gardens that drift off seamlessly into the wood
– very Gertrude Jekyll, and in fact she designed the water garden here. Delightful in spring with wood anemones and bluebells nestling under flowering cherries. There are five separate gardens, and a formal yew walk, a fine
new double border and an Arts and Crafts pergola leading to a lake. The
Caröe family maintain the garden to an admirably high standard, with very
little outside help.

3   WINKWORTH ARBORETUM (NT)

nr Godalming   Tel 01486 208477

Daily all year, dawn to dusk. £2.50
From Godalming go SE on B2130 for 2m; garden signed on L.

Like all arboretums, good all the year round, but at its best in spring when
the azaleas, magnolias, sorbus and hamamelis are under-planted with bluebells and wood anemones, or in the autumn for the glorious foliage. It
stands on a steep hillside, and slopes down to two lakes with far-reaching
views. The National Collection of sorbus is here.

4   CHILWORTH MANOR   nr Guildford   Tel 01483 561414

Sat–Wed, for 1 week only in the middle of each month, April–Aug, and by
appointment. £1.50
From Guildford town centre go S on A281 for 2m. Turn L on A248 for 2m,
then turn L into Blacksmiths Lane where signed.

There was originally an 11th-century monastery on this site, and the stewponds, full of golden carp, date from that period. Most of Lady Heald's
present garden was laid out in the 18th and 19th centuries, and is on seven
distinct levels. Herbaceous borders, banked by high walls swathed in wisteria and roses, a lavender walk and fine shrubs please the eye. Many tender
and rare plants shelter in the warm walled garden, laid out by Sarah,
Duchess of Marlborough before she moved on to the grandeur of Blenheim
Palace. The woodland garden is lovely in spring, with primulas planted in
the bog garden. Flower arrangers may wish to visit at weekends, when
flower clubs decorate the house.

5 CLANDON PARK (NT)   nr Guildford   Tel 01483 222482

Sat–Wed, April to Oct, 1.30–5.30 (BH Mons 11–5.30. Sat/Sun in March 12–5.30). House and garden £4.

From Guildford town centre go E on A25 for 4m. Turn L on A247 for ½m; garden signed in West Clandon village.

A painting by Kryff hanging in this memorable 18th-century mansion (by Leoni) shows the original Dutch-style garden. Alas, this is no longer here, having been summarily removed by Capability Brown. Now there is a parterre on the south side of the house, with box hedges and topiary. There is a green and drippy grotto, and a most interesting Maori meeting house. What, you might well ask, is that all about? The 4th Earl of Onslow was Governor General of New Zealand, and brought it back with him. I'd love to know what his gardeners had to say about it. While you are murmuring a Maori chant, have a look at the sensational views over the lake and park. Best time of year to visit is spring, for the bulbs.

6 HATCHLANDS PARK (NT)

East Clandon, nr Guildford   Tel 01483 222482

Tues–Thurs, Suns and BH Mons (and Fris in Aug), April to Oct, 2–5.30. £1.50

From Guildford go NE on A246 for 4½ m; garden signed on L in East Clandon village.

The garden and park surround a house built for Admiral Boscawen in 1750 by Stiff Leadbetter, with fine interiors by Robert Adam. Repton designed the park, and new walks have been opened up here. On the south side of the house is a terrace where Gertrude Jekyll's designs have been restored. They are at their loveliest in May and June, an edging of box framing roses, lupins and aquilegias. As well as the parterres, there are shrubberies, a temple and statues to enjoy.

7 POLESDEN LACEY (NT)

nr Leatherhead   Tel 01372 458203

Daily, all year, 11–6. £3

From Leatherhead go SW on A246 for 2m. At Great Bookham turn L on minor road for 2m; garden signed on R.

These gardens follow an Edwardian theme, with pergolas smothered with roses. Cleverly included over a large area are fine herbaceous borders, many old roses (some planted by Graham Thomas) and individual lavender, iris and peony gardens. The garden statues and sculptures are worth looking at, and there is a fascinating winter garden for those making an early visit. The Queen Mother spent part of her honeymoon in these beautiful surroundings.

8 PAINSHILL PARK Cobham Tel 01932 868113

Suns, early April to mid Oct, 11–6. £3.50
From Cobham go W on A245 for 1m; garden signed on L.

This is a huge (150-acre) landscaped park, designed around 1750 by the brilliant Charles Hamilton, who unfortunately ran out of money before he had completed it to his total satisfaction. However, his delicious extravaganzas have been meticulously restored by a private trust for our enjoyment. They include a lake with little islands reached by a Chinese bridge, a grotto, a ruined abbey and a ruined Roman arch; a Turkish pavilion of great beauty, a vast waterwheel, and a gothic tower on top of the hill (worth the climb for the views). Some of the ancient trees remain, the most impressive being a great Cedar of Lebanon, said to be the largest in England, and a *Juniperus virginiana*, said to be the tallest.

9 RHS GARDENS Wisley Tel 01483 224234

Mon–Sat all year, 10–7 or dusk (RHS members only on Suns). £4.20
From Cobham go SW on A3 for 2½m; garden signed on R.

It is impossible to describe so large and famous a garden in a short space. It is always worth visiting at any time of the year – but particularly in the winter and early spring, when one can learn so much about unusual plants showing off their character in a 'dead' season. Sometimes that can be more rewarding than being simply dazzled by herbaceous borders, roses ad infinitum and seemingly endless bedding schemes. It goes without saying that a visit here is a lovely day out, with splendid plants for sale, a great gift shop and good restaurants. But it is primarily a garden to look at, learn in, and come home feeling wiser.

Where to Stay

All B&B prices are approximate per person, sharing a double/twin room usually with private or en suite facilities. It is a good idea to ask for any special requirements when booking.

A KNAPHILL MANOR   Tel 01276 857962

Teresa & Kevin Leeper, Knaphill Manor, Carthouse Lane, Woking, Surrey GU21 4XT.

Here is a large, comfortable family home, dating back to the 1780s, set in a large (5½-acre) garden to enjoy. It has good views, a formal lily pond, herbaceous beds, croquet lawn and tennis court. Although in Surrey's stockbroker belt, and near to a number of motorways, it is secluded and quiet (you reach it via a farmyard). The 3 lavish double/twin bedrooms all look out on to the garden and the distant horizons beyond. Dinner (£22, bring your own wine) is special. Restricted smoking, no dogs, children should be over 8. B&B £30–£33.

B HIGH EDSER   Tel 01483 278214

Carol Franklin-Adams, High Edser, Shere Rd, Ewhurst, nr Cranleigh, Surrey GU6 7PG.

This early 16th-century farmhouse is set in an Area of Outstanding Natural Beauty, has extensive gardens and grounds including a tennis court which guests can use. You can't help but enjoy the house, and the lounge is just the sort of place to relax in. There are 3 well-furnished double/twin bedrooms. There are many places to eat out locally. Children and dogs welcome by prior arrangement, smoking restricted. B&B £20.

C DEERFELL   Tel 01428 653409

Elizabeth Carmichael, Deerfell, Fernden Lane, Blackdown Park, nr Haslemere, Surrey GU27 3LA.

There are scenic delights here, and the countryside is outstanding. Unspoilt NT land is nearby, and views from Blackdown (1,000 feet) over the Sussex Weald are spectacular, stretching as far as the eye can see past the South Downs towards the coast. In early summer there is a blaze of colour from rhododendrons and azaleas. Two comfortable bedrooms are large enough to be used as family rooms. Two-course evening meals (£8.50, bring your own wine), must be arranged in advance. No smoking, no dogs, children welcome. B&B £19.

D BOOKERS LEE   Tel 01483 272442

Margaret & Andrew Carr, Bookers Lee, Alfold, nr Cranleigh, Surrey GU6 8JS.

This comfortable late-Georgian house, dating from about 1840, stands in an acre of formal garden, partly walled. It includes a rose garden with more than 120 plants, 75 yds of herbaceous borders, heather and azalea beds, and an aviary cheeping with interesting birds. You are made to feel really at home here, in spacious and well-proportioned rooms. Two large double/ twin bedrooms, 1 with a private bathroom, 1 sharing. If you would like a glass of wine in the evening before going out to eat at a local restaurant or pub, Margaret is happy to pour one for you. No smoking. No dogs in the house, but there is a stable where they may be happy. No children under 7. B&B £18–£25.

E BULMER FARM   Tel 01306 730210

Gill Hill, Bulmer Farm, Holmbury St Mary, nr Dorking, Surrey RH5 6LG.

Holmbury St Mary is an exceptionally pretty village and Bulmer Farm, a 17th-century house with many beams and an inglenook fireplace, is on the edge of it. There are 8 double/twin rooms, some en suite, and 2 self-catering cottages of which one is adapted for use by the disabled. You can walk to the village to eat out in the evenings. Restricted smoking, dogs and children by arrangement. B&B £18–£22.

What Else to Enjoy

This is a short selection of the many good things recommended in the area by owners of places to stay. Your hosts will certainly be able to provide additional information.

Other Gardens/Nurseries

Art-lovers as well as regular garden visitors will find the **Hannah Peschar Sculpture Garden** both fascinating and challenging. An exotic and dramatic water-garden designed by Anthony Paul provides the background for sculpture and ceramics, which are mostly for sale. From Dorking, go S on

A24 for 4m and turn R on B2126 to **Ockley**. The garden is at Black and White Cottage in Standon Lane. Open Fri–Sun and BH Mons, mid May to Oct, 11–8 (Suns and BHs 2–5). Admission £3–£5. Tel 01306 627269.

Mr and Mrs Nicholas Calvert have a 4-acre landscaped woodland garden at **Walton Poor** which is well worth a visit on the half-dozen days a year it is open for charity. In addition, Mrs Calvert runs a cottage nursery alongside, mostly open Wed–Sun, Easter to Sept, 11–5, where you can buy aromatic and scented plants and herbs, which you see growing in her herb garden and potager. From **East Horsley** on the A246 W of Leatherhead, go S on minor roads for 1½ m. Ask Mrs Calvert for final directions when you check to make sure the nursery is open. Tel 01483 282273.

If It's Wet

All the NT mansions in this visit will keep you happy indoors for an extended visit.

Clandon Park (*see* Garden 5) is a Palladian beauty built for the 2nd Lord Onslow in the 1730s. It has a magnificent marble hall, family portraits and furniture, and a fine collection of porcelain and needlework.

Hatchlands Park (*see* Garden 6) has wonderful interiors by Robert Adam, and displays the Cobbe collection of keyboard instruments, paintings and furniture.

Polesden Lacey (*see* Garden 7) is an elegant 1820's Regency villa altered early this century by the Edwardian hostess, the Hon. Mrs Ronald Greville. Her collection of paintings, furniture, porcelain and silver are still displayed.

If you want to go shopping, **Dorking** has an antique centre and is a pleasant town to potter about in. **Wisley** (*see* Garden 9) has a shop where organised people go early to buy their Christmas presents for gardening friends (the restaurant, too, is very good).

Eating Out

Being part of London's affluent commuter belt, there are many high-quality restaurants in this visit. Perhaps the pick of them, and widely recommended, is **Michels**, at 13 High St, **Ripley**, off the A3 just S of Wisley. This comfortable Georgian house is run by Erik and Karen Michel, and Erik cooks constantly inventive food. There is a £28 4-course dinner menu (including glasses of wine) which offers a good choice. If you eat *à la carte*, you should expect to pay at least double this. Tel 01483 224777.

The Wiltshire Downs

Ancient monuments, burial grounds, Iron Age hill-forts and, of course, Stonehenge are all over Salisbury Plain (so is the Army, alas). The enchanting River Nadder flows down to Wilton, and the great angler and writer Izaak Walton loved the Wylye valley. The cathedral's close at Salisbury is full of tranquility and beauty. At Stourhead you will find one of the most ravishing landscape gardens ever made. Listening to Michael Tippett's 'Ritual Dances' from his opera *Midsummer Marriage* captures all that is strange and wonderful about the ancient civilization that had such an extraordinary impact on this area.

OS maps: Landrangers **183**, 184

Gardens

Opening times: in larger gardens, and in NT properties, last admissions are usually 30–45 minutes before the garden closes. Admission charges are a guide to what one adult can expect to pay to go round the garden. It sometimes varies with the season or days of the week. When the house is also open to the public, there is usually an additional charge.

I HADSPEN GARDEN   Castle Cary   Tel 01749 813707

Thurs–Sun and BH Mons, March to Sept, 9–6. £2.50
From Wincanton go NW on A371 for 6m; garden signed on R, ½m E of A359 junction.

The basic lines of this garden were laid down by Margaret Hobhouse in early Edwardian times. It was restored 70 years later by Penelope Hobhouse, who added a splendid new lily pool. It is now in the very able hands of Nori and Sandra Pope. The borders are renowned for their dazzlingly brilliant colours, and a splendid collection of hostas shaded by beech hedges. The National Collection of rodgersias is here, and the glorious nursery sells treasures galore. Time your visit around lunchtime or teatime and enjoy the

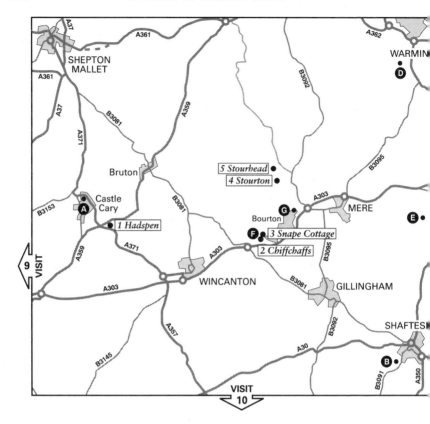

excellent and remarkably good value food (lunches £3–£4) served by Bond's Hotel (*see* Where to Stay).

2   CHIFFCHAFFS nr Bourton   Tel 01747 840841

Wed/Thurs, end March to end Sept; also BH weekends, and 1st and 3rd Sun each month, and by appointment, 2–5.30. £2
From Wincanton go NE on A303 for 3m. Turn L on minor road, signed Bourton, for 1m, then turn L in Chaffeymoor village; garden 300 yards on sharp bend, opposite Snape Cottage (below).

A garden full of interesting and colourful plants, created from scratch over 17 years. This is not a botanical collection, more a lovely garden divided into rooms, with many surprises and vistas. A walk through unusual trees and shrubs, with fine views over the Blackmoor Vale, takes you to a 2-acre

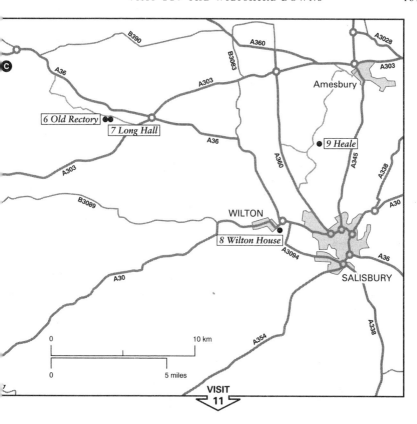

area of woodland, full of azaleas, rhododendrons, bulbs, and bog-loving plants such as primulas, meconopsis and iris. It is planted and maintained entirely by Mr and Mrs Potts, who have their own nursery (Abbey Nurseries) selling a wide range of their favourite plants.

3   SNAPE COTTAGE

nr Bourton (*see also* Where to Stay)   Tel 01747 840330 evenings
Wed, April to July, and Sept, charity Suns, and by appointment, 2–6. £1 From Wincanton go NE on A303 for 3m. Turn L on minor road, signed Bourton, for 1m, then turn L in Chaffeymoor village; garden 300 yards on sharp bend, opposite Chiffchaffs (above).

Angela Whinfield is a plantswoman with a mission – she loves old-fashioned cottage garden perennials, and historically ancient varieties of plants. She has amassed a large collection, and confesses to being totally self-taught, largely through the books of Margery Fish. If you buy a plant here she will give you excellent instructions on where to place it and how to make it flourish. Staying overnight at Snape Cottage is another treat. Ian Whinfield makes Windsor chairs – something else to watch and learn from.

4   STOURTON HOUSE GARDENS

nr Mere   Tel 01747 840417

Sun, Wed, Thurs and BHs, April to Nov, 11–6 (or dusk). £2
From Mere go NW on B3092 for 3m. Turn L, signed Stourton. Use Stourhead's
NT car park.

A garden with year round fascination, with unusual features and ideas – interesting bulbs, a vast collection of hydrangeas, magnolias and camellias. If you are planning a hedge of Leyland cypress, take a look at the imaginative way it has been handled here, with an immense wavy-topped hedge sheltering a herbaceous garden. Dried-flower enthusiasts can see them being grown, dried and sold here. Fond memories of an exceedingly good chocolate cake in Mrs Bullivant's tearoom.

5   STOURHEAD (NT)   nr Mere   Tel 01747 841348

Daily, all year, 9–7 (or dusk). £4.20
From Mere go NW on B3092 for 3m. Turn L, signed Stourton, to NT car park.

This justly world-famous landscape garden was the creation of banker Henry Hoare in the 1740s. It is perhaps at its best in spring, when the azaleas and bluebells light up the woodland; or in autumn for the leaf colours. There are many fine follies which are quietly reflected in the tranquil lake.

6   THE OLD RECTORY

Stockton, nr Warminster   Tel 01985 850607

By appointment April to July, and one charity afternoon. £1.50
From Salisbury go NW on A36 for 10m. Turn L on A303 for ½m, then turn
R on minor road, signed Stockton, for 1m; garden in village next to church.

Mr and Mrs David Harrison love this house and garden so much that, having left it in the 1970s, they bought it back in 1988 – and then set to work dedicatedly on the garden. It is an extremely pretty house, its frontage dating from 1799, with a huge sweeping lawn lorded over by a great cedar and a magnificent beech, plus a weeping pear and a weeping lime. The rear of the house is much earlier (c. 1550), and here are five separate garden rooms, the walled herb garden being handily placed by the back door. The orchard is home to old apple trees and a venerable walnut tree, and three more walled gardens follow, exuberantly planted with masses of roses, peonies, delphiniums, and Mr Harisson's favourite perovskia. The magnificent wisteria next door at Long Hall generously hangs over the wall and adds to the charm of this lovely garden.

7   LONG HALL GARDENS

Stockton, nr Warminster   Tel 01985 850424

1st Sat of month, May to early Aug, 2–6, and by appointment. £2
From Salisbury go NW on A36 for 10m. Turn L on A303 for ½m, then turn
R on minor road, signed Stockton, for 1m; garden in village near to church.

A 4-acre garden of great interest and charm – in fact, a series of gardens within a garden, set next to the village church. Along the churchyard wall, Susannah Yeatman-Biggs has planted an 'ecclesiastical' border, with lots of ecclesiastical purple, monkshood, madonna lilies and Jacob's ladder and, of course, the rose 'Rambling Rector'. A secret garden hedged with yew has a central lily pool and beds of old roses where soft feminine colours abound; in contrast, a bold red border looks heroic against a background of purple and coppery foliage. Great columns of Irish yew line the south terrace, adding to the air of graceful antiquity, nostalgia and beauty that pervade the garden.

Long Hall Nursery is run by James and Helen Dooley, who specialise in rare and beautiful chalk-tolerant plants. It is open Wed–Sat, mid March to end Sept, 9.30–5.30. Tel 01985 850914.

8   WILTON HOUSE   nr Salisbury   Tel 01722 743115

Daily, Easter to end Oct, 11–6. £2.75
From Salisbury go W on A30 for 2½m; signed on L.

This is the home of the Earl of Pembroke, and is impressively grand. A fine park surrounds an Inigo Jones house, and a wonderful Palladian bridge crosses the River Nadder. The north court has pleached limes and a box parterre. The east side has fine herbaceous borders backed by old walls swagged with climbers, and the walled garden has old-fashioned roses in profusion. There is also a riverside walk and nature trail, and children will love the adventure playgrounds. There are also plants for sale in the adjoining Wilton House garden centre.

9   HEALE GARDENS

Middle Woodford, nr Salisbury   Tel 01722 782504

Daily throughout year, 10–5. £2.50
From Salisbury go N on A360 for 4m. Turn R on minor road signed Middle Woodford for 4m; garden signed on R.

A most enchanting garden, absolutely not to be missed. If you can visit in June when the mass of shrub roses is out, it is magical – but it is both tranquil and sumptuous all the year round. A red Japanese bridge crosses the little Avon tributary that borders the garden, and there is a genuine Japanese tea-house next to it. Harold Peto designed some of the gardens in 1910, including the stone lily ponds and the terraces. The old clipped yews form the perfect backdrop to herbaceous borders and shrub roses. The kitchen garden is walled, with espaliered fruit trees and apple tunnels (ravishingly pretty). Fruit trees are under-planted with billowing flowers and clipped box balls. For many miles around, this is the garden for garden lovers, praised and recommended by all. The plant centre sells particularly good and interesting stock.

Where to Stay

All B&B prices are approximate per person, sharing a double/twin room usually with private or en suite facilities. It is a good idea to ask for any special requirements when booking.

A   BOND'S HOTEL   Tel 01963 350464

Yvonnne & Kevin Bond, Bond's Hotel, Ansford, nr Castle Cary, Somerset BA7 7JP.

Clad in Virginia creeper, with a small but charming garden, this 7-bedroom hotel formed out of a listed Georgian town house gets rave reviews from everyone (including hardened and cynical restaurant critics) for Yvonne's amazing cooking. The menus (a short one at £13.50, longer at £21.50, with reductions if you stay there) contain dishes of such eclectic imagination (Yvonne is self-trained) that they are hard to summarise. How about stir-fried chicken livers and chorizo in an orange and mint dressing? Or fillet of pork stuffed with cheddar and parsley, wrapped in cheese pastry with horse-radish cream? The cheeseboard and puddings are a dream. The 7 double/twin period bedrooms, carefully furnished, are mostly on the small side, but are very comfortable. Kevin is a garden lover (he has close associations with Garden 1 above) as well as a classic car collector. You are looked after by him and his staff attentively. Smoking allowed. No dogs. Babes in arms and children over 8 welome. B&B £30–£40.

B   THE OLD RECTORY   Tel 01747 853658

Rose Marie & Tony Haines, The Old Rectory, St James, nr Shaftesbury, Dorset SP7 8HG.

Since 1994, the garden at this fine 18th-century rectory has been trans-formed. Walled on all sides, it now has a paved terrace, two fountains, a bog garden and a pergola. The front garden overlooks an attractive old church. Inside the house, the architectural features have been carefully re-stored. Above all, guests find it friendly here – Tony, a doctor, with his pianola, books and gardening, Rose Marie with her language skills and a widely-travelled background, are great hosts. She was a teacher at the London Cordon Bleu Cookery School, and her terrific meals (£18–£22, licensed) reflect this. Three double/twin bedrooms. Smoking restricted, dogs and children welcome. B&B £30–£32.

C   THE OLD HOUSE   Tel 01985 840344

Bridget & Colin Thompson, The Old House, Sutton Veny, nr Warminster, Wiltshire BA12 7AQ.

A peaceful garden of 2 acres (with a further 3 acres of paddocks), with sweeping lawns, wide herbaceous borders and yew hedges, surrounds this lovely 300-year-old thatched house on the edge of Salisbury Plain. Bring your tennis rackets if you dare – Colin and Bridget are enthusiasts. Visitors comment on the warmth of the welcome they find here, and the tranquil atmosphere. Dinner (£18–£22) includes wine. There are 2 comfortable double bedrooms. No dogs, restricted smoking, children to be discussed. B&B £30.

D   SPRINGFIELD HOUSE   Tel 01985 213696

Rachel & Colin Singer, Springfield House, Crockerton, nr Warminster, Wiltshire BA12 8AU.

It would be hard to find a more beautiful setting than you have here, in a charming 17th-century village house in the Wylye valley, on the edge of the Longleat Estate. Rachel and Colin make sure you feel a welcome guest in their home, with its beams, open fires, fresh flowers, and well-furnished bedrooms (there are 3 double/twins). There is a lawn tennis court in which Rachel takes pride. Evening meals cost £14, and you should bring your own wine. No smoking, no dogs , and older children are preferred. B&B £25.

E   MILTON FARM   Tel 01747 830247

Janice Hyde, Milton Farm, East Knoyle, nr Salisbury, Wiltshire SP3 6BG.

There is a 300-acre working farm around this enchanting Queen Anne house where old beams, an inglenook fireplace, flagstone floors and un-plastered walls form the background to a comfortable home. Janice's hobby/business is importing ceramics and pottery from Portugal. You see it at meal-times and may also buy it. There are 2 lovely double/twin bed-rooms. B&B only, but there are many places locally where you can eat out in the evenings. Dogs and children by arrangement, smoking accepted. B&B £23–£25.

F   SNAPE COTTAGE   Tel 01747 840330 evenings

Angela & Ian Whinfield, Chaffeymoor, nr Bourton, Dorset SP8 5BY.

This old stone cottage has wonderful views, and a warm welcome from An-gela, who will discuss at length the merits of all the marvellous gardens around here, including her own, of course. You can walk to Stourhead from a footpath starting at her house. There is a very tempting selection of home-propagated plants for sale. Two double/twin rooms share a bathroom. B&B only: eat out at one of the many pubs and restaurants nearby. No smoking, no dogs, children should be over 12. B&B £19 (minimum 2 nights).

G   STAG COTTAGE   Tel 01747 840458

Marie & Peter Boxall, Stag Cottage, Fantley Lane, Zeals, Wiltshire BA12 6NX.

This unpretentious, friendly thatched cottage in a pretty village has a tea-room and tea-garden for tourists as well as being a modest B&B with 3 good double/twin bedrooms each with a bathroom. It is too small for a guest lounge, so if you want to spend your evenings here, a TV is moved into the tea-room. Otherwise – like most guests – you will probably walk down the road to the White Lion, a pub/restaurant that everyone enjoys. No smoking, well-behaved dogs and children welcome. B&B £14.

What Else to Enjoy

This is a short selection of the many good things recommended in the area by owners of places to stay. Your hosts will certainly be able to provide additional information.

If It's Wet

As a first choice, head for **Salisbury** with its unparalleled cathedral and close. You can potter around its old streets, with second-hand bookshops galore, for many happy hours.

Wilton House (*see* Garden 8) is as spectacular inside as its surroundings would suggest. Once a 9th-century nunnery, you may recognize Inigo Jones's magnificent 'Double Cube Room' from the films *The Madness of King George III* and *Sense and Sensibility*. As well as period furniture and furnishings, there are waxwork figures which help bring everything to life.

Another vast house, **Longleat**, is not far away, on the A362 between **Warminster** and Frome. It is ostentatious and popular, easy to find and perhaps should be visited once in your life.

Further W, find places which are cosier and, to me, more appealing. At The Old Brewery, **Wyke**, nr Gillingham, Talisman Antiques is one of the most amazing bargain-hunting centres you will ever come across. It includes many garden ornaments. **Castle Cary** is chocolate-box charming.

Eating Out

In **Castle Cary**, be sure to try **Bond's Hotel** (*see* 'A' Where to Stay). The food is daring and the service friendly. Dinner will cost about £20–£40 per person if you are not staying there overnight.

In **Shaftesbury,** looking out over the Blackmoor Vale, is a little restaurant which is constantly inventive in its range of differently-priced menus. **La Fleur de Lys**, 25 Salisbury St, is owned and run by David Shepherd, Mary Griffin and Marc Preston, and is delightfully informal. With wine and service, expect to spend upwards of £30 per person. No smoking in the dining-room. Tel 01747 853717.

Bath to Devizes

The jewel in this visit is Bath, with its Roman remains, perfect Georgian crescents and wonderful honey-coloured stone. Set in a bowl beneath surrounding hills, the town often feels soporific, and nowadays there can be horrendous traffic delays in high season. To remind you of the unhurried elegance there once was, play some music by John Field. He was born in Dublin, and his nocturnes and other pieces (best heard on a forte piano) were very popular in Bath's salons. Then go out into the countryside and villages beyond, and find their memorable gardens.

OS maps: Landrangers 172, **173**, 184

Gardens

Opening times: in larger gardens, and in NT properties, last admissions are usually 30–45 minutes before the garden closes. Admission charges are a guide to what one adult can expect to pay to go round the garden. It sometimes varies with the season or days of the week. When the house is also open to the public, there is usually an additional charge.

I   CROWE HALL   Bath   Tel 01225 310322

Six Suns, late March to mid July, 2–6, and by appointment. £1.50
From Bath railway station go S on A3062 for ½m; garden on L next to Widcombe church.

For the finest view over Bath, John Barratt's large varied garden is unsurpassed, and full of surprise on its steeply banked slopes. Views open up, archways, grottos and pools delight. An Italianate terrace is below the Regency-style house, and on the long walk there is amazing outlook across to Prior Park (*see* Garden 2), and the handiwork of Capability Brown. If that view hasn't taken your breath away, you can go and search for the ferny rock garden, the woodland garden and meadow garden.

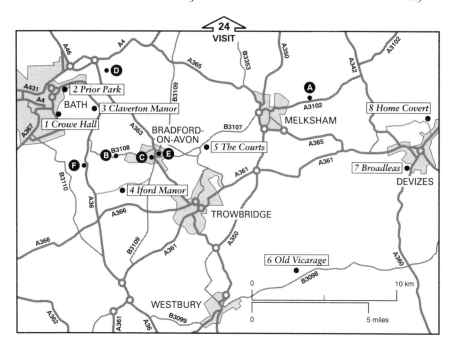

2   PRIOR PARK (NT)   Bath   Tel 01985 843600

Daily except Tues, all year, 12–5.30. £3.80
From Bath city centre to NE to Ralph Allen Drive. All visitors must walk or
use public transport as there is no parking at Prior Park or nearby. There is a
frequent bus service from the city centre.

After restoration work costing £500,000 over three years, this wonderful
18th-century garden reopened in 1996. Covering 28 acres, garden and park
design by Capability Brown, its most important architectural feature is a
pillared Palladian bridge across one of 3 lakes. Sweeping lawns, woods and
water, in a relatively compact area, show English landscape gardening at its
best.

3   CLAVERTON MANOR   Bath   Tel 01225 460503

Daily except Mons, end March to early Nov, 2–5 (BH Sun/Mon 11–5). £2
From Bath go SE on A36 for 2m; signed 'American Museum' on R.

Claverton Manor houses the American Museum, and more splendid views
across the Avon valley are waiting for you here. The garden has a histori-

cal American influence. The box-hedged herb garden contains a selection of plants used in colonial times, and there is a replica of George Washington's garden at Mount Vernon. Down the hill is a wood planted with American trees and shrubs, and the orchard has a collection of American apple trees. Despite losses in the great storms, other splendid old trees remain here.

4   IFORD MANOR   nr Bradford-on-Avon   Tel 01225 863146

Tues–Thurs, Sat/Sun and BH Mons, May to Sept, 2–5, and Suns in April and Oct. Other times by appointment. £2.20
From Bradford-on-Avon go S on B3109 for 1m. Turn R on minor road through Westwood, where garden signed.

Everyone keen on garden design will want to see this garden, the creation of Harold Peto, who made it his home in 1898. With steeply wooded slopes of the Frome Valley to exploit, he turned to Italy for inspiration. He terraced the slopes, with steps linking the different levels. Cypresses, fountains, pools, and a booty of classical statues, urns, colonnades and figures, surrounded by lush plantings, remind you of a theatrical garden set on the shores of Lake Como – until you see the pastoral English water meadows bordering the river below. The strong architectural features are softened by climbers, rampant wisteria and roses. Peto's splendid collection of architectural fragments and sculpture are housed in cloisters which he built in the Italian Romanesque style.

5   THE COURTS (NT)
Holt, nr Trowbridge   Tel 01225 782340

Daily except Sats, April to Oct, 2–5, and out of season by appointment. £2.80
From Bradford-on-Avon go E on B3107 for 2m; signed on R in Holt village.

Tucked away behind high walls in the village of Holt is this handsome house and mysterious, beautifully-kept 7-acre garden. Sir George Hastings laid it out originally at the beginning of this century, and it was greatly added to by Lady Cecilie Gott who, much influenced by Gertrude Jekyll and Lawrence Johnston, made a series of secret gardens hedged in with yew. A pleached lime avenue, topiary, herbaceous borders, a lily pond and fine conservatory are all there to be enjoyed.

Not far away is another NT property, **Great Chalfield Manor**, a ravishing moated 15th-century house with 7 acres of surrounding garden, which has memorable topiary, borders, terraces and an orchard.

6 THE OLD VICARAGE

Edington, nr Westbury   Tel 01380 830512

Charity Suns in June, and by appointment. £2.50
From Westbury go NE on B3098 for 4m. Turn L into Edington village; garden
by church.

John d'Arcy is a plant collector, and you can see the results of his travels
and passions, nurtured and grown to perfection in this garden. Interesting
at all times of the year, there are alpines, a scree garden, a sunken garden,
peat beds, and many unusual trees and shrubs. He also holds the National
Collection of evening primroses (*Oenothera).*

7 BROADLEAS GARDEN   Devizes   Tel 01380 722035

Sun, Wed, Thurs, April to Oct, 2–6. £2.50
From Devizes town centre go 1m S on A360; garden signed on R from Long St.

In this immaculately cared for garden, the great attraction is the densely
planted dell which reaches far down a valley, its steep sides planted with
magnolias, and fine specimens of *Paulownia fargesii,* azaleas, camellias,
hydrangeas, and one of my autumn favourites, a *Parrotia persica.* All these
beautiful flowering trees and shrubs are under-planted with drifts of bulbs,
hostas and erythoniums. Nearer to the house you can enjoy a rose garden,
herbaceous borders, and fine conifers. Something fascinating can be seen in
this garden all the year round. Excellent plants can be bought, propagated
by Lady Anne Cowdray, her specialities being salvias and euonymus.

8 HOME COVERT   nr Devizes   Tel 01380 723407

Charity Suns May and July, 2–6, and by appointment for garden-lovers. £2
From Devizes go NE on A361 for 1m. Turn L on minor road, signed Round-
way, for ½m; garden in village centre.

This highly imaginative and stimulating garden has been developed by Mr
and Mrs Phillips over the last 30 years. A large lawn in front of the house
is fringed with ornamental grasses, alpines and perennials, and there are
many unusual trees and shrubs to send you ferretting for labels. Then you
take a steep drop down to the waterfall, lake and bog garden, with a mouth-
watering collection of primulas, ferns and other bog-loving plants.

Where to Stay

All B&B prices are approximate per person, sharing a double/twin room usually with private or en suite facilities. It is a good idea to ask for any special requirements when booking.

A SANDRIDGE PARK   Tel 01225 706897

Annette & Andrew Hoogeweegen, Sandridge Park, nr Melksham, Wiltshire SN12 7QU.

Set on a hill in 30 acres of tranquil gardens and parkland including a bowling green and croquet lawn, this imposing mansion was a home to General Eisenhower during World War II. It is a marvellous spot for bird-watching. The 3 large double/twin bedrooms each have an individual flavour, furnished with objects collected by Annette and Andrew on their travels. Dinner (£18, licensed), is served in a stunning red dining-room and is cooked by Annette who ran her own catering company in London for many years. Smoking restricted, no dogs or children. B&B £40.

B BURGHOPE MANOR   Tel 01225 723557

Elizabeth & John Denning, Burghope Manor, Winsley, nr Bradford-on-Avon, Wiltshire BA15 2LA.

You will rarely – very rarely – be able to stay in a home with as much history as this one. Mainly dating from the 13th century, Henry VIII's prelate Archbishop Cranmer knew it well, and the fireplace in today's living-room is engraved with Elizabethan writing. Roots go back even further – excavations uncovered a curious leather shield dating to the reign of Alfred the Great in the 9th century. The manor has been the family home of the Dennings for many years, and they now welcome guests to their stunning house which has wonderful furniture and is adorned with family portraits. Outside, in 2½ acres of garden, are well-mown striped lawns, with some of the original borders still in place. The 5 large double/twin bedrooms have all the modern comforts. If you want self-catering, the Dower House sleeps 6. You can walk to a good village pub/restaurant in the evenings. Restricted smoking, no dogs, and children should behave as grown-ups. B&B £35.

C PRIORY STEPS   Tel 01225 862230

Diana & Carey Chapman, Priory Steps, Newtown, Bradford-on-Avon, Wiltshire BA15 1NQ.

Originally a terrace of six mellow stone 17th-century weavers' cottages, this is now a large house perched on a hill with great views of Salisbury Plain, yet Bradford-on-Avon's town centre is only three minutes' walk away. There is a sunny terraced garden, open for charity 3 or 4 times a year along with neighbouring gardens. You feel a sense of luxury and comfort here, with period furniture and a lovely library in which to relax. Diana's dinners (£16, licensed) are special, but don't happen every night as she has two young children to keep happy. Five double/twin bedrooms, all with good views. Smoking if other guests don't mind. No dogs or children. B&B £29.

D THE LODGE HOTEL   Tel 01225 858467

Keith & Mary Johnson, The Lodge Hotel, Bathford Hill, Bathford, Avon BA1 7SL.

The garden at this comfortable family-run hotel, in a village only 2½ miles from the centre of Bath, is special. Covering 2½ acres, the front gardens and lawns provide a loosely formed English garden with large, well-stocked rockeries and lily pond. Next comes a 'leisure area' with terraces, and a swimming pool heated from May to October, framed by trees, walls and colourfully-planted troughs. Then there is a typical cottage garden and lawn, leading into a meadow seeded with dozens of wild flowers and grasses, lovingly tended and weeded by hand so that in time, nature can take over. Luxuriously furnished, the Lodge has 5 double/twin bedrooms, 1 suitable for wheelchairs. B&B only, but the pub next door has good food, and there are many other places to eat out in the evenings nearby. Smoking, dogs and children are all OK. B&B £28–£55.

E BRADFORD OLD WINDMILL   Tel 01225 866842

Priscilla & Peter Roberts, Bradford Old Windmill, Masons Lane, Bradford-on-Avon, Wiltshire BA15 1QN.

There is a delightful eccentricity about staying in this converted windmill. Because the basic structure of the building is round, so are many of the features inside – a circular lounge, a spiral staircase, a circular bedroom with curved beams, even a king-sized round bed in one of the 4 double/

twin bedrooms, each of which is differently sized and shaped. The food here is unusual, too. Peter and Priscilla have travelled widely, learning how to cook dishes from faraway places. Ask in advance, and you can eat Mexican, Thai, Nepalese, Gambian, Jamaican and more (around £18, but not every night, licensed). No dogs, no children under 6, no smoking in the house (but there is a charming small garden for addicts). B&B £28–£36.

F   AVONSIDE   Tel 01225 722547

Ursula & Peter Challens, Avonside, Winsley Hill, Limpley Stoke, Wiltshire BA3 6EX.

This solid, stone-built house (18th-century, with 19th-century alterations and additions) is set in a 1½-acre garden bordered by tall trees and farm-land, with 120 yards of frontage onto the River Avon. On a light limestone soil, there are lawns and borders, a kitchen garden, tennis court, fruit trees, and five species of bamboo. Anyone fed up with television should come here – the valley situation prevents reception. Two good-sized double/twin bedrooms share a bathroom; 3-course suppers (£12, bring your own wine) include a free aperitif and coffee. No smoking in bedrooms, no dogs, children by arrangement. B&B £18–£20.

What Else to Enjoy

This is a short selection of the many good things recommended in the area by owners of places to stay. Your hosts will certainly be able to provide additional information.

Other Gardens/Nurseries

Hannays is famous for herbaceous shrubs and plants. The Hannays regu-larly go away on plant-collecting adventures, and some of their stock is grown from seeds they have brought back from distant lands. Their euphor-bia, sages and phlomis are particularly covetable. Open daily except Tues, March to Oct, 10–5, Find them at Sydney Wharf Nursery, **Bathwick**, Bath BA2 4ES. Tel 01225 462230.

People interested in exotic birds will enjoy themselves at **Rode Bird Gardens**, SE of Bath in the village of **Rode**. More than 200 species (about 1,200 birds in all) can be seen either in sensitively-designed aviaries or at liberty in the 17-acre landscaped gardens with ornamental lakes and woodlands which give pleasure in their own right for all of us who love gardens. There is a cafeteria, loos and good facilities for the disabled.

If It's Wet

The NT's **Great Chalfield Manor** is a marvellous old house, dating from 1480 and surrounded by a moat. Guided tours take no more than 25 people at a time. While you wait for one, the church and garden are inviting. Situated between Bradford-on-Avon and Melksham, it is open Tues/Wed, April to Oct, tours starting at 12.15. Tel 01985 843600 (regional office).

Gardeners shopping and sightseeing in **Bath** should head for Walcot St, where Walcot Reclamations have fascinating architectural salvage for sale, including garden seats, ornaments and sometimes pillars and statuary. Near-by is a fine cheese shop, good delicatessen and specialist craft shops.

And if it's crafts and collectables you're after, head for **Bradford-on-Avon**. This is an absolutely enchanting town, with a perfect Saxon church, its narrow streets tumbling steeply down the southernmost hill in the Cotswolds to a 14th-century bridge that spans the Avon. There are many antique shops (and a weekly antique collectors' fair), and good pubs and restaurants. At the helpful tourist information office at 34 Silver St (Tel 01225 865797) you can pick up a leaflet which guides you on an excellent round walk that takes you across a packhorse bridge to the south bank of the river. On the way you will pass the magnificent 14th-century tithe barn at **Barton Farm Country Park**, in the shadow of which are converted medieval cow byres that are now a series of individual craft shops and galleries, with a pleasant garden where you can have tea.

Eating Out

In **Bath**, the **Hole in the Wall** at 16 George St (Tel 01225 452242) keeps going after all these years, the standard under its latest owner/chef Christopher Chown still high. Prices are from £20–£35 per person. One mile NE of **Bradford-on-Avon** on the B3105 is a supremely well-run country house hotel, **Woolley Grange** (Tel 01225 864705), which I would love to have recommended as a place to stay, except that its B&B prices are a bit above our range. However, you can enjoy the ambience and excellent cooking with a set dinner menu costing £28, plus service and wine.

Around Chippenham

Historically, this area became wealthy because of the fine wool grown by the sheep reared on the chalky hills here. Castle Combe was a prosperous weaving town, and today has a picturesque market cross, trout stream, attractive bridges and well-preserved stone cottages – well worth visiting. If you go to Sheldon Manor, it is fascinating to walk in the lumpy fields around it. There is a deserted village here, and the Manor has produced a helpful guide to the site. I remember pottering around this visit on a very hot summer evening, stopping sometimes to look at butterflies on the wildflowers. As I drove away, I listened to Manuel de Falla's 'Nights in the Gardens of Spain'.

OS maps: Landrangers 172, **173**

Gardens

Opening times: in larger gardens, and in NT properties, last admissions are usually 30–45 minutes before the garden closes. Admission charges are a guide to what one adult can expect to pay to go round the garden. It sometimes varies with the season or days of the week. When the house is also open to the public, there is usually an additional charge.

I   BOWOOD HOUSE   nr Calne   Tel 01249 812102

Daily, April to Oct, 11–6 (or dusk). £4.80 (incl. house)
From Chippenham go SE on A4 for 1½m. Turn R on A342 for ½m; garden signed on L.

A very grand landscape garden designed by Capability Brown (who gave it his usual signature of a serpentine lake) and Humphry Repton. There are temples, follies, cascades, fine trees, sculpture, topiary, rose gardens, a woodland garden with bluebells, and in May and June the dazzling rhododendron walks are open. More than 700 varieties of trees are labelled, and can be identified with the *Bowood Tree Guide*. There is an adventure playground for children.

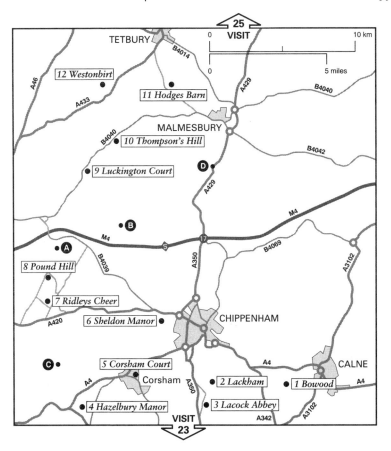

2 LACKHAM GARDENS   nr Chippenham   Tel 01249 443111

Daily, April to Oct, 11–5. £3
From Chippenham go S on A350 for 1½m; turn L where signed 'College of Agriculture'.

You could spend a whole day here, there is so much to see. This is a garden which educates whilst it enchants – you will definitely want your notebook and pencil. The greenhouses are within a walled garden, and contain ornamental pot plants, carnations, alstroemarias, etc, and a huge fruiting citrus tree. Gardeners will love the propagating house and the ornamental vegetable section; everything is clearly labelled. A major collection of roses – some are very old and rare – demonstrate how modern roses have evolved;

it is impossible not to admire the perfect herbaceous borders, herbs, lawns, shrubs and the woodland walk leading down to the river. Newly planned are gardens depicting the style of gardening in the 17th, 18th and 19th centuries, a maze and a pond. Children will love the adventure playground, sheep and piggies. There is a museum of old agricultural implements, plants for sale, and a coffee shop – you'll need that!

3   LACOCK ABBEY (NT)   nr Chippenham   Tel 01249 730227

Daily, April to Oct, 12–5.30 (closed Good Fri). £2.10
From Chippenham go S on A350 for 3m; abbey signed on L.

Nine acres of park surround the sleepy 13th-century abbey in this lovely NT-owned village, dominated by regal cedars, large black walnut trees and a tulip tree. It's best visited in the spring for sensational displays of snow-drops, aconites and crocus, followed by daffodils. A rose garden has been re-created from a very early photograph. This was the home of William Fox-Talbot, inventor of the camera (*see* If It's Wet).

4   HAZELBURY MANOR GARDENS
nr Box   Tel 01225 812952

Some charity afternoons, and by appointment with Head Gardener. £2.80
From Chippenham go SW on A4 for 3m. Turn L onto B3109 for 2m; garden signed on R.

The house and garden of this fascinating 15th-century fortified manor are currently under renovation. When a stately home, it was often visited by royalty, but later declined socially and became a school. Now, all is being reversed. Lime walks, pergola avenues, formal rose gardens, raised gardens, a peat garden, a decorative vegetable garden, shrub walk, archery walk, truly vast borders and the main lawn with most remarkable clipped yews around it (where Shakespeare plays are performed in summer in a magical setting) are evidence of the gardens' grand scale. I look forward to seeing progress. An interesting new idea was a star-shaped astrological border, with all the family's birthstone colours and flowers incorporated.

5   CORSHAM COURT   nr Chippenham   Tel 01249 701610

Daily except Mons, April to mid Oct, 11.30–5.30. Sats and Suns, mid Oct to March, 2–4.30 (closed Dec). £2
From Chippenham go SW on A4 for 2m; garden signed in centre of village.

No trip to Wiltshire is complete without visiting Corsham Court, a magnificent landscape garden started off by Capability Brown, completed by Repton, and with a modern arboretum recently planted. In spring daffodils bloom in their thousands beneath the many rare and exotic trees flourishing here. The fine trees are spread over smooth lawns, catalpas group around a lily pond, and great swags of old roses perfume the rose garden. A hornbeam *allée*, box-edged flower beds, urns and lovers' arbours make this an entrancing visit.

6   SHELDON MANOR   Chippenham   Tel 01249 653120
Suns, Thurs and BHs, Easter to early Oct, 12.30–6. £1.50
From Chippenham go W on A420 for ½m. Turn L at X-roads on minor road for ½m; garden signed on R.

Wiltshire's oldest inhabited manor, sole survivor of a deserted medieval village, and a family home for 700 years, the garden has a profusion of old roses in June and July. Of special interest, I found a *Rosa cooperi*, and a white Judas tree – but it's the calm atmosphere of quiet English life continuing here over the years that pervades the senses in this enchanting garden, enclosed by old barns and walls. Parts of the garden have intriguing old names: Sheep Sleight, Howes Rickyard, and Goatacre. On garden open days, there are good home-made buffet lunches in the barn (licensed).

7   RIDLEYS CHEER
Mountain Bower, nr Chippenham   Tel 01225 891204
4 charity days in May and June, 2–6, and by appointment. £1.50
From Chippenham go W on A420 for 7m. Turn R opposite Shoe Inn on minor road for ½m, turn L for ½m, then turn R to Mountain Bower village; garden at last house on R.

This is the garden of plantsman and designer Anthony Young, who truly cares about the placing of plants – so much so that he was bold enough to move a large Acer which he felt was in the wrong place. The garden has been greatly increased in size recently, creating an upper garden of mixed shrub and herbaceous plantings, with magnolias, willows, shrub roses and 20 different varieties of oak. This part of the garden has been very successfully united to the lower area by a flight of Cotswold stone steps Lutyens would have been proud of, flanked by flopping musk roses. Mr and Mrs Young have collected rare albas and hybrid musks, and the garden contains many more treasures. There are often interesting home-propagated plants for sale.

8 POUND HILL HOUSE

West Kington, nr Chipping Sodbury   Tel 01249 782781

Daily except Mons, and BH Mons, Feb to Dec, 2–6. £2
From Chippenham go W on A420 for 5m. Turn R into North Wraxall and follow minor roads for 2m to West Kington village; turn L at X-roads on no-through road.

A 15th-century house with a constantly developing 2-acre garden around it which is captivating all year round. It is divided into many small, charming gardens, which include a rose garden of David Austin's old-fashioned varieties, a topiary garden, a fascinating Victorian vegetable garden, and a pergola smothered with clematis, roses and wisteria. A new addition is a water garden with some interesting plants for shady places. If you ever have any doubts about what to plant in containers, have a careful look at the way Mr and Mrs Stockitt achieve such brilliance with theirs, and then pop into their nursery garden where there is a huge variety of rare and interesting plants, including topiary, at which they are so inventive.

9 LUCKINGTON COURT   nr Malmesbury   Tel 01666 840205

Weds, early May to end Sept, 2–5, and by appointment. £2
From Malmesbury go W on B4040 for 6m; garden signed L on edge of village, next to church.

A Queen Anne house of great beauty, based on an early medieval house (owned by Earl Harold before he became King Harold), next to a 12th-century church. Exquisite old walls, gate piers and outbuildings shelter this garden, which is best viewed in May when the drive is lined with flowering cherries, the lilac is out, and the wisteria draped over the south front of the house is in full glory. In a little walled garden by the stables, peonies (Molly the Witch) flank a silver weeping pear and a stone bench, while old apple trees lean over the rose beds. A pretty scalloped-edged border runs under the drawing-room window. Luckington Court featured largely in the BBC's film of *Pride and Prejudice*; the huge cedar tree across the lawn, from which Mr Darcy glowered so sullenly, looks very familiar. The Hon. Mrs Horn's home here is more atmospheric and romantic than heavily gardened – I loved it.

10 THOMPSON'S HILL

Sherston, nr Malmesbury   Tel 01666 840766

One charity Sun end June, 2–6.30, and by appointment. £1.50
From Malmesbury go W on B4040 for 5m. Turn L opposite Sherston church,
then R up Thompson's Hill. Garden at No. 1.

It's hard to believe this charming and personal garden was made only twelve years ago by Mr and Mrs Cooper. Clipped yew hedges form the basis, with three arches giving glimpses to lawns and herbaceous beds. There are numerous old roses (so the best season is June), and a lovely conservatory. This is a much photographed and written about garden, and you can understand why.

11 HODGES BARN

Shipton Moyne, nr Tetbury   Tel 01666 880202

Mon/Tues & Fri, April to mid Aug, 2–5, and by appointment. £2
From Tetbury go SW on A433 for ½m. Turn L on minor road for 1½m to
Shipton Moyne; garden 300 yds past Post Office on L.

You can feel how much Mrs Hornby loves this splendid garden as soon as you walk in. Against the backdrop of the house – once a columbarium built in the 15th century – are topiary and fine yew hedges giving strong lines to exuberant planting, particularly of exquisite old roses at their best in June. Visiting in the spring is a treat too, with bulbs and flowering shrubs, a little woodland, and splendid topiary all showing to advantage before you get side-tracked later in the year by the heavenly roses. The planting around the pond is extravagant and lush.

12 WESTONBIRT ARBORETUM

nr Tetbury   Tel 01666 880220

Daily, all year, 10–8 (or dusk). £2.50
From Tetbury go SW on A433 for 3m; arboretum signed on R.

I suggest that before starting your walk round here, you should stop at the visitors' centre near the entrance to this vast arboretum, and pick up some information and a map. Reckoned to be the most comprehensive collection of trees and shrubs in Europe, and covering 500 acres, it was started in 1829 by Robert Holford when plant collectors were at their busiest bringing back new specimens from foreign lands. In spring, bluebells in the silk wood, and camellias, magnolias and acers, are all lovely. Autumn colouring is, of course, spectacular – and winter walks, too, are marvellous. Try to visit it in every season; you can take your dog. The plants in the nursery are the best for miles around.

Where to Stay

All B&B prices are approximate per person, sharing a double/twin room usually with private or en suite facilities. It is a good idea to ask for any special requirements when booking.

A   FOSSE FARMHOUSE   Tel 01249 782286

Caron Cooper, Fosse Farmhouse, Nettleton Shrub, nr Chippenham, Wiltshire SN14 7NJ.

Caron is a writer and TV cook, and runs this lovely old farmhouse with her mother June. There is a wonderfully eclectic collection of furniture in the house, from art nouveau to antique pine; also a great rocking-horse. In the garden is a brightly-painted gypsy caravan. Ask Caron to describe the bedrooms to you because they vary a lot. There are 6 in total, including 1 single and a half-tester. Two have en suite bathrooms, others have showers or shared bathrooms. Dinner, as you might imagine, is extremely good (£22, licensed). Dogs by arrangement, children welcome, restricted smoking. B&B £38–£55.

B   CHURCH HOUSE   Tel 01249 782562

Anna Moore, Church House, Grittleton, nr Chippenham, Wiltshire SN14 6AP.

Grittleton village is a fairly well-kept secret – a delightful cluster of elegant Bath stone houses in immaculately kept surroundings. Church House, a large and handsome mid 18th-century Georgian rectory, fits in perfectly, with 11 acres of gardens and pastures, including a walled organically-cultivated kitchen garden and orchard. The copper beeches, floodlit at night, are among the finest in the county, and the lovely covered pool in a courtyard is heated to a pampering 84 degrees from May to October. You feel instantly at home in the wonderfully large rooms inside the house, and an impressive curved staircase takes you upstairs to 4 double/twin bedrooms furnished with antiques, all with good views. Dinner (£16, including wine, arrange in advance), has imaginative recipes. No children under 12, no smoking in the dining-room, no dogs. B&B £25–£36.

C PARSONAGE FARMHOUSE   Tel 01225 742811

Anne Daly, Parsonage Farmhouse, High Street, Colerne, nr Chippenham, Wiltshire SN14 8DN.

This 17th-century Grade II listed farmhouse is secluded in its own pretty courtyard in the centre of a village near Bath. There is a huge barn where great bargains can be found in china, glass and bric-à-brac. Anne's home is antique-filled, and gives out a warm and friendly atmosphere. Dinner (£16, bring your own wine) is cooked in the kitchen open to the dining-room. Two charming double/twin bedrooms. Smoking allowed, no children under 10, dogs if you talk about them beforehand. B&B £25–£30.

D MANOR FARM   Tel 01666 822148

Ross & John Eavis, Manor Farm, Corston, nr Malmesbury, Wiltshire SN16 0HF.

This charming 17th-century farmhouse lies alongside the A429 and is easy to find. Behind it, pleasant gardens include a pretty walled area with borders and a lawn, leading on to a working dairy/arable farm which John runs. Ross has been doing B&B for 18 years, regularly up-grades what she offers, and was a winner in the 1995 West Country Farm Holiday awards. Of the 6 bedrooms (1 single, with a shower, shares a loo), 4 are now en suite. Those which face the road are double-glazed to cut down traffic noise. Evening meals can be found in a friendly pub within walking distance, or you can drive 2m to Malmesbury. Restricted smoking, dogs and children by arrangement. B&B £18–£20.

What Else to Enjoy

This is a short selection of the many good things recommended in the area by owners of places to stay. Your hosts will certainly be able to provide additional information.

Other Gardens/Nurseries

Sherston Parva Nursery specialises in clematis (it always has about 150 varieties in stock), but also has many other unusual climbers and a large selection of conservatory plants. A large garden displays much of what is for sale, and the prices are reasonable. From Malmesbury, go W on B4040 for about 3m. It is signed on the L just before **Easton Grey**. Open daily except Mons, March to Oct, 10–5 (Suns 12–5). Tel 01666 841066.

If It's Wet

Bowood House (*see* Garden 1), home of the Earl and Countess of Shelburne, is a large Georgian house with an exhibition of family heirlooms, an Adam library, a 19th-century chapel and the laboratory where Joseph Priestley discovered oxygen. Open as for garden.

    Lacock Abbey (*see* Garden 3), founded as a nunnery in 1232, was converted into a country house in the 16th century. There are medieval cloisters, a Gothic hall and brewhouse. In the 16th-century barn you can see the Fox-Talbot museum of early photographs. Open as for garden.

    Corsham Court (*see* Garden 5) is on a different scale. Huge and hand-some, it is based on an Elizabethan house dating from 1582, and much enlarged in the 19th century to make room for collections of paintings and furniture. House open as for garden.

    Sheldon Manor (*see* Garden 6) won a national award for the historic house open to the public which has best preserved its character. There is a marvellous 13th-century porch, a 15th-century chapel and, inside the house, a 17th-century oak staircase, and collections of oak furniture, porce-lain and Nailsea glass. It is very welcoming here, and the home-made food is excellent. House open as for garden.

    If you want to potter about and shop, **Malmesbury** is my favourite town in this visit. Reputed to be England's oldest borough, its abbey, founded in the 7th century, is magnificent. The centre of the town has many architectural gems, and there are antique and other specialised shops. The little museum is fascinating, too, with illustrations of Malmesbury as it was, and lovely early bicycles.

Eating Out

You will probably want to visit the carefully preserved NT village of **Lacock**, and if so you shouldn't miss a meal at **At the Sign of the Angel**. I have stayed there overnight, and been charmed by the attention given by the Levis family who have owned it since 1944. It serves tradi-tional food to fit its traditional old-world surroundings, and will cost you about £30 per person. Tel 01249 730230.

South Cotswolds

In this book, there are perhaps half a dozen gardens which are supreme. Rosemary Verey's at Barnsley House is one of them. If you drive towards it on this visit from the north-east, you pass through Bibury, a camera-clicking chocolate box Cotswold village, its stream crossed by little bridges, ducks and ducklings posing obligingly beneath. In the north-west, you are in *Cider With Rosie* country. Laurie Lee, in his soft Gloucestershire accent, has put on tape a 'talking book' of his own masterpiece – great as an introduction to the area.

OS maps: Landrangers 162, **163**, 173

Gardens

Opening times: in larger gardens, and in NT properties, last admissions are usually 30–45 minutes before the garden closes. Admission charges are a guide to what one adult can expect to pay to go round the garden. It sometimes varies with the season or days of the week. When the house is also open to the public, there is usually an additional charge.

I   RODMARTON MANOR   Rodmarton   Tel 01285 841253

Sats, mid May to end Aug, 2–5, and by appointment. £2 Sats, £2.50 other days.
From Cirencester go SW on A429 and continue SW on A433 for 7m. Turn R on minor road, signed Rodmarton, for 1m; garden in village.

Mr and Mrs Simon Biddulph's house is a magnificent Arts and Crafts achievement, designed by Ernest Barnsley and Claud Biddulph at the beginning of this century on a marvellous site, with views across to Marlborough. Barnsley was also responsible for the garden design, and divided it up into a series of garden rooms, with Cotswold dry-stone walls and fine hedges. The topiary is stunning, and reflects the symmetry of the house. Masses of interest to see here, from the herbaceous borders to the

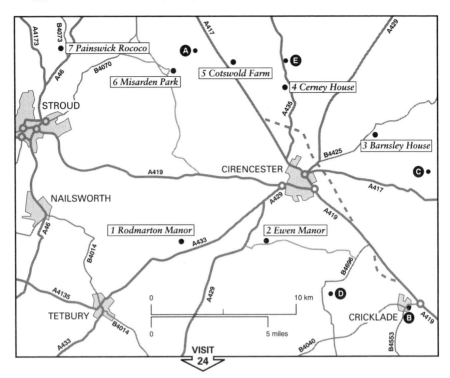

trough garden, which uses covetable old farm troughs as containers for alpines. The formal gardens give way gracefully to a woodland garden that tethers the estate seamlessly into its perfect setting. There is an eye-catching summer-house, a new rock garden, lots of old and new roses, and rare plants for plantsmen to ponder over. Please don't miss the giant chairs made of yew, in the herbaceous borders, just waiting for the Great Gardener in the sky to come and rest for a minute. Sometimes there are very good plants for sale.

2　EWEN MANOR　nr Cirencester　　　Tel 01285 770206

Wed–Fri, early May to early July, 11–4.30, and by appointment. £1.50
From Cirencester go SW on A429 for 3m. Turn L on minor road, signed Ewen,
for 1m; garden in village.

Amazingly, this house was physically moved from the opposite bank of the Thames in 1780, and the large cedar trees probably planted then. The maple trees up the drive were planted 25 years ago to replace an old avenue of limes. The old summer-house is a perfect place to sit and contemplate the pattern-mown lawn. A series of gardens features masses of shrub roses and ground cover, yew hedges, planted pots and a lily pool, all surrounded by fine trees in the woodland.

3 BARNSLEY HOUSE   nr Cirencester   Tel 01285 740281

Mon, Wed/Thurs, and Sat, all year, 10–6. £2
From Cirencester go NE on A429 for 1m. Fork R onto B4425 for 3m. Garden signed on R in Barnsley.

Justly, this is on everyone's must-visit list – the quintessential 'English-woman's Garden'. Created by Rosemary Verey, there is plenty of interest here all the year round. Indeed, if you live near enough you should visit several times a year to see the changes in season, and how a garden can be planned so that there is always something to attract the eye. My personal favourite is the potager (now everybody wants one) and the strictly mani-cured box hedges in the parterre. Home-propagated plants are one of the treats of going to Barnsley House, and so is lunch in the village pub opposite.

4 CERNEY HOUSE

North Cerney, nr Cirencester   Tel 01285 831300

Tues/Wed and Fri, Feb to Oct, 2–6, and parties by appointment. £2
From Cirencester go N on A435 for 4m. Turn L in North Cerney; garden behind church.

A romantic and exuberant garden of 3½ acres, with a walled garden over-flowing with roses and clematis, and fine trees and shrubs on the lawns around the house. Old fig trees grow up south-facing brick walls, together with a mass of roses. You can find lovely spring bulbs in the shady wood-land in spring (snowdrops especially); there is a herb garden, a kitchen garden and a rockery with a trickling waterfall. Goats and sheep graze the wildflower meadows. It poured with rain the day I visited, and I shared a summer-house by the herb garden with two damp peacocks – and then scampered to the shop for an excellent cup of coffee, with chocolate cake, and enjoyed masses of pictures of piggies. The best pig of all was rootling about in the orchard. Nothing could dampen my enthusiasm for this very personal garden made by Lady Angus and her daughter Barbara Johnston.

5 COTSWOLD FARM

nr Duntisbourne Abbots   Tel 01285 653856

By appointment (please give good notice). £2.50
From Cirencester go NW on A417 for 5m; garden signed on R immediately
after Five Mile Inn.

Major and Mrs P.D.Birchall's enchanting Cotswold house is set high above a valley, with fine views, and descends in terraces. Norman Jewson designed the terrace by the house, and it is unashamedly pretty, with good topiary and soft colour planting. In the walled garden a white seat is carefully sited by a *Cornus controversa* and a huge *Garrya elliptica*, with a charming view down to a small summer-house. Walk through this and you find yourself in a secret little box-edged parterre. Well-established shrub roses and lavender make this a nostalgic and very fragrant garden.

6 MISARDEN PARK   Miserden   Tel 01285 821303

Tues–Thurs, early April to Sept, 9.30–4.30. £2
From Stroud go NE on B4070 for 3m. Turn R on minor road for 2m, signed
Miserden. Fork L, and then fork L again.

A 17th-century house on a well nigh perfect site, looking down the Golden Valley. Marvellous yew hedges, wisteria romping over terraces, great herbaceous borders and formal rose gardens are some of the treats you can look forward to in this beautifully-maintained garden, which has Lutyens influence in its design. The adjoining nursery sells interesting plants, many of which you will have seen growing in the garden.

7 PAINSWICK ROCOCO GARDEN

Painswick   Tel 01452 813204

Wed–Sun and BH Mons, mid Jan to Nov, 11–5. £2.50
From Stroud go NE on A46 for 5m. Turn L on B4073 for ½m; garden signed
on L.

This amazing garden, which lay hidden by trees and brambles for centuries, has been under restoration for the last 10 years, largely copying a 1748 painting of it by Thomas Robins. It contains great treasures in the form of 18th-century garden buildings, now beautifully refurbished; a Gothic exedra (a kind of meeting-house), sparkling white like a wedding cake, the Eagle House, and many alcoves, temples, sculptures and pools. Paths wind between shrubs and a profusion of wild flowers on a steep site. Look for the magnificent snowdrops in early spring, the fish pond and the plunge pool. This is a brilliant renovation of a very important garden. The Rococo style marked the change from formal Italianate and French gardens to this more relaxed and informal style, with *allées*, vistas and surprises at the end of the serpentine paths. Dogs welcome on leads.

Where to Stay

All B&B prices are approximate per person, sharing a double/twin room usually with private or en suite facilities. It is a good idea to ask for any special requirements when booking.

A WINSTONE GLEBE   Tel 01285 821451

Susanna & Shaun Parsons, Winstone Glebe, Winstone, nr Cirencester, Gloucestershire GL7 7JU.

This small Georgian rectory is set in 5 acres of gardens and paddocks, and overlooks a Saxon church in a Domesday-listed village. Traditionally and comfortably furnished, it has spectacular views in an Area of Outstanding Natural Beauty, and is very quiet. Susanna trained as a professional cook, and it shows in her delicious dinners (£16, licensed). There are many good local walks, well-signed, if you have the energy after garden visiting. Three pleasant double/twin bedrooms, and dogs, children and smoking are all taken in good spirit. B&B £28.

B 23 HIGH ST   Tel 01793 750205

Patti & Robin Shield, 23 High St, Cricklade, Wiltshire SN6 6AP

Here is a classic Queen Anne town house, still with its gleaming flagstone floor and original ornate oak staircase. Superbly furnished with antiques (where Robin has a professional interest), it inspired one visitor to write: 'You feel you have stepped back 250 years'. In the centre of Cricklade, a market town since 1257, it has a walled garden behind, full of old urns, pots and statuary. There is also a kitchen garden whose produce is used for evening meals (£16, with wine) cooked by Patti, qualified Cordon Bleu. Two lovely double/twin bedrooms, restricted smoking, no dogs, children welcome. B&B £26.

C HAMPTON FIELDS   Tel 01285 850070

Jill & Richard Barry, Hampton Fields, Meysey Hampton, nr Cirencester, Gloucestershire GL7 5JL

This converted 19th-century barn has stunning views looking over beautiful open countryside, with horses grazing in the paddocks. When Richard and Jill bought the property in 1991, they immediately began to create a garden from a wilderness, planting hedges and specimen trees to enclose the boundaries. Trees, shrubs and roses are their main passion, but currently their energies are devoted to making a sunken garden at the back of the house, with an orchard beyond. Two double bedrooms and 1 single. B&B only, but there are many good places to eat out locally in the evenings. No smoking, and no dogs because of their own three springer spaniels. B&B £25–£28.

D 2 COVE HOUSE   Tel 01285 861221

Major & Mrs Peter Hartland, 2 Cove House, Ashton Keynes, nr Swindon, Wiltshire SN6 6NS.

Peter and Elizabeth live in the original half of a 17th-century manor house, its large rooms filled with Elizabeth's floral arrangements. The garden is occasionally open to the public, but guests can enjoy the well-kept lawns and borders on their own. Three double bedrooms, each with its own character. Dinner by arrangement (£18, bring your own wine) is usually taken *en famille*. Well-trained dogs and children welcome. Smoking discouraged. B&B £23–£25.

E SHAWSWELL COUNTRY HOUSE   Tel 01285 831779

Muriel & David Gomm, Shawswell Country House, Rendcomb, nr Cirencester, Gloucestershire GL7 7HD.

Muriel spends every spare moment gardening in this idyllic hillside spot overlooking the Churn valley. There are colourful borders, a vine-covered pergola, lovely lawns and many more gardening delights around this 17th-century creeper-clad house. Some garden-visiting guests spend a whole day wandering around the 25 acres of grounds. The 5 bedrooms (including 1 single) are all en suite, and beautifully furnished. Muriel has drawn up a guide of recommended places to eat out in the evenings, some only a few minutes' drive away. Restricted smoking, children and dogs by arrangement. B&B £23.

What Else to Enjoy

This is a short selection of the many good things recommended in the area by owners of places to stay. Your hosts will certainly be able to provide additional information.

Other Gardens/Nurseries

Just to the E of Stroud on the A419 is the village of **Chalford**. There is a memorable nursery here – **Crowcombe Farm Herbs**, in Gypsy Lane (Tel 01285 760544). It sells all the herbs you could ever want, specialises in wild flowers and is home of the Seed Bank and Exchange scheme.

If It's Wet

No great stately homes here, but plenty else. Head for **Cirencester**, called *Corinium* when it was at the heart of Roman Britain. The museum, in Park St, has one of the finest collections of Roman antiquities in the country. The parish church in the market square is a 13th-century spectacular, with a unique 3-storeyed vaulted porch of great beauty. The town also has great food shops, an open market, a good delicatessen and expensive clothes shops. It is easy to spend a whole pleasant day here.

For musical fun, one of my favourite places anywhere is Keith Harding's World of Mechanical Music in **Northleach**, about 1m off the NE edge of the visit map on the A429. It is a tiny, award-winning museum of rare clocks, musical boxes, automata and mechanical instruments, introduced and played for you in a lively (and scholarly) continuous entertainment that lasts about an hour.

Eating Out

In **Tetbury**, fans of Jilly Cooper's novels might want to lunch in the **Snooty Fox**, said to be the real-life setting for many of her fictional horsey affairs. Tel 01666 502436. **Calcot Manor**, just off the A4135 at **Beverston**, 4m W of Tetbury, is a major country house hotel with a major chef, Edward Portlock. The surroundings are grand, and it will be an evening out to remember. There is a set menu for dinner at £26 – but realistically, you are likely to finish up paying nearer £40 when you add the wine and service. Tel 01666 890391.

Around Oxford

To the north and west of Oxford, the villages are built with honey-coloured Cotswold stone, seen at its best in the Windrush valley which is steep and scenic. Burford is a ravishing town on a hill, with good shopping. South of Oxford, the Thames valley flattens out into lush water meadows, with grand house-boats and boat-houses along the river's banks. Haydn loved Oxford, especially the college quadrangles and gardens which you can visit today. He was honoured by the University which gave him a doctorate in music – so why not listen to his Oxford Symphony, No. 92 in G. If you visit Oxford, you will find good Park and Ride facilities on the outskirts. They are well worth using.

OS maps: Landrangers 163, **164**

Gardens

Opening times: in larger gardens, and in NT properties, last admissions are usually 30–45 minutes before the garden closes. Admission charges are a guide to what one adult can expect to pay to go round the garden. It sometimes varies with the season or days of the week. When the house is also open to the public, there is usually an additional charge.

| I | **FARINGDON HOUSE** | Faringdon | Tel 01367 240240 |

By appointment, and 1 charity Sun in April. £1
Next to the church in the centre of Faringdon.

Here you will find a large garden with a park behind, offering fine views across the county, and some pleasant garden features which include rose borders, a peony border, a marvellous fruit walk between two high sheltering walls, a great autumn border, and masses of bulbs in the spring. The owner, Dr Zinovieff, had a grandfather with a charmingly naughty sense of humour. He introduced amazing-coloured fantail doves, built the folly on the hill, and put a bust of fruity-looking old General Havelock in the middle of the pool by the Orangery.

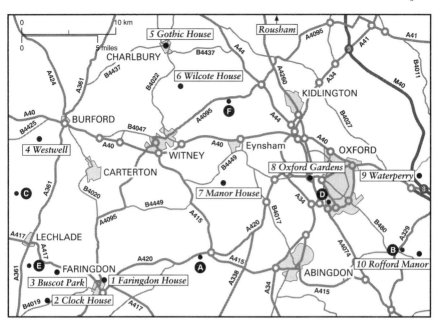

2   CLOCK HOUSE   Coleshill, nr Swindon   Tel 01793 762476

Thurs, May to Sept, 2–6, and 3 charity Suns. £1.50
From Faringdon, go SW on B4019 for 3½m. Garden is at far end of Coleshill.

There is plenty of interest in this artistic garden, with far-reaching views over the Vale of the White Horse. It has been created on the ground-plan of the original Coleshill House, burned down and demolished earlier this century. Intriguingly, the outline of the old house has been planted in box. An avenue of lime trees takes one's eye out to the hills beyond. In the sunny walled garden of the old laundry-yard roses scent the air and the green-house is filled with goodies. Plants in pots, all carefully tended by Mrs Denny Wickham, are set against warm walls.

3   BUSCOT PARK (NT)   nr Faringdon   Tel 01367 240786

Mon–Fri, and 2nd/4th weekends in month, April to Sept, 2–6. £3
From Faringdon go W on A417 for 3m. Garden well signed on L.

A dramatic feature here is the water garden, designed by Harold Peto in 1912. Water tumbles over rocks and rills into pools, under bridges, and finally reaches a lake. There are magnificent flower borders, too, planted by the late Peter Coats with a masterly eye for colour. Three allées, of lime and beech, fan out from the terrace, with prostrate junipers as the focal point at the end of each. Also enjoy an Egyptian Avenue with crouching sphinxes and graceful statues.

4   WESTWELL MANOR   nr Burford   Tel 01713 712718

Open occasional Suns in early summer for charity, 2–6.30. £1.50
From Burford go W on A40 for ½ m. Turn L down minor rd signed to Westwell.

Westwell Manor is one of my most favourite gardens anywhere, and although it is seldom open I must write about it. This year, I shall be along with everyone else to see the shrub roses, the wisteria pergola dripping with flowers, the peonies and the iris. Mrs Gibson is a garden designer, and has done wonders with this charming old Cotswold site. Up the hill from the house, opposite the decorative kitchen garden, is a gentle garden to be viewed in private by moonlight – a magical and romantic place.

5   GOTHIC HOUSE   Charlbury   Tel 01608 810654

Charity Suns in May and Sept, 2–6. £1.50 includes Priory Garden in same village.
In centre of Charlbury village, next to the Bell Inn.

Here is another house seldom open but which has to be visited if you are in the area at the time. Gothic House is the home of Andrew Lawson, one of Britain's best garden photographers, and his sculptress wife Briony. They have made brilliantly imaginative use of their smallish walled garden, with clever perspectives and tricks to draw the eye and enchant one. Sculptures and *trompe-l'oeils* are added delicious distractions from the design concepts of a man who truly knows his plants. Pots full of beautiful rarities fill the Gothic conservatory and are exquisitely placed on the terrace by the kitchen. (The Bell Inn is a good pub for lunch while you wait for the garden to open.)

6   WILCOTE HOUSE   nr Charlbury   Tel 01993 868606

Charity Suns in April/May and Oct, 2–5.30, and by appointment weekdays with the head gardener, Mr Pollard.
From Witney go N on B4022 for 4½m. Turn R through Finstock village. Garden is signed immediately on L.

Here are 7 acres of rolling parkland surrounding a fine old Cotswold stone house. There are all the features one would normally expect in a garden of this kind: splendid mixed borders, masses of lovely old shrub roses, and a laburnum tunnel. For me, the most pleasurable part is a new arboretum planted in an old orchard and criss-crossed by grass paths. There is a a tremendous variety of beautiful and interesting trees, which are under-planted with spring bulbs and are equally glorious in autumn.

7   THE MANOR HOUSE   Stanton Harcourt   Tel 01865 881930

Usually 2nd and 4th Tues of the month, and some charity Suns, April to Sept, 2–5. £1.50
From Witney go S on A415 for 2m. Turn L onto B4449 for 2m; garden in centre of Stanton Harcourt.

This picturesque stone manor house, the home of Mr Crispin and the Hon Mrs Gascoigne, has large formal and woodland gardens around it. A moat and medieval stew ponds are crossed by charming old rustic bridges. Clipped yews lead across the lawns to a chapel, and the old walls are draped with many roses, clematis and climbing hydrangeas. There are formal rosebeds and, in the walled kitchen garden, is a splendid collection of David Austin's new English roses alongside old and new espaliered apple trees. Unmissable are the scrummy teas, with big chocolate cakes, served in the historic Great Kitchen, with a shuttered roof designed to let out smoke and heat.

8   OXFORD GARDENS

Use local town maps to find your way from college to college.

You could easily spend a day wandering around Oxford's college gardens. However, I can't give you guaranteed opening times. Most can be readily visited during the long summer vacation, but even during this period, some colleges close unpredictably. It's so enjoyable wandering around Oxford that it's perhaps best to call in at the porter's lodge in each college, and ask.

New College is reliably open, and sometimes carries an admission fee of £1. It has absolutely brilliant wide borders, which have a new look each season with re-planting carried out by the Master of the Garden, Robin Lane Fox. You can see some of his best planting ideas here, backed by

climbers that grow high up the old city walls. An ancient Mound is also a
feature of this garden.

St John's College. You go through two quadrangles to reach this
garden, and it's difficult to believe that something so expansive and tranquil could exist just a couple of minutes away from a busy city centre. A
huge lawn is framed mainly by copper beeches, but with much else in the
way of foliage contrast. All around are smaller gardens backing on to old
walls covered with wisteria and other climbers.

Wadham College has good herbaceous borders and many old trees –
ginko, magnolia and limes. A scented white garden is in a courtyard.

Worcester College garden also amazes by its sheer scale. It is sub-
stantially landscaped with fine trees, and leads to a lake with the Oxford
Canal running behind it. The Provost's Garden, which has an old rose
garden and a charming orchard, is also sometimes open.

A few minutes walk to the N up the Banbury Rd, **St Hugh's College**
has no less than 10 acres of gardens with spectacular trees, shrubs, borders
and a dell garden.

Other gardens worth calling in on, if you have the time, are at
Somerville, Balliol, St Catherine's and Corpus Christi.

Try not to miss the marvellous **Botanic Gardens** which are Britain's
oldest, founded in 1621. Enormously high walls provide shelter to tender
climbing plants, including the best ceanothus I have ever seen, plus *Cytisus
battandieri* and wonderful climbing roses. Magnificent old trees spread their
branches over extensive lawns. Botanical beds of clearly-labelled plants are
very instructive. There is a huge collection of euphorbias, and excellent
greenhouses with tropical plants.

Finally in Oxford, there is the extraordinary **23 Beech Croft Road.** By
contrast to the grand-scale gardens above, here is a small jewel box started
by Mrs Dexter at the back of her house 40 years ago. She broke up concrete with her coal hammer, and laid stone walls to raise up the beds each
side of the narrow stone path that leads down the garden. How can she
manage to grow so many thousands of choice plants in so tiny a space? She
pushes them upwards – the colours now hanging like two richly-embroi-
dered tapestries, many-layered, always fascinating, from tiny choice alpines
nestling in the stones, to clematis, roses, honeysuckles and hydrangeas
swarming up the flowering shrubs. In the spring, ferns, fritillaries, hostas
and hellebores delight, with bulbs, under a *Clerodendrum fargesii*. Orchids
have come from her childhood home in Cumbria. A few well-chosen trees
supply background foliage colour. More than 70 clematis, as well as dozens

of climbing roses, ramp through this inspirational garden where no inch of space is wasted. Even the top of her coal bunker has been turned into a miniature roof garden. Phone Mrs Dexter on 01865 556020 for an appointment between April and September.

9   WATERPERRY GARDENS

nr Wheatley   Tel 01844 339226

Daily, all year, 10–5.30 (4.30 in winter). £2.30
From Oxford, go SE on A40 for 4m. Turn L briefly onto A418, and follow signs on minor roads via Wheatley,

Waterperry, widely signed in the area, started out as Miss Havergal's horticultural school 60 years ago, and is now primarily a large garden centre selling excellent and often rare plants. Some features of the old garden remain – borders, lawns and fine trees. You can find large collections of dwarf conifers, and excellent fruit bushes of anything you fancy munching.

10 ROFFORD MANOR   Little Milton

1 charity afternoon in Sept, and by written appointment. £2
From A4142 Oxford ring road go SE on B480 for 4m. In Stadhampton turn L and R and continue on B480 for 1½ m. Turn L onto minor road for 1m, then sharp R at sign 'Rofford only'.

This splendid garden, started from scratch twelve years ago by Hilary and Jeremy Mogford, has now matured into something very special. Yew hedges, tall, fat pleached limes past their adolescent stage, and the medlar walk look as if they have always been there. The box garden, with a square lily pool and trickles of water, now has 'dreaming spires' of box clipped to perfection. The new cottage garden is well established, with hot colours of purples and reds planted in gravel for a Mediterranean feel, while clematis and Virginia creeper cover the walls. The kitchen garden has a central arbour in the shape of a crown, covered with carefully pruned apples and pear trees. Low-trained step-over apple trees line the paths, and standard apple trees look perfect in large terracotta pots. Sweet peas entwined in wigwams provide white and purple. Veggies are immaculate. The swimming pool garden is one of the prettiest I have seen, its walls swagged with roses and purple clematis, with butterflies all over the buddleias. At the back of the house, the herb garden has central beds of roses – gallicas and Maiden's Blush – lined with santolina and catmint. All-white roses are in the rose garden, where the grey-flagged terrace is planted with thyme cushions.

From here you view the twin herbaceous borders, backed by clipped yew.Your eye carries on over the ha-ha to fields and woods beyond. Work is in progress to make two lakes and a woodland walk. The postal address for a written appointment is Rofford Manor, Little Milton, Oxfordshire OX44 7QQ

Where to Stay

All B&B prices are approximate per person, sharing a double/twin room usually with private or en suite facilities. It is a good idea to ask for any special requirements when booking.

A FALLOWFIELDS   Tel 01865 820416

Peta & Anthony Lloyd, Fallowfields, Kingston Bagpuize with Southmoor, nr Abingdon, Oxfordshire OX13 5BH.

Two acres of lawns, with fine specimen trees including *Sequoia wellingtonia*, a blue cedar and many oaks stretch south from this luxurious early Victorian Gothic house once owned by the Begum Aga Khan. Vegetable gardeners will drool over the 1-acre kitchen garden, half of it walled, which grows virtually all that is needed for Peta's lavish Aga-cooked dinners (5 courses, £23.50, including home-baked bread, licensed). There is a small heated swimming pool. Inside the house are treasured antiques, and the 3 bedrooms include a four-poster. No smoking, dogs welcome, children should be 10 or over. B&B £37–£40.

B STADHAMPTON MANOR   Tel 01865 891999

Anthea & Steven Savage, The Manor, Stadhampton, Oxfordshire OX44 7UL.

This peaceful 17th-century Cotswold stone manor, with mullioned windows, is approached across a village green with a pond. In the garden, a large lawn broken up by apple trees is bordered by a mature Wellingtonia, a vast copper beech and a south-facing mellow brick wall which backs a shrub and herbaceous border. In what used to be a Victorian vine house is a swimming pool. The house, with its oak floors, antiques and vast open fireplace in the drawing-room, is both elegant and ancient. Upstairs, the 2 spacious guest bedrooms overlook the garden. Anthea serves evening meals for parties of 4 (£22, bring your own wine), but guests are encouraged to eat out at the many excellent pubs and restaurants locally. No smoking, no dogs, well-behaved children welcome. B&B £30.

C KINGS HAY   Tel 01367 850239

Susie & Charles Hyde-Smith, Kings Hay, Eastleach Martin, nr Cirencester, Gloucestershire GL7 3NW.

Wide open vistas, with lawns and gardens stretching into the surrounding countryside, are a feature of this large stone house, wonderfully secluded on the edge of one of the Cotswolds' prettiest villages, renowned for two historic churches and a daffodil display in spring. Susie and Charles love entertaining friends, family and new guests, and are encyclopædic with local knowledge. There are 2 large guest bedrooms. Evening meals, licensed, cost £18.50. No smoking, dogs by arrangement, children welcome. B&B £27–£30.

D WOOTTEN HOUSE   Tel 01865 715594

Anne & Mark Phythian-Adams, Wootten House, Iffley Village, Oxford OX4 4DS.

Iffley Village is only 2m from the centre of Oxford (on the map it looks to be part of the city itself), but has managed to keep its rural atmosphere, with stone walls, thatched houses, a pub, and a marvellous 12th-century church. You can walk to the centre of Oxford along a canal towpath (and take a taxi back). Wootten House, partly 18th century, is a substantial and spacious home with a relaxed feel, set in 2 acres of mature garden with high stone walls and many trees. There are 2 guest bedrooms, and dinner (bring your own wine) costs £18. No smoking, dogs by arrangement, children welcome. B&B £25–£27.

E WESTON FARM   Tel 01367 252222

Jean Woof, Weston Farm, Buscot Wick, nr Faringdon, Oxfordshire SN7 8DJ.

This large 17th-century stone farmhouse is warm, comfortable and peaceful. Surrounded by its own 500-acre mixed farm, the garden is well-stocked and colourful, with climbers over the walls of the house, though it is not, says Jean, weed-free. Guests have their own dining- and sitting- rooms with log fires. Thick walls and two flights of stairs mean that you are never disturbed by what is going on in other parts of the house. The 2 double/ twin bedrooms, 1 a four-poster, have TV. No dogs, no smoking, children should be over 10. B&B £20.

F   THE OLD FARMHOUSE   Tel 01993 882097

Vanessa Maundrell, The Old Farmhouse, Station Hill, Long Hanborough, nr Oxford OX8 8JZ.

Beams, flagstone floors and an inglenook fireplace greet you at this low-built 17th-century farmhouse not far from Oxford. Outside, the garden is small but packed with goodies. In one-third of an acre, Vanessa has over-flowing herbaceous borders with old-fashioned cottage plants. She is a mine of local knowledge, constantly up-dating her computer file of lesser-known places to eat, and secluded round-trip walks or car drives to keep guests happily occupied. There are 2 guest double/twin bedrooms, one en suite. No smoking, no dogs, children should be over 12. B&B £19–£22.

What Else to Enjoy

This is a short selection of the many good things recommended in the area by owners of places to stay. Your hosts will certainly be able to provide additional information.

Other Gardens

About 10m N of Oxford, signed to the R of the A4260 Banbury Rd, is an enchanting large garden at **Rousham House** (Tel 01869 347110). Open Weds, Suns and BHs, April to Sept, 2–4, it is famous for the exquisite land-scaping by William Kent. The grounds slope down to the River Cherwell, and there are splendid statues, urns, follies, magnificent trees and *allées*. There are good borders, a rose garden, veggie plot and a pretty parterre. Mr and Mrs Charles Cottrell-Dormer are delighted if you want to take your picnic into the garden, but not your children.

If It's Wet

Blenheim Palace is vast and grandiose – one of those places you think you should come away admiring, but somehow leaves only impersonal memories. Except for the the Long Library, that is. This outstandingly beautiful room, 183 ft long, has some 10,000 books and a magnificent organ. Musical evenings here are magical. Otherwise, the house is more or less the biggest this and the hugest that. Designed by John Vanbrugh, and built by the nation for the 1st Duke of Marlborough in recognition of his victory over the French at the battle of Blenheim, you will get a month's exercise walking round the interior. The park, covering 2,100 acres, was laid out by Capability Brown (one of his better efforts). The formal gardens, too, are on a vast scale and include the Marlborough Maze which is, of course, the world's largest. Go and have your breath taken away. Open daily from mid March to October, 10.30–5.30. Tel 01993 811325.

On another damp day, head for **Oxford**. The best way to have a first look at the colleges is to take a gentle conducted tour, lasting about 2 hours, starting from the Tourist Information Office at the centre of the city in Gloucester Green. You can pick up details here, too, of the many museums and galleries, all outstanding. The Ashmolean, founded in 1683, is the oldest public museum in Britain. The Covered Market is a joy for shopping – wonderful food stalls and specialised shops. In the nearby streets, antiquarian bookshops abound.

Elsewhere, if you have time to explore just one Cotswold town, choose **Burford**. You can shop, gaze, dawdle, have lunch or tea and go to the charming little Tolsey Museum which has one of the best doll's houses you will ever see.

Eating Out

As a rest after going to Blenheim Palace, try **The Feathers** in **Woodstock**, the pretty little town at Blenheim's entrance gates. This timbered hotel is an architectural delight, and I have never been let down by the food which you can eat at the bar, in a courtyard or in the restaurant. It might cost you £25 or £60, depending on your mood. Tel 01993 812291.

If you want the best – perhaps the best in England – then you have to go to **Le Manoir aux Quat' Saisons** in **Great Milton**, S of Oxford (Tel 01844 278847). You must know its reputation so well that I don't need to encourage you. It's possible to eat at a (sort of) modest price at lunchtime – there is a set menu at £29.50. But really, don't count the cost, and hope someone else is paying. I remember every mouthful I've eaten there.

Fortunately, Raymond Blanc has also opened a wonderful brasserie in **Oxford** for those of us with lighter purses. **Le Petit Blanc** in Walton Street is small, light and airy (designed by Terence Conran), and became immediately popular when it opened in 1996. The food, served from 11 a.m. to 11 p.m., is constantly inventive (some recipes deriving from Maman Blanc), with main courses typically costing £7–£10. You can eat lavishly without getting fat and drink pleasant wine for no more than £25 per head. Tel 01865 510999.

Banbury Cross

This is my home stamping-ground, and I know and love every lane, hill and wood. The west is full of warm Hornton-stone villages, some thatched and some tiled with old grey Stonesfield slates. Once you get away from Banbury it is totally rural. I left my front door open one day, and a flock of sheep wandered in. Central to many tourist attractions – Oxford, Blenheim, Stratford-upon-Avon – it is popular with a large number of visitors. Favourite music in my car at the moment is Schumann's Fantasiestücke, Opus 12, played by Alfred Brendel. Oh, if only I could play it like that.

OS maps: Landrangers **151**, 152

Gardens

Opening times: in larger gardens, and in NT properties, last admissions are usually 30–45 minutes before the garden closes. Admission charges are a guide to what one adult can expect to pay to go round the garden. It sometimes varies with the season or days of the week. When the house is also open to the public, there is usually an additional charge.

I   **BROUGHTON CASTLE**   nr Banbury   Tel 01295 262624

Weds, Suns and BHs, mid May to mid Sept, (also Thurs, July/Aug), 2–5. £3.50 (includes house).
From Banbury go SW on B4035 for 2m. Garden signed on R.

This romantic moated castle has been in Lord Saye and Sele's family since 1451. It feels like (and is) a genuine home, not a great showplace. The gardens here have a perfect setting in gentle, sloping parkland where you are free to walk at any time. The Ladies Garden was laid out around 1890, and the fleur-de-lys pattern has not changed since (its shape looks wonderful if you climb to the top of the tower and look down on it). Lanning Roper advised on the gardens in 1969, and wisely suggested eliminating some fussy

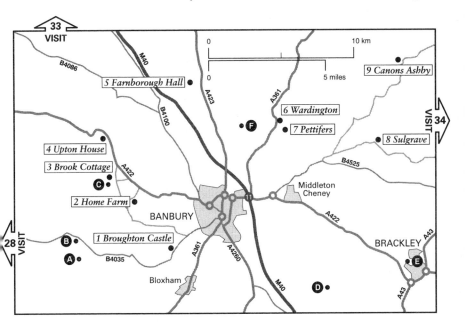

details. Shrub roses, honeysuckles, ceanothus and clematis festoon the centuries-old walls. The west-facing border is particularly splendid, with wide drifts of bold colours, starting in blues and yellows with purples, changing to reds, pinks and whites. Here is a brilliant garden, and a very personal one.

2 HOME FARM Balscote, nr Banbury   Tel 01295 738194

By appointment, April to Oct. £1.50
From Banbury go NW on A422 for 4m. Turn L on minor road where signed
to Balscote village. After ½m, garden signed on L.

There is plenty of interest, colour and rare plants in this sophisticated cottage garden, set on various levels behind a 17th-century house and barn. Mr and Mrs Royle found it as a farmyard, and have totally transformed it into a much-photographed garden of distinction. Contrasting foliage, flowering shrubs, roses, lilies, heathers, alpines and bulbs all ensure there is never a dull minute here. The views over farmland are tranquil.

3 BROOK COTTAGE

Alkerton, nr Banbury   Tel 01295 670303

Mon–Fri, April to Oct, 9–6, by appointment. £2.50
From Banbury go NW on A422 for 4½m. Turn L where signed on minor road
to Alkerton village. After ½m, turn L at war memorial into Well Lane, and
then fork R .

Gardening on a sloping site isn't easy, but Mr and Mrs Hodges have made a wonderful garden here, planting masses of old-fashioned shrub roses on the steeper parts, and using the springs on the hillside to great advantage. The landscaping has been designed to link the level areas of lawn and terrace with the natural slopes. Clumps of *Alchemilla mollis* and hostas soften the steps and stonework. The garden merges into the surrounding hilly countryside, with a lake fringed by irises and bog plants. Behind the house is a vegetable and cut-flower garden, so that it always has something to offer. Marvellous clematis scramble up arches, trees and hedges, and cleverly hide the tennis court. A curved copper beech hedge and some fine ornamental trees are noteworthy, as are the borders, one of which is white and silver, packed with unusual plants. Many of the most interesting plants are for sale.

4 UPTON HOUSE (NT)

Edgehill, nr Banbury   Tel 01295 670266

Sat–Wed, April to Oct, 2–6. £2.40
From Banbury go NW on A422 for 7m. Garden well signed on L.

Near the top of an escarpment with heady views towards Warwickshire, the garden is notable for some of the finest terracing in Britain. A long flight of stone steps beside the wide terraces leads to a lake and water garden stocked with ornamental fish. A sloping kitchen garden covering more than an acre is carefully maintained. Also worth seeing are the herbaceous borders and the National Collection of asters.

5 FARNBOROUGH HALL (NT)

Farnborough   Tel 01295 690202

Weds and Sats, April to Sept, 2–6. £1.50
From Banbury go N on A423 for 5m. Garden well signed on L.

For 300 years, Farnborough Hall has been the home of the Holbech family, who still occupy and administer it today. The design, including some well-placed temples, dates back to the 1750s, and is regarded by garden historians as the forerunner of the great landscaped parks later that century. The most original feature is an S-shaped terrace walk nearly a mile long, originally built to connect two family-owned properties (this is open on Thurs and Fri, admission £1, in addition to openings for the house and grounds as a whole).

6 WARDINGTON MANOR
Wardington, nr Banbury   Tel 01295 750202

Charity days in late May, and by appointment (groups preferred). £2
From Banbury go NE on A361 for 5m. Take sign R for Wardington. Garden in centre of village.

This is a beautifully maintained 4-acre garden with something to offer all gardening enthusiasts. In front of the wisteria-covered manor house, chic topiary birds are planted in impeccable lawns surrounded by clipped yew hedges, shrub borders and sheltering walls clothed in climbing plants. Behind the house, the ground slopes to an ornamental lake, with a pretty boathouse. The walk is through flowering shrubs, with lovely magnolias in late spring which is when Lord and Lady Wardington think their garden is at its best.

7 PETTIFERS Wardington, nr Banbury   Tel 01295 750232

Charity days May–July, and by appointment. £2
From Banbury, go NE on A361 for 5m. Take sign R for Wardington. Garden near church.

A stunning pastoral view over fields dotted with sheep, with fine old trees, dominates this garden – but look at the herbaceous border! Mrs Price strives to achieve here the prettiest plants so that they combine well with each other. A perfectionist, she is forever moving them around. Very good foliage plants give colour and interest throughout all seasons. Many unusual plants are here too, and you can borrow a helpful map and plant list to identify them. Beautifully laid brick paths, and good maintenance everywhere make visiting an added pleasúre. The herb garden, the green and white shrub border and the old rose borders are now maturing well.

8 SULGRAVE MANOR Sulgrave, nr Banbury
Tel 01295 760205

Daily except Weds, April to Sept, 10.30–5.30; Oct, 10.30–4; (closed 1–2).
£3.50 includes house
From Banbury go E over M40 on A422 for ½m. At roundabout, turn L on
B4525 for 1½m. Turn L onto minor road for 1½m to Thorpe Mandeville and
follow signs to garden.

Much-loved by Americans (it is endowed by the awesome-sounding
Colonial Dames of America), this is the ancestral home of George Washington, built in 1539. The gardens are formal, with lawns decorated by
flirty topiary birds, and there are flower borders set around the house. The
herb garden and rose garden help to give a 16th-century air to the charming old house.

9 CANONS ASHBY (NT) nr Daventry Tel 01327 860044

Sat–Wed, April to Sept, 1–5.30 or dusk. £3.40 includes house.
From Banbury go E over M40 on A422 for ½m. At roundabout, turn L on
B4525 for 1½m. Turn L on minor rd through Thorpe Mandeville for 6m. Car
park signed on L, 200 yds from garden.

The National Trust has been carefully restoring this formal garden, which
retains many of the features and plantings from its original design in the
early 18th century. The Green Court has splendid stone walls and gate
posts, clipped yews, and a statue by John Van Nost. A great cedar tree towers over the gardens, and old varieties of apple, pear and plum trees and
soft fruit have been planted.

Where to Stay

All B&B prices are approximate per person, sharing a double/twin room usually with private
or en suite facilities. It is a good idea to ask for any special requirements when booking.

A GOWER'S CLOSE Tel 01295 780348

Judith Hitching, Gower's Close, Sibford Gower, nr Banbury, Oxfordshire
OX15 5RW.

Here is where I live. It is an intriguing small 17th-century house, thatched
and beamed, set in a sleepy Cotswold village. My cottage garden, which I

began to re-awaken a couple of years ago, is coming along nicely. You must know from this book what sort of plants I like to grow – softly coloured treasures, climbers over a pergola, herbs in a parterre, old roses. You can expect good food, music, books, conversation, laughter, log fires and a very personal, informal atmosphere. There are 2 pretty double/twin guest bedrooms. I don't have time to do evening meals every night. They cost £20, wine to be discussed. There is a great village pub with a restaurant around the corner. No dogs, and it's not practical to bring young children. Strictly no smoking in bedrooms. B&B £25.

B HANDYWATER FARM   Tel 01295 780660

Sue Colquhoun, Handywater Farm, Sibford Gower, nr Banbury, Oxfordshire OX15 5AE.

Sue's 17th-century farmhouse has glorious views over the rolling country-side here. She is a very good gardener, and her lawns, with well-stocked borders alongside, slope via a stream seamlessly into the fields beyond. She has converted stables and outbuildings into self-contained suites sleeping 4-5 people; here you can cook your meals, or go out locally in the evenings. You can have breakfast with Sue in her house. It's best to discuss all the different possibilities with her. Restricted smoking, dogs and children by arrangement. B&B £25.

C MILL HOUSE   Tel 01295 670642

Maggie Hainsworth, Mill House, Shenington, nr Banbury, Oxfordshire OX15 6NH.

I can guarantee that you will find good company here with my friend Maggie and her jovial husband Keith. They have a fine stone farmhouse dating from 1650, set on the southern side of an exceptionally beautiful village, with spectacular views. It is meticulously restored, and is very com-fortable with traditional antiques everywhere. Keith may well challenge you to a game of snooker. 2 bedrooms. Several good places to eat out in the evenings, and sometimes Maggie does dinner. No dogs, children should be over 8, restricted smoking. B&B £25.

D HOME FARMHOUSE   Tel 01295 811683

Rosemary Grove-White, Home Farmhouse, Charlton, nr Banbury, Oxfordshire OX17 3DR.

This area is packed with tempting old Hornton-stone houses, with their slate roofs and climber-clad walls. Few are more attractive than Rosemary's which dates back at least 400 years, and has fascinating inglenooks, exposed beams and oak staircases. The courtyard is ablaze in summer with roses, clematis and begonias. Rosemary was an interior designer, and all her skills show in the comfort which the house offers. Two double bedrooms and 1 single. Dinner is £17.50 (bring your own wine). No smoking, dogs by arrangement, children should be over 10. B&B £23–£26.

E WALLTREE HOUSE   Tel 01295 811235

Pauline & Richard Harrison, Walltree House, Steane, Brackley, Northamptonshire NN13 5NS.

This splendid Victorian farmhouse is set in spacious grounds at the end of a long farm, with a pond, woodland walks and a private airfield. Pauline and Richard have done a great conversion job here, finding room in the house and courtyard buildings for 6 bedrooms that are comfortable and well-equipped. Usually you eat out in the evenings at one of the many local pubs. Dogs by arrangement, children welcome, smoking allowed. B&B £20–£28.

F THE OLD MANOR   Tel 01295 750235

John & Liz Atkins, The Old Manor, Cropredy, nr Banbury, Oxfordshire OX17 1PS.

Many of the guests who come here go garden-visiting in the area, attracted by the Old Manor, its Dovehouse Barn, and its own 2 acres of garden bounded by a medieval moat full of huge carp. The garden has been developed over the past 12 years or so from a reclaimed field, and has plenty of herbaceous beds, shrubs, a rose garden, orchard and spinneys. It is nice to know that wheelchair users can enjoy themselves here since the garden is on one level. The Barn, self-catering, is all at ground level too. Three double/twin bedrooms (one sharing a bathroom). Eat out locally in the evenings. Restricted smoking, dogs and children by arrangement. B&B £20–£24.

What Else to Enjoy

This is a short selection of the many good things recommended in the area by owners of places to stay. Your hosts will certainly be able to provide additional information.

If It's Wet

Upton House (*see* Garden 4) contains outstanding collections made in this century by the 2nd Lord Bearsted. There are fine Old Masters, tapestries and furniture, but the great joy is the porcelain and china. Open as garden. **Canons Ashby** (*see* Garden 9) has been the home of the Dryden family since the 16th century. The house dates from then, and although it was altered somewhat during the next 150 years, it has hardly been touched since 1710. The interior is, not to exaggerate, marvellous. There is wonderful panelling, Elizabethan wall-paintings and outstanding Jacobean plasterwork in wonderfully proportioned rooms that exude history. Open as garden.

If you want to potter about and shop, don't expect too much of **Banbury**, the main town in the area. The nursery rhyme cross is now a Victorian monument, its pagan origins long destroyed. Banbury cakes are a delicacy for the very sweet-toothed; buy them at R.S. Malcolm, 41 High Street. There is a picturesque market in the main square on Thursdays and Saturdays.

Or you might drive towards Chipping Norton, south-west from the corner of the visit map. On the way, visit Whichford Pottery, started from nothing 15 years ago by Jim Keeling, and now selling a range of magnificent terracotta garden urns internationally. Then take the back roads past the awe-inspiring prehistoric Rollright Stones. **Chipping Norton** itself has many antique shops, and one of the smallest theatres in Britain, with good live performances on most nights.

Eating Out

It may not be a meal you will remember for the rest of your life, but friends and I often go to the **Thai Orchid** in East Bar, **Banbury**, which serves generous helpings of authentically cooked food, and is inexpensive (about £18 per person). Book in advance – it is always busy. Tel 01295 270833.

North Cotswolds

Nearly all the gardens in this visit are built on hills and have outstanding views. They also include some of the best gardens in England: Hidcote, famous throughout the world; Kiftsgate, home of the monster prickly rose; and Sudeley, with a grim old history and brilliant new ideas. Cotswold brash isn't the easiest soil to manage because it dries out so quickly. Gardeners here have to mulch and enrich constantly. The tops of the Cotswolds have bitter winters and cruel winds. Despite these, here in the heart of England there is such a wealth of beautiful houses and gardens we should be listening to something very English: a tape of English choral music, sung by the Cambridge Singers and conducted by John Rutter – 'There is sweet music'.

OS maps: Landrangers **150**, 151, 163

Gardens

Opening times: in larger gardens, and in NT properties, last admissions are usually 30–45 minutes before the garden closes. Admission charges are a guide to what one adult can expect to pay to go round the garden. It sometimes varies with the season or days of the week. When the house is also open to the public, there is usually an additional charge.

I   SUDELEY CASTLE   Winchcombe   Tel 01242 602308

Daily, March to Oct, 10–5. £5.40

Going SE in Winchcombe on B4632, turn L onto minor road where signed; garden is ½m on R.

This historic 15th-century castle, once the home of Katherine Parr, is now a major tourist attraction, not the least reason being the superb garden. The sculptured yews in the Queen's Garden surround an excellent collection of shrub roses – indeed, Lady Ashcombe hopes her garden will become one of Britain's best rose gardens, and to this end has enlisted the help of Rose-

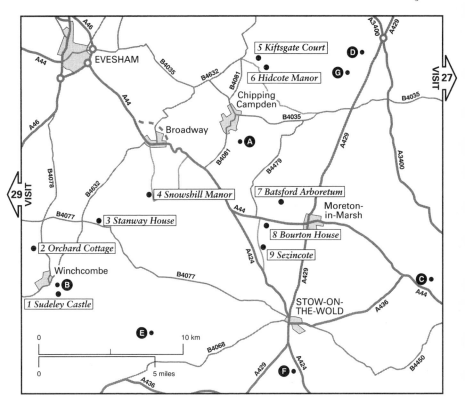

mary Verey and Jane Fearnley-Whittingstall. There are eight gardens in all, as well as manicured lawns and formal pools. Be sure not to miss the specialist nursery, which has good stock and many unusual plants on sale.

2 ORCHARD COTTAGE

Gretton, nr Winchcombe   Tel 01242 602491

All year, by appointment only to interested gardeners. £2
From Winchcombe go NW on B4078 for 100 yds. Follow minor rd signed on
L to Gretton village (1½m). Garden 300 yds on R in Duglinch Lane, next to
Bugatti Inn.

The garden here was made 50 years ago by Mrs Nancy Saunders, a great plant collector and intrepid traveller, with some help from her friend John Codrington. Her enthusiasm for rare plants lives on in her nephew Rory Stuart, who has continued to collect interesting plants from around the world. The lawns at the front of the cottage are bordered by hellebores, peonies, eryngiums, euphorbias and alliums. Behind them is the old orchard where lurks a collection of unusual shrubs and trees, including many different willows (one of them being Salix 'Nancy Saunders') and an intriguing elm with a variegated leaf. At the top of the orchard, there is a gothic tunnel of hazels leading to a remarkable view stretching over to the distant Malvern Hills. The orchard is under-planted with orchids, spring bulbs, fritillaries and white phlox to add a moonlight touch. Paul's Himalayan Musk has taken over the garage, and a Kiftsgate rose has enveloped an old perry pear. Behind the house are more borders of rare plants, and a very prickly wild gleditsia, planted from a seed which Rory brought back from Lesotho 12 years ago, and is now a substantial tree. A thyme seat is a fragrant place to sit and dream, and a medlar tree leans over the raised beds of vegetables, including asparagus.

3   STANWAY HOUSE   nr Winchcombe   Tel 01386 584469

Tues and Thurs, June to Sept, 2–5, and by appointment. £3.50
From Broadway go SW on B4632 for 5m. At Toddington roundabout, turn L on B4077 for 1m. Garden signed on L.

Stanway is an archetypical Cotswold village of mellow stone houses, (including a bakehouse which now serves good teas), a 14th-century tithe barn and a fine church. Stanway House remains, as it was when built in the early 18th century, the dominant feature of the village, with 20 acres of planted landscape and many fine trees. The current owner, Lord Neidpath, is starting to restore the original garden's most grandiose feature: a 185-yd-long waterfall (longer even than at Chatsworth), overlooked by a pyramid folly in which guests dined on summer evenings to watch the water cascading down. A new gardener is helping to renovate these romantic gardens with energy and flair.

4   SNOWSHILL MANOR (NT)
nr Broadway   Tel 01386 852410

Daily except Tues, April to Oct, 1–6. £5.20
From centre of Broadway go S for 2½m on minor road, following NT signs. Garden in centre of Snowshill.

Both house and garden reflect the rustic ideals of Charles Wade, the owner in the 1920s, who made this small terraced garden out of a wilderness, and

filled his house with a charming and eccentric collection of musical instruments, dolls, toys, craft tools, and much else. The garden is organically
grown, and owes much, on a smaller scale, to the Hidcote room concept.
The handcrafted garden furniture is coloured Wade blue, and much of the
planting, in blue, mauve, and purple, reflects this.

5 KIFTSGATE COURT

nr Chipping Campden   Tel 01386 438777

Wed/Thurs, Suns and BH Mons, April to Sept, 2–6; also Sats in Jun/July.
£3
From Chipping Campden go NW on B4081 for 1m. Turn R on minor road,
following NT signs to Hidcote (Garden 6) for 2½m. Kiftsgate is signed just N
of Hidcote.

Just below Hidcote (*see* Garden 6), and within easy walking distance, Kiftsgate Court offers a striking contrast in garden styles. Instead of Hidcote's
formality, Mr and Mrs Chambers are the third generation of a family
which over time has produced one of the most imaginative and sensitive
planting arrangements to be found anywhere. The spectacular siting, on
three levels facing south-west, has something of interest at all times of
the year, with a huge show of bulbs in the spring, and autumn colour
from many rare tree and shrub species. The garden is perhaps at its best in
June and July: this is when the multitude of roses bloom, and the borders
glow with colour variations that only supreme garden artists could have
achieved.

6 HIDCOTE MANOR GARDEN (NT)

nr Chipping Campden   Tel 01386 438333

Daily except Tues and Fri, April to Oct, 11–7; also Tues, June/July. £5.30
From Chipping Campden go NW on B4081 for 1m. Turn R on minor road,
following NT signs to Hidcote for 2½m.

This 10-acre garden was the extraordinary vision early this century of Major
Lawrence Johnston. He chose an apparently difficult, windy, isolated hilltop site, and turned it into one of Britain's best-known gardens. It is a must-
visit for every garden-lover at least once, despite the certainty that you will
never be on your own. He initiated and planted the now widely-used concept of garden rooms, self-contained gardens within gardens, protected by
high hedges, and with a surprise at every corner. I have visited it countless

times, and still find it wonderful. Good value restaurant, and a large NT shop.

7   BATSFORD ARBORETUM

nr Moreton-in-Marsh   Tel 01608 650722

Daily, March to early Nov, 10–5. £2.50
From Moreton-in-Marsh go W on A44 for 1½m. Turn R for ½m where signed.

If you want to stretch your legs, and buy some plants to take home, this is where you should come. The 50-acre arboretum and wild garden has more than 1,500 trees. It is spectacular in spring, with carpets of bulbs, followed by magnolias and cherries. In the autumn, you are overwhelmed by red and gold maples and sorbus. There is a fascinating collection of bronze statues and unusual shrubs brought back from Japan and other exotic eastern countries by Lord Redesdale. The nursery has the best stock for miles around. I often go there.

If you're lucky enough to be there (or at either of the nearby gardens 8 and 9) when **Abbotswood** is open, be sure to go there. It is only a couple of miles away, 1m W of Stow-on-the-Wold on B4077. It is a truly lovely garden, but only opens occasionally, on a few Sundays from April to June. At its best in spring, you approach by a walk beside a stream, planted with skunk cabbage, bulbs, primulas and masses of fritillaries. In the woods are magnolias, flowering shrubs and specimen trees, plus a large heather garden. The formal garden was laid out by Lutyens, and his lily pool is spectacular – as are the views. Tel 01451 830173 for opening times.

8   BOURTON HOUSE GARDEN   nr Moreton-in-Marsh

Thurs/Fri, end May to end Sept, 12–5. £3
From Moreton-in-Marsh go W on A44 for 2m. Garden signed on L.

Since moving to their beautiful 18th-century Cotswold village house in 1964, Mr and Mrs Richard Paice have designed this garden mostly on their own. Today, with marvellous views, it has well-kept lawns, fountains, a particularly good knot garden potager, and imaginatively planted borders set against stone walls. Each year there is something new to see, and everywhere the planting skills spark off ideas which can be carried back home. There is a 16th-century tithe barn where you can make your own teas, and where plants are for sale.

9   SEZINCOTE   nr Moreton-in-Marsh

Thurs/Fri and BH Mons, Jan to Nov, 2–6 or dusk. £3
From Moreton-in-Marsh go W on A44 for 2m. Garden is signed ½m on L.

A stone lodge with a white gate leads you up an avenue of holm oaks through a park that could only have been designed by Repton, and could not be more traditionally English. At the end, abruptly, the scene changes to that of India, with a country house built in the Moghul style, and fronted by formal Indian garden, fountains, a temple and huge trees. They give a fine backdrop and shelter to a profusion of exotic shrubs. A large orangery contains many tender plants. India and England in one place? It sounds a strange combination, but it works wonderfully.

Where to Stay

All B&B prices are approximate per person, sharing a double/twin room usually with private or en suite facilities. It is a good idea to ask for any special requirements when booking.

A   THE MALT HOUSE   Tel 01386 841334

Nick & Jean Brown, The Malt House, Broad Campden, nr Chipping Campden, Gloucestershire GL55 6UU.

This is at the top end in price of any accommodation in this guide, but it is beautifully situated for the visit, and very special. Nick and Jean have created, in their idyllic 17th-century Cotswold house, what feels like a year-round house party. Outside, there are 4 acres of wonderful gardens, open twice a year for the NGS, with a croquet lawn and a stream running through to old orchards. Inside, there are 7 superbly comfortable double/ twin bedrooms. Dinner, eaten round a large table with other guests, is cooked by the owners' son, John, who offers good choices on the £23.50 menu. Dogs and children welcome, restricted smoking. B&B £43.

B   WESTWARD   Tel 01242 604372

Susie & Jim Wilson, Westward, Sudeley Lodge, Winchcombe, Gloucestershire GL54 5JB.

This Georgian mansion, with its stately garden and wide sweeping lawns, has spectacular views over Sudeley Castle, and across the Cotswolds to the

Malvern Hills. It is surrounded by its own 550-acre farm. Susie and Jim have been taking in guests for a number of years now, she having been a professional cook after training at the Prue Leith school in London. An enthusiastic and widely-travelled couple, you can be sure of a warm welcome from them. The rooms are large, with 2 double bedrooms for guests. Evening meals cost £17.50, and there is a drinks licence. No smoking. Children over 10 and dogs welcome. B&B £29.

C RECTORY FARM   Tel 01608 643209

Nigel & Elizabeth Colston, Rectory Farm, Salford, nr Chipping Norton Oxfordshire OX7 5YZ.

Rectory Farm is a 200-year-old farmhouse, with a mature garden, set in its own unspoiled 450-acre valley. Nigel and Elizabeth have lived in the Cotswolds their entire lives and can pass on all their knowledge of the hidden villages untouched by tourism. They enjoy dining with their guests (dinner £17.50, bring your own wine), and can teach fly fishing on the two spring-fed trout lakes. One double and 2 single bedrooms. No smoking, no dogs, children welome. B&B £27.

D BLACKWELL GRANGE   Tel 01608 682357

Liz Vernon Miller, Blackwell Grange, Blackwell, nr Shipston-on-Stour, Warwickshire CV36 4PF.

A listed early 17th-century farmhouse on the edge of a sleepy market town, Blackwell Grange has great character with its low ceilings, stone-flagged floors, and deep-set windows. The beamed sitting-room has comfortable chairs, a log fire, and plenty of reading matter. The garden is attractive and well kept, with views of distant hills. Evening meals, by arrangement, costs from £12 (bring your own wine). The 3 double bedrooms have lovely views. No smoking, no dogs, children must be teenage. B&B £25.

E GUITING GUEST HOUSE   Tel 01451 850470

Yvonne & Bernie Sylvester, Guiting Guest House, Post Office Lane, Guiting Power, Gloucestershire GL54 5TZ.

Originally (some 450 years ago) a village pub, this is now an appealing home that has been sensitively modernised. Floorboards of elm come from the nearby Wychwood Forest; flagstones are covered with warming rugs. The bedrooms (4 double, 1 single) are mostly en suite, and some have four-posters. Order your dinner (from £13) when you book – you can rely on Yvonne's own taste for locally bought food. Bring your own wine. Children welcome, restricted smoking, dogs by arrangement. B&B £23.

F   WYCK HILL LODGE   Tel 01451 830141

Jackie Alderton, Wyck Hill Lodge, Wyck Hill, nr Stow-on-the-Wold, Gloucestershire GL54 1HT.

Once, at the beginning of the 19th century, this was the lodge to a local mansion. Today, it is comfortably furnished, and gives an atmosphere of warmth and relaxation. Jackie's garden has honeysuckle climbing over the walls, well-stocked island beds. The 3 double/twin bedrooms (2 on the ground floor are suitable for wheelchairs) are en suite, and the house is usually filled with flowers from the garden. Light suppers are served during summer months (from £13, unlicensed). No smoking, no children, no dogs. B&B £20–£22.

G   LOWER FARM   Tel 01608 682750

Jackie & Ken Smith, Lower Farm, Darlingscott, nr Shipston-on-Stour, Warwickshire CV36 4PN.

'A 16th-century ambience with 20th-century appointments' is how Jackie describes her lovely old farmhouse – stone-built, warm and welcoming, like so many of the houses round here. Her walled garden is profusely planted, well kept, and very peaceful. The 3 double en suite bedrooms are spacious and well furnished. There are many places to eat out in the evenings. No smoking; dogs and children by arrangement. B&B £20.

What Else to Enjoy

This is a short selection of the many good things recommended in the area by owners of places to stay. Your hosts will certainly be able to provide additional information.

Other Gardens/Nurseries

There are two town gardens well worth a look if you stop for a while in the lovely market town of **Chipping Campden.** You will find Mr and Mrs Lusty's garden behind her interior decorating shop, The Green Dragon

(Tel 01386 840379). It shows brilliantly what can be done with a long narrow space. The Ernest Wilson Memorial Garden, behind the church, is in
remembrance of the famous Victorian plant collector who introduced more
than 1,000 varieties of trees and shrubs to our country.

There is an outstanding specialist nursery in this visit. **Fibrex Nurseries**, Honeybourne Lane, **Pebworth** holds the National Collection of
pelargoniums, and its range of varieties for sale is unsurpassed. It is also
excellent for ivies and hardy ferns. All the plants are well displayed. Tel
01789 720788.

If It's Wet

Sudeley Castle (*see* Garden 1) should on no account be missed, even though
you will be among a crowd of people. The architecture, the surroundings
and the lavish interiors are all memorable. House open as for garden.

Snowshill Manor (*see* Garden 4) is enchantingly eclectic and personal.
You go from room to room in this lovely stone house wondering what on
earth you will find next. House open as for garden.

If you want to potter and shop, most of the small towns marked on the
visit map have something to offer. **Shipston-on-Stour** is calm and restful, with good pubs. Everyone seems to walk at about half the pace of the
rest of England. There are several antique shops with bargain buys, if you
hunt. **Chipping Campden** is a delight, with a long wide main street dominated by the gabled open-air Jacobean market hall. **Winchcombe** has re-
liable pub lunches and lots of atmosphere while you visit the three gardens
nearby. **Stow-on-the-Wold**, close to the enchanting villages of Lower
and Upper Slaughter, and Lower and Upper Swell, is a shopaholics delight.
The antique shops may be out of budget range, but have exquisite pieces
to tempt you.

Eating Out

At **Moreton-in-Marsh**, you will find one of my favourite restaurants.
The Marsh Goose, on the High Street offers inspired cooking by Sonya
Kidney in its two small dining-rooms, with attentive and knowledgeable
service. You should book; £13.50 for lunch and £24 for dinner. Tel 01865
590344.

Around Tewkesbury

The River Severn flows through this area between the Malverns and Bredon Hill, so there are lush, sheltered valleys where orchards and market gardens abound. In spring, there is an apple trail you can drive along, through pink and white clouds of blossom. Cotswold stone begins to give way to black-and-white cottages. We are right in Elgar country here, so his Cello Concerto is perfect – most hauntingly played by Jacqueline du Pré with Sir John Barbirolli conducting.

OS maps: Landrangers 149, **150**, 162,163

Gardens

Opening times: in larger gardens, and in NT properties, last admissions are usually 30–45 minutes before the garden closes. Admission charges are a guide to what one adult can expect to pay to go round the garden. It sometimes varies with the season or days of the week. When the house is also open to the public, there is usually an additional charge.

I   CAMP COTTAGE
Highleadon, nr Gloucester   Tel 01452 790352, after 6 p.m.

Sun/Mon, June/July, 2–5, and by appointment. Also 2 Suns late Feb and early March for hellebores and snowdrops. £1
From Gloucester go W on A40. 1m after roundabout with A417, turn R on B4215 signed Newent. After 2½m, turn R at Highleadon Garage. Cottage is 100 yds on L.

Hard to believe that this garden, packed with more than 400 roses, is only 10 years old. Mr Holmes and Mr O'Neill have lost count of how many clematis they have, all tumbling, scrambling, climbing up walls, trellis, pergolas and trees. It is a blissful, exuberant garden, with rambling paths. It feels secretive, while at the same time profusion rules. The air is heavy with scent. Moss roses are under-planted with pulmonarias, bulbs

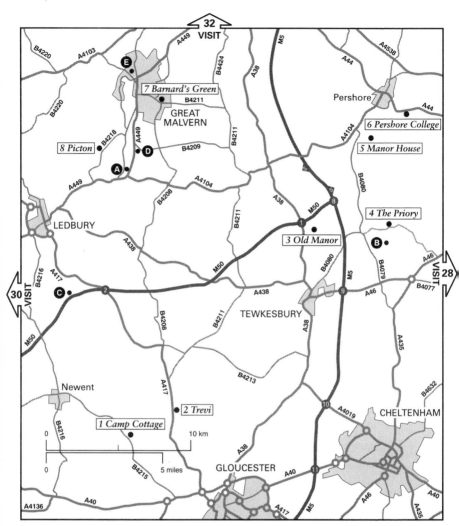

and a splendid selection of hellebores. By the front door of their black and white cottage are large tubs of scented geraniums, and roses in pots. Heavenly.

2 TREVI GARDEN

Hartpury, nr Gloucester   Tel 01452 700370

4 afternoons in late March, then most Thurs and Suns, April to Sept, and by appointment. £2
From Gloucester go NW on A417 for 5m to Hartpury. By war memorial, double back sharp R into Old Rd.

Sally and Gilbert Gough are true plant-lovers, and have designed a 1-acre garden to show off their remarkable collection of interesting plants. A tiny stream gives them scope to grow bog plants. Paths meander through a laburnum arch supporting clematis, which leads to an immaculate veggie patch with lovely field views. Varieties of jasmine scramble up trellis with honeysuckle and lathyrus, a little orchard has bold planting around the perimeter, and a second lawn has hot-colour plants in the surrounding borders. All is as neat as a new pin. There is a really splendid area selling plants under the trees by the kitchen door, and on Thursdays there are ample teas in the garden. Sally is most knowledgeable, and has words of wisdom for all interested gardeners.

3 THE OLD MANOR

Twyning, nr Tewkesbury   Tel 01684 293516

Mons (not BHs), March to Oct, 2–5, and by appointment except weekends. £1.50
From Tewkesbury go N on A38 for 3m. Turn R to Twyning; garden is opposite T-junction in village.

Covered with wisteria, the rosy brick house is what remains of a Queen Anne house which had fallen into such disrepair that it was demolished. The inheritance was lovely old walls to grow things up, and courtyards entrancingly paved with headstones made redundant at Birlingham and Bredon churchyards, together with old stone sinks that are now home to Mrs Wilder's large collection of alpines. It's a good garden to visit from mid April to mid June, when this courtyard is sensational. The garden, re-markably sheltered and warm behind the great walls, has thriving exotic and tender plants – peaches, kiwi fruit, *Colutea media*, sophera, fremontoden-dron and *Cytisus battandieri*, all normally found in conservatories. A partic-ularly fine Chilean jasmine romps over a wall, and hot borders flourish around the lawn. Five cherries, netted, grow on the warm walls, an old felled mulberry has sprouted anew from gnarled roots, dwarf apples grow in the orchard, handsome gate piers topped with stone pineapples introduce a pear arbour and a nut grove adds to the charm. Alpines are Mrs Wilder's speciality and her nursery has rare plants for sale. Look into the gardener's shed, once a gardener's bothy, and see the splendid double-seater garden loo – too good to miss.

4   THE PRIORY   Kemerton, nr Tewkesbury   Tel 01386 725258

Fri and charity Suns, June to Sept, 2–7, and groups of over 20 by appointment. £2.
From Tewkesbury go NE on B4080 for 3½m. In Bredon, turn R on minor road for 1m to garden in the centre of Kemerton.

The Hon. Mrs Healing and her late husband Peter redesigned this garden 30 years ago, having planted choice trees before this. The 4 acres contain several small enclosed areas – a sunken area with a water-lily pool and pots of daturas, alpines in raised beds, a splendid vegetable garden, masses of dahlias (Mr Healing won many prizes for these), pergolas smothered with roses, and fine shrubs. The great glory of The Priory is its borders. The June border has soft colours of grey, silver, pinks and whites, made ethereal with crambes and campanulas. The Red Border is striking from late to July to September when it sizzles with colour from dahlias, penstemons, red canna lilies, phlox and copper-foliaged shrubs. Mrs Healing propagates treasures from her garden, and always has rare and interesting plants for sale.

5   THE MANOR HOUSE
Birlingham, nr Pershore   Tel 01386 750005

Thurs, May and Sept; Wed/Thurs, June/July; 11–5. Closed August. £1.50
From Pershore go SW on A4104 for 1m. Turn L on B4080, and immediately L again into Birlingham village. Garden is beyond the church.

This delightful, spacious garden set on the banks of the Avon has long pastoral views and wide lawns where profuse borders blend into the countryside over the ha-ha. A series of garden rooms gives Jane Williams-Thomas the opportunity to indulge in her passion for perennial plants. Big clumps of euphorbia, symphytum, *Alchemilla mollis*, hardy geraniums and monkshood give shape and colour to bold herbaceous borders. Brick paths link the gardens, and at the heart of it all is the White Garden, where standard Iceberg roses, white campanulas, tall white phlox and white willow herb are woven into a tapestry with silver-leaved shrubs backed by dark green yew. Planting is prolific and energetic – a great lesson to be learned in the delicate use of colours in the garden. As if being such a talented gardener weren't enough, Mrs Williams-Thomas makes coracles as well. You can see them on the barn walls of the tearoom. Really good home-made cakes here, and very good plant sales as well.

6 PERSHORE COLLEGE   nr Pershore   Tel 01386 552443

Gardens: occasional open days. Nursery: daily except Tues, 11–6.
From Pershore go E on A44 for 1m. College well signed on R.

The RHS has its West Midlands Regional Centre at this College of Agriculture, and there are lectures and demonstrations throughout the year. Basically, this is an educational garden, set in a fine ornamental park. Here you can see fruit and vegetables perfectly grown, alpines, glasshouses, orchards and the Hardy Plant Society's garden. The plant centre sells many unusual plants, and if you are an RHS member you can get gardening advice and plant identification on certain days. Best to telephone first.

7 BARNARD'S GREEN HOUSE
Great Malvern   Tel 01684 574446

Thurs, 2 charity Suns, April to Sept, 2–6, and by appointment. £1.50
From the centre of Great Malvern go E on B4211 for ½m to Barnard's Green.
The garden is at 10 Poolbrook Rd, at junction with B4208.

The house dates from 1630, and looks out on to fine old cedars, immaculate lawns, a spring-flowering woodland area, a rose garden, splendid herbaceous borders and a kitchen garden with a great glasshouse. Mrs Nicholls is a dried-flower expert and has a thriving business, the flowers all being grown here. The brick paths and clipped yew and box hedges give good bones to this nice garden.

8 THE PICTON GARDEN
Colwall, nr Great Malvern   Tel 01684 540416

Wed–Sun, April to Oct, 10–1 and 2.15–5.30. Also Mon/Tues in Sept/Oct.
£1.50
From Great Malvern go SW on B4218 for 3m. In Colwall, look for sign 'Old
Court Nurseries' (adjoining the garden) on R.

This garden is famous for the National Collection of Michaelmas daisies (there are more than 350 varieties) which are worth a long detour to see in September and October. There is a fabulously rich tapestry of brilliant colours. However, the bulk of the plants displayed in the garden are unusual herbaceous perennials, including inulas, heleniums, euphorbias, aconitums and astrantias which are grown cottage-garden style in wide borders. There is a background of mature shrubs and a small woodland area with acers, a variegated ash and the rare elm *Ulmus* 'Jacqueline Hillier'. A small rose garden has old shrub rose favourites and David Austin roses, and there is a damp border for moisture-loving plants including meconopsis. This is very much a plantsman's garden, and Paul Picton sells all these desirable treasures in his adjoining **Old Court Nursery**.

Where to Stay

All B&B prices are approximate per person, sharing a double/twin room usually with private or en suite facilities. It is a good idea to ask for any special requirements when booking.

A   HOLDFAST COTTAGE HOTEL   Tel 01684 310288

Stephen & Jane Knowles, Holdfast Cottage Hotel, Little Malvern, nr Great Malvern, Worcestershire WR13 6NA.

An ancient wisteria covers the front of this friendly, white-painted, small hotel, surrounded by orchards and open farmland with magnificent views of the Malvern Hills. Two acres of flower-filled gardens go down to a woodland area with gentle pathways for an evening stroll. There is a luxurious conservatory, and a comfortable beamed lounge with an open fire. Evening meals (£18, licensed), the menu changed daily, are special – original and imaginative. The 8 cottagey bedrooms are light and airy. Restricted smoking, dogs and children welcome. B&B £40.

B   UPPER COURT   Tel 01386 725351

Bill & Diana Herford, Upper Court, Kemerton, nr Tewkesbury, Gloucestershire GL20 7HY.

Bill and Diana are long-time friends of mine, so I know their lovely house particularly well. It is a family home, an outstanding large Georgian manor in one of the prettiest villages on Bredon Hill. Their 15 acres of garden and grounds, sometimes open for charity, have an idyllic outlook, an enviable 13th-century dovecote and a Domesday-listed watermill. There is a beautiful lake where you can enjoy fly fishing, a swimming pool and tennis court. The house is filled with treasures – porcelain, china, needlework and antiques. It is a wonderful combination of the stately and the homely. The 3 bedrooms include one with a four-poster, and another in a garden room suitable for wheelchair users. If you bring children, the Coach House is ideal. Evening meals cost £27, and there is a drinks license. Dogs by arrangement, restricted smoking. B&B £38–43.

C GROVE HOUSE   Tel 01531 650584

Michael & Ellen Ross, Grove House, Bromsberrow Heath, nr Ledbury, Herefordshire HR8 1PE.

This substantial, square-built 15th-century house has spacious gardens of lawns and mature trees stretching over lawns to a small lake. The 13 acres of grounds are devoted to horses, and if you fancy a bit of riding, it is easily arranged. Inside the house are beams, panelling and open fires. The antique furniture makes you feel totally in tune with a historic home. Michael and Ellen are passionate about enjoying the best in food and wine. The 3 big bedrooms always have bowls of fruit, with home-made biscuits on the tea trays. Dinner is £20 (bring your own wine), usually with vegetables from the walled kitchen garden. Children and dogs welcome, restricted smoking. B&B £32.

D THE OLD VICARAGE   Tel 01684 572585

Michael & Maureen Gorvin, The Old Vicarage, Hanley Rd, Malvern Wells, Worcestershire WR14 4PH.

Two magnificent specimen cedars dominate the 1-acre garden of this splendid Victorian house on the slopes of the Malvern Hills, now totally transformed in atmosphere, inside and outside, from the suffocating darkness of times gone by. The large windows have been cleared of their heavy curtains, the woodwork stripped and lightened. It is friendly and relaxed here – let people enjoy themselves is the motto. There are 5 well-equipped family/double/twin bedrooms, one on the ground-floor for wheelchair users. Dinner, by arrangement, costs £14.50, licensed. Dogs and children are welcome, and you can smoke except in the dining-room. B&B £23.

E COWLEIGH PARK FARM   Tel 01684 566750

Sue Stringer, Cowleigh Park Farm, Cowleigh Rd, Great Malvern, Worcestershire WR13 5HJ.

This delightful black-and-white timber-framed farmhouse has a history dating back to the early 13th century. Beautifully restored, with more than 2 acres of landscaped gardens including an ornamental fish pond and a small lake, it is peacefully set at the foot of the Malvern Hills. The 3 comfortable bedrooms, as elsewhere in the house, are filled with period furnishings. Evening meals, by arrangement, are delicious 2-course affairs costing £11 (bring your own wine). No smoking, no small children, dogs by arrangement. B&B £20–£23.

What Else to Enjoy

This is a short selection of the many good things recommended in the area by owners of places to stay. Your hosts will certainly be able to provide additional information.

Other Gardens/Nurseries

Ledbury has a very good nursery – **Rushfields**, in Ross Rd. It specialises in choice herbaceous perennials and grasses and exquisite hellebores raised by Helen Ballard. Open Wed–Sat, and by appointment. Tel 01531 632004.

Perhaps not a garden, but a fascinating experience anyway, is the tour of the **Three Choirs Vineyard**. The excellent guided tour tells you much about grapes and the process of wine-making – with free wine-tastings, and a good lunch in the restaurant (which you pay for). Find it on the SW side of our map, just N of Newent on the B4216. Open daily all year, 10–5.30. Tel 01531 890223.

If It's Wet

Gloucester is the city to head for on a wet day. Although it is traffic-ridden and modern, there is much to do. The cathedral is a must. The Docks, an area restored and re-developed on the banks of the river, has many museums, restaurants and antique centres. You can take boat trips on the *Queen Boadicea II*.

Newent has plenty to offer on a rainy day. The Shambles, in Church St, is a charming museum set out to re-create life in a Victorian country town. A 4-storey house filled with furniture and costumes, it is surrounded by winding streets with specialist shops and craft centres.

Ledbury is another lovely maze of streets with black-and-white half-timbered houses leaning out over the cobbles. Don't be fooled into thinking that the towers and crenellations of nearby **Eastnor Castle** are in any way ancient. This imposing pile was built in 1820, and its interior, with fine furniture, furnishings and paintings, has recently been refurbished. It is open Suns and BH Mons from Easter to Sept, and on weekdays in July and Aug, 11–5. Admission £4.

In **Great Malvern**, do try to visit the Priory – a wonderfully calming place.

Eating Out

Two miles N of **Ledbury**, tucked away in hills just beyond the village of Wellington Heath, is Patricia Hegarty's renowned **Hope End**. A large, walled kitchen garden beside this lovely house provides most of the vegetables and all the herbs for her cooking, which is uncomplicated, justly praised and highly recommended. A set dinner costs £30 per person, service included, and there is a good wine list. Tel 01531 633613.

The Wye Valley

Here the River Wye flows through gentle fields which all seem to be full of stout black-and-white cows. There is the River Dore, too, flowing through the Golden Valley where black-and-white timbered houses become ever more ornate. The whole lovely area is lush, fertile and deeply rural, with no motorways or industrial estates to mar its beauty. From hilltops, you can often see the Welsh mountains in the distance, and stretching around you are cider orchards glowing with rosy apples (don't try them – they are sour). My drive-along music was the Sibelius Violin Concerto in D Minor, Opus 47. I like the version played by Itzhak Perlman, with André Previn conducting the Pittsburgh Symphony. The 1st movement, where Perlman sails through the fiendishly difficult passages with his showman's ease, has gutsy bravura. The 2nd movement is deliciously tender and warm – just like the countryside here.

OS maps: Landrangers 148, **149**, 161, 162

Gardens

Opening times: in larger gardens, and in NT properties, last admissions are usually 30–45 minutes before the garden closes. Admission charges are a guide to what one adult can expect to pay to go round the garden. It sometimes varies with the season or days of the week. When the house is also open to the public, there is usually an additional charge.

I **ABBEY DORE COURT**   Abbey Dore   Tel 01981 240419

Daily except Weds, March to Oct, 11–6, and by appointment earlier in year for hellebores. £2
From Hereford go SW on A465 for 10m. Turn R on B4347 where signed and garden is 2½m on R.

This garden will be loved by all plantswomen. It has formal lines, but overflows with flowers, trees, shrubs and climbers, all exuberantly planted to

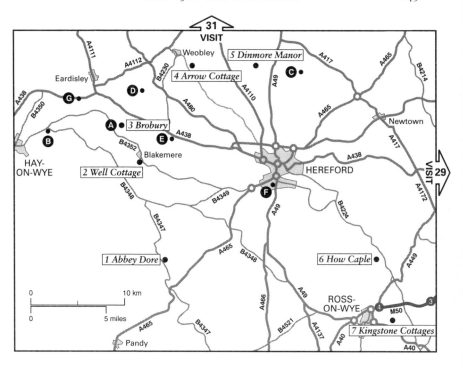

complement each other. Two large lawns are bordered by herbaceous plants, and dominated by two huge *Sequoiadendron giganteum* trees with a carved owl sitting under one of them. The formal garden runs the width of the top end of the garden, and has one of the prettiest (and must uncomfortable) Victorian garden seats I know. Here is a collection of viburnums, cornus, prunus, acers and salix all chosen for marvellous foliage interest in shades of bronze, copper and cream. The river walk beside the chattering Dore is ferny and shady, with many hostas. Across the bridge is a pond, a salix collection, a rock garden and some magnificent sorbus. A helpful map guides you round the garden and points out the major plants. Lunches and teas are served in the stable yard. There are good plant sales, a food shop with local delicacies, a gift shop and a teddy bear's loft. You can spend many happy hours here, and visit the Abbey as well.

2 WELL COTTAGE

Blakemere, nr Hereford   Tel 01981 500475

May to Aug, by appointment. £1.50
From Hereford go SW on A465 for 2m. Turn R on B4349 for 2m, then R
again on B4352 for 6m to Blakemere. Garden is on L by red phone box.

This 1½-acre garden nestles charmingly into the surrounding countryside, its boundary hedges blending perfectly with their wilder neighbours – hawthorn, hazel, ash and oak. At the front of the 17th-century cottage is an abundant, bosky cottage garden, with a fine *Davidia involucrata*, which has just started to produce the fluttering white hankies (which are bracts, not flowers) that it's famous for. The old well-head is smothered in ivy and campanulas, and astrantias add to the soft and gentle colour schemes. Mr Edwards gradually tamed the nettles and thistles at the back of the cottage, and dug out a pond, now brilliantly edged with primulas, hostas, rogersias, iris and lysichitons. The long strip of land was divided into three separate areas, with an upper and lower lawn, and wide borders using bold architectural plants.

3 BROBURY GARDENS

Brobury (*see also* Where to Stay)   Tel 01981 240419

Mon–Sat all year except Christmas and New Year, 10–4.30. £2
From Hereford go W on A438 for 10m. Turn L on minor road signed to
Brobury/Bredwardine for 1m. Garden is on L by Bredwardine Bridge.

Here are 8 acres of semi-formal gardens, with fine mature trees, herbaceous borders and terraces with great views. This is Kilvert country, and the garden is on the Kilvert Trail. The Gallery alongside the house is well worth visiting: it has a huge selection of antique maps and horticultural prints.

Close by, 5m W of Hereford, S of the A438 nr **Swainshill**, and well signed is the NT's **The Weir**, lovely to visit in spring when the walk along the banks of River Wye is a drift of bulbs. Open Wed–Sun, mid Feb to Oct, 11–6. £1.50.

4 ARROW COTTAGE

Ledgemoor, nr Weobley   Tel 01544 318468

Wed–Fri and Suns, April to July, and Sept, 2–5, and by appointment. £2
From Hereford go NW on A4110 for 8m. At Bush Bank, turn L on minor roads
for 3m through Kings Pyon to Ledgemoor, where garden is on L just before inn.

Here is a series of enchanting gardens, set in 2 acres of old apple orchards, which constantly changes mood and delights at each new turn. Ingenious planning and planting by Mr and Mrs Lance Hattatt encloses garden rooms with yew and beech hedges, and uses the best and most interesting varieties of plants, trees and shrubs, all maintained to a very high standard. Old brick paths lead through a green garden, then a magnificently moody purple Gothic garden over a Chinese bridge to a fountain garden, then a magnificent long rill garden with a tall plinth and urn at the end, and lastly a long grass walk by a contorted willow planted mainly for foliage effect. A shrub rose garden is a-billow with catmint, hardy geraniums and campanulas. Facing a rectangular lawn, the summer house has an inscription which (translated from Latin) reads: 'Here is everlasting spring and summer, in months which are not her own.' Virgil's words are perfect. The planting here is very gentle, with soft blues, pinks, silvers and lemon. A white cherry tree is in the middle of the lawn, and *Salvia turkestanica* and *Verbena bonariensis* are allowed to self-seed through the borders. You go through a gate to two hot-colour borders, orange socking you in the eye. Yet another small garden has a pond fringed with iris, astilbes and gunnera. The splendid area for plant sales has a formal border recently planted with *Prunus lusitanica* and box, which will eventually be clipped into round dumpling shapes. Teas are served in an attractive tearoom. This garden isn't suitable for children, and no dogs are allowed.

5   DINMORE MANOR   nr Leominster   Tel 01432 830322

Daily, all year, 9.30–5.30. £2.50
From Hereford go N on A49 for 6m. Garden well signposted on L.

These gardens are 550 ft above sea level, with outstanding views, and are dominated by the exuberant architecture of the house, its cloisters and chapel. Mr Murray's grandfather invented the reflective 'cat's eyes' for the road, and bought the estate in 1927. Many years have been spent restoring the medieval buildings and the gardens. A formidable yew tree, estimated to be more than 1,000 years old, is a major feature, along with a huge rock garden with fine old acers growing in it. There are mixed borders of unusual plants, old roses and a pool. The garden is especially good in autumn with stunning foliage colour. The plant centre mainly sells uncommon herbaceous plants.

6 HOW CAPLE COURT   nr Ross-on-Wye   Tel 01989 740626

Mon–Sat, all year, 9.30–5, and Suns, April–Oct, 10–5. £2.50
From Hereford go SE on B4224 for 10m. Turn R at How Caple X-rds. Garden
well signed.

A house on this site was mentioned in the Domesday Book, but the present garden dates from Edwardian times, its 11 acres set high above the
River Wye. Formal terraces, yew hedges, pools, statues and roses contrast
with the magnificent trees and shrubs in The Dell and less formal areas. The
water gardens are under restoration at the moment. The terrace is formidable, with eight clipped yews leaning together as if to whisper a joke
around a lily pool. A very pretty summer house and more lily ponds are
on the next terrace. A visit to the medieval church is well worthwhile.
Good plant sales in the stable yard, and a tearoom.

7 KINGSTONE COTTAGES
Weston under Penyard   Tel 01989 565267

Mon–Fri (not BHs), mid May to mid July, 9–4, and by appointment. £1
From Ross-on-Wye go E on A40 for 2m. At Weston Cross Inn, turn L to
Bollitree Castle, then L again to Rudhall. Garden well signed ½m on L.

Twenty years ago this was just a cottage in a field, now it's a treasure trove
of delight. Sophie Hughes is an expert on pinks, and holds the National
Collection here, with more than 100 varieties, beautifully displayed in a
parterre, and planted all around the rest of the garden. Herringbone brick
paths meander around serpentine beds, packed with architectural plants –
the sort which give height and bold shapes – and cottage garden favourites.
This is very much a well-used and much-loved family garden, rather than a
showplace, with hammocks, cosy seats for two, and splendid garden furniture made by Mike Hughes. He has also made a quirky grotto, and lined it
with shells, bones, and empty (alas) bottles which once held excellent wine,
with a brilliant surprise at the end. A pool is fringed with iris, and shrub
roses abound. The cottage is completely covered by climbing plants – figs,
jasmine, vines and roses. Very good plants for sale and, of course, masses
of pinks.

Where to Stay

All B&B prices are approximate per person, sharing a double/twin room usually with private or en suite facilities. It is a good idea to ask for any special requirements when booking.

A **BROBURY HOUSE** *(see also* Garden 3)   Tel 01981 500595

Leonora Weaver, Brobury House, Brobury, nr Hay-on-Wye, Herefordshire HR3 6BS.

This comfortable Victorian house has fine views beyond its garden to the Black Mountains in the distance. When you stay here, you get the feeling that you can spread yourself – the rooms are large, there is a TV lounge as well as a drawing-room, and you can enjoy the watercolours and prints (more than 200,000) filed and displayed in the Coach House gallery. There are 4 double/twin bedrooms, and, in an annex, 2 inexpensive (£20) single rooms with en suite shower and loo. There is a good choice of local restaurants and pubs where you can eat in the evenings. No smoking, children and dogs by arrangement. B&B £27–£30.

B **THE HAVEN**   Tel 01497 831254

Janet Robinson, The Haven, Hardwicke, nr Hay-on-Wye, Herefordshire HR3 5TA.

This early-Victorian vicarage, mentioned in Kilvert's diary, is surrounded by 11 acres of garden and paddocks. Janet says modestly that 'never is all the garden tidy at one time'. But you will find it abundantly and colourfully planted, with views across fields. Inside the house, the rooms are spacious, comfortable, lined with books and pictures and warmed by log fires. There are 9 bedrooms, including one single, mostly en suite or with private facilities. Four-course evening meals cost £13, licensed. Children welcome, smoking restricted, dogs treated as guests and must pay £5 per night. B&B £23–£27.

C   VAULD FARM   Tel 01568 797898

Mrs Jean Bengry, Vauld Farm, The Vauld, nr Hereford HR1 3HA.

You won't find a more heavily beamed black-and-white house in this book than here – at least, not one you can stay in. Be sure to take your camera because the reflections in the adjoining ponds are magical. Altogether there are 5 acres of gardens and grounds which include a converted barn in which you can sleep. Everywhere, the architecture is astounding. The 6 double/ twin bedrooms include a terrific four-poster – but get a description of the choices when you ring to book. Evening meals cost £15 (bring your own wine). Restricted smoking, no dogs, children should be over 12. B&B £20–£25.

D   DARKLEY HOUSE   Tel 01544 318121

Jill & Malcolm Ainslie, Darkley House, Norton Canon, nr Hereford HR4 7BT.

You know Jill and Malcolm are passionate gardeners from the moment you go up the driveway to their weather-boarded house. Evidence is everywhere of the way they have transformed 3½ acres of farmland since they started work on it in 1989. Growing into maturity are a scented wall garden, a pond garden, a wild garden, herbaceous borders and a brick-built pergola that look on to extensive views. The house, which has a lovely conservatory where you eat, has 3 double/twin bedrooms and one single, either in the house itself or in a converted barn and stables. Jill is a Cordon Bleu cook and provides evening meals (£14, bring your own wine) by arrangement. No smoking, no dogs, no children. B&B £20.

E   THE OLD RECTORY   Tel 01981 590218

Audrey Mayson, The Old Rectory, Byford, nr Hereford HR4 7LD.

Audrey and John are avid garden visitors, and can mark your map for even more places than I have described in this visit. Their own garden, about an acre around their Georgian house, is a joint effort, with Audrey choosing the herbaceous plants and shrubs, and John choosing the trees, looking after the veggie garden and cutting the grass. Now where have I heard that story before? From inside the house, there are good views through the deep sash windows in the sitting-room. You can arrange with Audrey to have an evening meal (£10–£12, bring your own wine), or there is a wide choice of local restaurants where you can eat out. Three large double/twin bedrooms. Children welcome, no smoking, no dogs in the house. B&B £19.

F GRAFTON VILLA FARM   Tel 01432 268689

Jennie Layton, Grafton Villa Farm, Grafton, nr Hereford HR2 8ED.

Although only just outside the southern outskirts of Hereford, this 18th-century farmhouse has panoramic views over its own farmland and hills, where sheepdogs greet you and hens lay eggs for your breakfast. The garden is perhaps best in spring, with a carpet of snowdrops and other bulbs. There is a large rockery, and a lawn dominated by a weeping ash. The house is comofrtably furnished, and has 3 double/twin bedrooms. Evening meals (£15, bring your own wine) are simply but imaginatively cooked, with portions large enough to satisfy a working farmer. No smoking, no dogs, children welcome. B&B £18–£19.

G WINFORTON COURT   Tel 01544 328498

Jackie Kingdon, Winforton Court, Winforton, nr Hay-on-Wye, Herefordshire HR3 6EA.

This fantastically-beamed house dates back to 1520, and exudes the history of this area. The massive studded front door was re-cycled from Eardisley Castle. Inside is some early stencilling. You eat breakfast in a room which was once the main Court House for the district, with a magnificent early 17th-century oak staircase and a huge stone fireplace. Outside is a delightful garden, with herbs and cottage flowers. Each of the 3 double/twin bedrooms (one a four-poster) has its own character. Flowers, antiques and collections of china and bygones are everywhere. B&B only, but Jackie has a list of places nearby where you can eat in the evenings. Restricted smoking, dogs and children welcome. B&B £17–£21.

What Else to Enjoy

This is a short selection of the many good things recommended in the area by owners of places to stay. Your hosts will certainly be able to provide additional information.

If It's Wet

As a first choice, head for **Hereford**. The 11th-century cathedral is superb, with its proudest possession, the Mappa Mundi, drawn in about 1290, now thankfully saved for the nation. You can see it, together with an accompanying exhibition, in the crypt.

The centre of the city has been pedestrianised, and much now consists of modern shops. However Capuchin Yard, just off the narrow Church St, has a feeling of antiquity and is home to craftspeople and a number of specialised shops. There are 90-minute walking tours round the historic parts of the city which start from the Tourist Information Office (Tel 01432 266867).

On the W edge of the visit, **Hay-on-Wye** claims to be the secondhand book centre of the world, with a literary festival there each summer. There are, I suppose, hundreds of thousands books to be bought from shops and open-air stalls, and I defy you to come away empty-handed.

On the E edge of the visit, **Much Marcle** is a village where you can travel back in time by visiting **Hellens House**. It dates from 1292 which makes it one of the oldest homes in England still lived in by the family who built it. There is wonderful stonework, an uncanny atmosphere and many historical curiosities. Open Weds, Sat/Sun and BHs, Easter to Sept, 2–6. Quench your thirst in the sampling room at **The Bounds**, where the old-established H. Weston and Sons will show you how perry and cider is made nowadays.

At **Ross-on-Wye**, the Lost Street Museum is a delightful re-creation of an Edwardian street, with authentic shops showing collections of dolls, toys, musical boxes, phonographs, early radios and motor bikes, plus period amusement machines (e.g. What The Butler Saw), games and quizzes. It's perfect for a wet afternoon.

Eating Out

Travelling around on this visit, I ate pleasantly and inexpensively at the **Salutation Inn** (Tel 01544 318443) and at **Jules Bistro** (Tel 01544 318206) in **Weobley**. In **Winforton**, you will certainly want to try Wendy Hibbard's cooking at the **Sun Inn**, where she offers an excellent range of local farmhouse cheeses to finish off menus which are inventive and original throughout (Tel 01544 327677).

Just off our map to the S (follow the A 465 towards Abergavenny, and turn L onto B4521 to **Llandewi Skirrid**) is the legendary **Walnut Tree Inn** where I have been fortunate enough to enjoy meals a number of times. The food and ambience here are extraordinary – a combination of pub, bistro and *haute cuisine*, with portions large enough to satisfy the most famished walker. It's crowded and fun, and you can spend as much or as little as you like. Main courses cost £10–£16, and you will probably get a bill for £25–£40 per head. You must book. Tel 01873 852797.

From Leominster to the Welsh Hills

It's border countryside here at its most beautiful, the valleys rich and strewn with cider apple orchards, divided from Wales by the River Lugg – an unlovely name for such a lovely river. The closer you get to Wales, the wilder and more rural it becomes. I have often heard nightingales sing in the woods here, so on my way to visit the gardens I played a tape of 'The Lover and the Nightingale', from *Goyescas* by Granados – magically evocative piano music.

OS maps: Landrangers 137, 138, 148, **149**

Gardens

Opening times: in larger gardens, and in NT properties, last admissions are usually 30–45 minutes before the garden closes. Admission charges are a guide to what one adult can expect to pay to go round the garden. It sometimes varies with the season or days of the week. When the house is also open to the public, there is usually an additional charge.

I   **HERGEST CROFT**   Kington   Tel 01544 230160
Daily, mid April to Oct, 1.30–6.30. £3
From Kington go W on A44 for ½m. Garden signed on L.

Hergest Croft has been gardened for three generations of the Banks family, all of them keen plantsmen and collectors. Construction of the house began in 1896, and the oldest of today's fine trees date from around then. Successive generations of the family have continued the tradition, so that there is now an exceptional collection of rare, exotic trees and shrubs. The National Collections of maples and birches are here. Park Wood is a hidden valley where huge rhododendrons grow. Magnolias and azaleas abound, lilies, roses and hydrangeas take the eye in summer, and from August onwards there are vivid colours from the maples and birches. The kitchen gardens should not be missed; the veggies are immaculate. The orchards of old espaliered apple trees are carpeted with bulbs in the spring, and in

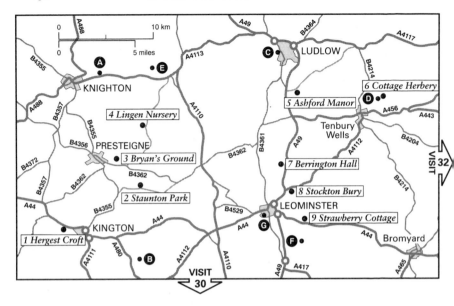

summer are the backdrop to herbaceous perennials and old roses. You may picnic in the orchards and dogs are allowed on leads. Rare plants are for sale, and there is a tea-room.

2 STAUNTON PARK

Staunton on Arrow, nr Leominster   Tel 01544 388474

Thurs and Suns, April to Sept, 2–6. £2
From Kington go N on B4355 for 3m. Turn R after Titley on minor road
signed Stansbatch and Staunton Park; the garden is 1½m on L.

There are 14 acres of grounds in this nostalgically Edwardian park. You enter through an avenue of Wellingtonias. There are good herbaceous borders to enjoy, plus Kate's Herb Garden, created by a younger daughter of the family, now sadly dead, who planted a wide range of decorative and medicinal herbs. A walk along the ha-ha leads to the lake, woodland walk and bog garden. There is also a rock garden, a scented walk and a shrubbery of golden foliage. Plants, mostly herbaceous and rockery, and herbs are for sale, and don't miss the delicious cream teas which are served in a pretty tea-room.

3   BRYAN'S GROUND   nr Presteigne   Tel 01544 260001

Sun/Mon, April to Sept, 2–5, and by appointment for groups. £1.50
From Presteigne go E on B4362 for 1½m. Turn L at sign to Kinsham/
Lingen. After ½m, turn left on minor road signed to Stapleton. Garden is 1m
on L (watch for pillarbox in gatepost, or you will miss it).

Work is still in its early stages here – a brilliant garden re-awakening being undertaken by David Wheeler and Simon Dorrell (who also produce *Hortus*, in my view the best gardening periodical in the country). They are knowledgeable, energetic and enthusiastic, and this will be a major English garden very soon. It's only just English – the Welsh border is across the River Lugg which flows through their 25 acres. Little of the old Edwardian garden remains, except for a fine herringbone brick terrace above a lily pool, with twelve fat dumplings of clipped box around it, enlivened with regale lilies. Hedges of beech and yew are planted, and crossed by an avenue of pleached limes, underplanted with alliums and alchemilla. Separate garden rooms have been created. Kiosks of trellis are at the corners of a formal garden, with plans for a rose garden and pergola. Other plans include a hornbeam cloister, a skating pool and a Dutch garden with canals and pots. Simon has built a classical temple, called the Sulking House, fronted by a sulky border of deep maroons, black pansies, knautia and heuchera. The former orchard in front of the house is being replanted, using old varieties whose names were found listed on the apple racks in the shed. The herb garden has larch poles with carved bears on top, as in medieval gardens, and a little beech hedge is growing to make a serpentine walk – a crinkle-crankle – aligned to a giant sequoiadendron in the field. By the front door are four stone parterres, with Portugese laurel as centrepieces and pots of hostas. Smooth pebbles from the river bed provide a contrast of textures. This is a hugely ambitious garden.

4   LINGEN NURSERY   nr Presteigne   Tel 01544 267720

Daily, Feb to Oct, 10–6. Admission free.
From Presteigne go E on B4362 for 1½m. Turn L and the garden is 3m in
middle of Lingen, on R opposite a chapel.

Kim Davies started growing alpines when he was a boy. He became an expert, and has branched out to include rare herbaceous perennials. He holds the National Collection of *Iris sibirica*, and has a comprehensive personal collection of herbaceous campanulas. I wanted to buy them all. He also has a mouth-watering number of alpine penstemons and auriculas. His garden is designed to show off his interesting plants to their best advantage, and includes a new large rock garden and perennial bed. Everything is well labelled, and he is a most knowledgeable gardener, willing to let you pick his brains.

5   ASHFORD MANOR

Ashford Carbonel, nr Ludlow   Tel 01584 872100

All year, by appointment. Donation to charity.
From Ludlow go S on A49 for 4m. Just after junction with B4361, turn L on minor road signed to Ashford Carbonel. Ignore sign to village: go 1m further; garden signed on R.

A short entry in the NGS guide says intriguingly that this garden 'has hardly any flowers'. Its owner, Mr Kit Hall, took up flower arranging after World War II, and grew mostly foliage plants he could use in his work. Now in his nineties, he showed me his glorious garden with enthusiasm. Blessed with soft pastoral views, and huge old walls as a perfect backdrop, most of the planting is of trees and shrubs, with many climbers. A silver and grey corner of the sunny terrace is particularly effective. The serpentine wall in rosy brick supports tender climbers and a huge yellow tree peony. A remarkable clump of yuccas, more than a century old, and a bed of scented white peonies are near the little orchard where a wild flower meadow has established itself. The stone terrace in front of the old manor is home to stone sinks and troughs. Colour from berberis, eucalyptus, bergenias, *Alchemilla mollis* and globe artichokes lights up the garden all through the year. Mr Hall looks after the garden entirely by himself – and he's the only gardener I've met who actually welcomes dogs.

6   THE COTTAGE HERBERY

nr Tenbury Wells   Tel 01584 781575

Suns, May to July, and by appointment on weekdays, 10–6. £1
From Tenbury Wells go E on A456 for 2m. Turn L at Peacock Inn to Boraston. Turn R in village where signed.

Here is a small specialist nursery run by Rob and Kim Hurst with help from their young daughter India, not yet in her teens. All the plants are grown organically in a wild and deliciously natural valley around their Mill House where the River Cornbrook runs through the garden, dividing Worcestershire and Shropshire. Variegated and other less usual herbs are a speciality here, together with a full range of herbs used for medicine, cooking and dyeing. There is a box-edged herb bed based on the theories of Nicholas Culpeper, the 17th-century herbalist. The cottage garden is full of old favourites – hollyhocks, astrantias, foxgloves, dianthus, violas and masses of shrub roses, with numerous rose arbours and honeysuckle-draped seats. Kim produces herb suppers for parties served in her conservatory. The sales area is full of desirable plants – but it's steep and often slippery to get there, so wear stout shoes. Everywhere you look, plants ramp and abound and, always in the background, there is the music of the brook chattering and the birds singing – joyful.

7 BERRINGTON HALL (NT)

nr Leominster   Tel 01568 615721

April, Fri–Sun and BH Mons; May to June and Sept, Wed–Sun and BH Mons; July to Aug, daily; Oct, Fri–Sun, 1.30–5 (4.30 in Oct). £1.70
From Leominster go N on A49 for 3m. Garden well signed on L.

If you are interested in old apple varieties, try to visit the walled garden here at picking time. There are more than 50 varieties of historic, pre-1900 apples. The house was designed by Henry Holland, set in a splendid park and landscaped by Capability Brown, with Berrington Pool as its centre-piece. Formal Edwardian gardens, originally laid out by Dobies of Chester, has rows of clipped golden yew and a splashy fountain. The woodland garden has a fine collection of rhododendrons.

8 STOCKTON BURY GARDENS

Kimbolton, nr Leominster   Tel 01568 613432

Thurs–Sun and BH Mons, April to Oct, 2–5. £2.50
From Leominster go NE on A49 for 1½m. Turn R on A4112. Garden is ½m on R; enter through 2nd gateway.

A dwelling has been on this site since 660 AD, and although this is a rela-tively newly-planted garden, the magnificent medieval walls, tithe barn and pigeon house give it tranquillity and a sense of history. Plum orchards, kitchen garden and chicken runs have been transformed into island beds with unusual shrubs and flowers. The south wall, more than 100 yds long, shelters tender climbing plants – figs, peaches and kiwi fruit, as well as roses, honeysuckle and clematis. A conservatory in a warm corner has a grindstone from the cider mill as a central table, and plumbago and clianthus ramp about. An Elizabethan garden is coloured by soft blues and pinks, the wall dripping with a 'Pink Ice' wisteria. There are lovely views across cider apple orchards to the monastic fish ponds, and a romantic gothic ruin is incorporated into a woodland walk, together with a bog garden and a water feature in an old quarry. Meticulously planted and maintained by Raymond Treasure and Gordon Fenn, this garden is lovely. The old cider press has been beautifully converted to form a new shop and plant centre. The new loos are out of this world – be sure not to miss them.

9   STRAWBERRY COTTAGE

Hamnish, nr Leominster   Tel 01568 760319

Thurs/Fri, Suns and BH Mons, end April to mid Sept, 2–5.30, and by appointment. £1.50

From Leominster go E on A44 for 3m. Turn L at X-roads signed Hamnish, then R on minor road signed Puddleston. Turn immediately R over cattle grid and along track for ½m to garden; park car by gate to house.

It is astonishing to find that this paradise garden is only eight years old. Mr and Mrs Philpott have created a hillside sensation out of 2 acres of steep fields, with lovely pastoral views. They spent all available funds on terracing the rockery, buying mature shrubs and more than 250 roses, and then grew the rest from seeds and cuttings. It's a natural, exuberant garden, fitting perfectly into the wild landscape, painted with soft colours. Bridges and pergolas are swathed with roses, honeysuckle and clematis. Colour-themed borders are of blues and greens, yellow and white. A cottage garden filled with sweet peas, aquilegias and poppies is backed by more shrub roses, clematis and honeysuckle. The world's most contented hens have a scratching place of their own. At the top of the hill there is a tea garden where you can choose to sit on a bench under a shady ash tree, or go to a table inside a cosy tea-room. A nursery area sells interesting home-propagated stock. The enterprising Philpotts have beaten a steep slope, windblast, frost pockets and clay soil to produce an elegant and exciting garden.

Where to Stay

All B&B prices are approximate per person, sharing a double/twin room usually with private or en suite facilities. It is a good idea to ask for any special requirements when booking.

A MILEBROOK HOUSE   Tel 01547 528632

Rodney & Beryl Marsden, Milebrook House, Milebrook, nr Knighton, Powys LD7 1LT.

From one side of this family-run hotel you look out over a croquet lawn backed with rhododendrons and gorgeous wooded hills. From another, there are profuse and well-kept herbaceous borders. You are on the border of England and Wales here, in the rolling Marches, much of the country-side designated an Area of Outstanding Natural Beauty. The 6 double/twin bedrooms are spacious. Meals (lunch or dinner, £17–£20) are in Rodney and Beryl's licensed restaurant, imaginatively cooked with mostly home-grown local produce. No dogs, restricted smoking, and a family bedroom for those with children. B&B £33.

B BROXWOOD COURT   Tel 01544 340245

Mike & Anne Allen, Broxwood Court, Broxwood, nr Pembridge, Herefordshire HR6 9JJ.

High on a hill within its own 1,200-acre estate, this is a spectacular place to stay, with superb views over the Black Mountains. The 29-acre garden was designed in 1860, and has magnificent trees, and sweeping lawns com-plete with peacocks. Anne's family have been here for 600 years. In 1954 the house was elegantly rebuilt by her father, retaining the original court-yard and clock tower. Dinner (£18, licensed) is often *en famille*, and is by arrangement. Two very comfortable double/twin bedrooms. Dogs OK if you ask first. Children should be 10 or over. Smoking restricted. B&B £30–£35.

C NUMBER ELEVEN   Tel 01584 878584

Guy Crawley & Michael Martin, Number Eleven, Dinham Lane, Ludlow, Shrop-shire SY8 1EJ.

Overlooking the walls of Ludlow's picturesque 11th-century castle, this is a 1770 townhouse of quite exceptional standard. Designed by Sir James Gibb (architect of Oxford's Radcliffe Library), it is in superb condition, with period antiques and an eye for detail and attention that marks out a stay with Guy and Michael here. Tucked behind the house, amazingly in the centre of this little town, is a 300-ft walled garden on two tiers, with ter-races, a fish pond and small fountain, herbaceous borders and fruit trees, all beautifully designed and maintained. In the middle of June, it is open to the public along with about a dozen more of Ludlow's 'secret gardens' hidden from the road. The master double bedroom, with a cast-iron four-poster, is part of a suite with another double bedroom and a sitting-room. There are 2 further twin rooms. Number Eleven is licensed, and you can eat dinner (£14) by arrangement. No smoking, no dogs, and no children under 14. B&B £28–£30.

D THE OLD RECTORY   Tel 01584 811088

Rosemary Matthews, The Old Rectory, Boraston, nr Tenbury Wells, Worcestershire WR15 8LH.

You go up an ancient tree-lined drive to this Georgian top-of-the-hill country house, surrounded by open countryside with magnificent views in all directions. The 3-acre garden is Rosemary's great love, particularly good in spring with a multitude of bulbs, but with a profusion of shrubs, borders and climbers that give year-round interest. There is a hard tennis court for the energetic. John tends the kitchen garden, growing produce for candlelit dinners (£15) in the dining-room – or in the courtyard if it's a balmy night: bring your own wine. Two spacious double/twin bedrooms. No smoking, dogs by arrangement, no babies. B&B £25.

E UPPER BUCKTON FARM   Tel 01547.540634

Hayden & Yvonne Lloyd, Upper Buckton Farm, Upper Buckton, Leintwardine, nr Craven Arms, Shropshire SY7 0JU.

The Georgian house here, set in 450 acres of family farmland, looks out on lovely gardens, informally designed and lovingly gardened, where Yvonne devotes attention to her favourite plants – hostas and lilies. The grounds, with wide lawns, slope gently to a mill stream and a motte. A ha-ha takes you to old-fashioned meadowland, the River Teme, and old woodlands beyond. Yvonne is a generous and imaginative cook (evening meals £18, bring your own wine), and you usually eat *en famille*, unless farming is particularly hectic. Three double/twin bedrooms. No dogs in the house, children under 12 to be discussed, no smoking. B&B £25.

F HEATH HOUSE   Tel 01568 760385

Margaret & Peter Neal, Heath House, Humber, nr Leominster, Herefordshire HR6 0NF.

Peter says he finds gardening here on light and fertile soil a joy after 50 years on Thames Basin clay. A weeping ash dominates one side of the lawn in front of this low, pretty stone house, and elsewhere there are herbaceous borders, many climbers, a formal garden, and a good vegetable garden with produce for evening meals. These are by arrangement, and cost from £13, depending on how elaborate they are, whether you want wine, etc. Three double/twin and 1 single bedroom. Restricted smoking, no dogs, and children should be discussed in advance. B&B £22.

G HIGHFIELD   Tel 01568 613216

> *Catherine & Marguerite Fothergill, Highfield, Ivington Road, Leominster, Here-fordshire HR6 8QD.*

This is a big, comfortable Edwardian house, with good furniture and carefully-chosen furnishings, set in an acre of garden surrounded by fields, with lovely views over the hills; great sunsets a speciality. Catherine and Marguerite are twins who found that cooking and entertaining was much more their passion than science teaching so moved from London for a different lifestyle. As gardeners, they say they are still learning, and like to talk to guests about it. With lovely mature trees, including an old walnut, herbaceous beds, a herb patio and a large greenhouse, there is room for ambition here. The food is special. Talk to either host about what you enjoy eating, and chances are it will be transformed into something better. Prices for evening meals are from £12, licensed. Three double/twin bedrooms. Restricted smoking, no dogs, no children. B&B £17–£20.

What Else to Enjoy

This is a short selection of the many good things recommended in the area by owners of places to stay. Your hosts will certainly be able to provide additional information.

Other Gardens/Nurseries

Queenswood Country Park is home to a well-forested arboretum with more than 500 unusual trees. The 170 acres of park are noted for an abundance of wild flowers and fungi. There is good car parking, a visitor centre with information leaflets, a café, shop and loos. Admission free. You will find it on the S edge of the visit map, signed off the A49.

If It's Wet

Two NT properties lie at the centre of this visit. **Berrington Hall** (*see* Garden 7) is an elegant late 18th-century house and you get a good insight into domestic life by visiting the recently restored bedroom suite and a nursery, laundry and Georgian dairy. House open as for garden.

The walls and corner towers of nearby **Croft Castle** were built in the 14th and 15th centuries. The interior, with a fine staircase and elaborate plasterwork ceilings, is mainly 18th century. Opening times as for Berrington Hall. The huge park with avenues of fine trees, the walled garden with herbaceous planting and a modern vineyard are also here.

People often call **Ludlow** the loveliest small town in England, and they may be right. It is unhurried, picturesque and friendly and there is a wealth of buildings to be explored – the ancient castle, the museum, the cathedral-like parish church, craft workshops, nice places to eat and many antique and curio shops.

Leominster, too, offers similar enjoyments. The Mousetrap stocks a good range of the mouth-watering cheeses made in the area, together with local cider, wine and other produce.

Drive W from here on the A44 and you come to two black-and-white villages which are absolute gems. **Eardisland** straddles the River Arrow and has the cosiest tea-room you will ever find, together with an inexpensive gift shop which carries a good range of countryside books. **Pembridge** is even better endowed with wonderful old oak buildings. The little covered market is enchanting and the old coaching inn makes you feel as if you are in another century. Be sure to call in at the visitor centre, which has a cafeteria, loos and gift-shop, and can set you out on walks or drives along the Black and White Villages Trail. And don't miss a bargain antique shop irresistibly called 'Junk and Disorderly'.

Eating Out

If you want to celebrate, the restaurant most widely recommended is at the **Marsh Country Hotel**. Jacqueline and Martin Gilleland spent seven years sensitively restoring this lovely medieval house, and creating a delightful garden round which you can wander before you settle down to one of Jacqueline's tasty dinners. The set dinner menu costs £20, and with wine and service you will end up paying £30–£35. You will find it at **Eyton**, 2m NW of Leominster off the B4361. Tel 01568 613952.

Around Worcester

Worcester, its glorious cathedral perched above the River Severn and the peaceful water meadows, has a variety of interesting gardens not far away. Stone House Cottage is especially fascinating, and shouldn't be missed. Musically we are in Elgar country – but it is also Gerald Finzi country. If you haven't become acquainted with his music, this is the perfect time to do so. He grew and treasured many old varieties of English apples, and his music is essentially English too, lyrical and nostalgic. For an introduction, try his Clarinet Concerto, Opus 31. Emma Johnson has made a sparkling recording.

OS maps: Landrangers 138, 139, **150**

Gardens

Opening times: in larger gardens, and in NT properties, last admissions are usually 30–45 minutes before the garden closes. Admission charges are a guide to what one adult can expect to pay to go round the garden. It sometimes varies with the season or days of the week. When the house is also open to the public, there is usually an additional charge.

I **LAKESIDE** nr Worcester Tel 01886 821119

Charity Suns in April and June, 2–6, and by appointment for groups. £2 From Worcester go W on A44 for 9m. Turn L on minor road signed to Linley Green. Garden is ½m further in Gaines Rd.

Whether you visit in April, when the bulbs and flowering shrubs are marvellous, or in June when the mixed beds and borders in the walled garden are at their best, the views here are so breathtaking they shouldn't be missed. Your eye goes down a steep slope to a lake and fountain, once three medieval stewponds, and beyond to ravishing countryside. There is a heather garden, and a newly-established bog garden. Unusual plants are for sale on open days. The owner, Chris Philip, is a plant specialist, having

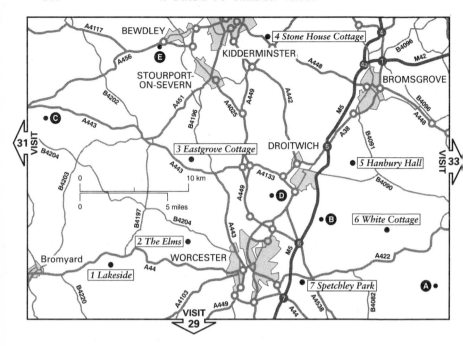

devised and compiled *The Plant Finder*, a directory of Britain's nurseries selling rare varieties.

2   THE ELMS   Lower Broadheath, nr Worcester   Tel 01905 640841

Tues/Wed, late June to Oct, 10–4, and by appointment. £1.50
From Worcester go NW on B4204 for 4m to Lower Broadheath. Turn L opposite school into Frenchlands Lane. Garden is ½m at end of track.

In this idyllic, isolated setting, a lovely 1½-acre garden is now maturing well. Started nine years ago around a Georgian farmhouse and old farm buildings, Mr and Mrs Stewart have used flair and imagination in creating a blue-and-white garden, a border of sizzling hot colours, a lily pool, mixed herbaceous borders and a rose walk. In the old fold yard, an ornamental kitchen garden contains a nursery selling cottage-garden treasures and rare herbaceous plants.

3   EASTGROVE COTTAGE NURSERY

Sankyn's Green, nr Droitwich   Tel 01299 896389

Thurs–Mon, April to July; Thurs–Sat, Sept to mid Oct, 2–5. £2
From Droitwich go W on A4133 for 4m. Turn R on B4196 for 1½m. Turn
L to Sankyn's Green (½m). Garden and nursery are signed on L.

Here, around a pretty black-and-white cottage, is a small, fascinating garden where every plant is a winner. Old brick paths meander through beds
of clever colour combinations and foliage interest. A small arboretum contains trees with especially interesting leaves. A magnificent honeysuckle,
Lonicera 'Anna Fletcher', grows up the old barn, along with an elegant tiny
rose 'Pom-Pom de Paris'. Malcolm and Carol Skinner give visitors a warm
welcome and are always at hand for advice. Splendid home-propagated
plants are for sale.

4   STONE HOUSE COTTAGE

nr Kidderminster   Tel 01562 69902

Wed–Sat, March to Oct, 10–6 (also Suns in May and June). £2
From Kidderminster go SE on A448 for 2½m to Stone village. Garden is on
L up drive next to church.

Here is a most remarkable garden. Set in an old walled kitchen garden, it
is now divided up into many smaller rooms, with vistas radiating out to
give it interest every way you turn. The design makes the garden feel much
larger than it actually is. Louisa Arbuthnott is a talented gardener and propagator. Not only does she raise thousands of desirable plants to sell, but has
managed five children as well. James Arbuthnott has a passion for building
towers, gazebos and arcades, all of them covered by climbing, scrambling
plants. A long yew walk is tempting; raised beds by the house nurture
alpines and tender treasures; interesting foliage plants form the backdrop to
the borders. Everything is labelled and you may be able to buy a rarity in
the excellent nursery – being so sheltered here, there are many tender
plants. This is an exceptionally personal and intriguingly romantic garden –
the perfect place for a grown-up game of hide-and-seek. On a couple of
evenings in June, you can take a picnic and listen to music wafting down
from the towers.

5 HANBURY HALL (NT)   nr Droitwich   Tel 01527 821214

Sun–Wed, April to Oct, 2–6. £2.50
From Droitwich go E on B4090 for 4½m. Garden is well signed on L.

This charming house, built in 1701 by the Vernon family, originally had a
garden designed by George London. It is his design that the NT is now busy
reconstructing. The sunken parterre, divided into four box-edged sections,
echoes the formality of the architecture, and is planted in blocks of bold
colour. Beyond this is a wilderness, and then a formal fruit garden. There
is a fine orangery, built in 1740, complete with cossetted orange trees, and
an 18th-century ice house. When fully restored, it will be a magnificent
garden.

6   WHITE COTTAGE
Stock Green, nr Redditch   Tel 01386 792414

Fri–Tues, mid April to Sept, 10–5, advance appointment appreciated. £1
From Worcester go E on A422 for 7m to Red Hart Inn. Turn L at brown tourist
sign to Stock Green (1½m), and L at T-junction in village. Garden is 100 yds
on L.

This tranquil 2-acre garden, a haven for wildlife, is chiefly known for its
collection of hardy geraniums. There are more than 150 varieties of these
adaptable flowers here, spilling out over paths and bulking out the herbaceous borders. A rock garden displays some of the smaller geraniums. Island beds burgeon with herbaceous perennials, and there is a pretty stream
with its bog garden. Mrs Bates's favourite plant (apart from her cranesbills)
are tree peonies, which she grows to perfection. In spring, the wild garden
is carpeted with cowslips, primroses, fritillaries and bluebells. Very good
plants are for sale here, and also at the nearby **Coneybury Plant Centre**,
run by the same Bates family. Here you can find many David Austin roses,
and flowering shrubs you have admired at White Cottage.

7   SPETCHLEY PARK   nr Worcester   Tel 01905 565224

Tues–Fri, Suns, BHs, April to Sept, 11–5 (Suns 2–5). £3
From Worcester go E on A422 for 2m. Park entrance well signed on R.

When I visited this garden several years ago it was overgrown and dank,
and seemed neglected. Not any more – it is being beautifully restored to
the grand design of Miss Ellen Wilmott and her sister Rose Berkeley. It is
very large, with charming yew-enclosed gardens full of shrub roses, mar-

vellous tree peonies and cranesbills. The wide borders under the sheltering rose-brick walls are splendid. A new garden with lily pool has been built, and will shortly mature into a romantic Edwardian rose garden. The park contains magnificent trees and a lake. In spring, the daffodils are justly famous, and I found a field of martagon lilies just coming out in May. Strangely, the house stands gauntly away from the gardens, surrounded by dark cedars, detached from the jewel colours in the yew-hedged main garden.

Where to Stay

All B&B prices are approximate per person, sharing a double/twin room usually with private or en suite facilities. It is a good idea to ask for any special requirements when booking.

A MANOR FARM HOUSE   Tel 01386 462226

Sheila Virr, Manor Farm House, Ab Lench, nr Evesham, Worcestershire WR11 4UP.

The soft bricks of this 200-year-old farmhouse are covered with climbers, and the large lawn in the garden sweeps away to borders, a duck pond, and a vegetable garden with enviable produce – all surrounded by trees and meadows in a tranquil part of England. Sheila was for many years a drama critic, and still keeps her links with the Royal Shakespeare Company. Now she follows some of her many other interests – antique-collecting, gardening, cooking, entertaining. There are two double/twin bedrooms with pretty views. Dinner (£17.50) is unlicensed. Dogs by arrangement, restricted smoking, children should be over 10. B&B £29–£30

B CHURCH FARM   Tel 01905 772387

Anne & Michael Dean, Church Farm, Oddingley, nr Droitwich, Worcestershire WR9 7NE.

There is plenty of room to stretch your legs around this large farmhouse beside the Worcester–Midland Canal. The gardens are spacious, leading to a cider orchard and open farmland. Play tennis on an all-weather court, if you feel energetic, or croquet, if you feel mean. You will be made very much at home by Anne (who comes from America) and Michael who entertain with enthusiasm. Evening meals are £15.50 (licensed). Two generous double bedrooms and 1 single. No dogs, children should be over 12, and smoking restricted. B&B £28.

C ROBINS END   Tel 01584 781592

Adrian & Sarah Worsley, Robins End, Eastham, nr Tenbury Wells,
Worcestershire WR15 8NW.

Sarah loves the 5 acres of gardens and woodlands around her Queen Anne rectory, and is justifiably proud of them. Lawns sweep down to a ha-ha and spectacular views over the Teme valley. Mixed borders are planted for scent as well as colour. There is a monumental copper beech, and magnificent yews. The kitchen garden and greenhouse are so productive that Sarah has a vegetable and fruit stall in her drive. If you're feeling at all sporty, there is a heated swimming pool, a hard tennis court, a croquet lawn – and, inside the house, a fine billiard room. The house is comfortably furnished, with 2 spacious double bedrooms and 1 single. Usually, you eat out in the evenings, the excellent nearby Peacock Inn being favourite. Restricted smoking, dogs and children by arrangement. B&B £28.

D CAULIN COURT   Tel 01905 756382

Sally Harfield, Caulin Court, Ladywood, nr Droitwich, Worcestershire
WR9 0AL.

Much of this large, handsome country house dates from the 18th century. It is set in 20 acres of grounds – much of it fields with horses – including a traditional English garden with lawns, old trees, herbaceous borders and many climbers. There are two delightful small orchards with old apples and perry pears. Inside, the house is full of home comfort, and if you are on your own and don't want to go out to the local pub/restaurant (which features a crown bowling green), Sally will cook you a modest evening meal (£10, bring your own wine). The 3 bedrooms, en suite, include 1 single. Dogs welcome, although they must sleep in the stable unless they are very small and well-behaved. Children welcome too. Restricted smoking. B&B £20–£23.

E TARN
Tel 01299 402243

Topsy Beeves, Tarn, Long Bank, Bewdley, Worcestershire DY12 2QT.

This comfortable country house has views over glorious wooded Worcestershire scenery. Topsy has worked every spare hour on her garden, which covers about 4 acres plus 13 acres of orchards, for thirty years, fighting a continual battle with rabbits and deer from the ancient oakwood which surrounds it. Exceptionally colourful, it has wonderful borders and informal planting. Inside the house, you can rest your legs and extend your mind in a lovely old library. There are 2 twin and 2 single bedrooms. Eat out in the evenings at good places nearby. No smoking. Dogs and children by arrangement. B&B £20.

What Else to Enjoy

This is a short selection of the many good things recommended in the area by owners of places to stay. Your hosts will certainly be able to provide additional information.

Other Gardens/Nurseries

At **Great Witley** are **Perhill Nurseries** which carry an enormous stock of alpines and herbaceous perennials, particularly campanulas and salvias. In all, more than 2,000 species and varieties are sold – and there is no mail order, so you have to visit; for directions, *see* below. Open daily, 9–6. Tel 01299 896329.

If It's Wet

The NT's **Hanbury Hall** (*see* Garden 5) is a William & Mary-style house built in 1701, with lovely interiors that include painted ceilings and an outstanding staircase. There is a good collection of porcelain. House open as garden.

Also at Hanbury is the Jinney Ring Craft Centre. Housed in lovely old farm buildings, it has a wide variety of craftsmen, including a rocking-horse maker, and several specialist shops that include needlework and stained glass. The restaurant there is tempting, too.

Witley Court, **Great Witley**, 10m NW of Worcester on the A443, is a spectacular ruined house, which caught fire earlier this century. Built on a grand scale, with lovely grounds, the dominating feature is a huge

Fountain of Perseus, now under restoration. Open daily April to Sept, and Wed–Sun in March and Oct.

Otherwise, if it looks like being a rainy day, head for **Worcester** where there is much to do and see, including the wonderful cathedral. The Royal Worcester porcelain factory in Severn Street runs fascinating tours, and the factory shop sells china at bargain prices. Its museum has some fine treasures, and there is a family restaurant. Opening hours vary. Tel 01905 23221.

Also worth visiting is the Museum of Local Life, in a 16th-century half-timbered building in Friar Street. The displays are vivid and realistic. Open daily (except Thurs and Suns) 10.30–5. Tel 01905 722349.

Elgar-lovers may want to make a pilgrimage to the little cottage in **Lower Broadheath** where he was born in 1857. From Worcester, go W on A44 for 2½m, and turn R at sign 'Broadheath – Elgar's Birthplace'. Open most days of the year except Weds. Opening times vary. Tel 01905 333224.

Eating Out

Most widely recommended is **Brown's**, at 24 Quay Street, **Worcester**. It is a converted grain mill overlooking the River Severn, with a stripped-down interior and a feeling of airy spaciousness. A set menu lunch costs £16, dinner £30. There are no extras except for wine, and the menus have many imaginative choices. Tel 01905 26263.

Shakespeare Country

I took my first toddling footsteps in the garden of Shakespeare's Birthplace because we lived next door. As you may guess, I know this area very well. Despite the huge number of tourists who come here, the countryside is still lovely, with its willow banks, pretty little villages and great gardens. You can enjoy the river by hiring a boat on the river at Stratford-upon-Avon (oh, those long-gone days when there were just half a dozen of us in a couple of punts, and had the river to ourselves), or take in the view of the whole Avon valley from the Tower at Warwick Castle. I suggest something suitably Shakespearian for your music here. William Walton's incidental music to Sir Laurence Olivier's film of *Henry V*, perhaps, or his brilliant opera *Troilus and Cressida*.

OS maps: Landrangers 139, 150, **151**

Gardens

Opening times: in larger gardens, and in NT properties, last admissions are usually 30–45 minutes before the garden closes. Admission charges are a guide to what one adult can expect to pay to go round the garden. It sometimes varies with the season or days of the week. When the house is also open to the public, there is usually an additional charge.

I   COUGHTON COURT (NT)   nr Alcester   Tel 01789 762435

Over Easter; then Sat–Wed, May to Sept; Sat/Sun in April and Oct; 11–5.30. £3

From Alcester go N on A435 for 1m. Garden well signed on R.

A stunning 16th-century house is the backdrop for a formal garden here that slides away over the River Arrow to a deer park. This is the home of the Throckmorton family, and with a burst of energy Mrs Clare Throckmorton's daughter, Christina Birch, has designed and planted a huge and magnificent new walled garden. You have to pay a little extra to see it, and

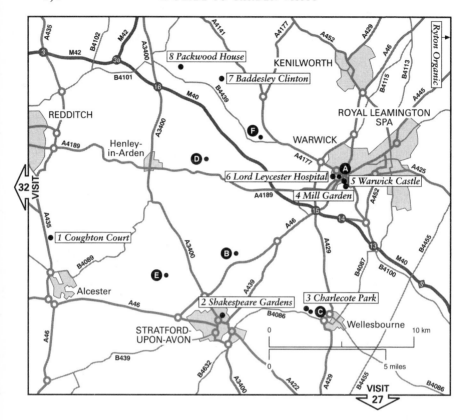

it is worth every penny. All sorts of brilliant ideas are contained inside. There is a rose labyrinth, based on the theme of 'Fair Rosamund', mistress of Henry II. Around a statue of this buxom local lady (Woodstock was her real strutting ground) are Rosamundi roses and blowsy catmint – a perfect combination. Little paths lead one through arbours, arches and gazebos, all beautifully made, and roses, clematis and honeysuckle are rapidly climbing to the tops of them. There is exciting use of colours. Soft peaches, apricots, lemons and creams are spiked with navy delphiniums, and cooled with grey and silver foliage plants. There is a scented garden, a marvellously moody red and purple garden, and past the sunken pool you can see through to two vast, sparkling herbaceous borders beyond the walls. Elsewhere, around the house, a courtyard garden has a group of box-enclosed parterres, with large pots of lilies making the air swoony with scent. Sit down here, and look down a pleached lime walk across the lawns, to black and white cows grazing in the park. It's lovely. There are very good plant sales, a restaurant, and exhibitions in the stable yard.

2 SHAKESPEARE GARDENS

Stratford-upon-Avon   Tel 01789 204016

All year (with rare exceptions), 9.30 or 10–5.30 or dusk. Various charges.
All gardens are in the vicinity of Stratford-upon-Avon, and well signed. There
is a good coach tour if you (advisedly) leave your car in a park.

At **Shakespeare's Birthplace** there is a town garden, with trees (notably a venerable mulberry), herbs and flowers mentioned by the Bard. **Mary Arden's House** is basically a farmhouse, with mixed, charming cottage borders, together with an exhibition of old farm implements in the barn. Sometimes you can watch falconry practised on the lawn. **Anne Hathaway's Cottage** is the quintessential cottage garden, dizzying American visitors unused to such prettiness. There are antique gardening tools to look at, and good plant sales. At **New Place** there is an Elizabethan knot garden, with a tunnel of apple trees, where sweetbriar scents the shady walk. **Halls Croft** is where Shakespeare's daughter Susannah Hall lived. It is charming when the wisteria is out, and the borders are bosky.

3 CHARLECOTE PARK (NT)

nr Wellesbourne   Tel 01789 470277

Fri–Tues, April to Oct, 11–6. £4.40
From Stratford-upon-Avon go E on B4086 for 5m. Turn L on B4088. Garden
signed on L after ½m.

This is the family home of the Lucy family, famous because Shakespeare is supposed to have been caught poaching deer in the park here. His alleged misconduct has been commemorated by planting a Shakespeare border with plants mentioned in his plays and sonnets. He must have known and loved flowers and the countryside, because he wrote about them so often – 'oxlips and nodding violets', and all those herbs poor Ophelia ranted on about. Today's park was laid out by Capability Brown, and the River Avon meanders through it. There is a fine riverside terrace beside the house, clipped yews, wonderful urns and an orangery in the formal gardens. The statues were collected by the family on a Grand Tour of Europe in the 19th century.

4   THE MILL GARDEN   Warwick   Tel 01926 492877

Suns, Easter to early Oct, 11–6, and by appointment. Donation for charity.
At 55 Mill St, immediately next to Warwick Castle

Over many years, Arthur Measures has created a jewel of a garden, tucked under the towering walls of Warwick Castle and dropping down to the River Avon. Reflected light from the river makes the garden sparkle. A ruined 14th-century bridge and magnificent trees on the opposite bank make this setting dramatic and theatrical, matched by exuberant foliage planting. The sound effects come from water rushing continuously over the weir. By the water's edge are gunnera, kingcups, astilbes and ox-eye daisies. Bold planting includes large architectural clumps of *Euphorbia wulfenii*, alliums and bamboos. A rose hedge planted thirty years ago now towers 25 ft high, cascading like a creamy waterfall. Honeysuckles have climbed to the top of tall holly trees. An enchanting summer-house has a marvellous carved door with ornamental hinges – a castle reject. Close to the house is a sheltered terrace covered with sinks and pots full of tender treasures, all jostling for space with rampant campanulas, pansies, astrantias, heathers and sedums.

5   WARWICK CASTLE   Warwick   Tel 01926 408000

All year except Christmas day, 10–6 or dusk. £8.50
Car park well signed in centre of Warwick.

Centuries old, rising high above the town and dominating the scenery with its formidable towers, Warwick Castle has been home to the Greville family until a few years ago when it was bought by the Madame Tussaud company. Fear not – the changes they have made here are all to the good. Everyone who visits seems to come away admiring the way that they have been able to enhance some of the richest historical heritage we have. The castle stands in 60 acres of grounds, landscaped by Capability Brown who was given a site of extraordinary natural beauty, dropping down a slope to the River Avon. Magnificent Cedars of Lebanon frame a famous view, and successive Earls of Warwick added their personal touches to the gardens. An orangery, a formal parterre, and a magnificently restored Victorian rose garden are all there to be enjoyed. Some snobby peacocks have a lawn all to themselves. It would be worth crossing the Atlantic just for the views from the walls to the river beneath.

6 LORD LEYCESTER HOSPITAL
(THE MASTER'S GARDEN)   Warwick   Tel 01929 491422

Daily except Mons, Easter to end Sept, 10–4.30. £1 donation to charity.
In the centre of Warwick, at corner of Westgate and High St. Small car park
behind in Brook St.

Hidden behind a unique group of medieval buildings lies The Master's
Garden at Lord Leycester Hospital, secret and very old. Enclosed by the
town walls, it was the home created by the Earl of Dudley for twelve
ageing soldiers – The Brethren – with a Master in charge. This was in 1571,
and there are still twelve Brethren and a Master living here. (You can buy
jolly good lunches and teas in the Brethren's Kitchen.) Restoration of the
gardens began in 1993, under the careful direction of Dr Susan Rhodes,
garden designer and historian. It has been a community effort, with towns-
people giving plants and seeds, old garden implements and flowerpots, and
most importantly their time and skills. Original herringbone brick paths
have been uncovered, and new plantings of box and yew are already well
established. There is a pleached lime hedge, herbaceous beds of soft colours
and a thatched summer-house, while a restored pineapple pit was found
under a gazebo with a hypocaust (an ancient underfloor heating system). An
ornamental vegetable garden with standard gooseberries, old wheelbarrows
and rhubarb forcers add to the feeling of antiquity. A Norman arch found
in the chapel frames a vast 2,000-year-old Egyptian vase brought back from
the banks of the Nile. Fitting in with the atmosphere of this marvellous
place, but new, is a rose pergola and a bowling green for the Brethren.
Lucky them.

7 BADDESLEY CLINTON (NT)
Chadwick End, nr Solihull   Tel 01564 783294

Wed–Sun and BH Mons, March to Oct, 2–6 (Oct 12.30–4.30). £2.25
From Warwick go NW on A4177 for 1m. At roundabout, branch L on A4141
for 1½m. In Baddesley Clinton village follow signs L to garden.

The moat around this 14th-century manor mirrors gardens here which echo
that age, although the Victorians planted some rhododendrons along the
lovely walk that leads around the ancient fish ponds; the spring daffodil display is incomparable. The walled garden is formal, with good colours in the
borders, the moat is dreamy with waterlilies and the Fenners family has its
coat of arms created by plants in the lawn. There is a charming herb

garden. Best to avoid weekends – it's very popular, partly because of the excellent licensed restaurant here for lunch.

8   PACKWOOD HOUSE (NT)

Lapworth, nr Solihull   Tel 01564 782024

Wed–Sun and BH Mons, April to Oct, 2–6 (Oct 12.30–4.30). £2.50
From Warwick go NW on A4177 for 3m. Fork L on B4439 for 5m. Garden
is well signed on R.

This Carolean garden is famous for its 'Sermon on the Mount' represented in old yew trees which were originally set out in 1650 by John Fetherston. One commands the top of a mound, reached by a spiral path, and twelve 'apostle' yews are on the terrace below. Other yews, planted in an old orchard, represent 'the multitude'. Elsewhere, brick walls enclose a formal garden with a gazebo at each corner, there are magnificent herbaceous borders and a sunken pool. In spring, drifts of bulbs are marvellous in the woodland.

Where to Stay

All B&B prices are approximate per person, sharing a double/twin room usually with private or en suite facilities. It is a good idea to ask for any special requirements when booking.

A   BROME HOUSE   Tel 01926 491069

Cherrie & Ray Chandley, Brome House, Bridge End, Warwick, Warwickshire CV34 6PB.

You couldn't be in a prettier part of the town of Warwick here. Tucked down a little road facing directly on to the river and the castle walls, Brome House is 15th-century, traditionally half-timbered, and has a well-kept long narrow 'old English' garden on three tiers at the back. There are 2 double/twin bedrooms with much character. You eat out in the evenings at any of a huge choice of places in the town. Children welcome, no dogs, and no smoking in bedrooms. B&B £28.

B INGON GRANGE   Tel 01789 731122

Margaret Watkins, Ingon Grange, Ingon Lane, Snitterfield, Stratford-upon-Avon, Warwickshire CV37 0QF.

This large, comfortable family home, on the outskirts of the village, has a 4-acre garden constantly being improved, with splendid views in all directions, and a ha-ha linking it to meadowland beyond. There is a tennis court. Television is banned from the spacious lounge set aside for guests, so expect to do some friendly talking. The airy bedrooms (2 double, 1 single) have nice outlooks. Margaret will suggest many places to eat out in the evenings. No smoking, no dogs, and children should be over 10. B&B £24.

C KINGSMEAD FARM   Tel 01789 840254

Jennifer Seccombe, Kingsmead Farm, Stratford Rd, Charlecote, nr Wellesbourne, Warwickshire CV35 9ES.

You overlook Charlecote Park (Garden 3) from this wisteria-covered old house with its attractive garden. There is a range of good accommodation here because the owners have sensitively and imaginatively converted the coach house and two cottages into self-catering suites. Otherwise, there are 3 double/twin bedrooms in the house itself. No smoking, no dogs, children OK depending on which accommodation you choose. B&B £23.

D OAKTREE FARM   Tel 01926 842413

Louise & David Smith, Oaktree Farm, Yarningale Common, Claverdon, nr Warwick, Warwickshire CV35 9EB.

The garden around this comfortable farmhouse is perhaps unique among all those described in this book: it looks wild, and is designed to be so. David, besides farming the 34 acres of meadow and woodland here, is a wildlife photographer, and works with the Warwickshire Wildlife Trust. So if you wonder what a big clump of thistles is doing so near the house, it's because it is encouraged to be there. Staying here is very good value. The 3 double/twin bedrooms are all en suite and have TV. There are log fires. Evening meals (bring your own wine) cost £8, a price made possible because all the ingredients (including meat) come from the farm. Children welcome, dogs by arrangement, restricted smoking. B&B £21.

E PEAR TREE COTTAGE   Tel 01789 262282

Ted & Margaret Mander, Pear Tree Cottage, Church Rd, Wilmcote,
nr Stratford-upon-Avon, Warwickshire CV37 9UX.

This stone and half-timbered listed building has enormous character and
charm. Set in a large country garden, well-tended and with plenty of plants
to enjoy, it overlooks Mary Arden's House (one of the Shakespeare
Gardens, 2 above). The bedrooms (6 double, 1 single, some in a later
extension) are of a high standard. No dogs, restricted smoking, children
welcome. B&B £20–£23.

F SHREWLEY POOLS FARM   Tel 01926 484315

Cathy Dodd, Shrewley Pools Farm, Haseley, nr Warwick, Warwickshire
CV35 7HB.

The 1-acre garden attached to this working farm was lovingly created by
Cathy's mother-in-law, whose hobby was collecting unusual specimens
from specialist nurseries all over the country – trees, shrubs, climbers,
herbaceous plants. It is a plantsman's joy. The house is 16th century, with
beams, open fireplaces, oak floors and many original features. You get a
warm welcome from Cathy, and very comfortable rooms to sit and relax
in. She is flexible about cooking evening meals (unlicensed). There are 2
guest bedrooms (1 family, 1 twin). No smoking, no dogs, children welcome.
B&B £20–23.

What Else to Enjoy

This is a short selection of the many good things recommended in the area by owners
of places to stay. Your hosts will certainly be able to provide additional information.

Other Gardens/Nurseries

Ryton Organic Gardens is the place to learn all about mulching, green
manure crops and how to attract the right sort of wildlife to your garden.
The 7 acres include a wood, a wildflower meadow, soft fruit, a rose
garden, herbaceous and shrub borders, herbs, veggies with interesting old
varieties growing and a bee garden. There is also a lovely scented garden
for the blind, a children's play area and picnic places. The restaurant

serves delicious lunches and teas (organic, of course). Open daily except Christmas, 9–5.30. It is just off the visit map. From Leamington Spa, go NE on A445 for 9m. Cross over A45, and the garden is signed ½ m on R. Tel 01203 303517.

If It's Wet

Warwick Castle (*see* Garden 5) is much the best place to head for, and the town of **Warwick** is compact and full of antique shops and antiquities. Call in at the friendly tourist information centre in the Court House, Jury Street (Tel 01926 492212), where you will be helped on your way. The local guide leaflet is charmingly written.

Otherwise, you will no doubt want to go to **Stratford-upon-Avon**. This is now so much a tourist centre that you will find it hard not to get caught up in the crowds. Definitely park your car in one of the numerous signed car parks, and then forget it for the day. You can walk across the old tram bridge over the River Avon, and enjoy the best introductory view of the theatre and the low-slung town. Along Waterside, you will find the Parish church and Shakespeare's grave. For old times' sake (mine, not yours), enjoy a drink on the terrace of the pub nick-named the Dirty Duck near the theatre, and look out on to the gardens, trees and river beyond.

There are four NT properties described above – **Coughton Court** (*see* Garden 1), **Charlecote Park** (Garden 3), **Baddesley Clinton** (Garden 7) and **Packwood House** (Garden 8) whose houses are open to the public approximately during garden hours.

Eating Out

Places to eat change hands pretty regularly in this area (and the restaurant I was going to recommend in Stratford-upon-Avon has recently closed). Instead, walk up Sheep Street and see which of the many menus displayed might suit your taste that night. A pub/restaurant you can trust is **The Bell** at **Alderminster**, just off the S edge of the visit map on the A3400. Tel 01789 450414.

Northamptonshire

The south-western end of this visit has lovely rolling hills and good views. North-east of the M1 it becomes busier and more industrial. Reservoirs are dotted about, giving good opportunities for bird-watching (including flamingos at Coton Manor, which is a particularly good garden to visit). You will be spending quite a bit of time in the car if you intend to look at all the gardens here. A tape I often play is Max Bruch's Violin Concerto No. 1 in G minor. There are dozens of recordings, from Sir Yehudi Menuhin to Nigel Kennedy. It's such a wonderful piece that it's hard to find a dull interpretation. Drive along and enjoy it.

OS maps: Landrangers 140, 141, **152**, 153

Gardens

Opening times: in larger gardens, and in NT properties, last admissions are usually 30–45 minutes before the garden closes. Admission charges are a guide to what one adult can expect to pay to go round the garden. It sometimes varies with the season or days of the week. When the house is also open to the public, there is usually an additional charge.

I   THE MENAGERIE
Horton, nr Northampton   Tel 01604 870957

Thurs, April to Sept, 10–4, and groups by appointment. £2.50
From Northampton go SE on B526 for 7m. Garden entrance is 1m after Horton village. Turn L opposite lay-by through a field. There is a small sign on farm gate. Difficult to find; owner helpful with final directions.

The Menagerie has its name because it is on the site where Lord Halifax kept his private zoo, surrounded by a moat, in the 18th century. An outstanding rococo folly was built in the grounds, and this was restored to its former glory in 1975 by the late Gervase Jackson-Stops, the architectural historian and writer who made it his home. The garden was mainly devel-

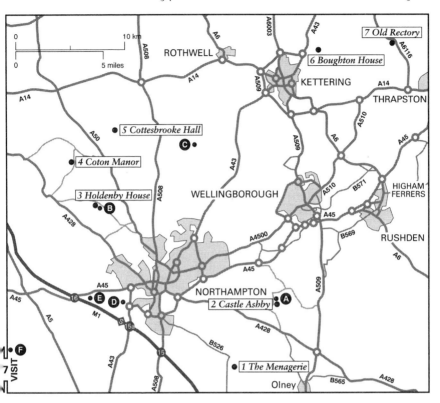

oped from 1992 by Ian Kirby, incorporating four of the earlier fishponds, and giving them fountains. There are two remarkable thatched arbours, a bog garden, heavenly shrubberies with serpentine paths and awash with colour, herbaceous borders and formal planting around the house. There is an enchanted grotto, a shell-lined cave where Orpheus plays to the animals: it's not always open, but you can ask the gardener to let you peep in. The south front of the house is planted with herbs and Mediterranean plants, and lots of lavender. Espaliered fruit trees are trained up wires to echo the ornamental scrolls decorating the house. Plans for the future development of this rare house and garden continue. I'm looking forward to the Wicked Garden which promises to be full of poisonous plants and Nasty Things. There is a very good nursery garden attached to the property, mostly selling perennials propagated from here by the affable head gardener, Mike Brown.

2   CASTLE ASHBY GARDENS

nr Northampton   Tel 01604 696696

Daily, 10–dusk (occasionally closed for events). £2.50 in ticket machine
From Northampton go SE on A428 for 7m. Turn L to Castle Ashby. Garden
(1½m) well signed on R.

The grand home of the Marquess of Northampton is set in a magnificent park landscaped by Capability Brown, who also built the Temple seen across the Menagerie Pond. The views across the park are stunning, with avenues of beech, horse chestnut and lime, and extensive lawns. The Terrace Garden, designed by Matthew Digby Wyatt, has more than 100 urns – what a job to plant and water them all. The fountains here are being restored; indeed, much restoration work is going on in the garden, and will continue for some years. The Italian Garden has cones of clipped yews, more than 30 terracotta urns – more watering – and a triumphant archway, or Gloriette'. The orangery is stocked with *Cytisus battandieri*, figs, jasmines and magnolias. The Summerhouse Garden has colourful bedding schemes, a pond with great crested newts, and yet more especially beautiful urns. The walled kitchen garden is now a field, with deserted bee boles. Try to find the energy to stroll round the lake and woodland walk. It has marvellous trees, bulbs in spring, marsh iris, a Capability Brown bridge, masses of wildflowers and orange-tipped butterflies. The church in the grounds is worth visiting. Supposedly, there is a witch's grave which nobody tends but is always immaculate.

3   HOLDENBY HOUSE GARDENS

nr Northampton   Tel 01604 770074

Suns, BH Mons, and Thurs in July/Aug, April to Sept, 2–6. £3
From Northampton go N on A50 for 3m. Turn L on minor road via Church
Brampton for 3m. Garden signed on L.

Sir Christopher Hatton built this 16th-century house and created around it a large garden. Little remains of the original plan, but Rosemary Verey has planted a replica of an Elizabethan garden, using period plants. It is very charming. Also enjoy a fragrant border, silver borders and some lovely piggies in the rare breeds farmstead.

4 COTON MANOR GARDENS

Ravensthorpe, nr Northampton   Tel 01604 740219

Wed–Sun and BH Mons, mid April to early Oct, 12–6. £2.70
From Northampton go NW on A50 for 7m. Turn L to Hollowell and follow
brown tourist signs to garden (1½ m).

This garden looks good all the year round, mostly because of its strong
bones – holly hedges, dark and glistening and immaculately clipped, yews
and velvet lawns. Little springs dash down the hill, a glistening pool is over-
hung by a double pink cherry. Around the house, dated 1662, is a terrace
filled with pots and sinks of tender plants, and heavenly scented geraniums.
A round rosebed has a petticoat edging of *Stachys lanata,* and flourishing
along the stream bank are candelabra primulas, Welsh poppies, alliums and
astilbes, together with azaleas and acers. A series of small linked ponds are
home to duck, geese and flamingos, next to a goosey haven of meadowland
under old apple and pear trees. The herbaceous borders are packed with
interesting plants, and happily the less well-known are labelled. In the
kitchen garden there is a splendid selection of herbs. The tropical house has
more water, gushing from a cherub's fat face, and vibrant colours from
exotic plants. Very good home-propagated plants are always for sale. You
get a warm welcome from Mr and Mrs Pasley-Tyler, the third generation
in a family of gardeners here.

5 COTTESBROOKE HALL

nr Northampton   Tel 01604 505808

Wed–Fri, BH Mons and Suns in Sept, Easter to Sept, 2–5.30. £2.50
From Northampton go NW on A50 for 6m. Turn R to Cottesbrooke (1½m)
where the garden is signed.

This magnificent Queen Anne house, dating from 1702, is set in a splendid
park with long pastoral views over lakes and sheep-grazed meadows. The
gardens around the house, and the wild garden, have been developed during
this century by a number of notable designers including Dame Sylvia Crowe
and Sir Geoffrey Jellicoe, the latter being responsible for the formal Fore-
court garden. There is a great deal to enjoy here. As you go in, there is a
long statue walk, with statues of philosophers flanked by a tapestry hedge
and clipped yews. Elsewhere is a Dutch Garden with two sundials, the
Dilemma Garden, Pool Garden – peaceful and tranquil with gentle water
splashes – a pair of splendid herbaceous borders, and walls and pergolas

draped with white wisterias, roses and clematis, all carefully trained so that architectural features are not lost. Two magnificent cedars rule the lawn. The whole garden has an air of extreme elegance and refinement, and is immaculately kept.The urns and planters are spectacular. Lovely teas in the laundry yard, with sticky cakes made by the cook at the great house.

6 BOUGHTON HOUSE   nr Kettering   Tel 01536 515731

Daily except Friday, May to mid Sept, 1–5. £1.50
From Kettering go N on A4300/A43 for 3m. Turn R at Geddington and follow signs to garden (1½m).

This vast 16th- and 17th-century house is home to the Duke and Duchess of Buccleuch and Queensberry, with a magnificent park, lakes and great avenues of trees. Around the house are herbaceous borders and a circular rose garden with a central sundial. The old monastic ponds are now lily pools. A walled kitchen garden is beautiful as well as fruitful and functional, and has a nursery raising good plants for sale. Wisteria and roses embroider the west front of the house, and yew hedges give a fine dark background to the statues. The 300-acre park has walks and trails, and an adventure playground for children.

7 THE OLD RECTORY
Sudborough, nr Kettering   Tel 01832 733247

All year by appointment. £2.50
From Thrapston go W on A14 for 1m. Turn R at roundabout on A6116 for 3m. Garden is on L in Sudborourgh, next to church.

Surrounding Mr and Mrs Huntington's peaceful Georgian rectory is a garden packed with unusual plants and brilliantly conceived colour themes. Particularly fine is the potager designed by Rosemary Verey, with her signature of standard gooseberries, little brick paths and an arbour in the middle. The container planting is masterly – I detect the influence of Rupert Golby here. Hellebores are marvellous in spring. Lovely herbaceous borders, a woodland walk and a formal rose garden are all beautifully maintained.

Where to Stay

All B&B prices are approximate per person, sharing a double/twin room usually with private or en suite facilities. It is a good idea to ask for any special requirements when booking.

A THE FALCON   Tel 01604 696200

Jo & Neville Watson, The Falcon, Castle Ashby, nr Northampton, Northamptonshire NN7 1LF.

This is a cottage hotel rather than a country house, but Jo and Neville Watson give such a warm welcome you feel very much as if you are visiting their home. There are masses of fresh flowers and good furnishings. Outside, a large lawn is surrounded by willow and walnut trees, and a vegetable garden with produce for the kitchen. There are 16 fully-equipped comfortable double/twin bedrooms. The dining-room is usually very busy in the evenings (dinners £19.50, licensed, with a lot of choice) because the chef has a high reputation locally. You can eat outside on warm summer evenings beneath a pavilion marquee. Smoking allowed, children and well-behaved dogs welcome. B&B £38.

B LYNTON HOUSE   Tel 01604 770777

Carlo & Carol Bertozzi, Lynton House, Holdenby, nr Northampton, Northamptonshire NN6 8DJ.

This is a highly acclaimed, but not expensive, restaurant-with-rooms. Lynton House was originally built as a rectory for one of the chaplains to Queen Victoria in 1853. It stands in 3 acres of grounds with mature trees and shrubs, and makes a good herbaceous show. The dining-room and a new conservatory, where you eat breakfast, look out on them. Carlo is an engaging host and Carol is the chef, making many Italian dishes. The set dinner menu, if you choose it, is £24 plus wine. There is a bedroom suite, 2 doubles and 1 single. No small children, restricted smoking, and no dogs. B&B £28.

C WOLD FARM   Tel 01604 781258

Anne Engler, Wold Farm, Old, nr Northampton, Northamptonshire NN6 9RJ.

There are charming gardens behind this 18th-century house, with a colourful pergola, well-stocked herbaceous borders, terraces and lawns. Anne Engler is a vivacious host, and you are likely to have good fun here in spacious and well-furnished rooms, one of which has a billiard table. She cooks an evening meal for £15 (bring your own wine if you like, although it is available here). There are 6 double/twin bedrooms; one on the ground floor of a garden cottage is suitable for wheelchairs. Children welcome, restricted smoking, and dogs by arrangement. B&B £22–£24.

D UPTON MILL   Tel 01604 753277

Jane Spokes, Upton Mill, Upton, nr Northampton, Northamptonshire NN5 4UY.

This old mill house straddles the fast-flowing River Nene, and has picturesque surroundings. In summer it is wonderful, in winter it can be flooded and somewhat bleak – but Jane thinks garden visitors will stay with her between April and October anyway. There is a wildlife garden on the river bank, a pond for moorhens and miles of open farmland beyond with good country walks. Jane cooks evening meals (£10, bring your own wine) which you should talk about in advance. There are 2 twin bedrooms and 1 single. There is only 1 bathroom, but Jane makes sure you have it to yourself by not letting spare rooms except to friends coming as a party. Children welcome, restricted smoking, dogs by arrangement. B&B £18–£20.

E THE ELMS   Tel 01604 830326

Primrose & David Saunders, The Elms, Kislingbury, nr Northampton, Northamptonshire NN7 4AH.

Rooms in this pleasant house look out over the Saunders's working farm. There is a friendly and informal atmosphere, and lavish breakfasts. There are 3 comfortable double/twin bedrooms, sharing facilities, and two pubs in the village where you can eat out in the evening. No smoking, children welcome, dogs by arrangement. B&B £18.

F TIVY FARM   Tel 01327 830874

Celia & Michael Judge, Tivy Farm, Litchborough, nr Towcester, Northamptonshire NN12 8JH.

When Celia and Michael moved to this farmhouse, they decided that their 6 acres of grounds needed some loving care and improvement. Keeping everything worthwhile, they planted trees, created borders and dug out a lake, now thriving with trout and crayfish. It is a very good 1½-acre garden-in-the-making. There are 2 double/twin rooms with showers, sharing a loo. Eat out at local pubs in the evenings. No smoking, children welcome, dogs by arrangement. B&B £18.

What Else to Enjoy

This is a short selection of the many good things recommended in the area by owners of places to stay. Your hosts will certainly be able to provide additional information.

If It's Wet

There are many stately homes in this visit, the most popular (in the month when it is open) being **Althorp House**, home of the Spencer family since 1508. Diana, Princess of Wales, grew up here. Set in 550 acres of undulating parkland, it is lavishly furnished and has good paintings and china. Open daily in Aug, 2–5.30. Find it 6m NW of **Northampton**, L off the A428. Admission £5.

Two gardens described above also open the homes attached to them. **Holdenby House** (*see* Garden 3) was built from Elizabethan remains of what was formerly the largest house in England, and later became the prison of Charles I. It is architecturally fascinating. House open as garden.

Boughton House (*see* Garden 6), home of the Duke of Buccleuch and his Montagu ancestors since 1528, has been called the 'English Versailles'. It contains outstanding fine art collections. Open in August, 2–4.30.

In the village of **Castle Ashby** (Garden 2) there is a good craft centre and what is called a 'rural shopping yard' with country furniture, tiles, ceramics, leather goods and much else, including a restaurant with wholesome food.

Eating Out

The **French Partridge** in **Horton**, 5m SE of Northampton on B526, was a coaching inn in the 16th century. Changed gradually over the years, it has a comforting air of solidity brought by the Partridge family both to the surroundings and to the assured cooking. Their ideas for new dishes are taken from many sources (and are only offered when the family as a whole has approved them). A set dinner menu, with a good choice, costs £23 including service. Wine is extra, and if you eat outside the menu you could spend £30–£35 per head. Tel 01604 870033.

Around Cambridge

On the flat, dry plains around Cambridge are some very grand gardens, often with hundreds of acres of landscaped parks; and by contrast there is one brilliant little garden, set against a railway line, which enchanted me. The Cambridge college gardens are always a tranquil treat. I like to listen to something orderly and scholarly in this atmosphere. Cambridge is where I first seriously heard Beethoven's string quartets, which many of my musical friends think to be the supreme example of composing. For an introduction, try listening to his Grosse Fugue in B Flat, Opus 133; there are many recordings.

OS map: Landranger **154**

Gardens

Opening times: in larger gardens, and in NT properties, last admissions are usually 30–45 minutes before the garden closes. Admission charges are a guide to what one adult can expect to pay to go round the garden. It sometimes varies with the season or days of the week. When the house is also open to the public, there is usually an additional charge.

I   NUNS MANOR   Shepreth, nr Royston   Tel 01763 260313

April to July, by appointment. £1.50
From Cambridge go SW on A10 for 7m. Ignore first R turn to Shepreth, take second. Go through Frog End (½m). Garden is at last house on R.

A gravel drive with a splendid massed bed of lavenders and tumbling rock roses greets you at this 16th-century farmhouse which formerly belonged to the Nuns of Chatteris. The garden was designed in 1986, by the son of Mr and Mrs Brashaw, so that it could be enjoyed from the drawing-room windows. Now there are 2 acres of fine plants, beautifully judged colours, an immaculate croquet lawn, a small woodland walk under-planted with bulbs and wildflowers and an orderly kitchen garden. The eye is led away

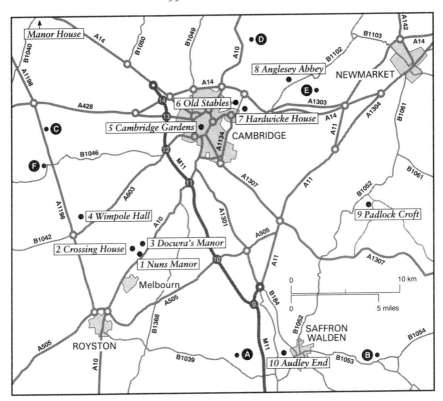

from the garden and over a ha-ha to the fields beyond, making a most peaceful setting. Twin herbaceous borders to boast about are Mrs Brashaw's great triumph. Plants are tightly packed in, well fed and perfectly staked. She has used verbascums, crambes, foxgloves, allium and euphorbias – all strong architectural shapes – to give form, filled successfully with a riot of knautia, poppies and penstemons. Mr Brashaw is a compost addict (and grows perfect courgettes on top of the heaps), and his dedication shows in this marvellously well-nourished garden. A small nursery area for interesting and good-value home-propagated plants is by the kitchen garden.

2   THE CROSSING HOUSE

Shepreth, nr Royston   Tel 01763 261071

Daily, all year, dawn to dusk. Collecting box.
From Cambridge go SW on A10 for 8m. Turn R to Shepreth. Garden is ½m further on at 78 Meldreth Rd, by railway crossing.

This plant-lover's garden is crammed full of colour and interest, with a vast assortment of plants, some rare, some old-loved favourites. By the door of the house is a pretty double arch of clipped yew, leading you to the lawn – which is getting smaller and smaller – and to box-edged borders, little ponds, streams and raised rock beds. A fine selection of trees, including a copper 'Dawyck' beech, and a crab apple supporting a lovely yellow rose, 'Easleas Golden Rambler'. Many treasures, including Mrs Fuller's favourite pansies and violas, are closely planted in this fascinating small garden. One recent visitor spent 4 hours looking at everything he could find, and then came back the next day to see what he had missed. There are three greenhouses, with splendid pelargoniums, orchids and other exotics and alpines. For trainspotters, there is a country garden seat, sheltered by espaliered pear trees, where you can sit and watch trains whistle by on the adjoining track. Mr Fuller can tell you everything you ever wanted to know about trains.

3   DOCWRA'S MANOR

Shepreth, nr Royston   Tel 01763 261473

Weds and Fri, all year, 10–4, many charity Suns, and by appointment. £2 From Cambridge go SW on A10 for 7m. Turn R to Shepreth where signed; garden is ½m, opposite War Memorial. Park behind village hall.

Old buildings, walls and hedges here form a series of enclosed gardens, each with its own character, and sheltering tender plants. A cobbled path to the front of the house has standard roses, alstroemerias, euphorbias, lilies and lovely old stone sinks planted with alpines. By the side of the main lawn are splendid beeches, an old mulberry, and a classical temple for quiet afternoon snoozes. Tall box and yew hedges lead into a shrub-rose garden, with grass paths where hardy geraniums and ox-eye daises tumble alongside. There is an overpowering perfume of philadelphus on the air, together with old roses that scramble to the top of apple trees. A gate in the wall leads to a paved courtyard, with a fountain and pool surrounded by large terracotta pots. A walled garden and paved garden are very exciting: patchworks of colours are made by many different plants from many countries. There are plenty of Mediterranean species, jostling each other, closely planted and with associations that are always well thought out – crambes, penstemons, poppies, roses, lavenders, acanthus and huge thistles swagger through the garden as you make your way along narrow stone paths exuberantly overgrown. In the orchard, pear arches have clematis adorning them, with feathery asparagus beds beside. A crinkle-crankle beech hedge hides the fertile veggie garden, where flowers for picking grow alongside peas and beans. The plant sales area is full of home-propagated stock, including some rarities. Mrs Craven also has a garden at Ardtonish in Scotland with a totally different climate and soil. I can't wait to go there and compare it with the garden here – a delightful, unpretentious creation of a botanical scholar and a skilled plantswoman. John Craven died in 1980, but his book *A Botanist's Garden* has been republished, and has become, for me, favourite bed-time reading.

4   WIMPOLE HALL (NT)

Arrington, nr Royston   Tel 01223 207257

Daily except Mon and Fri, mid March to early Nov, 1–5 (BHs 11–5). £4.80 From Cambridge go SW on A603 for 7m; garden well signed on R.

In the 17th century, there was a great formal garden here, with a 2-mile avenue of elms planted in 1720. Alas, these died of Dutch elm disease, and have now been replaced by limes. Capability Brown and Humphry Repton both worked here, and reduced a little of the formality. Now the NT has restored some parterres and the Dutch garden, and created a new informal rose garden. Fine specimen trees are in the pleasure grounds to the E of the house, with an under-planting of many varieties of daffodils, narcissi and wildflowers in the spring.

5   CAMBRIDGE GARDENS

Use local town maps to find your way from college to college.

It is difficult to rely on opening times and days to see these striking gardens, but some will always be open; ask at the Porter's Lodges. Colleges often prefer not to have visitors in term time, or during exam weeks, or if they are holding a private function. Among the best are at **St John's College**, approached across the Wren bridge; **Clare College** has magnificent herbaceous borders; **Emmanuel College** has a charming herb garden designed by John Codrington; **Peterhouse** has a fascinating paved octagonal courtyard. All the colleges have great lawns, fine trees and the River Cam quietly flows between them. They are architecturally magnificent at any time of year.

The instructive and beautiful **Botanic Garden** is in Trumpington Rd, ¾ m S of the city centre, with a great rock garden, a huge collection of plants and fine trees in an attractive setting.

6 THE OLD STABLES

Fen Ditton, nr Cambridge   Tel 01223 292507

Some charity Suns, and by written appointment. £1.50
From Cambridge city centre go E on A1303 for 1m and over roundabout junc-
tion with A1134. Turn immediately L on B1047. At X-rds in Fen Ditton
(½m), turn L into High St. Garden is at No 54, just past the church.

This is an unusual and informal garden where the owners, Mr and Mrs
Zavros, have a rare talent for propagation – nearly everything has been
grown from seed or a small cutting. It is very sheltered, with rich soil, and
the river close by helps to keep it damp. There is a collection of iris, and
lots of small botanical beds are packed with plants – carpentarias, lilies,
peonies, cistus. Shrubs are interesting too – a *Corylus avellana* 'Contorta',
kolwitzia, arbutus and cornus in variety. The kitchen garden is full of of
kitschy jokes, with a plastic cucumber, a giant onion and an elegant scare-
crow. Old implements and wheelbarrows loll about. Two huge and rare
black poplars are in the adjoining river meadow. There is a small area of
Mediterranean plants, to make Mr Zavros feel at home. Everywhere are
charming and original ideas.

7 HARDWICKE HOUSE

Fen Ditton, nr Cambridge   Tel 01223 292246

Occasional charity days and by written appointment. £1.50
From Cambridge city centre go E on A1303 for 1m and over roundabout junc-
tion with A1134. Turn immediately L on B1047. At X-rds in Fen Ditton
(½m), turn R into High Ditch Rd. Garden is at last house on R.

This nicely wild garden has great interest for those who love aquilegias –
the National Collection is held here, and every delightful variation on
'Granny's Bonnet' can be seen. They are mostly grown in an enclosed
garden, sheltered by high beech hedges, along with plants that associate well
– salvias, phlomis, shrub roses, lilies, iris and acanthus. Mr Drake is a plant
collector and a selection of plants he has grown from seeds gathered in
Turkey and Greece are planted near two Turkish-inspired gazebos, called
tourbés. His garden is divided into four by tall hedges (necessary windbreaks
here) and a charming *allée* of silver birch, under-planted with snowdrops
and narcissi in spring, and crossed by eight large dumplings of clipped box.
Shrubs and climbing roses scramble up trees. Mr Drake has been trying to
grow most of the plants on Tradescant's list, so it's a great place to see old

varieties. I learned a fascinating hint from him: he dangles bars of cheap soap, threaded with string, from the perimeter hedge which keep out muntjac deer who don't like the smell of carbolic.

8 ANGLESEY ABBEY (NT)

Lode, nr Cambridge   Tel 01223 811200

Wed–Sun and BHs (daily July/Aug), Easter to Oct, 11–5.30. £3.20
From Cambridge city centre, go E on A1303 for 4m and over junction with
A14. Continue on B1102 to Lode; garden (2m) signed on L.

This splendid park has majestic trees, walks and avenues which you go through to approach the house and the formal gardens around it. Beyond, the planting becomes more natural, with meadows, woodland and wild-flowers taking over the the man-made features. Of much interest are the statues, many of which came from Stowe. I had fun wondering which Lord Fairhaven had chosen them. There are lots of satyrs, grinning with naughty thoughts. Narcissus is by a pool. In the pinetum I came across a limp-wristed Saracen, and a splendid Pan with pipes, grapes, pomegranates and a huge leer on his face – I knew why when I looked at his behind. Tucked away in a shady avenue of box and yew, I found a virgin and two bishops, safely miles away from the libidinous goat-footed satyrs. This garden specializes in dahlias, and has a vast collection of old and rare roses in a semi-circular walk, backed by a beech hedge. Beautifully maintained borders are set around a large lawn, with a more serious statue trying to tell the time by a sundial that was a bit inaccurate. The gardens would look lovely in spring when snowdrops abound, and the parterre is planted out with thousands of hyacinths. There is a formal rose garden, at which one is only allowed to peep over the gate. The roses looked modern and in garish colours, so I didn't mind. There is a plant sales-area, restaurant and places to picnic.

9 PADLOCK CROFT   West Wratting   Tel 01223 290383

Wed–Sat and BH Mons, April to mid Oct, 10–6. £1.50
From Cambridge go SE on A1307 for 9m. At Linton, turn L on B1052 for 4m
to West Wratting village. At Chestnut Inn, turn R on minor road for ¼m,
branch R, then R again up lane. Garden is first house on L.

This garden, based on the collections of the Bellflower family, was started seventeen years ago on a weedy old allotment. Now it is a calm and tran-quil plantsman's cottage garden, with sinks, troughs, rock gardens, alpine houses and a potager – all to house their National Collection of campanulas, symphyandras, adenophoras and platycodon. There are also some most desirable codonopsis. This a brilliant garden, with a nursery catalogue among the best in the country.

10 AUDLEY END   Saffron Walden   Tel 01799 522842

Wed–Sun and BH Mons, April to Sept, 12–6. £3
From the centre of Saffron Walden go W on B1052 for 1m, well signed.

This huge Jacobean mansion is set in a park designed by Capability Brown from around 1760. Robert Adam added the beautiful bridge over the River Cam. The parterre designed by William Sawney Gilpin has been restored. The flowers growing here, in more than 100 beds, were all known in the 1830s. They include iris, astrantia, peonies and massed displays of annuals. Old roses scent the rose garden. There is a rock garden. Fine trees grace the park, which has a temple and Lady Portsmouth's Column, both designed by Robert Adam.

Where to Stay

All B&B prices are approximate per person, sharing a double/twin room usually with private or en suite facilities. It is a good idea to ask for any special requirements when booking.

A ELMDON LEE   Tel 01763 838237

Diana Duke, Elmdon Lee, Littlebury Green, nr Saffron Walden, Essex CB11 4XB.

It is comfortable and homely here, in an 18th-century farmhouse with many of its Georgian features intact. An acre of garden, mainly lawns, clipped hedges and mature trees, surrounds the house, peacefully set within a 900-acre estate. The rooms are comfortably furnished, with many antiques, and guests find it easy to relax. Evening meals (£16, licensed) are served *en famille* around a large dining table. Of the 3 spacious double/twin bedrooms, two look out over the garden and farmland beyond. No dogs in the house, smoking allowed, children welcome. B&B £28–£30.

B LITTLE BROCKHOLDS FARM   Tel 01799 599458

Anthony & Anne Wordsworth, Little Brockholds Farm, Radwinter, Saffron Walden, Essex CB10 2TF.

The 7-acre garden around this Elizabethan farmhouse (some of it is 14th-century), covered with climbing roses, is very special. Old roses, ponds, trees, orchards, an avenue of walnuts, a knot garden, a potager and decorative kitchen garden with organically-grown vegetables – it's worth a garden visit in its own right. Anthony and Anne started taking guests into their home quite recently, because they enjoy making new friends. They have 3 double/twin bedrooms, all with a good outlook. Dinner (bring your own wine) costs £18. No smoking, no dogs, children welcome. B&B £28.

C CHURCH FARM   Tel 01954 719543

Peter & Maggie Scott, Church Farm, Gransden Road, Caxton, nr Cambridge, Cambridgeshire CB3 8PL.

This spacious, listed white-painted farmhouse is set in 3 acres of gardens looking on to a pond with weeping willows, towering horse chestnuts and an old church – truly a scene of rural peace. It is mainly Peter, a historian, who tends the garden. The terraces are covered with pots and tubs, wisteria and honeysuckle clamber wherever they can find space. There is a croquet lawn, tennis court, herbaceous borders and rose beds – all very casual. There are 2 double/twin bedrooms, both with a good outlook. Maggie's dinners cost £17.50 (discuss wine in advance). No dogs, no smoking, no children. B&B £26–£28.

D BERRY HOUSE   Tel 01223 860702

Sally & Phil Myburgh, Berry House, High Street, Waterbeach, Cambridgeshire CB5 9JU.

If there's one thing Sally has, it's energy. Escaping from the advertising world in London, she moved to this Georgian village house and turned it into a home which welcomes people from all over the world. She bakes her own bread, invents new dishes, finds special places for guests to go and enjoy themselves, grows herbs and tomatoes – and recently, decided to marry Phil. Her garden, including a pond and bog garden, is full of wildlife and there is a feeling of abundance everywhere. A beamed coach house is set aside for guests. Downstairs is a comfortable drawing-room with a piano, and in the old hayloft above are 2 luxurious double/twin bedrooms, one with a 6-ft bed. In the evening, you can have delicious suppers for £10–£12.50, or dinner for £18 (bring your own wine). No dogs, smoking allowed, children should be over 12. B&B £25–£30.

E　THE MERCHANT'S HOUSE　　　Tel 01223 812777

Loder & Julia Bevington, The Merchant's House, Commercial End, Swaffham Bulbeck, Cambridgeshire CB5 0ND.

This mellow brick 17th-century house has a lovely feeling of antiquity. Loder and Julia have done wonders with it since moving here six years ago, putting in all the comforts that we need today while restoring all the old features that had been neglected in the previous forty years. The same applies to the garden. An overgrown shambles now has a formal potager with lavender hedges and quinces. More than 100 roses have been planted, and the old walled garden, with ancient box hedges, is being brought to life again. There are 2 en suite double bedrooms. Julia will give you an ample list of suggested places to eat out in the evenings. No smoking, no dogs, children should be over 10. B&B £23.

F　GLEBE HOUSE　　　Tel 01954 719509

Brian & Charlotte Murray, Glebe House, Park Lane, Longstowe, Cambridgeshire CB3 7UJ.

Woods on one side of this 16th-century house, and open farmland on the other, with a pretty garden, make this a wonderfully attractive retreat. Charlotte has a gift for making visitors feel welcome at her home, which is comfortably furnished and painted in soft colours. You can choose either a family room with 4 beds, or an en suite double. She is a Cordon Bleu-trained cook; the cost of her evening meals starting at £9 (bring your own wine). No smoking, no dogs, children welcome. B&B £19.

What Else to Enjoy

This is a short selection of the many good things recommended in the area by owners of places to stay. Your hosts will certainly be able to provide additional information.

Other Gardens/Nurseries

Just off the NW edge of the visit map is one of the most entrancing houses and gardens you will ever find – **The Manor House**, in the middle of **Hemingford Grey**. Created by the children's author Lucy Boston, her *Green Knowe* books were set here. Built around 1100 AD, the house is moated, backs on to a river and has many wild and secret areas beyond the bosky formal areas whose clipped yew hedges and topiary enclose splendid collections of old roses. Diana and Peter Boston welcome garden enthusiasts by appointment all year. Tel 01480 563134. To find the garden, follow the A14 NW towards Huntingdon, and turn R on A1096 and then L to Hemingford Grey.

Monksilver Nursery, on the N edge of the visit, is truly exceptional. It has one of the country's largest selections of herbaceous perennials, many of them very rare, as well as desirable shrubs. The nursery holds the National Collections of galeobdolon, lamium and vinca. Their catalogue is amazingly detailed. Open Fri/Sat, April to June, and on 2nd Sat in month, July to Oct, 10–4. Find it in Oakington Rd, **Cottenham**, on the B1049. Tel 01954 251555.

If It's Wet

Cambridge is packed with museums, of which the Fitzwilliam in Trumpington St is pre-eminent. If you want to visit the colleges, don't forget that most are closed for examinations from mid April to mid June. At other times, you can explore them yourself, or join a 2-hour guided walking tour from the Tourist Information Office in Wheeler St. Tel 01223 322640.

Eating Out

At **Fen Ditton** (*see* Gardens 6 and 7), enjoy a splendid lunch at the **Ancient Shepherd** in the High St. Tel 01223 293280. For a gourmet celebration that won't break the bank, there are strong recommendations for **Sycamore House** in Church St, **Little Shelford**, just S of Cambridge off the A1301. Michael and Susan Sharpe have converted a pretty pub into their homely restaurant, with a 4-course set menu that has plenty of imaginative choices, priced at about £20. With wine and service, you will probably end up paying a bit more than £30 per head. Tel 01223 843396.

Constable Country

John Betjeman called Essex 'sweet uneventful countryside'. It is gentle, with flat fertile fields perfect for market gardening. Beth Chatto's garden is here – a must for gardeners. Did you know that Colchester was named after merry Old King Cole? In the north of the visit you come to the country-side loved and painted by John Constable. He captured the long-ago rural charm of this area for us, and many of the scenes he painted are almost unchanged. It's fun to visit Flatford Mill or Dedham, and have yourself pho-tographed by a friend in the scene of one of his paintings. Driving around, try listening to some truly English music by Herbert Howells. His *Hymnus Paradisi*, an English mass, is hauntingly written.

OS maps: Landrangers 155, 167, **168**

Gardens

Opening times: in larger gardens, and in NT properties, last admissions are usually 30–45 minutes before the garden closes. Admission charges are a guide to what one adult can ex-pect to pay to go round the garden. It sometimes varies with the season or days of the week. When the house is also open to the public, there is usually an additional charge.

I GLEN CHANTRY
Wickham Bishops, nr Witham   Tel 01621 891342
Fri/Sat, April to end Sept, 10–4, and many charity days, 2–5. £1.50
From Witham go S on B1018 for 1m. Immediately after crossing A12 by-pass, turn L on lane signed Wickham Bishops. After Benton Hall Golf Club (½m), cross narrow bridge and turn immediately L up track in Blue Mills hamlet.

Once you've found Glen Chantry, you will be thrilled by the unusual perennials and mixed borders, the white garden and rock gardens with a stream and waterfalls running through it, and the mastery with which Sue and Wol Staines have made their garden from scratch over the last twenty

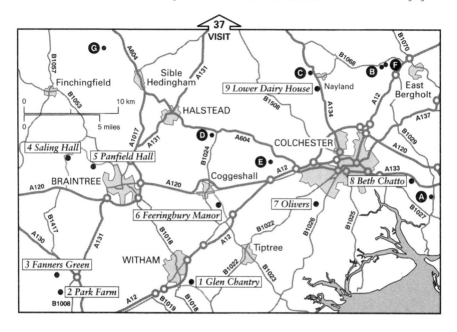

years. Sue now spends a great deal of her time in the nursery attached to the garden, where she propagates her specialities – alpines, white flowers and rare perennials.

2 PARK FARM

nr Great Waltham, nr Chelmsford   Tel 01245 360871

Mid April to July, by appointment. £1.50

From Braintree go SW on A131 for 6m. At roundabout junction with A130, go briefly S on B1008, then turn R into Chatham Hall Lane signposted to Howe Street. Park Farm is ½m on L.

Jill Cowley is an amazing gardener. Not only does she write and broadcast about gardens widely, but has found time to create an exuberant, energetic garden herself, bursting with interest and surprises at every corner – and all this on land that had concrete and bricks from old farm buildings just below the soil. Holes for trees had to be pick-axed out. There are three pools with water-lilies, and lots of hot colours around them: thalias, fennels and towering plumes of dark burgundy 'Fat Red Hen' seeding itself freely. Little gravel paths meander around this garden. I got quite lost in it, but found a delightful winter garden under an old walnut tree where aconites, snowdrops, mahonias, camellias and clipped box make for winter cheerfulness. Long vistas have been made between fat box hedges over the neighbouring park. A new water feature has a wooden viewing bridge, and a willow sculpture of a Loch Ness Monster lurks in the water. The garden is full of delightful touches – and some humorous ones like a wicked-looking sprite which spits water from a barrel – interesting plants and shrubs. Don't be surprised to be escorted around by any number of the nine resident cats.

3   6, FANNERS GREEN   Great Waltham   Tel 01245 360035

3 charity weekends mid month in each of May, June and July, and groups by appointment. £1
From Braintree go SW on A131 for 6m. At roundabout junction with A130, go S briefly on B1008. After 1m, turn R signed to Great Waltham. Opposite the church, turn L into South St. After 1½m, turn R into lane by a row of cottages. Garden has neat topiary at the gate.

A windy third of an acre with poor soil was what garden designer Gunilla Pickard found when she moved here fifteen years ago with her doctor husband. Hedges were planted in box, beech and privet to create shelter and make small garden rooms, each one with a different character. The strong formal design has relaxed and exuberant planting. The path by the front door is lined with formal patterns of clipped box, in-filled with blue and white flowers. The cottage is black-boarded, and plants look stunning against it. A blue 'Prince Charles' clematis, white 'Iceberg' roses and a vine dangling green grapes showed up to perfection. Two clipped standard viburnums are under-planted with the flax *Linum perenne*, alliums and blue salvias. In front of a beech hedge is a border of pinks, purples and blues. In the yellow, lime and white border, two fat topiary hens look out over the lawn. Windows have been cut into the hedge to give glimpses of pastoral views. This is very much a designer's garden, full of interest and attention to detail. The veggie and herb plot is tiny but perfect. The conservatory houses exotic tender plants, and a giant cactus that won't stop growing.

4   SALING HALL   Great Saling, nr Braintree

Weds, May to July, 2–5. £1
From Braintree go W on A120 for 5m. At Saling Oak Inn, turn R signed to Great Saling. Garden is 2m on R.

All readers of the RHS magazine should know that the 'Tradescant' column is written by Hugh Johnson, and this is the glorious garden he and his family have made. His great passion is for trees, and he has turned 12 acres of alkaline clay into an arboretum of great beauty and rare specimens. Collections of oaks, beeches, pines, birches, prunus, robinias and sorbus are planted to give walks and vistas. There is a pretty walled garden where box pyramids vie with mushroom-shaped fruit trees for attention, and the borders are informally planted. There is also a Japanese garden and a veggie garden, and the old water gardens have been restored.

5   PANFIELD HALL   nr Braintree   Tel 01376 324512

April to Oct, by appointment. £1.50
From Braintree go NW on B1053 for 2m. Turn L on minor rd for ½m; garden
in Hall Road.

This is a magnificent old house, built in 1520 and partly moated. The garden is under restoration, and a new terrace with raised beds is nearly finished, the herringbone brickwork repeating the pattern on the house. In the old orchard, roses grow up pillars. In front of the house are rose beds hedged with lavender, with four very pretty standard salix. Fine trees have been planted to replace those lost in the great gales, including 'Dawyck' copper beeches and a catalpa by one of the stewponds. Generous herbaceous borders brim with soft, gentle colours, and there is a maze of box. Mr Newman found a cupola that was being demolished at a Victorian school, and it now makes the most charming folly. He calls it 'the biggest fly-trap in Essex'.

6   FEERINGBURY MANOR   nr Colchester   Tel 01376 561946

Mon–Fri, end April to end July, 8a.m.–1p.m., and by appointment but not
Sat/Sun or BHs. £2
From Colchester go W on A12 and then A120 for 7m. In Coggeshall, turn L
on minor rd to Feering. Garden is in Feeringbury village (1m) on R.

Here is a 7-acre garden, bordering on the River Blackwater, which looks as though it has been carved out of an encroaching wilderness. Beds, hedges and paths are strictly formal. Outside these confines, exuberance rules – frothing cow-parsley, rambling honeysuckle, and willows by the water. The garden is planted for colour and interest all the year round, with masses of bulbs, bog-loving plants and a wide variety of honeysuckle and clematis. A large central bed of shrub roses is magnificent in summer, then ignored until autumn produces a show of hips. Two ponds and a small stream are home to many primulas and other plants which revel in damp conditions.

7   OLIVERS   Colchester   Tel 01206 330575

All year, by appointment. £2
From Colchester go SW on B1022 for 3m towards zoo (signed). At roundabout on outskirts of town, turn L into Cunobelin Drive, then R into Olivers Lane. After 1m, garden is at last house.

This charming 18th-century houses is perched above the valley of the Roman River, with fields gently sloping down to it. Philip Morant, in his 1780 *History of Essex*, described it as 'a retired and agreeable place, with handsome gardens, canals and fish ponds'. Very apt then – and today, David and Gay Edwards have made a stupendous garden here, despite suffering cruel damage in the great storms of '87 and '90 when the woods were devastated. The west front of the house is covered with wisteria and *Magnolia grandiflora*. On the S side is a wide terrace, planted with soft colours where silver- and grey-leaved plants glitter in the sun. A yellow border against a side wall has euphorbias, hostas, variegated ivy, *Lonicera* 'Baggesen's Gold', yellow allium and daylilies. Two box-edged parterres, with fat dumplings of box, are planted in summer with cool lime and white nicotiana. Against a warm south wall, a Banksia rose has reached the roof, together with another huge *Magnolia grandiflora*. At their feet nestle mertensias, white agapanthus and *convolvulus cneorum*. A Ride has been cut through the woods where you can find rhododendrons, azaleas, amelanchiers and shrub roses, under-planted with bluebells, snowdrops and cowslips. At the end of the Ride stands Bacchus, a figleaf coyly defying all the breezes. Wildflowers, including many tiny red specie tulips, grow under white cherry trees. Around the lawn are curved beds of shrubs and old roses. A yew walk has 5 buttresses. Between each one is a herbaceous bed using blocks of different colours – very effective. There are six acres of wonderful gardens to explore here.

8   THE BETH CHATTO GARDENS
Elmstead Market   Tel 01206 822007

Daily except Suns, March to Oct, 9–6; Mon–Fri, Feb and Nov, 9–4. £2
From Colchester go E on A133 for 3m. Garden is on R just after Elmstead Market.

Beth Chatto designed this garden thirty years ago, on a boggy field with exceedingly dry perimeters. Her great knowledge of which plants will grow in difficult situations, and her excellently written books about her garden have made her something of a high priestess among gardeners. Herbaceous borders are particularly striking here, as plants are chosen for their foliage as much as their flowers. A dry Mediterranean garden is planted in gravel on a sunny slope, and water and bog gardens are down in the valley. Next to the garden, Mrs Chatto has one of the best nurseries ever, full of unusual plants.

9 LOWER DAIRY HOUSE

Nayland, nr Colchester   Tel 01206 262220

Many charity days, end March to early July, 2–6, and by appointment. £1.50 From Colchester go N on A134 for 7m. Just before Nayland, take lane on L signed Little Horkesley. Garden is ½m on L past farm buildings.

This is a 1½-acre plantsman's cottage garden crammed with plants – some unusual, many self-sown, nearly all old-fashioned. A stream runs along one side, giving Mr and Mrs Burnett ample scope to plant some of their favourite primulas, hostas and mimulus. There is a woodland dell, and banks of glorious shrub roses. Sun-worshipping plants are here in profusion too – cistus and diascias. The garden displays a glorious carpet of flowering spring bulbs.

Where to Stay

All B&B prices are approximate per person, sharing a double/twin room usually with private or en suite facilities. It is a good idea to ask for any special requirements when booking.

A HOCKLEY PLACE   Tel 01206 251703

Helen & Humphrey Bowles, Hockley Place, Frating, nr Colchester, Essex CO7 7HF.

Beth Chatto's garden (*see* Garden 8) is only a 3-minute drive away from this supremely comfortable Lutyens-style house whose own garden is renowned for its rhododendron walk set among 5 acres of park, apple orchards and farmland. You will get healthy here – along with energetic croquet and a heated swimming pool, there is a gym. Then, of course, you will spoil it all by pigging yourself on Helen's delicious dinners (£18–£20, licensed) in her beamed dining-room. Tall people have a treat here since the 3 double/ twin bedrooms having extra-long beds. No smoking, dogs by arrangement, children should be over 12. B&B £30.

B   THE OLD VICARAGE   Tel 01206 337248

Meg Parker, The Old Vicarage, Higham, nr Colchester, Essex CO7 6JY.

The views from here are pure Constable: open fields, trees punctuating the distant landscape, the rivers Brett and Stour, low horizons – marvellous. Somehow the beamed Tudor house measures up to this. The Parkers have lived here in style for many years and it all feels very settled, with comfortable furniture and antiques collected over time. The back of the house is wisteria-clad, facing south over lawns with a large herbaceous border, and an old wall with fig, peach and plum trees bordering the swimming pool. There is a tennis court, too. B&B only, so you eat out in the evening at one of the many excellent pubs and restaurants in the area. There are 4 double/twin guest bedrooms. Smoking allowed, dogs by arrangement, children welcome. B&B £27.

C   GLADWINS FARM   Tel 01206 262261

Robert & Pauline Dossor, Gladwins Farm, Harper's Hill, Nayland, nr Colchester, Essex CO6 4NU.

This traditional black-and-white timbered farmhouse, just over the border into Suffolk, looks out onto acres of lawn, grassland, woodland and water. It is always busy and jolly here – stables and barns have been converted into self-catering cottages, usually full of children who enjoy watching the farm animals and jumping into the indoor swimming pool (grown-ups can use the sauna). There is a tennis court, and private fishing. In the main house, the 4 double/twin bedrooms have comfortable modern furnishings. B&B only, but there are excellent pubs close by for evening meals. Dogs and children welcome, restricted smoking. B&B £25.

D   ELM HOUSE   Tel 01206 240456

Lady Larcom, Elm House, 14 Upper Holt St, Earls Colne, nr Colchester, Essex CO6 2PG.

For a number of years now, Lady Larcom has welcomed guests to her fine, square-built, red-brick Queen Anne house in this outstandingly handsome village. Her garden is walled, with good borders and many climbers. An attractive terrace is used for summer barbecues. She knows the area well, and can guide you to specialist gardens not often open to the public, as well as vineyards and craft shops in which she takes an interest. There are 2 elegant double/twin guest bedrooms. Dinner is £15 (bring your own wine). Dogs by arrangement, restricted smoking, children welcome. B&B £20–£25.

E OLD HOUSE   Tel 01206 240456

Patricia & Richard Mitchell, Old House, Fordstreet, nr Colchester, Essex CO6 3PH.

Behind this fascinating 14th-century hall house is a friendly, wandering garden, cottagey in style but extending to 2 acres. Somewhat neglected while the Mitchells' children were growing up, it is now back in shape with long, contoured lawns backed by wide borders and fine trees. Patricia fights a never-ending battle with the lack of rain here – but you wouldn't think it from the abundance which her garden shows. Inside the house are oak beams, log fires and a long history. There are 2 double/twin guest bedrooms and 1 single. In the evening, you can eat at any of three pubs within 100 yds. No dogs, smoking allowed, children welcome. B&B £20–£23.

F THE BAUBLE   Tel 01206 337263

Nowell & Penny Watkins, The Bauble, Higham, nr Colchester, Essex CO7 6LA.

You can enjoy 1½ acres of good gardens here, together with a tennis court and heated swimming pool. The period cottage is full of antiques, is heavily beamed and has a big fireplace blazing with logs if the weather turns chilly. The 3 comfortable double/twin bedrooms are well equipped, and there are many places to eat out locally in the evening. Smoking discouraged, no dogs, and children should be over 12. B&B £20.

G OLLIVERS FARM   Tel 01787 237642

James & Sue Blackie, Ollivers Farm, Toppesfield, nr Halstead, Essex CO9 4LS.

A well-kept, peaceful 2-acre garden with lovely views lies behind this 17th-century farmhouse. A lime avenue in the paddock leads to a small woodland garden. Nearer the house is a large mixed white border well worth studying. There are many climbers, colourful herbaceous borders, roses, clipped yew hedges, shrubs, a pond – altogether, it is a place all garden-lovers will enjoy. The 2 double/twin bedrooms have a good outlook. For evening meals, there are plenty of local pubs, and good restaurants within 5m. No smoking, no dogs, children to be discussed. B&B £20.

What Else to Enjoy

This is a short selection of the many good things recommended in the area by owners of places to stay. Your hosts will certainly be able to provide additional information.

Other Gardens/Nurseries

Near **Coggeshall** are two historic estates. **Marks Hall** gives you lovely walks round ornamental lakes, cascades and ancient woodlands. From Coggeshall, go W on A120 for 2m, where it is signed on R. Open daily except Mons, Easter to Oct. **Cressing Temple**, built by the Knights Templar, has two magnificent medieval barns now containing rural exhibitions. There is a newly-created Tudor walled garden alongside. From Braintree, go SE on B1018 for 3m. Open daily except Sats, Easter to Sept. There is a nursery I am fond of at 1 Steps Farm, **Polstead**. It is small and personal, the creation of Frances Mount who sells hardy herbaceous perennials and more than 50 varieties of hardy geraniums. Tel 01206 262811 to make sure she is open. To find the village, go N from from Colchester on A134 for 4m. At Nayland, turn R on B1087 for Stoke-by-Nayland, then on a minor rd to Polstead.

If It's Wet

There are so many parks, gardens and historic buildings in this part of Britain that, as well as the ones I have written about above, there are others which I'm sure you will enjoy. You can climb **Layer Marney Tower,** the tallest Tudor gatehouse in Britain – an absolutely stunning display of ornate brickwork, surrounded by pleasant yew-hedged gardens and a large park and farm with many rare breeds of animals. Open daily except Sats in July/Aug, and Thurs and Sats, April to June and Sept, 2–6. From Colchester, go SW on B1022 for 4m and turn L after the village of **Birch** where signed. The NT has some fascinating properties in the area. Bourne Mill, in Bourne Lane, **Colchester**, still has most of the old mill machinery intact inside a 16th-century gabled flint house next to a large millpond, with a pretty cottage garden alongside. At **Coggeshall**, you will find the vast Grange Barn, built around 1140, and thought to be the oldest in the country. In West St, Paycocke's is a Tudor merchant's house with fine carved panelling and a display of lace. The garden is worth a stroll.

Colchester, the first capital of Roman Britain, has a long history, excellent museums and good shopping. The Castle Museum is entertaining and popular with children who can find plenty of hands-on activity. Walking tours start from the Tourist Information Centre in Queen St. Tel 01206 282290.

In **Braintree**, there is a unique working Silk Museum, using hand looms rescued from what used to be a thriving industry in the area. You can buy as well as watch. Open Mon–Fri, 10–5 (closed 12.30–1.30). Find it in South St, off the A131 London Rd.

Eating Out

The **Angel Inn** at **Nayland** (near Garden 9) is the most widely recommended. A pub which has become more a restaurant, it has a good atmosphere, 16th-century surroundings and affordable good food. Expect to spend £25–£30 per head. Tel 01206 337324.

Suffolk

There are absolutely stunning locations here. Long Melford is a pretty village with two great gardens – Melford Hall and Kentwell. Sun House, nearby, does B&B and has one of the most colourful gardens in this book. Helmingham Hall's garden, to the east, is among the best in Britain. It is mostly flat countryside, with windmills dotting the broad sky-line, reminding me of loveable Don Quixote and his romantic quest. I am very fond of Richard Strauss's symphonic poem about the eccentric old knight – 'Don Quixote', Opus 35 – and played it as I drove around.

OS maps: Landrangers **155**, 156, 169

Gardens

Opening times: in larger gardens, and in NT properties, last admissions are usually 30–45 minutes before the garden closes. Admission charges are a guide to what one adult can expect to pay to go round the garden. It sometimes varies with the season or days of the week. When the house is also open to the public, there is usually an additional charge.

I   MELFORD HALL (NT)   nr Sudbury   Tel 01787 880286

Wed–Sun and BH Mons, May to Sept, 2–5; Sat/Sun, April and Oct, 2–5.
£4 includes principal rooms in house
From Sudbury go N on A134 for 1m. At roundabout, branch L on B1508 for 3m. Garden well signed on R.

The park is very splendid, and many new oaks have been planted recently. The moat is dry and is now a sunken garden with espaliered apples trained up the sheltering walls, with iris and agapanthus making a blue and white splash of colour. The big lawn is dominated by a copper beech, a weeping ash, a Judas tree and a mulberry tree leaning on its elbows. Two big dumplings of box are huge enough for children to climb in and hide, and there are some very chic topiary trees. Inside a clipped yew enclosure is a lily pool and fountain; fragrant plants surround it – lavender, rue and

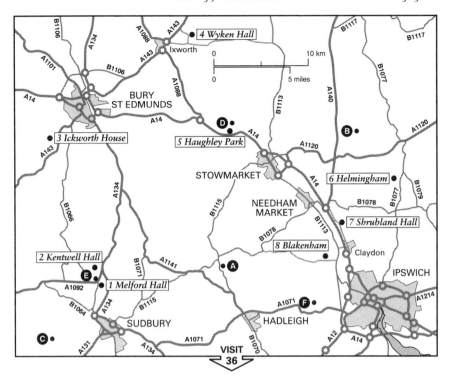

germander. Vines and wisterias ramble over the garden walls, with a wide herbaceous border in front, planted in original Victorian and Edwardian designs. By far the best thing here is the octagonal gazebo, devastatingly pretty and eccentric, giving a good view of the garden and park. Maddeningly, it is sometimes locked.

2   KENTWELL HALL

Long Melford, nr Sudbury   Tel 01787 310207

Daily, early July to mid Sept, 12–5; also BHs in April and May; also Suns, early March to early June and late Sept to late Oct. £2.90
From Sudbury go N on A134 for 1m. At roundabout, branch L on B1508 for 3m. Continue briefly on A1092. Garden well signed on L.

A fascinating and atmospheric trip back in time to Tudor England here. The rosy brick house, in classic Elizabethan E-shape, was built in 1520, and is completely surrounded by a moat. a ½m-long avenue of 300-yr-old limes leads through the park from the road. Dovecote and stocks are to the L as you enter. In the courtyard in front of the house, a modern maze has been laid out in ornamental brickwork, in the shape of a Tudor rose. At the back of the house is an old walled garden, and here Patrick and Judith Phillips, the bold couple who are making it their life's work to restore Kentwell, have planted a Tudor garden. Many of the espaliered fruit trees are ancient indeed, and old varieties of vegetables, flowers and herbs are grown here in glorious profusion and great charm. No, it's not immaculate, and I don't expect Tudor gardens were either. The atmosphere, tranquillity and age of this charming garden and its setting appealed to me enormously. Also, the Phillips's keep rare breeds in the farmyard, and have restored some old barns brilliantly.

3   ICKWORTH HOUSE (NT)

nr Bury St Edmunds   Tel 01284 735270

Daily, Easter to Oct, 10–5. £1.75
From Bury St Edmunds go SW on A143 for 3m. Garden well signed on R.

Very grand here, in the setting of a huge 1,800-acre park with woods and farmland. Capability Brown was responsible for tinkering with the landscape. The 4th Earl of Bristol built the present house. He was an eccentric and impassioned art collector, and Bishop of Derry. The garden is impersonal, but contains many good trees and shrubs. Long *allées* of box give distant views of temples or urns; curved beds of catmint and roses echo the line of the Rotunda. A silver garden has interesting silvery variegated trees and shrubs, and is next to a stump garden. I hate stumperies – nasty, ugly Victorian monstrosities. Burn 'em all, I say. There are long walks around the estate, and you can get a map out of a machine in the car park for £1. There is a restaurant in the basement of the Rotunda. Marvellous giant terracotta pots of agapanthus line the orangery steps.

4   WYKEN HALL

Stanton, nr Bury St Edmunds   Tel 01359 250287

Thurs, Suns and BH Mons, May to Sept, 11–5.30. £1.50
From Bury St Edmunds go NE on A143 for 8m. At Alecock's Grave X-rds turn R on minor road, signed to Wyken Hall.

This lovely Elizabethan house, the home of Kenneth Carlisle, has an exciting and vibrant garden round it, mostly planted in the last few years. Hedges of hornbeam and yew divide it up into a series of garden rooms. The rose garden has a long pergola drenched with flowers, and Arabella

Lennox-Boyd has designed a ravishing knot garden and formal herb garden. Along an outside wall of the kitchen garden is a border of hot colours. The kitchen garden is traditional and lovely, with a greenhouse and fruit trees. On the other side of the garden you can find a nuttery, and a maze of copper beech. I think you could happily spend a whole day here. There is a vineyard, now producing very drinkable wine which you can buy in the Leaping Hare Country Store in the medieval barn, along with many desirable baskets, quilts and other presents. Here too is the café, which serves meat and fish smoked over vine cuttings, home-grown veggies and lots of teas, coffees, squidgy cakes – all good country food.

5 HAUGHLEY PARK nr Stowmarket Tel 01359 40205

Tues, May to Sept, 3–5.30. £2
From Stowmarket go NW on A14 for 4m. Garden well signed on R.

This pretty house, owned by the Williams family, was built around 1620. The parkland has fine old trees, and is backed by 100 acres of woodland. On the N side of the house, a spacious lawn is surrounded by mixed herbaceous borders, and smaller gardens are enclosed by perfectly clipped hedges. The old lime avenue marches out into the countryside, and in spring a profusion of rhododendrons and azaleas bloom, under-planted with bluebells and lilies-of-the-valley – ah, Diorissimo! An old oak with a 30-ft trunk, reputed to be over 1,000 years old, is still flourishing, as is a great *Davidia involucrata*.

6 HELMINGHAM HALL nr Stowmarket Tel 01473 890363

Suns, end April to mid Sept, and groups on Weds by appointment. £3
From Ipswich go N on B1077 for 9m. Garden well signed on L.

This is a jewel of a garden – one of the best in England. It is great at any time of the year, but fantastic when the musk roses are bloming. These were planted in 1965 by the present Lord Tollemache's mother, and the collection is still being added to. They grow in wide borders beneath the walls, and are edged with Hidcote lavender and under-planted with London Pride. The walled garden has eight beds, divided by grass paths and arched tunnels that are draped with sweet peas, runner beans and gourds – a magnificent sight. Climbing roses, some so old that they haven't been identified, are trained along wires. A sublime double herbaceous border runs down the middle, and serried rows of perfect vegetables are behind wonderful pink and purple climbing roses. Between the walls and the surrounding moat are long beds with different planting schemes, including plenty of iris, peonies, tulips and roses. The west border is full of silver, pink and white scented flowers to enhance perfect summer evenings. In 1982, Lady Tollemache asked Lady Salisbury for advice on planning a Tudor garden to the E of the house. The resulting garden is a triumph, and looks as though it has been there for centuries. Low hedges of lavender or box are planted in a knot design which incorporates the Tollemache fret found in the brickwork of the house. The beds are in-filled with plants known to be grown before 1780. A statue of Flora stands in a bed of golden thyme. There is informal planting in profusion within a formal structure, including many more old roses, white foxgloves, campanulas, violas and *Alchemilla mollis*. This garden is enclosed by a yew hedge, and paths lead out to the old stables and tea-rooms in the Coach House. Plants and vegetables from the gardens are for sale in the farm shop. In the park are large herds of red and fallow deer whose ancestors have been roaming here since 1600, while some of the oak trees are thought to be 900 years old. The drawbridge is still pulled up every night, as it has been for the last four centuries.

7   SHRUBLAND HALL   nr Ipswich   Tel 01473 830221

Suns and BH Mons, end March to early Sept, 2–5. £2.50
From Ipswich go N on A14 for 3m. Turn R at roundabout into Claydon. Turn L onto minor road alongside A14 for 2½m. Garden signed on R.

Here is an important Victorian garden, undergoing restoration by Lord and Lady de Saumarez. It was designed by Charles Barry, and later on William Robinson advised about the planting. The chief glory is the stunning Italian staircase which descends from the top terrace to the formal gardens below. There are follies, a Swiss chalet, a loggia and a maze of box where you can happily lose your children for a while. The wild garden leads into the park, with many fine and very old trees.

8   BLAKENHAM WOODLANDS
Little Blakenham, nr Ipswich   Tel 01714 112201

Daily except Sats, March to June, 1–5. £1
From Ipswich go N on A14 for 3m. At Claydon roundabout, turn L briefly on B1113, then L at Great Blakenham onto minor rd signed to Little Blakenham. Garden signed on R just before village.

This is a woodland garden well worth visiting in late spring – a 5-acre paradise of camellias, magnolias, cornus, rhododendrons and azaleas, all under-planted with a sea of bluebells. Later in the year, there are roses and hydrangeas to enjoy.

Where to Stay

All B&B prices are approximate per person, sharing a double/twin room usually with private or en suite facilities. It is a good idea to ask for any special requirements when booking.

A THE OLD RECTORY   Tel 01449 740745

Tess & Rupert Chetwynd, The Old Rectory, Nedging, nr Hadleigh, Suffolk IP7 7HQ.

Two acres of landscaped gardens lie around this elegant, pink-washed Georgian house which has been carefully restored and filled with period and antique furniture. Rolling lawns and carefully sited trees take the eye to distant views over the Suffolk countryside. Nedging is a tiny hamlet, and there is perfect peace and quiet here. The 3 double rooms are each decorated in an individual style. Dinner, *en famille*, is served most evenings, costing £17.50–£20 (bring your own wine). No smoking, no dogs, and children should be over 12. B&B £28–£33.

B THE OLD RECTORY   Tel 01449 711283

Patricia Currie, The Old Rectory, Mickfield, nr Stowmarket, Suffolk IP14 5LR.

When Patricia arrived here in 1987, she hired a bulldozer and then spent the next 18 months staring at expanses of black polythene as it killed off a wilderness of bindweed and ground elder where she wanted to make beds in the 1½-acre grounds. She is a passionate gardener, as you may gather. Blessed with fine specimen trees, and a foaming mass of apple blossom and a carpet of cowslips in spring, her garden today is a triumph, mainly planted for foliage effect. Colour on the terrace around the old timber-framed house, which has medieval origins, comes from lavishly-planted urns and containers. Inside the house is a beamed Tudor dining-room, a gracious Georgian drawing-room, and 3 comfortable and spacious double/twin bedrooms. Dinner (£18, licensed) is served by arrangement. No smoking, no dogs, and children should be over 8. B&B £26.

C ST MARY HALL   Tel 01787 237202

David & Katy Morse, St Mary Hall, Belchamp Water, nr Sudbury, Suffolk CO10 7BB.

This medieval manor house, handsome with white paint, is surrounded by 5 acres of lovely gardens, with quiet countryside beyond. A huge lawn, with fine trees, leads to a large pond and a kitchen garden which provides fresh vegetables for Katy's expertly-cooked dinners (£16, licensed). There is a tennis court and heated swimming pool. The 2 double/twin bedrooms are luxuriously furnished. No smoking, children welcome, dogs by arrangement. B&B £25–£30.

D THE OLD RECTORY   Tel 01359 240144

Pamela Bowden, The Old Rectory, Wetherden, nr Stowmarket, Suffolk IP14 3LS.

Three acres of informally planted gardens, blooming with old-fashioned roses in June, surround this square-built part-Elizabethan, part-Georgian house, with a further 10 acres of orchards and grounds. Pamela is a well-known gardener locally, and can introduce you to a number of private gardens not normally open to the public. The 3 double/twin bedrooms (sometimes a bathroom is shared) include 1 with a four-poster. There are several pubs and restaurants locally where you can eat out in the evening. No smoking, no dogs, and children should be over 14. B&B £25–£28.

E SUN HOUSE   Tel 01787 378252

Maureen Thompson, Sun House, Hall Street, Long Melford, Suffolk CO10 9HZ.

Spectacular – that's the first word which comes to mind when trying to describe the marvellous garden here. Created over the last dozen or so years, it overflows with colour and foliage, from the terraces crammed with summer flowers and urns, past a lily-pool where plants burst through the surrounding paving to a lawn backed by decorative trees, shrubs and borders. It has won many awards, and was runner-up (shame) in a national newspaper competition that drew 2,800 entrants. Maureen is an expert on specialist nurseries locally, and can introduce you to private gardens in the area. Accommodation – a twin room with a sitting-room – is in a studio cottage attached to the main house, furnished with antiques, and old glass and porcelain. There are numerous pubs and restaurants within walking distance where you can eat out in the evening, and Long Melford itself, with its magnificent church and many antique shops, is worth a visit in its own right. No smoking, no dogs, no children. B&B £25.

F MULBERRY HALL   Tel 01473 652348

Penny Debenham, Mulberry Hall, Burstall, nr Ipswich, Suffolk IP8 3DP.

This lovely 16th-century house, once owned by Cardinal Wolsey, has an enviable garden, including the old apple tunnel I've always longed for but never planted. Lawns and clipped yew hedges lead to fields where cattle graze contentedly. A pergola and rose garden leads you to a tennis court. Inside the house is an unmistakeable sense of history, with Henry VIII's coat of arms on the inglenook fireplace, and a winding staircase to 3 double/twin bedrooms. Dinner, if requested in advance, costs £15 (bring your own wine). Home-baked bread accompanies a lavish breakfast. No smoking, dogs by arrangement, children welcome. B&B £18.

What Else to Enjoy

This is a short selection of the many good things recommended in the area by owners of places to stay. Your hosts will certainly be able to provide additional information.

Other Gardens/Nurseries

Hartshall Nursery is special, and you have to visit there in order to buy. Renowned for its trees and shrubs (particularly cherries, maples and birches), a careful look round will uncover treasures of all sorts – the plants you never knew about and suddenly seem irresistible. Open Tues–Sat all year except July and BHs, 10–4.30. Find it near Garden 4. From Ixworth go E on minor rd for 4m to **Walsham Le Willows**. Continue east on rd towards Westhorpe. Hartshall Farm is signed on L after 1m. Tel 01359 259238.

If It's Wet

The NT's **Melford Hall** (*see* Garden 1), has the reputation of being one of the finest Elizabethan houses in the area, with a splendid banqueting hall and good collections of pictures, furniture and porcelain. Open as garden. The village of **Long Melford** is lovely in its own right, with good pubs, art galleries and antique shops.

Kentwell Hall (*see* Garden 2) is equally popular, and has much more of a family feel after all the personal effort Patrick and Judith Phillips have put in so as to bring the house and gardens back to order after more than 50 years of neglect. It has been a labour of love – but what a labour! Don't miss it. Open as garden.

At **Ickworth House** (*see* Garden 3) you are back again to display and formality in the curious Italianate design of this huge house with its curving corridors. It contains magnificent Georgian silver, and paintings by Titian and Velasquez, together with family portraits including some by Gainsborough. Open as garden.

Bury St Edmunds, with an historic town centre, is definitely worth exploring. In Honey Hill, a fascinating museum has been created in the Manor House. Here, with the aid of much modern technology, you can discover clocks, watches, paintings, furniture, costume and ceramics made during the last 400 years. Open daily all year, 10–5 (Suns 2–5).

Corn Craft is fun. Set up 18 years ago by Winifred and Roystan Gage, it is in part a craft shop with an endless array of hand-made cottage crafts, from corn dollies and baskets to pottery. But in summer you can wander through their 70 acres given over to the cultivation of flowers for drying. There are countless displays which you can buy in the shop, but you can also pick them from the fields and take them home to make your own arrangements. Open daily all year, 10–5, there is a tea-room with excellent home-made goodies. From Hadleigh, go NW on A1141 for 5m, where it is signed on the R, just before **Monks Eleigh**.

If you just feel like a wander around what is said to be the finest medieval town in England, **Lavenham** is the place. Fine timber-framed houses intermingle with small cottages and crooked town houses, with more than 300 listed buildings and the medieval street pattern still intact. There are many good places to eat and shop.

Eating Out

Mr Underhill's, run by Chris and Judy Bradley, has been in business for many years now, and still gets high recommendations for the way it buys prime seasonal produce and turns it into dishes you will remember for their uncomplicated but imaginative simplicity. Set dinner menus are £26–£35, so count on spending a bit more than this per head. Find it at **Earl Stonham**, on the A140 E of Stowmarket just S of the junction with the A1120. Tel 01449 711206.

Around Norwich

The Broads cover more than 5,000 acres of lakes and rivers – a haven for botanists, bird-watchers and what is known as inland cruising (I call it a jolly good holiday). Some grand and imposing estates are here, with a wonderful garden at Raveningham Hall which alone makes the area worth visiting. You will find a choice of great places to stay, too. Ralph Vaughan Williams loved it. He wrote 'In the Fen Country' and 'Norfolk Rhapsody' as an appreciation – surely the right music to get you in the mood.

OS maps: Landrangers 133, **134**, 144

Gardens

Opening times: in larger gardens, and in NT properties, last admissions are usually 30–45 minutes before the garden closes. Admission charges are a guide to what one adult can expect to pay to go round the garden. It sometimes varies with the season or days of the week. When the house is also open to the public, there is usually an additional charge.

1   SOMERLEYTON HALL   nr Lowestoft   Tel 01502 730224

Thurs, Suns and BH Mons, mid April to Sept, 12.30–5 (also Tues/Wed in July/Aug). £3.95 includes house
From Lowestoft go NW on B1074 for 6m. Garden signed on R.

It's very popular here, and justifiably so. There are 12 acres of superbly kept gardens with magnificent old trees, and a Victorian conservatory stuffed with colourful pot plants. Flowerbeds are formal, and the treasure in this garden is a splendid maze – put Granny and the children in there for half an hour while you have a quiet cuppa in the tea-room. Schoolboys of all ages will love the miniature railway, which runs on Suns and Thurs. There are extensive lawns and interesting shrubs, and the house is surrounded by an old deer park.

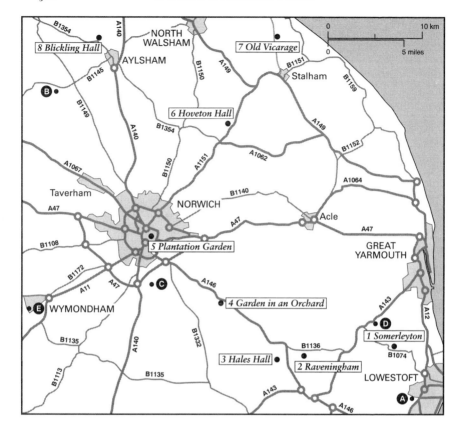

2 RAVENINGHAM HALL

Raveningham, nr Hales   Tel 01508 548206

Wed, Sun and BH Mons, April to Sept, 2–5 (Wed 1–4). £2
From Norwich go SE on A146 for 12m. At Hales, turn L on B1136 for 1m.
Garden signed on R.

Raveningham is the home of Sir Nicholas Bacon and his family. There is a fascinating plantsman's garden here, crammed with rare plants, shrubs and trees, all grown so seductively. Parts of the 18th-century garden remain, but this is predominantly a 20th-century masterpiece. Old melon pits and a Victorian conservatory are being restored. The gardens grow masses of flowers for florists, and Lady Bacon, mother of Sir Nicholas, is the indomitable driving force behind a garden that exports daffodils and snowdrops, and raises many rare plants and shrubs available through her catalogue. Everything is unusual and interesting. There is masses to enjoy in this old country house garden – wonderful yew hedges backing wide herbaceous borders, collections of old roses under-planted with lilies (more than fifty varieties). The kitchen garden is 200 years old, and has a gnarled and aged apple tree from the original planting, of a variety not known today. Figs, peaches, vines and cucumbers jostle for space in the greenhouse, with jasmines and *Clianthus maurandias*. This is a great garden, worth driving a long way to see.

3   HALES HALL   Hales, nr Loddon   Tel 01508 548395

Daily except Mons, April to Oct, 10–5; Suns 2–5. By donation.
From Norwich go SE on A146 for 12m. 1m after junction with B1136, turn
R on minor road to Hales.

A moat flows around the remains of an Elizabethan house here. The garden, with its wide mixed borders and excellent topiary, is being restored. Mr and Mrs Terence Read specialise in growing figs and greenhouse grapes, and hold the National Collection of citrus. Lovely conservatory plants are for sale, and I'm going there to buy my mulberry tree – another of their specialities.

4   GARDEN IN AN ORCHARD
Bergh Apton, nr Norwich   Tel 01508 480322

Most Sat/Suns and BH Mons, May to Sept, 11–6 (phone to confirm). £1
From Norwich go SE on A146 for 6m. Turn R where signed to Bergh Apton.
Garden is at Wyke House in Mill Rd, 300 yds on L.

This is very much a plantsman's garden, started in 1972 by Mr and Mrs Boardman, and now extending to 3½ acres, with many island beds and wandering paths. Rare plants, trees and shrubs thrive here, including nine species of eucalyptus, eight sorts of buddleia, many bamboos, salvias and wonderful clumps of specie roses, which clamber up trees together with the clematis. You will find colour and form in the garden all the year round, and a ½-acre of wildflowers in the meadow in May.

About 2½m N of here is **Rosemary Cottage**, Daphne ffiske's famous herb garden. It is a treat, with a huge choice of herbs and medicinal plants for sale. Open Thurs–Sun, March to Sept, 10–4. Go on minor roads through Yelverton to **Bramerton**. Garden is signed in The Street. Tel 01508 538187.

5   THE PLANTATION GARDEN
Norwich   Tel 01603 621868

Suns, mid April to Oct, 2–5, and by appointment. £1.50
In centre of Norwich, nr St John's RC Cathedral. Entrance between Crofters and
Beeches Hotels. Garden at 4 Earlham Rd.

If you are staying in Norwich, or passing through, make a point of visiting
this Victorian garden, made in a disused chalk quarry nearly 150 years ago.
Volunteers have been nobly restoring it. There are some remarkable architectural features, including a long Italian terrace, ornaments and a 30-ft
fountain. People who garden on chalk will be particularly interested to see
which plants thrive and flourish here.

6   HOVETON HALL GARDENS
nr Wroxham   Tel 01603 782798

Wed, Fri, Sun, and BH Mons, Easter to mid Sept, 11–5.30. £2.50
From Norwich go NE on A1151 for 8m. Signed on L 1m past Wroxham.

Hoveton Hall, the home of Mr and Mrs Andrew Buxton, is singularly lucky
to have so much water in one of England's dryest locations. Many aquatic
plants thrive along the dykes, streams and lakes, and in May there are magnificent azaleas and rhododendrons, primulas, giant gunneras and new plantings
of camellias and magnolias. The Hall is attributed to Repton, and it looks
very grand from the Lakeside Walk. The Spider Garden has an intriguing
spider's-web gate, designed and made by Eric Stevens. It has classical
English herbaceous borders, and particularly fine peonies in June. The walled
kitchen garden shelters some fine old fruit trees, masses of veggies and an
excellent display of home-propagated plants for sale. A nice tea-room in the
old milking parlour has ploughman's lunches and gooey cakes.

7   THE OLD VICARAGE
East Ruston, nr Stalham   Tel 01603 632350

Suns and Weds, early May to Oct, 2–5. £3
From Norwich go NE on A1151/A149 for 12m. Turn L briefly on B1151,
then L again on minor rd N for 3m, signed to Walcott. After East Ruston
church turn R into lane. Garden is 200 yds on R.

This garden, made by owners Alan Gray and Graham Robeson, will surprise and delight you. Although the North Sea is close and plants can be
wind–whipped, hard frosts are rare. Within high sheltering hedges, exotic

plants thrive – bananas, palm trees, agaves and cannas. A Mediterranean garden glitters with silvery foliage and aromatic plants, the herbaceous borders are sumptuous and a box parterre is neatly clipped. Not a thing is out of place, while wildflowers abound in the meadows around. The old church spire is set against the long Norfolk views, full of sky.

8   BLICKLING HALL (NT)   nr Aylsham   Tel 01263 733084

Daily except Mon and Thurs (open BH Mons), end March to early Nov, 10.30–5 (July/Aug, 10.30–6). £5.50 includes house
From Norwich go N on A140 for 10m. At roundabout, turn L on B1354 for 2m. Garden well signed on R.

This magnificent Jacobean house is surrounded by an old landscaped park, with oak, beech and chestnuts, and a lovely lake. The gardens around the house have some huge fat yew hedges, probably part of the original planting, and a parterre with topiary pillars designed by Nesfield around 1870. The Victorian sunken garden was re-modelled by Norah Lindsay in the 1930s, with four herbaceous borders and yew topiary around a 17th-century fountain. There are *allées*, a Doric temple and a superb orangery designed by Samuel Wyatt, with camellias, ferns and (of course) oranges in it. Other architectural features are a mausoleum, a pyramid and a Gothic tower. Norah Lindsay also planted the dry moat, and a shrub walk which leads to the secret garden. In spring, there are great drifts of bluebells in the wilderness garden, and a fine collection of magnolias. In the orchard is an extensive plant centre, selling plants all grown at Blickling.

Where to Stay

All B&B prices are approximate per person, sharing a double/twin room usually with private or en suite facilities. It is a good idea to ask for any special requirements when booking.

A   IVY HOUSE FARM   Tel 01502 501353

Caroline Sterry, Ivy House Farm, Ivy Lane, Oulton Broad, Lowestoft, Suffolk NR33 8HY.

This substantial farmhouse, with its low-slung converted outbuildings around a courtyard, now has 10 double/twin bedrooms in all, and its own licensed restaurant, the Crooked Barn, where you dine and eat breakfast.

Caroline loves her 2-acre country garden, flanked by two large lily-ponds, although she admits it is her mother who does most of the gardening. Herbaceous beds intertwine through lawns, edged by rose beds and mixed borders, leading to Oulton Broad. The guest bedrooms are generously-sized, and 2 have special facilities for wheelchair users. A 3-course dinner costs £20. Dogs welcome, smoking generally allowed, children by arrangement. B&B £40.

B   GREY GABLES   Tel 01823 672603

James & Rosalind Snaith, Grey Gables, Norwich Road, Cawston, nr Norwich, Norfolk NR10 4EY.

This substantial former rectory has 3 acres of garden, formally planted near the house, leading to orchards and a woodland walk. All around is open countryside. It is a handsomely-furnished house with a great mahogany stair-case, and a Victorian sitting-room looking out to the garden. There are 7 spacious guest bedrooms. Excellent evening meals (a 3-course menu costs £15) would satisfy the most demanding gourmet. James and Rosalind travel abroad each year to find new wines, and now offer a choice of no less than 300, all reasonably priced. Dogs and children welcome, restricted smoking. B&B £29.

C   THE OLD RECTORY   Tel 01508 492490

Kassy & Jonathan Pusey, The Old Rectory, Caistor St Edmund, nr Norwich, Norfolk NR14 8QS.

This fine, creeper-clad Georgian house was once the residence of the Bishop of Thetford. Today it is filled with antiques and fine old paintings, Kassy's skills as an interior and television designer showing everywhere. Mature in-formal gardens have herbaceous borders, heathers and many old roses. The courtyard has raised herb beds and a water garden with colourful trailing and climbing annuals in pots and baskets. The bedrooms – 2 double/twin, 1 single – are luxurious. Kassy loves cooking, and her 4-course evening meals cost £17 (bring your own wine). No smoking, children welcome, dogs by arrangement. B&B £26.

D DECOY BARN
Tel 01493 488392

Barry & Janet Spurr, Decoy Barn, Beccles Rd, Fritton, nr Great Yarmouth, Norfolk NR31 9AB.

Well-kept gardens, with paddocks and orchards giving lovely views to un-spoiled countryside surround this comfortable converted barn in the Broads National Park. The 2 double/twin bedrooms are on the ground floor, and are en suite. The breakfast-room has numerous board games, maps and local tourist literature. For evening meals, there is a village pub immediately opposite, and restaurants a short drive away. Children welcome, no dogs, no smoking. B&B £25.

E KIMBERLEY HOME FARM
Tel 01953 603137

Jenny Bloom, Kimberley Home Farm, Wymondham, Norfolk NR18 0RW.

You get a warm welcome here from Jenny who is one of the most gener-ous hosts you will ever meet. Her handsomely furnished farmhouse looks out to a large garden with a tennis court, and stables where racehorses are kept and trained. There are 4 attractive double/twin bedrooms (two some-times share a bathroom) and a family suite in the attic. Jenny's generosity extends to the food she so amply cooks. There is always an offer of second helpings from the roasts and game which she serves in the evening (3 cours-es from £15, bring your own wine). Children welcome, dogs by arrange-ment, no smoking. B&B £25

What Else to Enjoy

This is a short selection of the many good things recommended in the area by owners of places to stay. Your hosts will certainly be able to provide additional information.

Other Gardens/Nurseries

The name of **Bressingham Nursery** must surely be known to everyone who has gardened for any length of time. Alan Bloom's 5-acre gardens have huge island beds which display more than 5,000 herbaceous species and varieties, many of them to be found in the adjoining nursery. Open daily, April to Oct, 10–5.30. To find it, continue on A140 S of visit map for 6m to Diss; turn R on A1066 for 3m, and nursery is signed on R in the village of Bressingham. Tel 01379 88464.

Peter Beales, the rose specialist and author, has a wonderful display of old-fashioned, specie and shrub roses at his nursery grounds – best visited in June, of course. The scent is heavenly. Open daily all year, 9–5 (earlier closing on Sat/Sun). Find it by continuing SW on A11 past Wymondham for 7m. It is 1m SW of **Attleborough**, signed on L of A11. Tel 01953 454707.

If It's Wet

When you visit Garden 1, **Somerleyton Hall**, it is well worth going round the interior (included in admission price). It is an Elizabethan houses, much expanded in the mid 19th century, with elaborate plaster-work in the Italian style. Open as garden.

The NT property in this visit is **Blickling Hall** (*see* Garden 8). Built in the early 17th century, this is one of East Anglia's greatest house, with collections of fine furniture, pictures and tapestries. The long gallery is renowned, and there is a spectacular Jacobean plaster ceiling.

Wet or dry, **Norwich** has much to offer, its centre being perhaps the most complete remaining medieval city in England. Dominated by the cathedral, which should be on every visitor's must-see list, it is a maze of half-timbered shops, merchants' houses and more than 30 flint-built churches. There is a 6-day open air market, and a wealth of specialist shops. Guided walking tours start from the Tourist Information Centre in Gaol Hill (Tel 01603 666071), but it is just as easy to enjoy on your own. Of many museums and art galleries, the Castle Museum is the largest, with major archeological and other collections in the former dungeons. Dragon Hall in King St is also good, with an outstanding timber-framed Great Hall.

Eating Out

There are many restaurants in **Norwich**, and one of the most widely recommended is **Tatlers**, a Georgian house at 21 Tombland, a small cobbled street with an archway leading to the cathedral. Cooking is imaginative, the surroundings friendly. Expect to pay £25–£35 per head. Tel 01603 766670. Another recommendation in Norwich is the well-established **Adlard's**, at 79 Upper St Giles St. David Adlard is rated as one of the area's most talented chefs, renowned for never using produce out of season, and meat that is always cooked to perfection. It is a pleasant 18th-century house with a relaxed feel to it. Your bill will probably be £30–£45. Tel 01603 633522.

South Lincolnshire

Gardeners thinking of Lincolnshire will probably associate the county immediately with its bulb fields, particularly tulips. In fact, these are on flatlands to the east of this visit. Here you will find the grand castles and mansions which the landed gentry made their own because of the rolling landscape on which they could impose their designs, and its handy position for the stage coach to London. There are historic market towns, and on higher ground some ancient woodlands. William Byrd (1543–1623) was a Lincolnshire man, and the gentry danced in their stately way to his music. Try recapturing times past by listening to his pavanes and galliards, played on a harpsichord.

OS maps: Landrangers 121, 129, **130**

Gardens

Opening times: in larger gardens, and in NT properties, last admissions are usually 30–45 minutes before the garden closes. Admission charges are a guide to what one adult can expect to pay to go round the garden. It sometimes varies with the season or days of the week. When the house is also open to the public, there is usually an additional charge.

I   21, CHAPEL STREET

Haconby, nr Bourne   Tel 01778 570314

Many charity Suns, April to Oct, and by appointment. Also Sat/Sun in late Feb for snowdrops and hellebores. £1
From Bourne go N on A15 for 3m. At X-rds, turn R to Haconby (½m). Garden on R in centre of village, before church.

In contrast to all the grand, stately, formal parks you will find in this visit, here is a cottage haven. Cliff and Joan Curtis are fanatical growers of alpines and bulbs, but their garden is fascinating at any time of year. In February, over 200 varieties of snowdrops can be seen, along with the hellebores.

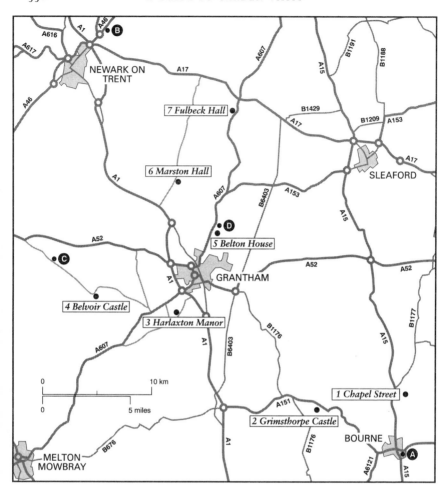

In spring, you find alpines of every sort planted in rockeries and scree beds. Summer months are sumptuous with herbaceous borders, roses and clematis. A marvellous selection of bulbs takes off again in the autumn. Sometimes, you will be lucky enough to find rarities on sale.

2   GRIMSTHORPE CASTLE   nr Bourne   Tel 01778 591295

Thurs, Sun and BH Mons, Easter to Sept, 11–6. £2
From Bourne go NW on A151 for 4m. Castle signed on L in Grimsthorpe village.

This is the Tudor castle of the de Eresby family, the North Front added by Vanbrugh. The stewponds and deer park were smartened up by Capability Brown, and the landscape has many fine trees. Around the castle are formal gardens – rose gardens and herbaceous borders with yew hedges and topiary clipped to perfection. I greatly enjoyed the geometric ornamental vegetable garden, created by the Countess of Ancaster and John Fowler in 1961. There are two nature trails, a new woodland adventure playground for children and deer to feed by the Coach House, where you can buy tea.

3 HARLAXTON MANOR nr Grantham Tel 01476 592101

Daily except Mons (open BH Mons), April to Oct, 11–5. £2.50
From Grantham go SW on A607 for 2m. Garden well signed down drive on L just before Harlaxton village.

The manor and its garden were created by Squire Gregory Gregory around 1830, and it is thought probable that Gregory's illustrious relative Prince Charles Joseph de Ligne inspired the design. The Prince had a garden in Belgium which was considered second only to Versailles, and his grandiose ideas were brought to Harlaxton. Overgrown and neglected for years, the importance of this garden became apparent when restoration was started by TV gardener Alan Mason. You may have seen some of the programmes about what he has already achieved, halfway through a 10-year plan. The formal gardens were designed to be a stroll around Europe, with French terraces, a Dutch-style canal reflecting the manor and statuary, and Italian colonnades. The *pièce de résistance* currently is a ½-acre walled garden, with a series of show and theme gardens within, packed with a vast collection of rare and unusual plants.

4 BELVOIR CASTLE Tel 01476 870262

Tues to Thurs, Sat/Sun, April to Oct, 11–5 (Sun only in Oct). £5 includes castle interior
From Grantham go SW on A607 for 3m. Turn R in Denton, and follow signs for 4m. Gardens on L.

The awesome interior of the Duke of Rutland's spectacular castle is perhaps what most people come here to see, but the gardens on their own are well worth a wander, and perhaps a picnic on the curved stone seats. Designed to show off the extravagant crenellated 19th-century castle at its best, there are walkways, many rose beds, fine trees and acres of grass. The

most notable feature is the terraced Statue Garden (or rather, gardens) leading down from the castle to the park beyond, with a carefully sited collection of 17th-century sculptures by Caius Cibber, royal sculptor to Charles II.

5   BELTON HOUSE (NT)   nr Grantham   Tel 01476 66116

Wed–Sun and BH Mons, April to Oct, 11–5.30. £4.50 includes house
From Grantham go NE on A607 for 3m. Garden well signed on R.

Belton is terribly grand and impressive. Built in the last years of Charles II's
reign, it is the perfect Restoration house, and the garden reflects this formality. It has two architectural gems: an orangery designed by Sir Jeffrey
Wyatville, and a little Palladian temple facing a mirror pond. There are
follies, fine urns, glasshouses and conservatories, rose gardens, sculptures,
topiary and an impressive Dutch garden. Around all this is a deer park of
1,000 acres, and a splendid adventure playground where your children can
let off steam if they've behaved themselves round the gardens. As in many
large NT properties, there is a gift shop and restaurant.

6   MARSTON HALL   nr Grantham   Tel 01400 250225

3 charity Suns in June, 2–5, and by appointment. £2.50
From Grantham go N on A1 for 4½m. Turn R for Marston; garden is 1½m
on R.

Marston is the ancient home of the Rev. Henry Thorold, whose family have
lived here since the 14th century. The beauty and serenity of the house and
garden show no signs of the battering they took from Cromwell's troops.
A venerable laburnum, reputedly the oldest and largest in England, and a
400-year-old wych elm are in the garden at the front of the house, with
many other interesting plants and shrubs. Walls and high hedges divide up
the 3 acres into romantic walks, rose beds, a cottage garden, herbaceous
borders, kitchen garden and a knot garden planted with herbs. A Gothic
gazebo is decorated with murals by Barbara Jones.

7   FULBECK HALL   nr Grantham   Tel 01400 272205

Easter, BH Mons, and daily end June to end July, 2–5. £1.50
From Grantham go N on A607 for 11m. Garden on L in Fulbeck.

Smooth and spacious lawns, fine trees and and hedges with abundantly
planted borders make a superb formal setting for this imposing 18th-

century stone mansion. The 11-acre garden is on a limestone ridge so plants never get waterlogged, and Lincolnshire has a low rainfall anyway. So while Michael and Mary Fry have kept the basic structure of the gardens laid out nearly a century ago, they have cut out annuals, hybrid tea roses and bedding schemes, and concentrated on plants which thrive here. This means numerous climbers and clematis which are encouraged to romp through the yews, hollies and laurustinus. Many old trees are contemporary with the house, however. The Arnhem Museum is here, and in July there is an Arts Festival. Interesting herbaceous stock goes on sale in the same month.

Where to Stay

All B&B prices are approximate per person, sharing a double/twin room usually with private or en suite facilities. It is a good idea to ask for any special requirements when booking.

A BOURNE EAU HOUSE   Tel 01778 423621

George & Dawn Bishop, Bourne Eau House, South Street, Bourne, Lincolnshire PE10 9LY.

For all its modern comforts, you feel as if you have stepped back in history in this part-Elizabethan, part-Georgian house. Across the Bourne Eau is a 12th-century abbey. There is a lovely, well-stocked garden. George and Dawn, having lived abroad for many years, delight in making new friends among guests who come to stay. You eat Dawn's delicious evening meals (£22 including wine) in an entrancing Elizabethan dining-room. There are 2 well-furnished double/twin bedrooms. Children welcome, dogs by arrangement, restricted smoking. B&B £33.

B THE OLD VICARAGE   Tel 01636 705031

Jeremy & Julie Steele, The Old Vicarage, Langford, nr Newark, Nottinghamshire NG23 7RT.

Spacious well-kept grounds surround this handsome red-brick Victorian vicarage, set next to one of the oldest and prettiest churches in Nottinghamshire. You will love the style, comfort and warmth of welcome here. There are 3 excellent double/twin guest bedrooms. Imaginative evening meals (£17.50, licensed) are served in a splendid dining-room. Restricted smoking, no dogs, children should be over 12. B&B £30–33.

C PEACOCK FARM   Tel 01949 842475

Nicky Need, Peacock Farm, Redmile, nr Grantham, Nottinghamshire
NG13 0GQ.

There is a wonderful informality about this award-winning B&B, a 300-year-old white stucco farmhouse with an assortment of farm buildings marked by a giant topiary peacock. Nicky, who has mostly taken over running the place from her parents Marjorie and Peter, chats amiably to people who wander in and out of her kitchen. There are comfortable chintzy furnishings, and you get to the 5 double/twin bedrooms either through the kitchen or from the courtyard, because they are mostly on the ground floor. You eat generously in Nicky's small, inexpensive locally-popular restaurant – either à la carte or a 3-course menu at £13.50, licensed. Dogs and children welcome (and lots of outdoor things for them to enjoy), smoking allowed. B&B £23.

D COACH HOUSE   Tel 01476 573636

Bernard & Sue Norton, Coach House, Belton-by-Grantham, Lincolnshire
NG32 2LS.

Bernie spends a great deal of his spare time tending, improving and landscaping the luxuriant 1½-acre garden backing on to this handsome stone house. The dining-room looks on to a lovely 'secret' courtyard and fountain which he has built. Bernie and Sue are very knowledgeable about local gardens and hidden beauty spots. There are 4 double/twin bedrooms, all en suite, with masses of character. You can arrange to stay in for evening meals (from £12.50, order your wine in advance or bring your own), but guests are encouraged to try the many good pubs and restaurants nearby. No smoking, dogs and children by arrangement. B&B £17–£20.

What Else to Enjoy

This is a short selection of the many good things recommended in the area by owners of places to stay. Your hosts will certainly be able to provide additional information.

Other Gardens/Nurseries

If you are staying at Bourne Eau House (*see* 'A' – Where to Stay), make a point of ringing Dick Sellars (Tel 01778 422241) for an appointment to see his enchanting, tiny garden about 1m to the N, in which not an inch of space is wasted. What he has created at the back of 32 Main St, **Dyke** is a lesson to us all.

On the S edge of the visit map, just E of the A1, is the little village of **Clipsham** – aptly named, because in Yew Tree Avenue you will find some 70 trees clipped into amazing topiary shapes. Maybe it's not a garden – but it's something all gardeners should see.

If It's Wet

Most of the gardens described above surround stately homes whose interiors are as important as their parks. Starting with Garden 2, here's a quick run-down. **Grimsthorpe Castle** has to be seen to be believed. It is unimaginably grandiose with superb paintings and furniture. **Harlaxton Manor** is an architectural masterpiece, but the interior is not often open; telephone to find out when. **Belvoir Castle**, home of the Dukes of Rutland since Norman times, has paintings by Holbein, Poussin, Reynolds and Rubens. **Fulbeck Hall,** family home of the Fanes since the 17th century, has arts and treasures collected over the years, including period furniture, china and *objets d'art*.

Woolsthorpe Manor is another NT property, but on a different scale. A small 17th-century farmhouse, it was the birthplace of Sir Isaac Newton. Today the old kitchen, bedchamber and study have been furnished in the style of the period. In the garden is an apple tree grafted from the one which supposedly inspired his theory on the law of gravity. Open Wed–Sun and BH Mons, April to Oct, 1–5.30. From Grantham go S on A1 for 7m to **Colsterworth**. Turn R on B676 and follow signs in village.

Eating Out

Towards the N of the visit, the **Black Swan** is recommended. Pleasantly furnished in a 400-year-old house by the banks of the River Witham, Anton and Alison Indans have been running their restaurant for more than 10 years. You are well looked after, and the dinner menu is based on excellent local produce. Expect to spend £25–£35 per person. Find it 6m E of Newark-on-Trent, just S of the A17. Tel 01636 636474.

Around Derby

It is perhaps porcelain that you first think of in this area – Royal Crown Derby the best-known of all – and it came as a surprise to me when I found that, historically, silk production was almost as big an industry. As I was heading for lovely Dove Dale, north of Ashbourne, where the great angler Izaak Walton loved to fish for trout, I was reminded of Schubert's rippling, joyful Piano Quintet in A, 'The Trout', in its famous recording by Jacqueline du Pré, Daniel Barenboim et al.

OS maps: Landrangers 119, **128**

Gardens

Opening times: in larger gardens, and in NT properties, last admissions are usually 30–45 minutes before the garden closes. Admission charges are a guide to what one adult can expect to pay to go round the garden. It sometimes varies with the season or days of the week. When the house is also open to the public, there is usually an additional charge.

I   CALKE ABBEY (NT)   Ticknall   Tel 01332 863822
Sat–Wed and BH Mons, April to Oct, 11–5. £2.50
From Derby go S on A514 for 4m from city outskirts. Turn L at Ticknall, and follow signs for 1m.

Calke interests me particularly because in the walled garden is a genuine auricula theatre, originally built to show off these beautiful plants – and I'm an auricula fancier. The garden is under restoration by the NT. Already finished are herbaceous borders, dahlia borders, Victorian bedding schemes, the fruit and vegetable garden and the Orchard House. Later plans include the physic garden, and apple and plum orchards growing old varieties of fruit. An ancient parkland surrounds this splendid 18th-century house.

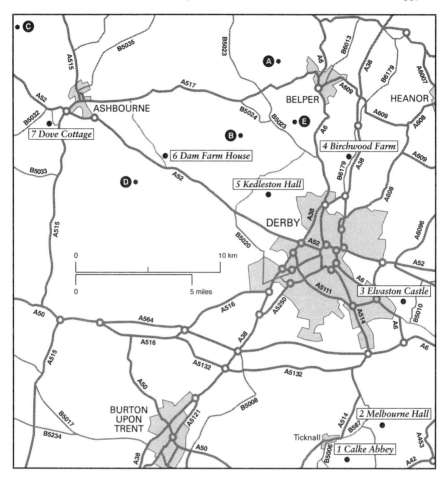

2   MELBOURNE HALL GARDENS

Melbourne, nr Derby   Tel 01332 862502

Wed, Sat/Sun and BH Mons, April to Sept, 2–6
From Derby go S on A514 for 3m from city outskirts. At Stanton by Bridge
turn L on B587 for 1m. Garden well signed in Melbourne.

Historically fascinating, and beautifully maintained, this late 17th-century
garden has not been meddled with. It was laid out in the style of Le Nôtre
by Henry Wise and George London. Wise was gardener to Queen Anne,
and madly fashionable at the time – he and London had a hand in the gardens at Hampton Court, Kensington Palace, Bushey Park, Longleat, Petworth

and Chatsworth. There are regal avenues, and long vistas with statues. Turfed terraces stretch down to the lake. A dark tunnel of yew stretches to the west, and on the S side of the house are mixed borders.

3   ELVASTON CASTLE PARK   nr Derby   Tel 01332 571342

Daily, Easter to Oct, 9–5. Free (car park 60p weekdays, £1.20 weekends)
From Derby go SE to city outskirts to join A6. After ½m, turn L to Elvaston; castle 1m on L.

This historic garden was in a state of great neglect 25 years ago, and was rescued and restored by Derbyshire County Council. You will find an Italian garden – very formal, with clipped yews, wide herbaceous borders, a lake and parterres. The old walled garden is now named the Old English Garden where there are herbaceous borders, a rose garden and a herb garden. The good topiary and the large number of evergreen trees and shrubs make this a garden enjoyable to visit in winter as well as summer. Well-behaved dogs are allowed on leads, there is a café and the Information Centre has a fascinating history of the place.

4   BIRCHWOOD FARM   nr Derby   Tel 01332 880685

Daily except Suns, March to Oct, by appointment. £1.50
From Derby go N on A38 for 2m. At roundabout junction with A38, turn L on B6179. After 1m, turn L onto minor road for 1m. Park in field at top of drive to garden and nursery on L.

This is a garden for plant enthusiasts, and is contained within old walls covered by shrubs and climbers, with winding paths leading round a wide range of unusual hardy plants. Hardy geraniums, penstemons, silver plants, campanulas and delphiniums are much favoured here. There are old and modern English roses in profusion. Perfumed plants are also much in evidence, their colours carefully blended to complement each other. The garden is peaceful and is surrounded by a wood; this gives home to the many different birds which Mr and Mrs Coates so much enjoy watching. A nursery is attached to the garden, specialising in interesting hardy perennials and shrubs.

5   KEDLESTON HALL (NT)   nr Derby   Tel 01332 842191

Sat–Wed, April to Oct, 11–6. £2
From Derby go NW on A52 for 5m. At Kirk Langley, turn R where signed.
Garden 1½m on R.

A very grand place indeed – built by Robert Adams around 1760, and the ancient family home of the Curzons. Adams was also influential in the layout of the park, and built some attractive features – the elegant bridge over the lake, the hexagonal summer-house by the formal rose garden, an orangery, and a fishing-room with nearby boat-house. The woodlands are best visited in late spring when the dogwoods and rhododendrons are at their peak. To be truthful, the park and gardens simply cannot compete with the beautiful house.

6   DAM FARM HOUSE

Ednaston, nr Ashbourne   Tel 01335 360291

Some charity Suns, April to Oct, 1.30–5, and by appointment. £2
From Ashbourne go SE on A52 for 5m. Just after sign to Ednaston (on R), look
for Yeldersley Lane on L. Garden entrance is 500 yds up this lane on R.

Dam Farm House is beautifully situated down a long drive past a 6-acre lake. The garden was made from a field sixteen years ago, and the 2-acre garden contains a scree bed with many alpines, mixed borders, many climbers up walls and pergolas, and unusual and interesting shrubs carefully tended by Mrs Player.

7   DOVE COTTAGE   nr Ashbourne   Tel 01335 343545

Charity Suns, April to Oct, 1.30–5, and by appointment. £2
From Ashbourne go S on A515 for 1½m. Turn R at X-roads in Clifton, then
then L down lane signed 'Mayfield Yarns'. Garden is 200 yds on L.

Ann Liverman is a well-known horticulturalist – she lectures and broadcasts, and with her husband Stephen has made their riverside garden into an enchanting series of small cottage gardens. Her particular favourite plants are campanulas, astrantias, alliums, geraniums and euphorbias. She has fine collections of these, along with variegated and silver foliage plants. An arboretum is being created in the old orchard, and a *Prunus serrula* grove. The River Dove beside the garden attracts swans, ducks, herons and kingfishers. Mrs Liverman finds time to propagate her plants which are for sale on open days, and at local plant fairs.

Where to Stay

All B&B prices are approximate per person, sharing a double/twin room usually with private or en suite facilities. It is a good idea to ask for any special requirements when booking.

A DANNAH FARM   Tel 01773 550273

Joan & Martin Slack, Dannah Farm, Bowmans Lane, Shottle, nr Belper, Derbyshire DE56 2DR.

Although a working 128-acre farm complete with pot-bellied pigs, this is also a friendly and professionally-run B&B with meals – an award-winner nationally and locally both for accommodation and its small, beamed farmhouse restaurant, The Mixing Place. There are 8 double/twin bedrooms, most with fantastic views over the Ecclestone valley. The two comfortable sitting-rooms include a bar. A set menu in the evening costs £16, licensed, and there are plenty of other à la carte choices. Children welcome, restricted smoking, no dogs. B&B £30–£38.

B PARKVIEW FARM   Tel 01335 360352

Linda & Michael Adams, Park View Farm, Weston Underwood, nr Ashbourne, Derbyshire DE6 4PA.

This large, 3-storey Victorian farmhouse is smothered with creepers and climbers, and surrounded by long lawns, including one for croquet, leading to a 370-acre farm. There are 3 comfortable and spacious double/twin bedrooms with antique four-posters. There are many pubs and restaurants locally where you can eat out in the evening. Breakfast is a treat – and if you are bored with toast, there are pancakes, scones and croissants. No dogs, no smoking, children should be over 10. B&B £23–£25.

C BEECHENHILL FARM   Tel 01335 310274

Sue Prince, Beechenhill Farm, Ilam, nr Ashbourne, Derbyshire DE6 2BD.

Beechenhill Farm is a treasure. Sue, an artist and book illustrator, has produced a brochure about her house and self-catering cottage which is perhaps the most delightful of the hundreds I have seen. Recently, she has devoted her designing talents to her garden where she has many plans which she loves to discuss with other garden-lovers. Colourful planting

around the farmhouse leads to a little wildflower valley which is spectacular from June to early August. Wire sculptures of chasing cats sit above the
trellis-work. Beyond are some of the most wonderful views you will ever
find. There are 2 excellent double/twin bedrooms, and the cottage – with
flexible twin/single sleeping arrangement can take six guests. There are
many pubs and restaurants locally where you can eat out in the evenings.
Breakfasts are lavish, and include great porridge. No smoking, no dogs in
the house (allowed in cottage if well-behaved), children welcome. B&B
£18–£25.

D   SHIRLEY HALL FARM   Tel 01335 360346

Sylvia Foster, Shirley Hall Farm, Shirley, nr Ashbourne, Derbyshire DE6 3AS.

You step back in history here. This peaceful old farmhouse, with large lawns
and a large carp-filled pond, has an oak-panelled sitting-room with Tudor
beams, a family coat-of-arms, and period furniture. Sylvia can arrange for
you to visit Ednaston Manor nearby, a Lutyens house with a great private
garden. The 3 double/twin bedrooms are handsomely furnished, and mostly have wonderful views, as do the 3 self-catering cottages. The village pub,
where you can eat out in the evenings, is only a short walk away. No smoking, no dogs, and children should be over 8. B&B £17–£22.

E   CHEVIN GREEN FARM   Tel 01773 822328

*Carl & Joan Postles, Chevin Green Farm, Chevin Rd, nr Belper, Derbyshire
DE56 2DN.*

This 300-year-old house, plentifully beamed, is backed by a small, colourful walled garden. Carl and Joan have been welcoming people to their home
for many years, and can point you towards all the local attractions. There
is a choice of single, twin, double and family bedrooms, all en suite, as well
as 5 self-catering cottages. There are many pubs and restaurants in the area
for evening meals. Generous breakfasts come with free-range eggs from the
farm. No smoking, no dogs, children welcome. B&B £15–£18.

What Else to Enjoy

This is a short selection of the many good things recommended in the area by owners of places to stay. Your hosts will certainly be able to provide additional information.

Other Gardens/Nurseries

Bluebell Nursery is one you may well have come across at RHS Westminster shows, at Hampton Court or at the Chelsea Flower Show, where there are often splendid displays of trees and shrubs from this excellent nursery. It is well worth a visit. You find it on just S of the visit map, taking the A514 towards Swadlincote, turning L briefly on the A50, and then R where signed to **Blackfordby**. The nursery is behind the Bluebell Inn. Tel 01283 222091 to check opening times.

Other Places to Stay

Just N of the visit map is Mollie McKinley's absolutely stunning house and garden. **Babington House**, Greenhill, Wirksworth, Derbyshire DE4 4EN, has been featured many times in glossy magazines. Dating from 1558 with many original details, it is long, low and expansive, and beautifully furnished. The garden is a dream, with many architectural features enhanced by sumptuous and colourful planting. There are 3 luxurious double/twin bedrooms. Find it by taking the B5023 N from near Derby to **Wirksworth**. It is at the upper end of our price range: B&B starts at £40, dinner is from £17.50, and wines are mostly chateau-bottled French. No dogs, restricted smoking, children should be over 12 and well-behaved. Tel 01629 824665.

If It's Wet

Calke Abbey (*see* Garden 1) is described by the NT as the house that time forgot. Built around 1700, its contents have been virtually undisturbed since the death of the last owner in 1924. The gold and white drawing room, Sir Vauncey Harpur's childhood bedroom, the library and beer cellar are particularly fascinating and there are also natural history collections and a magnificent early 18th-century state bed. Open as for garden.

Another wonderful NT mansion is the Palladian **Kedleston Hall** (*see* Garden 5). It has the most complete number of Robert Adams interiors in

England, and contains a huge collection of family portraits, Old Masters and original furniture. House open as garden.

Derby, although heavily industrialized, has a city centre with traditional markets and specialist shops. The Museum and Art Gallery gives a good insight into the history of the city, and contains wonderful porcelain together with paintings by Joseph Wright. Open daily all year, admission free. Tours of the Royal Crown Derby Porcelain Company, close to the city centre, take about 90 minutes and demonstrate just how the exceptional hand-crafted tradition is kept up. They take place twice daily on weekdays, at 10.30 and 2.45. The museum and factory shop is also open daily. Tel 01332 712800.

Out in the country, **Ashbourne** is good for antique-hunting, and also has two renowned places for tea – The Gingerbread Shop, and Peter Cook's Tea Shop. While you are in Ashbourne, check in the Tourist Information Centre (13 Market Place, tel 01335 343666) for details of local well dressing, an old custom almost unique to Derbyshire. Originating from pagan times, then banned, then re-sanctified as a Christian ritual, it is the art of decorating wells or springs (or street water taps, come to that) with natural growing things. In one village or another, it goes on from May to September.

Eating Out

If you fancy a pub lunch in the middle of **Derby**, look out for **Ye Olde Dolphin** (1530) in Queen St, near the cathedral. Tel 01332 349115.

Go to **Ashbourne** for a meal to remember at **Callow Hall** where the same family, the Spencers, has been cooking and catering since the late 18th century. All the smoking, curing and baking is done on the premises, and the menus reflect this love of local produce. A set dinner menu, with plenty of choice, costs £30, plus service and wine. Find it at Mapleton Rd, ½m NW of Ashbourne turning L off the A515. You can stay luxuriously here too. B&B costs £45–£60 per person. Tel 01335 343403.

The Shropshire Plain

This fertile plain has some superb gardens – indeed, I think Wollerton Old Hall deserves soon to be as famous as Hidcote. Bridgemere Garden World aims to be the nursery which offers the largest variety of garden plants in Britain. Then there is a rocky outcrop with steep hills that is home to the most quirky and eccentric place in this book: the Hawkstone Follies. Don't take them too seriously, and try to get a head for their heights by listening to Richard Strauss's Alpine Symphony, Opus 64.

OS maps: Landrangers 117, 118, 126, **127**

Gardens

Opening times: in larger gardens, and in NT properties, last admissions are usually 30–45 minutes before the garden closes. Admission charges are a guide to what one adult can expect to pay to go round the garden. It sometimes varies with the season or days of the week. When the house is also open to the public, there is usually an additional charge.

1 HAWKSTONE HISTORIC PARK AND FOLLIES

Weston-under Redcastle   Tel 01939 200601/01630 685242

Daily, April to Oct, 10–6. £4.50
From Market Drayton go SW on A53 for 5m. In Hodnet, turn R on A442 for 1½m, then L on minor rd for 1½m to Weston; garden is well signed on R.

These amazing follies are being restored to their wonderfully dotty 18th-century splendour by English Heritage and the owners of Hawkstone Park Hotel. You reach the follies along tunnels and winding paths, with lots of steps and precipitous edges. Let me warn faint hearts, and anyone with rickety legs or prone to vertigo, that they should stay at home, or at least stay and have a nice lunch at the hotel. There used to be a mechanical hermit in the grotto (now being mended), there's a death-defying Swiss bridge, a White tower, a Red castle, an Indian rock passage and Gingerbread hall. A

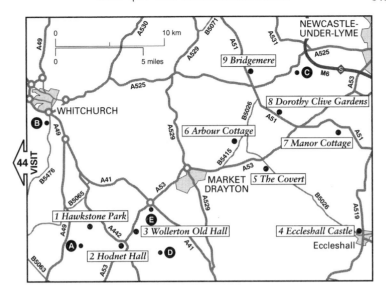

rumour that King Arthur may have been buried here has supplied visitors with the self-same king in one of the amazing caves. Standing over everything is a tall monument topped with the glittering statue of Sir Rowland Hill, who in the 18th century created this fascinating fantasy world.

Nearby are **Hawkstone Hall Gardens**, open only in August, but worth a visit at that time. The Victorian rose gardens are in front of a lily-pool, and a hot wall shelters climbers and backs a fine herbaceous border. There is a Winter Garden and a Courtyard Garden, and the earlier pleasure grounds, laid out around 1700, have woodland walks through splendid old trees and shrubs.

2 HODNET HALL

Hodnet, nr Market Drayton   Tel 01630 685202

Tues–Sat 2–5, Suns and BH Mons 12–5.30, April to Sept. £2.80
From Market Drayton go SW on A53 for 5m. Garden well signed in centre of Hodnet.

Hodnet Hall was built in the Elizabeth style in 1870, on a flat plateau above a marshy bog. The late A.G.W. Heber-Percy started to make this wonderful garden in 1922. The marshes were dug into a charming series of lakes and pools that form the central spine of the garden. The soil is rich and lime-free, so magnificent magnolias, acers, azaleas and rhododendrons grow here, together with kalmias and stuartias. Fringing the lake are some of the best astilbes I've seen, plust vast gunneras, rogersias, skunk cabbages, iris and candelabra primula. Magnificent oaks, beeches and limes adorn the surrounding park, under-planted with masses of daffodils and bluebells in spring. A broad walk runs along the terrace in front of the house, with splendidly planted borders. Broad steps flanked by lavender lead down to the lake. A large dovecot, built in 1656, stands on the sky-line. Warm walls shelter an ornamental kitchen garden where fruit trees – cherries, apples, pears greengages and peaches – are beautifully trained against the walls. Box-lined beds contain veggies and flowers for picking. In July, when I was there, it was a mass of delphiniums, sweet peas and roses – and kittens playing under the gooseberry bushes. Good plants are for sale in the kitchen garden, and the tea-room is a haven. And dogs are allowed on leads – hurrah.

3   WOLLERTON OLD HALL

nr Market Drayton   Tel 01630 685769

Fris and Suns, June to Aug, 1–5. £2
From Market Drayton go SW on A53 for 4m. Garden well signed on L in Wollerton.

It is absolutely amazing to find that Lesley and John Jenkins have created this masterpiece in only ten years. The old black-and-white hall demands straight lines and achieves them with clipped yew, beech hedges and pleached limes. A series of garden rooms inevitably invites comparison with Hidcote. But here the planting is much more exuberant and experimental, without losing the classic English charm – borders feature old favourites such as campanulas, artemisias, alchemilla, valerian and masses of old roses. The hot-colour garden is sensational in a balanced riot of copper, red, soft oranges and yellow, cooled down with greys and silvers. The central lime *allée*, under-planted with purple sage, has the gable end of the house as a geometric back-drop, and is perfect in its simplicity. My favourite border is in purple, pink and dark blue, with velvet clematis winding their way through it. I have to plant one.

4   ECCLESHALL CASTLE   Eccleshall   Tel 01785 850151

Daily for 1 week in early April, then Weds and Suns mid May to late Aug, 1–5.30. Donation to charity.
From Eccleshall go ½m N on A519. Garden well signed on L.

The gardens surround a William and Mary house and medieval castle ruins, its walls providing perfect support for climbing roses and shrubs. The dry moat is now a sunken garden. The old bridge is draped with *Hydrangea petiolaris* and solanum, and in summer the rose garden and herbaceous borders are charming. A lime avenue leads you through the grounds, while behind it are many other fine old trees and Mr and Mrs Mark Carter are planting even more. There are great drifts of snowdrops and daffodils in spring.

5 THE COVERT

Loggerheads, nr Market Drayton   Tel 01630 672677

2 charity afternoons in July/August, 2–5.30, and by appointment. £2.50
From Market Drayton go E on A53 for 3m. At Loggerheads X-rds, turn R on
B5026 for ½m. Ask owners for final directions.

How exciting to find a modern house with a contemporary and totally original garden around it. Leslie and Diana Standeven have pulled off a designer's coup with their Mediterranean-feeling front garden. Architectural shapes and plants are artfully combined. Agaves, corylines, sandstone chippings, carefully arranged stones and clipped standard balls of ligustrum make a dramatic statement. A good collection of euphorbias and a small trickling stream add to the effect, while glaucous foliage plants glisten in the sun. Go into the garden behind the house, and the scene changes for Act II. Here is a dazzling collection of rare plants collected from all over the world. Long vistas are achieved with garden walks that lead one around borders crammed with treasures. There are rare orchids, rockeries – one was formerly a large stone fireplace in the house – scree beds and a pool. Diana's great joy is an alpine house with an eclectic collection growing in tiny pots set into sand. I had to put my glasses on to appreciate some of these alpine jewels. Wherever you look in this garden, even familiar plants are used with such stunning effect that they take on a new life.

6 ARBOUR COTTAGE

Napley, nr Market Drayton   Tel 01630 672852

Some charity days, late April to June, 2–5.30, and weekdays by appointment.
£2
From Market Drayton go E on A53 for 1½m. Turn L on B5415 for 1½m.
Opposite telephone box turn L along a narrow lane for ½m. Garden is on R.

Twelve years ago, this was a field with a rubbish tip and a dump of big stones from neighbouring fields. Now, Mr and Mrs Hewitt have created a plantsman's garden with colour and interest all the year round. Protected on one side by an oak wood, they planted a shelter belt of hedges and ornamental trees to shield them from the winds that whistle across open farmland here. Many varieties of acers, silver birches, eucalyptus, sorbus, maples, prunus and some unusual beeches went in. Island beds curve round the trees and ornamental shrubs, and are filled with hellebores, hostas, ferns, alpines, and masses of shrub roses and clematis. On open days, Mrs Hewitt makes famously delicious scones, and has unusual plants for sale.

7   MANOR COTTAGE

Chapel Chorlton, nr Newcastle-under-Lyme   Tel 01782 680206

Mons, Easter to mid Sept, 2–5, and by appointment. £1.50
From Market Drayton go E on A53 for 6m. At junction with A51, turn R and after 3m, in Stableford, turn R at Cock Inn. After ½m, garden is at promi-nent white house on far side of Chapel Chorlton's village green.

Mrs Heywood started off with a flat patch and two apple trees. She has developed it now into an exciting garden, with thousands – yes, thousands – of unusual plants among the better-known. The garden is strong on coloured foliage, using hostas, euphorbias, geraniums and ferns. She is a flower arranger, and has a special talent for placing plants harmoniously in association with one another. Little paths wind round the garden, giving constant surprises, taking you to yet another grouping of unusual plants. At the front of the house, bold variegated conifers are prettily swagged with *Tropæolum speciosum. Rosa* 'Glauca' stood next to a coppery berberis, hy-pericums nestled into eunonymus. The original apple trees are still there, but swagged with roses now. Alpine enthusiasts will find many treasures in this plantsman's immaculate garden.

8   DOROTHY CLIVE GARDENS

Willoughbridge, nr Market Drayton   Tel 01630 647237

Daily, April to Oct, 10–5.30. £2.60
From Market Drayton go E on A53 for 6m. At junction with A51 turn L. Garden well signed on R after 1½m.

Dorothy Clive lived here from the time of her marriage in 1907 until her untimely death in 1942. It was her husband, Colonel Clive, who first made inroads into tangled woodland for her to enjoy walks round their property. So began the famous garden now named in her memory. The gravelly soil and lack of lime has made it ideal for huge collections of rhododendrons, azaleas, heathers in massed plantings and beautiful magnolias, all flowering with drifts of bulbs beneath. In summer, there are roses everywhere, herbaceous plants, ornamental grasses and pool-side bog plants. And, of course, wonderful autumn foliage colours. A booklet available will guide you round the different walks and help with plant information. The tea-room specialises in squidgy home-made cakes.

9   BRIDGEMERE GARDEN WORLD

nr Nantwich   Tel 01270 520381

Daily, all year, 10-dusk. Free.
From Market Drayton, go E on A53 for 6m. At junction with A51, turn L. Garden well signed on R after 6m.

When John and Elizabeth Ravencroft grew their first roses here in 1962, they had one aim – to offer more varieties of good and well-loved plants than anywhere else in Britain. They have achieved it. If it hadn't bucketed with rain when I visited, I might still be there. Apart from displaying absolutely everything a keen gardener might desire, there are six different gardens designed to inspire you: a French rose garden, a Victorian garden, a woodland garden, a rock garden, a water garden and a cottage garden. There is also a good bookshop, food hall, flower arrangers' centre, aquatic house and glasshouses stuffed with house plants. The restaurant and coffee shop was bright, in spite of the rain, and the food was delicious. Lots of families seemed to be having a whole day there.

Where to Stay

All B&B prices are approximate per person, sharing a double/twin room usually with private or en suite facilities. It is a good idea to ask for any special requirements when booking.

A   THE CITADEL   Tel 01630 685204

Sylvia Griffiths, The Citadel, Weston-under-Redcastle, nr Shrewsbury, Shropshire SY4 5JY.

Sylvia is a friend, and her amazing crenellated house, built in 1820 for local grandees, is set spectacularly in wonderful north Shropshire countryside, with views to the Welsh hills. The garden, particularly good for its azaleas and rhododendrons, stretches seamlessly into parkland and hills. Inside, the house is among the most imposing you will find in this book, with a round hall, a sweeping staircase, an octagonal drawing-room of great elegance, a billiard room, and 3 luxurious double/twin bedrooms (2 of them in the turrets). Sylvia's gift is to make this quite matter-of-fact, as if you had been here many times before. You dine, so long as you arrange it in advance, at a large table with other guests (£17.50, bring your own wine). Restricted smoking, no dogs in the house, children should be over 12. B&B £30–£33.

B   DEARNFORD HALL   Tel 01948 662319

Jane & Charles Babbington, Dearnford Hall, Whitchurch, Shropshire SY13 3JJ.

Last year, when their children left home and their parents retired from farming, Jane and Charles decided their splendid large house in large grounds was too quiet, and needed visitors. They started offering B&B, with enormous success. The 2 well-furnished double/twin bedrooms are en suite, the furnishings are old, the views are lovely and – although only a ½m from the Whitchurch by-pass – it is extremely quiet. As well as running the 500-acre farm, Jane and Charles have created a 15-acre trout fishery lake, professionally run, where you can learn or practise your fishing skills. There are many places locally to eat out in the evenings. No smoking, dogs or young children. B&B £25–£30.

C   THE OLD HALL   Tel 01782 750209

Mary Hugh, The Old Hall, Madeley, nr Newcastle-under-Lyme, Staffordshire CW3 9DX.

When there's a drought, Mary despairs of her garden which is on light, sandy soil. Mostly, however, it is wonderfully rich and colourful, with 2 acres of borders, lawns and old trees, a tennis court, wisteria-covered pergola and a tranquil pool. It is thought that King Charles, escaping from the Roundheads, hid here. A heavily-beamed black-and-white house, the interior is full of wonderful old oak furniture, panelling and woodwork. Mary is a professional musician and the sitting-room has a piano. Evening meals, which should be arranged in advance, are cooked by Ann O'Leary and cost £12 (bring your own wine). The oak-panelled dining-room can seat as many as 18 guests on special occasions. Breakfast is served in a Victorian conservatory. There is a variety of accommodation – 3 double/twin bedrooms in the Hall (2 sharing an amazing 1920s bathroom), and 3 further double/twin bedrooms in a converted stable block. No smoking, children welcome, dogs by arrangement. B&B £20–£25.

D   STOKE MANOR   Tel 01630 685222

Julia & Mike Thomas, Stoke Manor, Stoke upon Tern, nr Market Drayton, Shropshire TF9 2DU.

Stoke Manor is a comfortable, 3-storey Victorian house with ample lawns, mature trees and distant views. There is a footpath round Mike and Julia's 250 acres of farmland and a reservoir where tasty crayfish are farmed. There is a family, a double and a twin room for guests. There is a drawing-room with plenty of books and magazines, and a cellar bar. B&B only, so you eat out in the evenings at local pubs or restaurants. Children and dogs welcome, smoking allowed. B&B £20–£25.

E   MICKLEY HOUSE   Tel 01630 638505

Pauline Williamson, Mickley House, Tern Hill, nr Market Drayton, Shropshire TF9 3QW.

Pauline's landscaped gardens are barely two years old, but already look established. A long, rose-covered pergola runs alongside a series of rockeries, a fountain and lily-pools. The low-slung Victorian house is newly furnished, with 2 ground-floor double/twin bedrooms, one of them with a Louis XIV king-sized bed. There are many places to eat out in the evenings. No smoking, no dogs, children welcome. B&B £18–£25.

What Else to Enjoy

This is a short selection of the many good things recommended in the area by owners of places to stay. Your hosts will certainly be able to provide additional information.

If It's Wet

If you're hoping for a wealth of stately homes to put a roof over your head on a rainy day, I have to say this isn't the visit for you (although you could, of course, drive further afield). **Hawkstone Hall** (*see* Garden 1) is owned by the Redemptorists who vacate it during August and allow visitors to tour their impressive Georgian mansion, with good interiors and furnishings. Or go and enjoy tea and a guided tour at the stunning **Old Colehurst Manor** (*see* Eating Out).

Otherwise, **Whitchurch** is a market town to enjoy, and is particularly good for local produce to take home – cheeses especially. **Market Drayton** is full of elaborate half-timbered buildings. Its claim to fame is partly as the birthplace of Clive of India, but more quaintly as the home of gingerbread men. The tradition (and a supposedly secret recipe) for making this sweet biscuit goes back 200 years, and is celebrated all over town, along with a street market whose history goes back 750 years, and many specialist food shops.

Eating Out

When Bjorn and Maria Teksnes bought **Old Colehurst Manor**, they decided to go the whole hog. They spent the first seven years restoring this glorious, heavily-beamed black-and-white 17th-century mansion and its gardens. When they opened it as a restaurant and hotel, they didn't just go for authentic furniture and put its staff into costume, but purchased a wardrobe of Elizabethan clothes which guests, too, could wear if they dared. If this sounds kitsch, I can assure you it isn't – it's a riot of fun. The menus, while based on recipes from long ago, have been brought up to date for 20th-century tastes, and are excellent. A six-course dinner costs £35 per head, plus wine and service, and if you want to dress up, it costs an extra £10. On evenings when there is entertainment, there is a £15 surcharge. You can stay here, too, although it is a bit pricey compared with most entries in this book: £35 per person if you sleep in the twin-bedded prison cell, up to £85 in the great chamber. You will find it well signed at **Sutton**, 2m S of Market Drayton between the A41 and A529. Tel 01630 638833.

More restrained (where wouldn't be?) is **Goldstone Hall** which has an outstanding reputation, and many awards, for its food and ambience. Chef Simon Smith is truly imaginative in what he achieves with mostly local produce. Main courses cost around £18, and with wine and service you can expect to spend about £35–£40 per head. You can also stay here. B&B costs £42–£47 per person, and there is a good value weekend break which costs £125 per person and includes dinner on both nights. The postal address is simply **Market Drayton**, Shropshire TF9 2NA. You find it to the SE of Market Drayton, near the village of Cheswardine. Tel 01630 661202.

Wenlock Edge

There is an amazing variety of countryside in this visit, with the Welsh hills to be seen distantly in the west from Wenlock Edge, while in the east you come close to the industrial Midlands (and it is there that you will find perhaps the most famous rose breeder of modern times, David Austin). In most towns and villages, the houses are traditionally built in black-and-white half-timbered oak, and are sometimes amazingly elaborate. We are firmly in A. E. Housman territory here, and if you haven't read his poem *Shropshire Lad*, now would be a good time to get acquainted. George Butterworth set it enchantingly to music, making it into a song-cycle which is pure essence of England. Benjamin Luxon, crisply enunciating the verse, made an excellent recording.

OS maps: Landrangers 126, 127, **138**

Gardens

Opening times: in larger gardens, and in NT properties, last admissions are usually 30–45 minutes before the garden closes. Admission charges are a guide to what one adult can expect to pay to go round the garden. It sometimes varies with the season or days of the week. When the house is also open to the public, there is usually an additional charge.

I   DUDMASTON HALL (NT)

Quatt, nr Bridgnorth   Tel 01746 780866

Weds and Suns, April to Sept, 2–5.30. £2.50
From Bridgnorth go SE on A442 for 4m. Garden well signed on R.

The house is late 17th century, and garden-lovers might find it especially attractive as it contains many fine old Dutch flower paintings, and other botanical art. Outside, you will find 8 acres, with good trees and lovely views over a pool. Around the pool are many bog-loving plants – gunneras, ligularias and primulas. The Dingle Walk goes along the lake and through

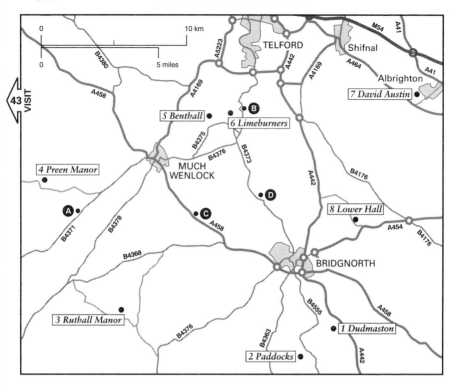

a wooded valley with streams and dense plantings of rhododendrons and scented azaleas. So it's best to visit in May – but if you go later, you will find masses of shrubs and nice old roses, as well as ancient mulberries and medlar.

2   THE PADDOCKS

Chelmarsh Common, nr Bridgnorth   Tel 01746 861271

By appointment late spring and summer. £1
From Bridgnorth go S on B4555 for 3m. Turn R to Chelmarsh Common where signed after Chelmarsh. Ask owner for final directions.

Typical old-fashioned plants thrive in this charming cottage garden which is divided into separate garden rooms. Mrs Hales hopes to give you a surprise round every corner. She delights in letting things grow naturally, and flowers are allowed (within reason) to seed themselves anywhere. Mr and Mrs Hales have made a pretty knot garden and a herb garden. The pond has an

island and a small waterfall, and where the stream flows through the garden at the back of the house, they are making a second wildlife pond. A
wooded area and a little orchard burst with bulbs and wild flowers in
spring. This is a delightful blend of the natural and artful, the work of skil-
ful gardeners.

3   RUTHALL MANOR   nr Bridgnorth   Tel 01746 712216

April to Sept, by appointment. £2
From Bridgnorth go SW on B4376 for 7m. At Cleobury North, turn R on minor
road signed to Ditton Priors (2m). Continue for ½m to Ruthall, where garden
is in centre of the village.

Mr and Mrs Clarke have created this garden with easy maintenance in mind.
They have planted groups of specimen trees – sorbus, robinias, salix and
birches under-planted with ground-cover plants. The pool has fringe planting of primulas, iris, astilbes and hostas. There are a lot of rare shrubs. This
garden will delight any plantsman.

4   PREEN MANOR
Church Preen, nr Church Stretton   Tel 01694 771207

5 charity Thurs May to July, 2–6, and groups of 13+ by appointment. £2
From Much Wenlock go SW on B4371 for 3m. At Presthope, turn R on minor
road signed to Church Preen (2m). Garden in centre of village.

The monks came to Church Preen in 1150 and chose a site with a fine view
of Wenlock Edge. Although high up, it was protected on three sides by ancient woodland. About 830 years later, the site was discovered by Mr and
Mrs Trevor-Jones who saw the potential for making a garden amongst its
ruined walls. As well as the remains of the monastery, there was a ruined
Norman Shaw manor. What they have now achieved is of great beauty and
interest. There are 18 different small garden rooms which lead from one
to another, full of surprises, planted with a plantsman's knowledge and an
artist's eye. The kitchen garden leads to grassed terraces below, the park
and a water garden. The veggies are grown in a parterre, and there is a
separate bog garden and fernery – enough here, for sure, to keep anyone
happy for an extended visit.

5   BENTHALL HALL (NT)   Broseley   Tel 01952 882159

Wed, Sun and BH Mons, April to Sept, 1.30–5.30. £2
From Much Wenlock go E on B4376 for 1m, branching L on B4375 for 2m.
Garden well signed on L before Broseley.

You are experiencing a little bit of garden history in this charming old
garden set around the 16th-century house. In the 18th century George
Maw, one of England's most renowned botanists and plant collectors, and
famous for his book *The Genus Crocus*, lived here. Then the gardens were
filled with rare bulbs and alpines from his plant-hunting expeditions, and
some still remain. Small stone terraces beside the house are planted with
roses in a design laid out by Graham Thomas, with tree peonies, potentil-
las and masses of hardy geraniums as ground-cover. The old kitchen garden
feels happy and domestic with crab apples and roses, and climbers up the
walls. There are fine trees on either side of the lawn, including an *Aralia
elata* – the Japanese angelica tree. And of course, in spring, don't miss the
crocuses.

6   LIMEBURNERS   Ironbridge   Tel 01952 433715

April to Sept, by appointment. £1.50
From Much Wenlock go E on B4376 for 1m, branching L on B4375 for 2m.
Approaching Broseley, turn L on minor road signed to Ironbridge. Ask owner
for final directions.

It's quite unbelievable when you see it, but this 9-acre garden was a council
tip twenty years ago. Mr and Mrs Derry have worked hard to create a natural garden particularly attractive to wildlife. A broad lawn on the south-
facing slope has lovely views over woodland, with many unusual trees and
shrubs. These are under-planted with differing ground-cover which not only
gives interest and colour but is home to many little creeping things. Butterflies, birds and insects are here in profusion, and the garden is more
beautiful for their presence. Limeburners is quite famous now, having been
seen on TV several times. The achievement is a triumph for Mr and Mrs
Derry.

7   DAVID AUSTIN ROSES   Albrighton   Tel 01902 373931

Daily except Christmas and New Year BHs, 9–5 (12–dusk in winter). Free.
From M54 junction 3, go S on A41 for 3m. In Albrighton, turn R at sign
'Roses and Shrubs', then second R down Bowling Green Lane to garden.

Visit here in June and July and choose some of the best roses you'll ever see, laid out in large borders and up pergolas and pillars. This leading rose breeder offers more than 900 varieties – old roses, shrub roses and his own roses, along with peonies, iris and other hardy perennials. Take a rich sugar-daddy with you, and give in to the urge to have yet more roses in your garden.

8   LOWER HALL   Worfield, nr Bridgnorth   Tel 01746 716607

April to July, by appointment. £2.50
From Bridgnorth go E on A454 for 3m. Turn L on minor road to Worfield (½m). Garden in centre of village.

Lower Hall was once described as one of Britain's most romantic gardens, and this is the atmosphere that Mr and Mrs Dumbell strive to maintain. They have been helped enormously by the design which Lanning Roper originally put in place. Courtyard gardens with fountains surround two sides of the house, containing plantings which flow over the brick paths to soften the lines. The walled garden is rich in colour, with many shrub roses, climbers ramping up the walls and through the trees, and a marvellous collection of iris. One of the courtyard gardens is an oasis of peace – just cool greens, whites, limes and creams are used in the borders. Across the lawn is the River Worfe, and here the water garden is planted with iris, hostas, astilbes, daylilies, ferns and magnificent primulas. There is a choice of two wooden bridges to take you across the river which bisects the garden. The woodland garden is planted with magnolias, birches, acers, amelanchiers, rhododendrons and azaleas, under-planted with bulbs and trilliums so there is splendid spring and autumn colouring.

Where to Stay

All B&B prices are approximate per person, sharing a double/twin room usually with private or en suite facilities. It is a good idea to ask for any special requirements when booking.

A   WENLOCK EDGE INN   Tel 01746 785678

Stephen Waring, Wenlock Edge Inn, Hill Top, nr Much Wenlock, Shropshire TF13 6DJ.

The Waring family's award-winning 18th-century inn is in a spectacular position, near one of the highest points of Wenlock Edge, which is largely owned by the NT. Plenty of hanging baskets make this listed building an attractive sight, and a wildlife pond has been created, attracting damsel-flies and dragon-flies. It is often busy and always fun here. The bars are beamed and friendly and you can eat well for about £12. The 5 double/twin bedrooms, including 1 on the ground floor, are extremely comfortable. Dogs, children and smokers are all welcome. B&B £25–£30.

B   THE SEVERN TROW   Tel 01952 883551

Pauline Hannigan, Church Road, Jackfield, nr Ironbridge, Shropshire TF8 7ND.

This house is fascinating. Built about 400 years ago on the bank of the River Severn, it was a hostelry, dormitory and brothel for working travellers on the river. Today, it has been brilliantly and sensitively restored by the Hannigans. Climbers ramp over the white-painted exterior. Inside, the old brewhouse is now a cosy sitting-room with a low, vaulted ceiling. Another guest lounge faces the river, and has an open fire with a wooden surround dating from 1680. There is a small bar, and a dining-room with a magnificent Jackfield mosaic tile floor. The 3 double/twin bedrooms, 1 a four-poster, are all en suite. For wheelchair uses, there is a ground-floor suite of rooms with its own access from the road, where breakfast can be served. You eat out locally in the evenings at your choice from a huge list of pubs and restaurants. Strictly no smoking, no dogs, and children must be well-behaved and discussed in advance. B&B £20–£22.

C   ALDENHAM WEIR   Tel 01746 714352

Jennifer & Stephen Coldicott, Aldenham Weir, Muckley Cross, nr Bridgnorth, Shropshire WV16 4RR.

This is an extremely comfortable, handsomely designed modern country house set in 11 acres of lush and prolific gardens, where paths wander through lawns and mature trees to woodland and a trout stream. Foxes, kingfishers and woodpeckers can regularly be seen round the pool and weir. 'Paradise gardens', one guest called them. There are 2 large sitting-rooms for guests to use. The 5 double/twin bedrooms all have en suite shower and loo. Generally, you eat out locally in the evenings, although Jennifer will cook light suppers if you ask in advance (from £10, bring your own wine). Children welcome, dogs by arrangement, no smoking. B&B £20.

D ALBYNES   Tel 01746 762261

Cynthia Woolley, Albynes, Nordley, nr Bridgnorth, Shropshire WV16 4SX.

Cynthia is a flower arranger, and in her 1-acre woodland garden, its large
pools occupied by mallard and moorhens, she mainly grows foliage plants
to give shape and texture to her arrangements for exhibitions. The substantial stone house was built in 1823, and looks out over lawns to sheep-
dotted fields beyond. The dining-room has marvellous panelling taken from
a Tudor house not far away, and there is a splendid oak staircase. Sylvia
cooks evening meals by prior arrangement, the price depending on how
many courses you have. There are also many places to eat out locally. The
3 guest bedrooms, including 1 single, are en suite. No smoking, no dogs,
children welcome. B&B £18–£20.

What Else to Enjoy

*This is a short selection of the many good things recommended in the area by owners
of places to stay. Your hosts will certainly be able to provide additional information.*

Other Places to Stay

I came across the excellent B&B **Church Farm**, run by Jo and Bob Savage,
through a friend who is passionate about snowdrops. So is Bob and Jo's son
Simon, a plant collector who has cultivated more than 65 named varieties
here, and has about 70 unnamed selections on trial. Early spring is a good
time to come here, although there is a lovely garden throughout the year.
It includes many rare and unusual plants, and a fern collection in a sunken
garden where the foundations of the 12th-century manor house have been
exposed. The Savage family has lived in the parish for centuries, and know
all the best places to go and buy plants. Three of the 5 guest bedrooms in
their red-brick Georgian house are en suite. Unusually, the sash windows open
sideways. Jo cooks dinner by arrangement, and there are also many pubs
locally, a particularly good one being only 1½ m away. Dogs and children
by arrangement, restricted smoking. B&B £20–£25. Find it just N of the
visit in **Wrockwardine**, Wellington, nr Telford, Shropshire TF6 5DG.
Tel 01952 244917.

If It's Wet

There are two NT properties in this visit whose interiors are worth visiting when you go to their gardens. **Dudmaston Hall** (*see* Garden 1) has collections of modern art and sculpture as well as fine period furniture and botanical art. House open as garden. At **Benthall Hall** (*see* Garden 5) the mullion windows are marvellous. So also are the elaborate carved staircase, the decorated plaster ceilings and oak panelling. It has a lived-in feel, with family collections of furniture, ceramics and paintings.

The main town of **Bridgnorth** is fascinating, steeply set on two levels with Low Town in the valley by the River Severn and High Town full of streets with half-timbered buildings leading to the ruined castle. It is so steep that you need to negotiate seven sets of steps and winding alleys to walk between the two – or take the cliff railway. It is a lovely place to explore, and if all that climbing makes you feel thirsty, the 17th-century Swan Inn, in High St, is full of atmosphere.

Ironbridge Gorge is a world heritage site. The great bridge across the River Severn, first of its kind and cast in 1779, is the focal point for a series of exceptional museums which bring to life the area's industrial and domestic past. It would take more than a day to visit them all. I loved Jackfield tile museum, with a collection of wonderful Victorian tiles and much else, and Blists Hill open air museum where a 50-acre site recreates town life at the turn of the last century. You will take about 90 minutes to go round the first, and 3 hours the second, but there are pubs and cafés to keep you going.

Eating Out

The Old Vicarage Hotel, a former Edwardian parsonage with period furniture and a friendly atmosphere, is the most widely recommended. It has a 2-acre garden with great views where you can wander before dinner, when set menus with lots of imaginative choice cost £24–£35 (it's more expensive at weekends). Find it off the A454, 2m NE of Bridgnorth, in the village of **Worfield**. Tel 01746 716497.

Around Welshpool

There is a truly Welsh feel about much of this visit, with its grey stone buildings, grey stone walls lining the hilly fields and grey slate roof-tops. You find, too, an intense local pride in the Welshness of all things beautiful. So you could listen to Welsh choirs, or perhaps put on a talking book. There is a good tape of Dylan Thomas reading his own poems, and many versions of his magical *Under Milk Wood*. If you are on your way to north Wales and just passing through the area, do find time to visit the wonderful gardens at Powis Castle.

OS maps: Landrangers **126**, 136, 137

Gardens

Opening times: in larger gardens, and in NT properties, last admissions are usually 30–45 minutes before the garden closes. Admission charges are a guide to what one adult can expect to pay to go round the garden. It sometimes varies with the season or days of the week. When the house is also open to the public, there is usually an additional charge.

I   MAENLLWYD ISAF

Abermule, nr Montgomery   Tel 01686 639294

All year by appointment. £1
From Montgomery go W on B4385 and B4386 for 5m. The garden is signed on L 1½m before Abermule.

This garden, on acid soil, blends in perfectly with the surrounding hills. There is nothing formal, just plenty of rhododendrons and azaleas and other lovely calcifuge shrubs, all under-planted with smaller plants and bulbs – *Viola labradorica*, hellebores, trilliums, hepaticas – and, in spring, the beauty of uncurling ferns and bright Welsh poppies. The alpine lawn, consisting of alpine plants grown on a slope, is home to damson trees and is bright with crocus, spring-flowering tulips, fritillaries and narcissus. Mrs Hatchard

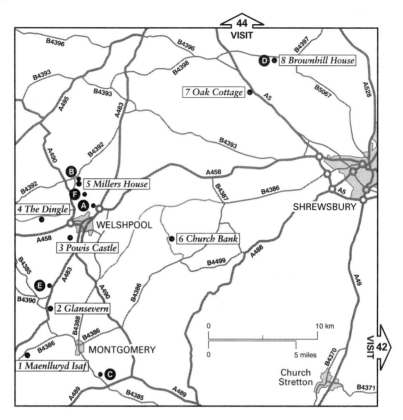

bought the house, with 20 wild acres, on an impulse in 1956. The beautiful garden you can now visit is still being developed by her. The latest addition is a calm, long pool to offset the noisy, babbling River Mule below.

2   GLANSEVERN HALL   nr Welshpool   Tel 01686 640200

Fri/Sat and BH Mons, May to Sept, 2–6. £2
From Welshpool go S on A483 for 5m. The garden is reached through an imposing gateway set in a grey stone estate wall on the L.

A grand entrance down a drive lined with Spanish chestnuts leads to this romantically sited house, c. 1800, on the banks of the Severn, and fronted by a 4-acre lake complete with a little island and masses of Canada geese, ducks and moorhens. Around the house is a formal garden. A rose garden has far-reaching views over gentle hills and the lawns have some magnificent trees – a *Gingko biloba, Cunninghamia lanceolata* and a fascinating *Magnolia acuminata*. Neville and Jenny Thomas acquired the hall thirteen years ago when they began to develop the gardens, keeping the best of the previous plantings but adding a vast new collection of ornamental trees around the lakeside walk, with splendid beds of herbaceous perennials. The recently re-discovered rock garden has a ghostly grotto which you can see by the light of an oil lamp. A charming wisteria walk leads to a fountain. The walled garden has a nursery, run by the Thomas's talented gardener, selling rare perennials. The tea-room, garden shop and gallery are in the pretty stable yard.

3   POWIS CASTLE (NT)   Welshpool   Tel 01938 554336

Wed–Sun, April to Oct, 11–6 (also Tues, July/Aug, and BH Mons). £4
From Welshpool go S on A483 for 1m. Garden well signed on R.

The terraces here are the finest surviving example in Britain of a late 17th century terraced garden. The designer is unknown, but work started around 1680 under William Herbert, 1st Marquess of Powis. The gigantic yew hedges bulge and lean and are totalling amazing. The topiary gives the splendid urns and statues a perfect back-drop. The orangery terrace has a border of bold planting in hot colours. The apple slope terrace has an acer collection, with bulbs, so is best seen in spring and autumn. The formal garden has a striking vine pergola, under-planted very prettily with golden marjoram. Beautifully planted borders surround the croquet lawn, and if you are not too tired, there is the fountain garden, the yew walk, the great lawn – 2½ acres of it – the garden pool, the wilderness, the wild garden and daffodil paddock. The garden is steep, so you will be delighted to know that lunches and teas are available. Have both.

4   THE DINGLE NURSERIES AND GARDENS

nr Welshpool   Tel 01938 555145

Daily except Tues, spring to autumn, 9–5. £1 in donation box
From Welshpool go N on A490 for 1m. Turn L on minor road signed to Dingle Nurseries, and fork L after 1½m. Garden up track on L.

Mr and Mrs Joseph have a splendid nursery, selling the very best selection of ornamental trees and shrubs. From it, a little gate takes you into their exciting garden, planted on a steep hillside, plunging down to a placid lake shimmering with water-lilies and with bog-loving plants around the fringe.

To get to the lake you descend zig-zag paths past flower-beds of carefully chosen harmonising plants. It's a tough walk, not advised for anyone with a weak heart or legs. Fine foliage shrubs are under-planted with large clumps of hostas, campanulas and cranesbills. Colours are subtle and complementary, and one's eye is constantly drawn across the lake to the hills beyond. Well mulched to try to stop the water running off the hill, this was an immaculate garden on an extremely difficult steep site. As for the walk, there are lots of seats along the way, so you can take it slowly.

5   THE MILLERS HOUSE

Guilsfield, nr Welshpool   Tel 01938 555432

All year by appointment. £1
From Welshpool go N on A490 for 1½m. Turn R on B4392 to Guilsfield (1m). In village, turn R at Windmill Lane. Garden is at 4th cottage on R.

Now, nearly nine years since they started it, Rozel and Mark Kneale have reason to be proud of their 1½-acre garden, situated with superb views on a south-facing slope. Closely planted mixed borders are full of colour. Masses of roses, old and new, a pond with a damp garden, a rockery, a herb garden and a pergola covered with roses and honeysuckle make this an informal garden of great charm.

6   CHURCH BANK   Rowley, nr Welshpool   Tel 01743 891661

May to Sept, by appointment. £1.50
From Montgomery go NE on B4386 for 7m. At Brockton, turn L on minor road signed to Rowley (1½m). The garden has metal farm gates on R just before village.

Here is a south-facing 2½-acre garden on a sloping site, with a pool at the bottom. Mr and Mrs Kavanagh are keen plant collectors, and the main focus is on the geometric beds at the rear of the house. This area has a Mediterranean feel, with plenty of grey-leaved plants basking in the sun and a nice collection of terracotta pots. In midsummer, the garden is a riot of colour from Mrs Kavanagh's favourite plants – poppies, penstemons, roses, alliums, aquilegias, geraniums and daylilies. She cunningly achieves a heavily-scented tapestry of colour. Also a great propagator, she often has interesting plants to sell.

7 OAK COTTAGE HERB GARDEN

Nesscliffe   Tel 01743 741262

Daily, Easter to mid Sept, 11.30—6 (but phone to confirm). £1.50
From Shrewsbury go NW on A5 for 7m. At Nesscliffe Hotel, turn L on minor
road. Garden is immediately on L, by car park.

Edward and Jane Bygott bought the cottage eight years ago and began herb gardening as a hobby – since when it has taken over. Retaining almost all the original design at Oak Cottage, but extending and laying out a new garden where Jane can grow her flowers, they now concentrate on herbs, wildflowers and cottage garden plants. Visitors come from all over Europe, also from Japan. The Bygotts grow and sell culinary, aromatic and medicinal herb plants and as many old-fashioned plants as possible.

8 BROWNHILL HOUSE

Ruyton-XI-Towns (*see also* Where to Stay)   Tel 01939 260626

Many charity days May to Aug, and by appointment. £1.50
From Shrewsbury go NW on A5 for 9m. At junction with B4397, turn R for
2m to Ruyton-XI-Towns. Near end of village, park at Bridge Inn, 100 yds from
garden.

Not many people have the guts and the talent to turn a north-facing cliff, covered in rubbish, into a fascinating garden – but Roger and Yoland Brown have plenty of both, and since 1972 have been busy terracing and planting. There are 550 steps so far, with a series of formal terraces and small enclosed gardens on each level. They have incorporated influences from other favourite gardens, so there is a bit of Bodnant, a miniature garden from Bangkok, a French parterre, an Arabic arch, a Chinese grave and a folly – all put together with more than 450 different shrubs and trees, masses of roses making a wonderful summer display, a major collection of ivies and a huge sense of humour. The River Perry is at the bottom, with a bog garden, and when you climb back up they kindly revive you with a cuppa. Plants can be bought here too.

Where to Stay

All B&B prices are approximate per person, sharing a double/twin room usually with private
or en suite facilities. It is a good idea to ask for any special requirements when booking.

A GUNGROG HOUSE   Tel 01938 553381

Eira & Stan Jones, Gungrog House, Rhallt, nr Welshpool, Powys SY21 9HS.

This grey stone 16th-century farmhouse stands high on a hill, with magnificent views of the Severn Valley and Powis Castle. The sloping garden is full of colour in the borders round lawns. Eira has taken in guests for a number of years now, and knows how to make you feel at home. There are beamed ceilings, and a polished oak staircase that leads to 2 en suite double/twin bedrooms. Everywhere is comfortably furnished, and Eira's evening meals cost £10 (bring your own wine). No dogs, no smoking, children welcome. B&B £20.

B LOWER TRELYDAN FARM   Tel 01938 553105

Sue Jones, Lower Trelydan Farm, Guilsfield, nr Welshpool, Powys SY21 9PH.

This 16th-century black-and-white house, once home to the Civil War diarist John Gwyn, has won many awards, including one for the best B&B in Wales. Covered with creepers and climbing roses, there are well-kept lawns with borders around. You come to the house up a private drive through parkland with grazing cattle, and have open views in every direction. Inside, the house is lovely, with masses of oak furniture, beamed ceilings, a great staircase and 3 very comfortable guest bedrooms – family, double and twin. Evening meals, licensed and usually with a traditional roast, cost £13. There are also self-catering cottages. No dogs, children welcome in the house, smoking only if other guests don't mind. B&B £20.

C LITTLE BROMPTON FARM   Tel 01686 668371

Gaynor Bright, Little Brompton Farm, nr Montgomery, Powys SY15 6HY.

A pretty little garden with wonderful views is at the back of this charming old white-painted farmhouse, built in the early 18th century. Offa's Dyke long-distance footpath goes through the farm's 100 acres, and there is also a nature trail where you can wander. There are 3 cosy en suite double/twin bedrooms, and a comfortable lounge with lots of books and an inglenook fireplace. The dining-room has an outstanding oak Welsh dresser, and evening meals (bring your own wine) cost from £8, depending on the number of courses, mostly using fresh farm-grown ingredients. No smoking, children welcome, dogs by arrangement. B&B £18–£20.

D BROWNHILL HOUSE   Tel 01939 260626

Roger & Yoland Brown, Brownhill House, Ruyton-XI-Towns, Shropshire SY4 1LR.

This is a lovely place to stay – an informal, rambling family home, built in the 17th century but now pleasantly modernised, with a large kitchen where meals are served, and a beamed lounge with an inglenook fireplace. The 3 bedrooms include 1 single and a ground-floor twin. A 4-course dinner (bring your own wine), with roast Welsh lamb a speciality, costs £10, served in the early evening, and there are 3 pubs within ½ m, where you are often invited to join the Browns when Roger finishes farming later. Breakfasts are extraordinarily lavish. There is a huge traditionally English fry-up with wonderful ingredients – but you can also arrange to have fish cakes, kippers or lamb chops. Try walking round gardens after that? No dogs, children welcome, restricted smoking. B&B £17–£18.

E TREFNANT HALL FARM   Tel 01686 640262

Jane Jones, Trefnant Hall Farm, Berriew, nr Welshpool, Montgomeryshire SY21 8AS.

This large, listed farmhouse was built in 1742. Its well-kept terraced gardens have glorious views over rolling countryside. The sitting-room in the house is a treat, by any standards, with a huge oak fireplace and a wonderful staircase leading to 3 double/twin bedrooms, all en suite. B&B only, so you eat out in the evenings at a good pub 2m away, or in Berriew village. It is wonderful walking country round here, but if you have a dog, it will not be allowed in the house. Smoking is discouraged, and children should be over 10. B&B £17–£18.

F BURNT HOUSE   Tel 01938 552827

Tricia Wykes, Burnt House, Trelydan, nr Welshpool, Powys SY21 9HU.

For garden-lovers (indeed, B&B-lovers), here is a treasure. I defy you to find, in high summer, a place with more colour and profusion than there is here, with – at the last count – 58 hanging baskets drenched with annuals, and more than 100 troughs and tubs set on terraces, lawns and steps around this creeper-clad, white-painted, 15th-century Tudor long-house. Heaven knows why this twenty-year-old 1½ -acre garden, with pools and an arched potager, is not open under the NGS. Tricia says she has never been asked. There are just 2 double/twin bedrooms (sharing a bathroom if you come with friends, otherwise you have it to yourself). A large beamed lounge furnished with sumptuous settees and good antiques leads to a lovely dining-room where Tricia's evening meals cost only £10 (bring your own wine). No small children, smoking allowed, dogs by arrangement. B&B £16.

What Else to Enjoy

This is a short selection of the many good things recommended in the area by owners of places to stay. Your hosts will certainly be able to provide additional information.

Other Gardens/Nurseries

Mrs Williams, at **Perrybrook Nursery**, grows hardy perennials, including a large range of primulas and other shade-loving plants, especially tricyrtis. She is at Brook Cottage, **Wykey**, nr Ruyton XI Towns, and is open most afternoons from March to Sept. Telephone to check: 01939 261120.

If It's Wet

Powis Castle (*see* Garden 3) was built in the 13th century by Welsh princes, and has been owned and altered by generations of Herberts and Clives for 400 years. The NT says it contains the finest country house collection in Wales. There is also a Clive Museum displaying treasures from India. Open same days as garden, but 12–5.

Another NT property is **Attingham Park**, an elegant late 18th-century mansion where you can see Regency taste at its best. There are magnificent state rooms and a remarkable picture gallery by Nash. The park was landscaped by Humphry Repton. Open Sat–Wed, April to Sept, BHs and Sat/Sun in Oct, 1.30–5. Admission £3.50. From Shrewsbury, go SE on B4380 for 4m, where it is signed just E of the visit map.

Eating Out

Like so many of the places to stay and eat in this area, there is nothing pretentious about **Edderton Hall**, run by Evelyn Hawksley. The dinner menu, at £22, could be described as enhanced home cooking – good ingredients and vibrant sauces. Evelyn does B&B too, so you must be sure to book a meal with her in advance. Find her house up a track near the village of **Forden**, on the Welshpool to Montgomery road. Tel 01938 580339.

Welsh Borders

There are views of the Welsh mountains all the time in this visit, where the names of villages get more and more difficult to pronounce. To the west is Offa's Dyke, and old castle and forts stand along the borders. Chirk Castle is one of the most forbidding of these, and I couldn't help thinking about all the prisoners who had been held there. Large chunks of Beethoven's *Fidelio* went through my head; the Act I quartet is heart-rending. Thank heavens, the atmosphere in the gardens at Chirk is just the opposite – heavenly, peaceful and serene.

OS maps: Landrangers **117, 126**

Gardens

Opening times: in larger gardens, and in NT properties, last admissions are usually 30–45 minutes before the garden closes. Admission charges are a guide to what one adult can expect to pay to go round the garden. It sometimes varies with the season or days of the week. When the house is also open to the public, there is usually an additional charge.

I OTELEY   Ellesmere, nr Oswestry   Tel 01691 622514

May to Sept, by appointment. £1.50
From outskirts of Oswestry go NE on A495 for 7 miles. In Ellesmere turn R on A528 for ½ m, passing The Mere car park on L. After 100 yds, turn L over cattle grids. Ask owner for final directions.

As you drive up through the old park with marvellous trees, views of the Mere open up. Go through the farmyard to the house, and the first thing you will find is a large walled kitchen garden, a white wisteria over the gateway, with figs, pears and plums beautifully trained up the walls. Around the back of the house are extensive lawns and venerably vast trees – cedars, holm oaks, ginkhos and a weeping lime of great beauty. They dwarf the folly tower set among them. Oteley was very grand indeed in its Edwardian hey-day, and Mr and Mrs Mainwaring make a valiant attempt to keep

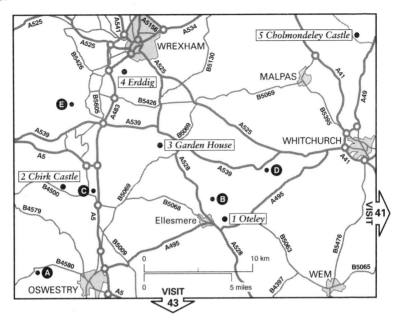

up this huge estate, but the waterside gardens have become very wild. I found that, in a way, this added to the charm. There are splendid terraces, one of them, with a beautiful pattern of pebbles, making a flat roof for a creepy old boat-house which would be the perfect setting for a Gothic thriller. They were probably designed by William Sawrey Gilpin. The terraces and steps climb back up the hill through overgrown rhododendrons and flowering shrubs, with loggias and summer-houses along the way. Back by the house, the borders are lovely, with roses and exotic romneyas. The high walls shelter magnificent *Magnolia grandifloras*.

2   CHIRK CASTLE (NT)

Chirk, nr Oswestry   Tel 01691 777701

Daily except Mons and Sats, April to Sept, 11–6 (also BH Mons and Mons in July and Aug). £4

From Oswestry go N on A5 for 5m. At roundabout, turn L on B5070 which joins with B4500. Castle is 1m ahead on R.

Chirk has a vast and magnificent garden, but hasn't lost its family feel. As you walk up the hill to it, the great gaunt castle looks severe and forbidding, but on the garden side it is much homelier, with roses, jasmine, clematis and *Hydrangea petiolaris* scrambling to reach the battlements. Marvellous cedars, copper beeches, weeping limes and cherries line the lawns from where there are splendid views over Cheshire and Shropshire. Rhododendrons, azaleas and bulbs are good in spring, together with magnolias and flowering cherries. A lime avenue, under-planted with daffodils, leads to an 18th-century statue of Hercules, and there are other beautiful statues of nymphs by Luccesi – all in rather humiliating states of bondage. Some staggeringly good hydrangeas are by a lily pool and the rockery is magnificent. But pride of place must go to the immense yew hedges and topiary. If you are not able to manage the uphill slog from the car park, there is a courtesy coach.

3   THE GARDEN HOUSE

Erbistock, nr Wrexham   Tel 01978 780472

Many charity days June/July, and by appointment. £1
From Wrexham go S on A528 for 5m. At Overton Bridge, turn R on minor
road to Erbistock (1m). Garden well signed.

Erbistock is a local beauty spot, and the Garden House situated above the River Dee has a wonderful air of tranquility about it. This is a new house, and an exciting new garden, with a good nursery garden attached. Formally planted, it has been developed to emphasize the visual pleasure which planned planting achieves. A colour circle is bordered by low clipped box, within an outer circle of hydrangeas. Along a pergola avenue, smothered with roses and clematis, are more than 140 species of hydrangeas. The walled garden has espaliered apples, pears, plums, cherries and red currants up the walls. A small parterre is in front of a dovecot. Nursery stock and flowers for florists are growing in fields and in the walled garden. This is definitely a garden to watch develop and mature – all carefully worked and planned by Simon Dyson-Wingett and his mother.

4   ERDDIG (NT)   nr Wrexham   Tel 01978 355314

Sat–Wed, April to Oct, 11–6 (Oct, 11–5). £3.20
On S outskirts of Wrexham, well signed from either A483 or A525.

This early 18th-century formal garden was almost lost through neglect, but has been brilliantly restored by the NT from archival material. A collection of old apple varieties are espaliered around the large walled garden – there is an Apple Day in the autumn when you can go and taste them – and fine wall shrubs and climbers are under-planted with old varieties of narcissi, daffodils and old-fashioned herbaceous plants. A pleached lime walk leads to a central canal and fish pool. Below this is a Victorian parterre, numerous shrub roses and a nice little herb garden. The National Collection of ivy is here.

5   CHOLMONDELEY CASTLE

nr Whitchurch   Tel 01829 720383

Wed/Thur, Suns, BH Mons and Good Friday, Easter to Sept, 12–5. £2.50
From Whitchurch go N on A49 for 5m. Castle well signed on L.

Although the Cholmondeley family has lived here for 800 years, this hilltop castle was built as recently as 1800. Around it is one of the most romantically-planted gardens you can find. There is colour and interest all the year, starting with spring bulbs and rhododendrons, azaleas, magnolias and camellias. Double herbaceous borders and a rose garden take over in high summer when the Temple Garden, with two ornamental bridges crossing a lake, offers quiet cool shade and a place to sit and watch the koi carp. Below the castle, the terrace was planted to celebrate the Queen's Silver Jubilee. In the paddocks are rare breeds of farm animals: sheep, piggies, cows, pygmy goats – and llamas. There is an enticing tea-room which is hard to resist.

Where to Stay

All B&B prices are approximate per person, sharing a double/twin room usually with private or en suite facilities. It is a good idea to ask for any special requirements when booking.

A   PEN-Y-DYFFRYN

Tel 01691 653700

Miles & Audrey Hunter, Pen-y-Dyffryn, Rhydycroesau, nr Oswestry, Shropshire SY10 7DT.

Guests come back again and again to this lovely old Georgian house, once a rectory, set on southern slopes in the Welsh border hills in 5 acres of gardens and grounds. All around are gentle green fields and hedges – wonderful walking country, with a circular walk that includes some of Offa's Dyke. Think Laura Ashley, and you will get a feel for what the inside of this award-winning B&B is like, with large rooms, log fires, extremely comfortable furniture and patterned furnishings. It is welcoming, well-organised and immaculate. There are 8 bedrooms of varying sizes, including a four-poster suite and a ground-floor room suitable for wheelchairs, whose French windows open into the gardens. Dinner, with classic puddings, costs £14.50, licensed. Dogs, smokers and children are all welcome. B&B £33–£40.

B GREENBANKS   Tel 01691 623420

Christopher & Tanda Wilson-Clarke, Greenbanks, Coptiviney, nr Ellesmere, Shropshire SY12 0ND.

Twenty acres of gardens and grounds surround this large, red-brick Victorian house, where Christopher and Tanda make sure you feel at home. Borders, shrubs and mature trees edge a substantial lawn, part of it set aside for croquet. There is a tennis court, too. There is good walking and horse-riding in the area. The 2 double/twin bedrooms have lovely views across fields. Evening meals (£13–£17, bring your own wine) are *en famille* in a dining-room with traditional country-house luxuries of candlelight and good silver. No smoking, dogs by arrangement, children should be over 12. B&B £27–£30.

C THE LODGE   Tel 01691 774424

Lindsay Davenport, The Lodge, Halton, nr Wrexham LL14 5AU.

This handsome Georgian mansion was once the hunting lodge for the Chirk Castle Estate. The 7 acres of grounds and mature gardens include two paddocks, a walled kitchen garden and lawns with many old shrubs and trees. A gardener keeps it all in good order – Lindsay says she prefers sitting out and enjoying it, or picking fruit. There is a high standard of furnishings inside, and 3 good double/twin bedrooms (1 on the ground floor for wheelchair users). Evening meals, often with game in season, cost £10–£18, licensed. Children, dogs and smokers are all welcome. B&B £18–£20.

D BUCK FARM   Tel 01948 830339

Frances Williams-Lee & Cedric Sumner, Hanmer, nr Whitchurch, Clwyd SY14 7LX.

When Frances and Cedric first came here twenty years ago, they found a ramshackle 450-year-old black-and-white house set in a concrete yard. At that stage, knowing nothing about gardening, they dug up the paving and then planted many trees which have now matured into a charming dell full of wildlife, beneath which flowers and roses bloom. The house has a great atmosphere of warmth and comfort, with numerous books and music, and everyone staying there is welcome to come and go as they please. Evening meals are special, using organically-grown ingredients and home-baked bread. The menus (vegetarian if you ask in advance) are highly original. Frances is of Chinese ancestry, but first learned her cookery in Trinidad, a melting-pot of international cuisine. Meals cost from £11.50 (bring your own wine). There are 4 double/twin bedrooms (sharing bathrooms). No smoking, children welcome, dogs by arrangement. B&B £18.

E   WYNN HALL   Tel 01978 822106

Elian & Ian Forster, Wynn Hall, Penycae, Clwyd LL14 1TW.

Elian and Ian have carefully restored this black-and-white timbered house, built in 1649, to keep its historic feel. Around it is a 1-acre garden enclosed by old yews, deciduous trees and shrubs, with extensive lawns where you can play croquet – or badminton, if you're feeling energetic. Inside the house is lovely old oak furniture, inglenook fireplaces and an oak staircase leading to 3 double/twin bedrooms with beamed ceilings (1 is en suite, the others occasionally share a bathroom). There are so many pubs within a couple of miles that evening meals are not often served nowadays. No smoking, children should be over 12, and dogs are not allowed in bedrooms. B&B £16–£18.

What Else to Enjoy

This is a short selection of the many good things recommended in the area by owners of places to stay. Your hosts will certainly be able to provide additional information.

Other Gardens/Nurseries

Hall Farm Nursery is well worth a visit if you want to take something home for your garden. It has good, reasonably priced herbaceous perennials, geraniums, alpines and carnivorous plants. It is in the little village of **Kinnerley**, just S of the visit map. Go SE from Oswestry on the A5, and turn R on B4398 for 1m. Kinnerley is signed on L. Open daily except Mons, 10–5. Tel 01691 682219.

Other Places to Stay

Just past Llangollen, off the visit map to the W, is the tiny hamlet of Rhewl, on the N bank of the River Dee. Here Mary Harman has 2 twin rooms (1 en suite) and 1 single in **Dee Farm**. Her pretty little garden is terraced like a large balcony to look out on stunning views to the Llantysilio Mountain. Depending on how hungry you are, a light supper here can cost as little as £5 (bring your own wine). Address: Dee Farm, Rhewl, nr **Llangollen** LL20 7YT. Tel 01978 861598. B&B £16–£18.

If It's Wet

The NT's **Chirk Castle** (*see* Garden 2), built as a border fortress by Edward I, has been continuously lived in since 1330 and is still largely intact. Elegant state rooms have Adam-style furniture and elaborate plasterwork. You can visit the dungeons, too. Castle open same days as garden, but 12–5.

The vast **Erddig** (*see* Garden 4), dating from the 17th century, is described by the NT as the most evocative upstairs-downstairs house in Britain. The staterooms still have most of the original furniture and furnishings, while the 'working' part of the buildings – kitchen, laundry, bakehouse, stables and so on – can also be seen. Opening days as garden, but house opens one hour later.

Eating Out

If it's interesting – sometimes experimental – food you're after, you might well try **Starlings Castle**, a restaurant with rooms that may be called a castle, but actually has only a central turret to justify the word. What you find, instead, are some low-slung 18th-century farm buildings with stone floors where Anthony Pitt, the owner and chef, offers an international range of dishes gathered during his extensive travels. It is off the A5 at **Bronygarth**, N of Oswestry, and quite hard to find. Ask for final directions when you book. Tel 01691 718464. Expect to spend £25–£35 per person.

For a different kind of experience, you could try dining on a narrowboat as it glides from **Llangollen** along the Shropshire Union Canal, crossing 120 ft above the River Dee on the Pontcysyllte aqueduct, the biggest in Britain. Tel 01978 823215 for details and prices.

Around Snowdonia

Many of these gardens are grouped along the Menai Straits where the mild climate and staggering views across to the Snowdonia National Park make them very special. Bodnant, on the other hand, is in a valley leading to the Conwy estuary. The soil is rich, moist and acid, so it is RAC country – rhododendrons, azaleas and camellias. I occasionally drive across here on the way to Holyhead where I catch the boat to Ireland and the Wexford opera festival. Will you join me in listening to some great chunks of Wagner? *Die Meistersinger* is the easiest opera to start with, if you're not yet an addict. Its plot, too, about a local choir, is apposite for Wales.

OS maps: Landrangers **115**, 116

Gardens

Opening times: in larger gardens, and in NT properties, last admissions are usually 30–45 minutes before the garden closes. Admission charges are a guide to what one adult can expect to pay to go round the garden. It sometimes varies with the season or days of the week. When the house is also open to the public, there is usually an additional charge.

I PLAS NEWYDD (NT)
Llanfairpwll, Anglesey   Tel 01248 714795

Daily exc Sat, end March to Sept, 12–5 (also Fri and Sun in Oct). £4 includes house.

After crossing the Menai Straits via the A5 to Llanfairpwll, turn L on A4080 for 1m. Turn L onto minor rd for 1m to Plas Newydd, signed on R.

I love Plas Newydd because of the large mural by Rex Whistler, my favourite artist. Please pop inside and look at it. The house and gardens are in a magical setting above the Menai Straits, with stunning views of Snowdon. The largely informal garden is best seen in late spring, when the rhododendrons, azaleas, magnolias and acers show their character in this

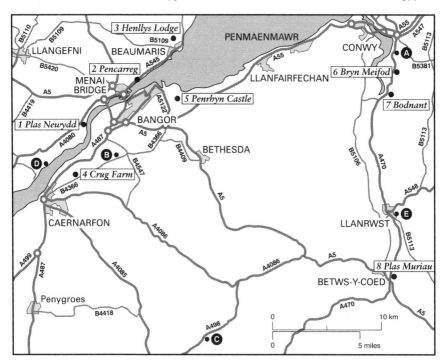

landscape designed by Repton. Exotic plants thrive in the mild climate, and
an arboretum of nothofagus and eucalyptus is under-planted with wildflowers.
Close to the house is an Italianate terrace and a formal rose garden.

2 PENCARREG   nr Menai Bridge, Anglesey   Tel 01248 713545

All year by appointment. Charity box.
From Menai Bridge go NE on A545 for 1½m. Garden is 100 yds up Glan y
Menai Drive on R. Best parking is in lay-by on A545.

Miss Jones started here in 1966 by clearing neglected ground. Now you see
a plantswoman's garden of year-round interest, with a wide selection of unusual shrubs – particularly cornus species and pittosporums. It is blessed
with marvellous views and a mild climate, while a bubbling stream gives
added beauty. Miss Jones strives to emulate the natural beauty of her
beloved Wales here with natural planting, so there are no annuals or
bedding plants, but plenty of perennials. Miss Jones and her collie dogs
welcome gardeners from all over the world, and her garden has been
featured 3 times on TV.

3   HENLLYS LODGE

nr Beaumaris, Anglesey   Tel 01248 810106

3 charity days, and by appointment. Charity box.
From Beaumaris go N past castle on B5109 for ½ m. Turn L, and L again, signed
to Henllys Hall Hotel. Garden is at lodge by hotel entrance.

Mrs Jones has a cottage garden here with stupendous views across the Menai
Straits to the mountains. Her favourite roses, mostly hybrid musks, are
under-planted with more than 80 varieties of hardy geraniums which bloom
from May to November, rare frosts permitting. A long double herbaceous
border is planted in the Edwardian style, with lupins, polemoniums and
monkshood (it's too windy for delphiniums). The woodland area is under-
planted with double-flowered periwinkles, and a little spring gives a boggy
place where trollius, astilbes and primulas grow to perfection.

4   CRUG FARM

Griffiths Crossing, nr Caernarfon   Tel 01248 670232

Thurs–Sun and BH Mons, April to end Sept, 10–6. Charity box.
From Caernarfon go NE on A487 for 2m. At roundabout, turn R on minor
road for ½ m to Crug Farm Plants, signed.

Crug Farm is the home of Mr and Mrs Wynn-Jones who are great gardeners and widely-travelled plant collectors. You will find highly unusual
shrubs, climbers and perennials, and more than 300 species of hardy geraniums. It is particularly interesting to visit in early spring to see the many
varieties of hellebores and daphnes. Display gardens help you in your choice
of plants from the nursery which specializes in shade-tolerant plants.

5   PENRHYN CASTLE (NT)   nr Bangor   Tel 01248 353084

Daily except Tues, April to Oct, 11–6. £4.50
From Britannia Bridge across the Menai Straits, go E on A5 for 5m. Turn L
on A5122 for ½ m, then R onto minor rd for 1m, following NT signs to castle.

All the good gardens in this area are blessed with magnificent views: to the
sea or to Snowdonia National Park or both – as here. The setting may be
the chief glory, but the gardens have interest in their own right. Although
exposed to the prevailing winds, exotics such as eucryphias thrive. The Victorian walled garden contains terraces and a well-kept parterre, while the
bog garden has tree ferns, palms and huge gunnera. There are huge drifts
of daffodils and wildflowers in the spring.

6 BRYN MEIFOD nr Conwy Tel 01492 580875

Garden: Fris, April to Sept (not Aug), 2–5, and by appointment. £1.50 Nursery: daily except Mons (open BH Mons), all year, 9–5.
From Conwy go E on A55 for 1½m. Turn R on A470 for 2½m. Just after Llansanffraid, Aberconwy Nursery signed on L.

The garden here provides an oasis of calm in the centre of a very busy and excellent plant centre. Dr and Mrs Lever are noted for the quality and variety of their plants, and are specialist growers of alpines, trees, shrubs and herbaceous plants. Each section of the garden is planted to provide interest throughout the year, using winter-flowering shrubs, trees with good bark, hellebores and spring bulbs, succeeded by epimediums and hostas. Trees and shrubs are chosen for fine autumn colour when there are gentians and cyclamen too. Scree beds nurture rare alpines, and other beds are for ericaceous plants. If your garden has months when it is dull and lacks interest, you can learn how to overcome the problem here, and then buy the right plants in a splendid nursery.

7 BODNANT GARDEN (NT) nr Conwy Tel 01492 650460

Daily, mid March to Oct, 10–5. £4.20
From Conwy go E on A55 for 1½m. Turn R on A470 for 3½m. Garden well signed on L.

The Aberconway family have made Bodnant, magnificently set above the River Conway looking across to Snowdon, one of Europe's most famous gardens. There is family continuity here. Two successive Lord Aberconways have been President of the RHS, and three generations of the Puddle family have provided the Head Gardener. You can see outstanding rhododendrons, camellias and magnolias in April and May, and in the 80 acres you will see plant collections from all over the world. The laburnum tunnel is famous (and has been copied by many great gardens). The Italian terrace above the woodland dell is imposing. Immaculately-clipped yew hedges, lily ponds, herbaceous borders, huge trees and National Collections of *Embothrium encryphia*, magnolia and rhododendron are all here. Put aside a whole day for Bodnant, and wear comfortable shoes; some of the garden is on a steep slope. There is a restaurant, and a good stock of home-propagated plants for sale.

8 PLAS MURIAU   Betws-y-coed   Tel 01690 710201

Daily except Mons (open BH Mons), March to Oct, 11–6. Phone to confirm. £1
From Betws-y-coed go E over Waterloo Bridge and N on A470 for ½ m. Gar-
den entrance on R by minor road signed to Capel Garmon and Gwydir Plants.

Gwydir Plants is a small nursery specialising in wildflowers, herbs, cottage
plants and unusual hardy perennials. Next to the nursery is the garden of
Plas Muriau which Tony and Lorna Scharer have been restoring. The site,
on a wooded hillside, has great views across the Conway Valley to Snowdonia National Park, and in spring the woodland atmosphere dominates
with a profusion of primroses, bulbs, flowering trees and shrubs. Brilliant
borders come to life in summer, stuffed with roses, perennials, herbs and
wildflowers. Tony and Lorna have a fine collection of damp-loving primulas, best seen in June.

Where to Stay

All B&B prices are approximate per person, sharing a double/twin room usually with private
or en suite facilities. It is a good idea to ask for any special requirements when booking.

A THE OLD RECTORY   Tel 01492 580611

Michael & Wendy Vaughan, The Old Rectory, Llansanffraid Glan Conwy,
nr Conwy, Gwynedd LL28 5LF.

It is all very luxurious and up-market here, but at the same time the house
hasn't lost the feeling of being a family home. It is idyllically situated, with
breath-taking views from a glorious garden (a 'mini-Bodnant', as it has been
described) across the Conwy estuary and towards Snowdonia. The 6 double/
twin bedrooms include half-testers and a four-poster. Wendy is Wales's
most-renowned female chef, and has won countless awards. A set-menu
dinner in the restaurant, which is open to the public, costs £27.50, licensed.
A coach house alongside has a ground-floor double bedroom where small
dogs and smokers are allowed. The main house itself is non-smoking, and
children should be over 5. B&B £37–£45.

B TY'N RHOS   Tel 01248 670479

Lynda & Nigel Kettle, Ty'n Rhos, Seion, nr Caernarfon, Gwynned LL55 3AE.

Many birdwatchers visit here as two nearby lakes are home to numerous varieties of birds. There are 2 guest lounges, 1 with a bar, the other with a warming log stove in a great fireplace. The 11 bedrooms of varying sizes are nearly all en suite. You eat in a restaurant which is always open to the public, a set meal costing £19. No dogs, children should be over 6, restricted smoking. B&B £28–£33.

C   PEN-Y-GWRYD HOTEL   Tel 01286 870211

Jane & Brian Pullee, Pen-y-Gwryd Hotel, Nantgwynant, nr Llanberis, Gwynedd LL55 4NT.

This inn has been voted the best mountain hotel in Britain, and is usually full of walkers and climbers enjoying the stupendous scenery round here. As a treat for tired legs, you can swim in a natural swimming pool at the end of the 2-acre garden, and then take a sauna hidden in the trees alongside. Jane and and Brian are enthusiastic hosts, and make sure that the friendly bar is always full of conversation about the day's happenings. The 19 bedrooms include 3 singles. They are plain, simple and comfortable. Only 1 is en suite, but there are plenty of bathrooms near. Hugely-generous evening meals cost £15. Breakfasts are on an equally gigantic scale. A games room for children, dogs by arrangement, no smoking in the dining room. B&B £21–£25.

D   PLAS TREFARTHEN   Tel 01248 430379

Marian Roberts, Plas Trefarthen, Brynsiencyn, Anglesey, Gwynedd LL61 6SZ.

This substantial and elegant 18th-century house is surrounded by its own 200-acre farm, and has panoramic views over a large garden and across the Menai Straits to Snowdonia. Marian has a wonderful singing voice: before taking on this extremely friendly B&B, she was a soprano soloist with Welsh choirs which toured all over the world. If you're lucky, the hills will come alive to the sound of her music. There are 8 double/twin bedrooms, some sharing bathrooms. There is a large guest lounge, and elsewhere a full-size snooker table, plus table tennis. Evening meals (2 courses for £10.50, bring your own wine) are taken early. Children welcome, restricted smoking, no dogs in the house. B&B £19–£21.

E   BRON EIRIAN   Tel 01492 641741

Anne & Michael Gibson, Bron Eirian, Town Hill, Llanrwst, Gwynedd LL26 0NF.

Anne and Michael's attractive, comfortable house is on the edge of the town, and has spectacular views from its well-kept garden. There are 3 double/twin en suite bedrooms, and a general air of peace and comfort. Evening meals are £12.50 (bring your own wine). No smoking, dogs by arrangement, children should be over 10. B&B £18–£20.

What Else to Enjoy

This is a short selection of the many good things recommended in the area by owners of places to stay. Your hosts will certainly be able to provide additional information.

If It's Wet

The NT's **Aberconwy House** is the only medieval merchant's house in **Conwy** to have survived the battles which raged through this walled town over the centuries. Dating from the 14th century, there is period furniture and an audio-visual presentation showing its history. A warning, though – there is no electric light, so on wet days the rooms are a bit dark.

Plas Newydd (*see* Garden 1) is an 18th-century house which, besides my favourite Rex Whistler mural, has an exhibition devoted to his work, and a military museum including campaign relics from the battle of Waterloo.

Penrhyn Castle (*see* Garden 5) looks Norman, but was in fact built between 1820 and 1845. You could happily spend a long time here. The reproduction interiors are all faithful to 11th-century originals, and there is the best private collections of paintings in North Wales. There is also an industrial railway museum, a doll museum and a countryside exhibition.

Eating Out

On the Isle of Anglesey, **Ye Olde Bull's Head,** in Castle St, **Beaumaris**, is a widely recommended restaurant-with-rooms. Higgledy-piggledy stone floors and old beams give plenty of atmosphere. Local produce provides memorable meals at prices which don't break the bank. A set lunch menu is £15, dinner £20. With wine and service, you can spend £25–£40 per head. B&B costs £38–£43. Tel 01248 810329.

On the mainland, **The Old Rectory** and **Ty'n Rhos** (*see* Where to Stay, 'A' and 'B') each have restaurants open to the public where you will eat well. At the first, set price dinners are £19–£23; at the second, £28.

The Cheshire Countryside

Welsh hills to the west, Pennines to the east, and in the middle is the the Cheshire plain, fertile, charming and wooded – when you can get away from the industrial towns. The black-and-white timbered houses are more extravagant than anywhere in the country. The best of all is Little Moreton Hall, its elaborately patterned exterior reflected in the calm moat below. When I visited this area the M6 was being repaired and I spent hours fuming in traffic jams on a hot day. The solution – as always – was to play some calming Bach. I listened to Christopher Hogwood playing the French Suites on a Ruckers harpsichord made around 1650. It restored my sanity, and the dog liked it too (she groans when I put on Bruckner or Wagner).

OS maps: Landrangers **109**, 110, **118**, 119

Gardens

Opening times: in larger gardens, and in NT properties, last admissions are usually 30–45 minutes before the garden closes. Admission charges are a guide to what one adult can expect to pay to go round the garden. It sometimes varies with the season or days of the week. When the house is also open to the public, there is usually an additional charge.

I   LITTLE MORETON HALL (NT)

nr Congleton   Tel 01260 272018

Wed–Sun and BH Mons, Easter to Oct, 12–5.30. Sat/Sun in Nov/Dec, 12–4. £3.60

From Congleton go SW on A34 for 4m. Garden well signed on L.

This house is one of the most enchanting timber-framed moated houses in the land, sparkling with the light reflected back from the moat. The garden wonderfully complements it, with gentle colours and plants known to have been around in medieval times. A long grass mound remains from the original garden. Graham Stuart Thomas has laid out a splendid knot garden in 17th-century style, with box hedges infilled with gravel. Around this, little

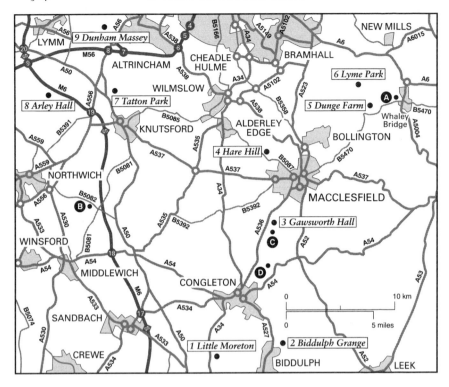

beds contain germander, herbs and woodruff, with standard gooseberries standing above them. There is a trellised walk, a yew tunnel and a charming orchard planted with medlars, quinces and rose-swagged pear trees. Behind the yew hedges you will find a small vegetable patch growing some of the earliest known varieties of salsify, beets, radishes, beans and peas. Herbaceous beds around the house are planted with big clumps of hostas, astrantias, cranesbills, catmint, pale irises and *Alchemilla mollis* – all very subtle and subdued, and perfectly suited to this marvellous house.

2 BIDDULPH GRANGE GARDEN (NT)

nr Congleton Tel 01782 517999

Wed–Sun and BH Mons, Easter to late Oct, 12–6 (Sat/Sun and BHs 11–6). £4 From Congleton go SE on A527 for 4m. Garden well signed on L.

This garden is being reconstructed on a vast scale by the NT. Made by James Bateman and Edward Cooke from 1842, it embodies all the Victorian enthusiasm for plant-collecting. Not only are there hundreds of plants from what were then exotic new places, but different parts of the garden depict foreign lands – Egypt and China for example. There is a long dahlia walk, a rose and verbena parterre, leafy tunnels, rocky outcrops and a fascinatingly horrible stumpery. When restoration is finished, it will be a truly remarkable garden.

3   GAWSWORTH HALL   nr Macclesfield   Tel 01260 223456

Daily, Easter to early Oct, 2–5.30. £2
From Macclesfield go SW on A536 for 3m. Garden signed on L.

Sir Edward Fitton made an important garden here in the 16th century, wishing to impress Elizabeth I. Legend has it that Mary Fitton, daughter of Sir Edward, may have been the 'Dark Lady' of Shakespeare's sonnets. The ravishing black-and-white timbered house is still here, but only the skeleton of the garden remains – lovely old Tudor walls, a canal, lakes and formal terraces. A great deal of labour went into making the terraces; the archeological dig that unearthed this information is interestingly written about in the handbook you can buy. Today the house is surrounded by formal rose beds, pools and fountains, summer bedding plants, statues and ornaments and lovely hedges of holly and yew. There is a charming tombstone marking the resting place of 'Maggotty' Johnson – wit, actor, poet, singer, dancer, and the last-known jester, otherwise called Lord Flame. Tim and Elizabeth Richards, who live here now, have been tireless in their efforts to discover the extent of the old garden.

4   HARE HILL GARDENS (NT)

Over Alderley, nr Macclesfield   Tel 01625 828981

Wed/Thurs, Sat/Sun and BH Mons, April to Oct, 10–5. £2.50
From Macclesfield go NW on B5087 for 3m. Garden well signed on R.

There is a walled garden here, ceanothus, vines and roses scrambling up the brickwork, with statues, a pergola and rosebeds below. But the woodland garden is the star attraction. Visit in May or June to see rhododendrons, azaleas and magnolias in profusion. There is also a fine collection of more than 50 different hollies – a shame we can't see them in December when their berries are out.

5 DUNGE FARM GARDENS

Kettleshulme, nr Whaley Bridge   Tel 01663 733787

Daily, April to Aug, 10.30–6. £2.50
From Macclesfield go NE on B5470 for 8m. In Kettlesfield, turn R on minor
rd for ½m signed 'Dunge Farm Gardens', then R down lane to garden.

In 1979 Elizabeth and David Ketley bought a derelict farm with a wonderful view over a wild valley with a stream at the bottom. They were blessed with some fine old beech trees, mountain ash and pines. Today, this is very much a plantsman's garden, informally winding its way up the valley, frequently crossing the stream, with a plethora of rhododendrons and azaleas under-planted with bulbs. Around the house are informal beds, with shrubs giving strong foliage colours and shapes, including *Acer palmatum* 'Bloodgood', *Eucalyptus gunnii*, embrothrium, *Prunus serrula*, and many shrub roses and tree peonies. The Ketleys admit to being almost obsessively keen on plant-collecting. Many rare and unusual plants are here, and the Ketleys propagate enthusiastically, so you can find marvellous varieties at most reasonable prices in their plant sales area. A sunny tea-room has a terrace enclosed with foxgloves and shrub roses. Bliss!

6 LYME PARK (NT)   Disley, nr Bramhall   Tel 01663 762023

Daily, April to Oct, 11–5. £1.50
From Whaley Bridge go NW on A6 for 4½m. In Disley turn L at entrance to
park and go S for 1m to car park.

Here are 17 acres of garden set in more than 1,000 acres of parkland with magnificent trees and grazing deer. The Palladian mansion is currently enjoying huge popularity after starring as 'Pemberley' in BBC TV's adaptation of *Pride and Prejudice*. Darcy's famous pool and the rides through the park will look familiar to many. In the garden are formal parterres, and a rose garden with a cherubic fountain, pool and a pretty gazebo bordered by hostas. A delightful herbaceous border, backed by hollies and beeches, has gentle, very appealing soft colours, designed by Graham Stuart Thomas. There is a valley garden with streams surrounded by rhodoendrons, azaleas and ferns. Most striking of all is the sunken Dutch garden. Viewed from above, it looks like a vibrant tapestry, with trimmed double hedges of box and ivy outlining the pattern, and a fountain splashing in the pool in the centre. Sheltered by high stone walls, with vines scrambling up them, the surrounding terraces are planted with shrub roses and philadelphus. Visited in July, it was hot and deliciously swoony with scent. The drive through the park is wonderful, and the lake reflects the fine old trees at the back of the house. Four young gardeners were busy weeding, but Mr Darcy was nowhere to be seen. Sigh.

7 TATTON PARK nr Knutsford Tel 01565 654822

Daily except Mons (open BH Mons), April to Sept, 10.30–6. £2.50
From Knutsford go N on A50 for 2m. Turn R on A5034 for 1½m. Garden entrance signed on R in Ashley Rd.

There are more than 50 acres of gardens and parks here, designed in the early 19th century for the Egerton family. A formal parterre, with bright summer bedding plants, was designed by Sir Joseph Paxton. The Orangery was the work of Lewis Wright (who also designed the house), and still contains outstanding citrus trees. Paxton's Fernery has been restored to glory, and near this is a formal rose garden, and herbaceous and shrub borders. By the lake is a Japanese garden (built by Japanese-born gardeners in 1910), with an arched bridge and temple. It shows Japanese restraint in the use of colour. You can also find a maze, woodland walks and miles of parkland to walk over. So thankfully, there is a restaurant, loos, a shop and plant sales.

8 ARLEY HALL nr Great Budworth Tel 01565 777353

Daily except Mons (open BH Mons), mid April to Sept, 12–5. £3
From Knutsford go W on A5033 for 2m. Turn R onto A556 for ½m. Turn L before M5 briefly onto B5391, then R on minor roads for 3m following signs.

The ancestral home of the Warburton family was originally built in the 15th century, but the present Arley Hall and gardens date from 1850. The magnificent double herbaceous borders were a novelty then, and remain much as they were to this day, backed by yew and with splendid fat yew buttresses dividing up the borders. A series of smaller gardens and courtyards allow for delightful changes in character in this 12-acre garden which has a definite family feel. Here you can enjoy shrub roses, old walled gardens with espaliered fruit trees, a clipped ilex avenue, a herb garden, a rockery with maples, willows and damp-loving plants, and a formal garden complete with heraldic beasts and Dawyck copper beeches. Another walled kitchen garden contains greenhouses growing tender pot plants for the house, plus vines, figs and peaches. The gardens have belonged to one caring family for nearly 500 years, and this continuity has lent a sense of settled peace.

9   DUNHAM MASSEY (NT)

nr Altrincham   Tel 01619 411025

Daily, April to Oct, 11–5.30. £2.50
From Altrincham go SW on A556 for 2m. Turn R on A56 for 1m. Garden
signed on R.

The NT has done wonders to restore this garden whose history spans
several centuries. The moat surrounding the Tudor mount is planted with
bog-loving plants – astilbes, ferns, irises and rodgersias which reflect their
colour in the water. There is an Edwardian parterre planted with bold
colours in the summer, and an 18th-century orangery. The surrounding
park dates from the 18th century too. There are now woodland walks, and
an energetic programme of tree-planting is in progress.

Where to Stay

*All B&B prices are approximate per person, sharing a double/twin room usually with private
or en suite facilities. It is a good idea to ask for any special requirements when booking.*

A   COTE BANK FARM

                                            Tel 01663 750566

Pamela Broadhurst, Cote Bank Farm, Buxworth, nr Whaley Bridge, Derbyshire
SK12 7NP.

Pamela admits to being a compulsive gardener, forever acquiring more
plants and extending up and down the hill on which the garden sits, 800 ft
up with glorious views to the Goyt valley and beyond. Guests have a large
sitting-room with a log fire, and plenty of books and magazines. There are
2 double/twin bedrooms. No evening meals, but there are masses of good
pubs and restaurants locally. No smoking, children welcome, dogs by
arrangement. B&B £20–£25.

B   SCULSHAW WILLOWS

                                            Tel 01565 722377

Elizabeth Grayling, Sculshaw Willows, Allostock, nr Knutsford, Cheshire
WA16 9JZ.

This peaceful and comfortable family home is set in 3 acres of gardens and
paddocks with a hard tennis court. The garden has been developed bit by
bit over the years, and has a great show of daffodils in spring. There is a

lawn big enough for croquet. Elizabeth is very knowledgeable about local gardens. She cooks evening meals (£15, bring your own wine) if ordered in advance. Two double bedrooms. No smoking, no small children, and dogs by arrangement. B&B £20–£25.

C ROUGH HEY FARM Tel 01260 252296

Phyllis Worth, Rough Hey Farm, Leek Rd, Gawsworth, nr Macclesfield, Cheshire CW12 0JQ.

This farmhouse, in a tranquil valley sheltering a 300-acre sheep farm, is old enough to have been mentioned in the Domesday Book. Rebuilt in 1360, from which much of the structure remains today, it was extended in 1790. There is a charming sitting-room for guests, and 3 double and 3 single bedrooms. Some share bathrooms. Plenty of pubs to eat out at in the evenings. Children welcome, no smoking, no dogs. B&B £18.

D YEW TREE FARM Tel 01260 223569

Sheila Kidd, Yew Tree Farm, North Rode, nr Congleton, Cheshire CW12 2PF.

This is a working farm that is easily found from the M6, yet has a peaceful setting in wooded parkland. There are lovely walks beside a stream down to the lake frequented by many wildfowl, or along the nearby canal. Sheila loves cooking, and provides great, straightforward evening meals for £10 (bring your own wine), using local farm produce. There are 3 double/twin bedrooms, 1 sharing a bathroom. Children welcome, smoking allowed, dogs by arrangement. B&B £16–£18.

What Else to Enjoy

This is a short selection of the many good things recommended in the area by owners of places to stay. Your hosts will certainly be able to provide additional information.

Other Gardens/Nurseries

Caddick's Clematis Nursery, Lynn Rd, **Thelwall**, nr Warrington, off the M6 and off the NW corner of the visit map, is what its name would suggest. Harry Caddick offers more than 300 desirable varieties of clematis, reasonably priced. Open daily except Mons, 10–5. Tel 01925 757196.

Other Places to Stay

Charlotte Walsh has a substantial 16th-century farmhouse with 7 modestly priced double/twin bedrooms, mostly en suite, at her home in **Needhams Farm**. You will find it off the N edge of the visit map, E of Stockport. The rooms range from a single to twin/doubles to a family room. There are inexpensive evening meals at £7, licensed. Dogs, children and smokers all welcome. B&B £16–£18. Address: Uplands Rd, Werneth Low, **Gee Cross**, nr Hyde, Cheshire SK14 3AQ. Tel 01613 684610.

If It's Wet

The NT properties in this visit are outstanding, despite the area being rather built up. **Little Moreton Hall** (*see* Garden 1) has a great hall, parlour and long gallery which are as fascinating as its amazingly ornate half-timbered exterior. **Lyme Park** (*see* Garden 6) is one of the largest houses in Cheshire, with 18th- and 19th-century additions to the original Elizabethan mansion. Inside, you can see four centuries of period furnishings and decoration, with Grinling Gibbons' carvings and a unique collection of English clocks. **Dunham Massey** (*see* Garden 9) is mainly Georgian. You can wander round more than 30 rooms that contain fine paintings and outstanding Huguenot silver.

All these houses are open on the same days as the gardens, but usually let you in an hour after garden opening times.

Another NT property if you want a break from from garden visiting is **Quarry Bank Mill**, at **Styal**, just N of Wilmslow off the B5166. This old cotton mill has been restored by the NT as a working museum, with demonstrations of weaving and spinning and galleries illustrating the mill-workers' world. There is a good shop selling cotton goods made there, and a coffee shop and licensed restaurant.

Eating Out

The **Brasserie Belle Epoque** at 60 King St, **Knutsford** is jolly, and not too expensive. In Edwardian surroundings, you can enjoy dishes that owe their inspiration to many sources – local dishes vie with recipes from France, Spain and Italy. About £20–£35 per head. Tel 01565 633060.

The Peak District

Most of this visit is within the National Park, with lush fields and sheltered valleys. Dovedale is a truly picturesque valley with marvellous walks. There are some splendid castles, houses and manors to visit, from the grandest of all, Chatsworth, to a charming 1-acre cottage garden at Oaks Lane Farm. It is, of course, very crowded, so it is best to plan a short holiday in the middle of the week. Let's listen to something noble here: Grieg's Piano Concerto in A minor, Opus 16. You probably know it backwards (but it sounds better forwards).

OS maps: Landrangers **119**, 120

Gardens

Opening times: in larger gardens, and in NT properties, last admissions are usually 30–45 minutes before the garden closes. Admission charges are a guide to what one adult can expect to pay to go round the garden. It sometimes varies with the season or days of the week. When the house is also open to the public, there is usually an additional charge.

I   BIRCHFIELD
Ashford in the Water, nr Bakewell   Tel 01629 813800

April to Sept by appointment. £1
From Bakewell go NW on A6 to Ashford in the Water. Ask owner for final directions to garden in Dukes Drive.

Mr Parker started making his garden out of a steep field nine years ago. First came the JCB, then he killed the weeds. Now it is a colourful paradise, with informal beds of peonies, dahlias and annuals against a background of fine foliage shrubs. A tunnel of roses and clematis hides the greenhouse. Valerian and cranesbill spill over the garden paths. The rockery by a small pond is planted with iris, kingcups, lilies, rock-roses and phlomis. Further up the hill, through a laburnum arch, is another lawn surrounded by

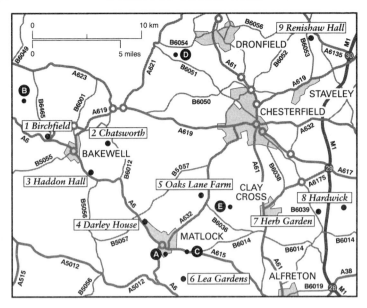

sparkling flower beds and flowering shrubs. An arboretum has been planted, with ginkgo, red oaks, liriodendrons and metasequoia, all fighting for
existence with Mr Parker's nibbling donkeys. The terraced garden has
charming views, and aims to have colour all the year round.

2 CHATSWORTH nr Bakewell Tel 01246 582204

Daily, March to Nov, 11–5. £3.50
From Bakewell go SE on A6 for 6m. At Rowsley turn L onto B6012 and follow
signs for 2½ m to car park.

The exciting approach to this great house, through Capability Brown's park,
is heightened by the spectacular water-jet, nearly 300 ft high, leaping into
the sky above the huge lime trees. My heart sank when I saw how many
people were there, but on the whole, they were clustered around the shop
and restaurant. I took a brisk walk up the hill and felt happy again. Happy
indeed – the kitchen garden was sublime, its raised beds intersected by
paths, with apple and pear tunnels, veggies arranged decoratively, and acres
of food and fruit growing alongside flowers for picking and drying. Nearby
was a quirky cottage garden, with ivy clipped into the shape of a four-poster
bed, and a table and two chairs, a fireplace and stairs created out of privet,
yew and ivy.The 'carpet' in this pretend room came from different shades

of thyme. All very odd, I have to say, but it delighted other visitors. The woodland walk was enchanting, with splendid beeches under-planted with rhododendrons and azaleas. There are huge borders, of course, great statues, Paxton's magnificent water cascade flowing down the hillside, long walks and vistas. It is huge and impressive and very well maintained. You need a whole day, and strong legs, if you want to see it all.

3   HADDON HALL   nr Bakewell   Tel 01629 812855

Daily, April to Sept (except Suns in July/Aug) 11–5. £4.50 includes house
From Bakewell go SE on A6 for 2m. Hall well signed on L.

Pause on the bridge as you walk up the path that takes you towards this house and its gardens, and drink in the serenity of the scene – a wildflower meadow, the river with ducks bobbing about, amazing topiary at the gardener's cottage, and the medieval house itself perching at the top of a steep hill. It is utterly wonderful. Alas, it would be difficult for the elderly and disabled to go much further. Many steps and levels have to be negotiated. This – to me the most romantic house in England – is home to the Duke of Rutland and his family, and you go through it to reach the gardens on the other side. Here, billowing roses tumble from walls and terraces, down balustrades and stone steps, with philadelphus in fragrant clouds and massed planting of tall delphiniums. Although best when the roses are out in June and July, the bones of the garden are so good that it would be brilliant on a misty day in March, with its clipped yew columns, smooth lawns, splashing fountains – and such views in any light. From each terrace, you can look down and across lush countryside and water-meadows. The tall walls shelter many tender plants. Carpenterias, *Cytisus battandieri*, clematis, ceanothus, santolina and lavender dangle from the buttresses beneath you. It won the Christies 'Garden of the Year' award in 1993, and it wins my heart every time I go there.

4   DARLEY HOUSE
Darley Dale, nr Matlock   Tel 01629 733341

End May to June, and September, by appointment. £1.50
From Matlock go NW on A6 for 2m. In Darley Dale the garden is on R, just past the hospital, on the corner of Old Hackney Lane.

Darley House, a Georgian residence standing in a beautiful 1½ -acre garden, was bought by Joseph Paxton and his daughter in 1845, and bears the hallmark of the great gardener and engineer. He probably lived here when working on the massive schemes at Chatsworth and it is known that he planted the huge copper beech which dominates the garden. A flight of stone steps with its balustrade echoes a similar one strewn with roses at Haddon Hall. Many fine trees grow here, including a ginkgo. Mr and Mrs Briscoe have lovingly restored the garden, whose tall walls shelter *Cytisus battandieri, Carpenteria californica, Fremontodendron californicum,* a large Chilean Firebush, pittosporums and tender hebes. On the south wall of the house, a large *Magnolia grandiflora* and wisterias are entwined with *Rosa* 'Cécile Brunner'. The borders are planted in soft colours of pinks, purples, blue delphiniums, and blue and white campanulas. Splendid meconopsis grow in a bed with foxgloves and old pinks. Mrs Briscoe is very knowledgeable about plants and their history, and gave me fascinating insights into her garden.

5   OAKS LANE FARM

Brockhurst, nr Matlock   Tel 01246 590324

2 charity days, and by appointment May to Aug. £1.50
From Matlock go NE on A632 for 3½m. Just past Kelstedge Inn, turn L up narrow lane, then first R; garden is ½m on R.

Mr and Mrs Hunter came to a small stone cottage in a barren field thirty years ago. Now it is a comfortable house with staggeringly good views and a great garden – and all because Mr Hunter likes to build walls, terraces and bridges, lay paths and alter the course of streams, while Mrs Hunter is a knowledgeable plantaholic. The combination is a winner. They have created a garden of sophistication, about 1 acre in size, meandering around the house and barn, with a new surprise at each turn. It has unusual plants, strong shrub foliage colour, with masses of shrub roses and acid loving plants. A small stream, with fat trout waiting to be hand-fed, trickles by the gate and forms a little bog garden. It is all a marvellous contrast to the grandiosities of Chatsworth and Hardwick Hall.

6   LEA GARDENS   Lea, nr Matlock   Tel 01629 534380

Daily, mid March to July, rest of year by appointment. £1.50
From Matlock go S on A6 for 2m. At Cromford, turn L onto minor roads for 2½m to Lea. Garden is at E end of village on L.

Mr and Mrs Tye have a valuable collection (more than 500 varieties) of rare rhododendrons and azaleas, together with lovely kalmias, in their 4-acre wooded hillside garden. A medieval mill-stone quarry was here originally, so there is an excellent rock garden with a huge number of alpines, acers, dwarf conifers, heathers and spring bulbs. There are new woodland walks planted with ornamental trees, many of which have bird-boxes attached to them; bird song is sweet on the air.

7 THE HERB GARDEN
Hardstoft, nr Chesterfield   Tel 01246 854268

Daily, March to Sept, 10–6. Donation box.
From Chesterfield go SE on B6039 for 6m. In Hardstoft turn L and garden is at Hall View Cottage, signed in village.

Lynne and Steve Raynor are herbalists, and here they have have created one of the foremost herb gardens in the country. Posters around the garden give information about the history and use of herbs in medicine, cooking and perfumery. There are four distinct sections within high, sheltering beech hedges. Culinary herbs are in box-lined beds divided by brick paths, with standard roses and sweet peas, and backed by a mass of shrub roses and foxgloves. The pot-pourri garden is small and heavenly, with scented geraniums and scented salvias. The physic garden is fascinating but more sinister – if the herb didn't cure your dropsy, purge you, give you spasms or produce energetic vomiting, it would probably poison you. In the lavender garden there are more than 30 different species. Did you know there were that many? This is an excellent place to learn about herbs, and buy them.

8 HARDWICK HALL (NT)
nr Chesterfield   Tel 01246 850430

Daily, April to Oct, 12.30–5. £2.50
From Chesterfield go SE on B6039 for 6m. At Hardstoft, turn L onto minor road for 2m crossing M1 and following signs to car park.

Bess of Hardwick, a famously powerful personality, built this magnificent 16th-century house after marrying her fourth husband, and had her initials ES carved along the parapet of the house. Along with coronets, coats of arms and oddly shaped chimneys, the roof-top looks to me a bit of a mess. However, the gardens have grandeur, and are divided into large courts. Borders are planted with huge clumps of architectural plants with strong colours. A delightful orchard has crab apples, medlars, mulberries, damsons and plums. Big hedges of yew and beech make *allées* and give a dark background to some lovely statues. The chief attraction for gardeners, I think, will be the herb garden. Set in a sheltered walled garden, with a nut walk along one side, it is the largest and most comprehensive I know. Golden hops grow up poles to give height and formality, and the the square beds – culinary, medical, domestic and perfumed – are prettily edged with lavender, box, germander and santolina. There are lovely names to conjure with – skirret, woad, alecost, comfrey, orach and lovage. The surrounding park and avenues of limes are what we would expect of a grand house.

9   RENISHAW HALL   nr Sheffield   Tel 01246 432042

Fri–Sun and BH Mons, Easter to mid Sept, 10.30–4.30. £3
From Chesterfield go NE on A619 for 4m. In Staveley, turn L onto B6053 for 2½ m; garden and hall entrance signed on R.

Here, high in the hills of northern England, but with a southerly aspect and shelter from fine trees and magnificent yew hedges, Sir George Sitwell brought alive his passion for Italian gardens. That was 100 years ago, when it was considered frivolous to spoil architecture with colour and flower-beds. Today, Sir Reresby Sitwell has enlarged and enhanced the borders, and added excitement with a leaping jet of water not unlike the one at Chatsworth. Wonderful fountains splash and sparkle, shrub roses delight and statues look on approvingly. A woodland walk has been opened. The Sitwell Museum gives a delightful insight into the lives of this eccentric and unconventional family whose talents for gardens and writing enchant me.

Where to Stay

All B&B prices are approximate per person, sharing a double/twin room usually with private or en suite facilities. It is a good idea to ask for any special requirements when booking.

A   HODKINSON'S HOTEL   Tel 01629 582170

Malcolm Archer & Nigel Shelley, Hodgkinson's Hotel, 150 South Parade, Matlock Bath, Derbyshire DE4 3NR.

The first hotel to be built in this spa town, at the very end of the 17th century, it takes its name from a certain Job Hodgkinson who bought it in the 1830s. He would recognize the carefully-restored architecture today, but surely not the amazing assortment of china, knick-knacks, Victorian clothes,

Dinky toys, art nouveau figurines and other collectable kitsch – you name it, Malcolm and Nigel have found it, and packed it into this immaculate 4-storey town house, fronting the river and with a lovely small hillside garden behind, at roof-top level, smothered with roses. Expect originality in the very good evening meals (£19.50–£24.50, licensed). There are 7 exceptionally comfortable bedrooms, including 1 single. No children, dogs welcome, restricted smoking. B&B £25–£40.

B   CRESSBROOK HALL   Tel 01298 871289

Bobby Hull-Bailey, Cressbrook Hall, Cressbrook, nr Buxton, Derbyshire SK17 8SY.

Bobby runs B&B in this huge, spectacular house on a scale much grander than most you will find in this book. Formal gardens, with splendid topiary, lead to a deep limestone gorge and wonderful views. A recently-discovered 1843 planting plan for the gardens, printed in Edward Kemp's 1858 *How to lay out a Garden*, has inspired her to start re-creating the original – an ambitious undertaking indeed. The Hall itself, still a family home, has wonderful interiors and just 3 double/twin bedrooms, but there are 7 cottages with further accommodation where you can self-cater or eat at the Hall. Dinner costs £16.50 (licensed), and in the summer there are often barbecues. There are all sorts of add-ons if you want to indulge yourself here – sauna, sun-bed, massage, aromatherapy, beauty treatment. Children welcome (there is a well-equipped play area), smoking restricted, dogs allowed in the cottages. B&B £25–£35.

C   LANE END HOUSE   Tel 01629 583981

Marion & David Smith, Lane End House, Green Lane, Tansley, nr Matlock, Derbyshire DE4 5FJ.

This is a beautifully presented former Georgian farmhouse where Marion and David give meticulous and friendly service to their guests. Around the pretty garden, with a fountain, colourful beds, water garden and a croquet lawn, are gentle strolls to ruined mills, ponds and waterfalls. The 4 double/ twin bedrooms – 1 with a canopied bed and another on the ground floor for people who find stairs difficult – are lavishly furnished (bathrobes beckon invitingly when one returns to the Hall, exhausted after garden-visiting). A low-slung attached building, looking out to the garden, is used as a comfortable lounge to rest your legs. There is a good choice on the dinner menu

(£15.50, licensed). No smoking, children welcome (but discuss first), dogs by arrangement. B&B £24–£28.

D   HORSLEYGATE HALL   Tel 01142 890333

Margaret Ford, Horsleygate Hall, Horsleygate Lane, nr Holmesfield, Derbyshire S18 5WD.

Gardening is Margaret's passion. When she came to this large house, part-Georgian, part-Victorian, in 1989 it was a mammoth job to clear the 2½ acres of brambles and self-sown trees. Only the best mature trees remain now of that jungle – and, instead, there is a sloping luxuriance of paths, shrubs, borders, a rockery, pool and an orchard. The vegetable garden is laid out surrounding a central herb wheel; a sun terrace encourages Mediterranean plants. Small wonder that many of Margaret's guests come back year after year to see how work is progressing. There are 3 large double/twin bedrooms (1 en suite), and everywhere inside the house is pleasantly furnished. You eat out in the evenings at a good pub only a couple of minutes away, or at nearby restaurants. No smoking, no dogs, children should be over 5. B&B £19–£22.

E   OLD SCHOOL FARM   Tel 01246 590813

Jonathan Wootton, Old School Farm, Uppertown, Ashover, nr Chesterfield, Derbyshire S45 0JF.

There is usually plenty of colour in the little garden on this working farm set in the Derbyshire moors. It has pleasantly furnished, good-sized rooms with lovely views. Evening meals (from £10, bring your own wine) can be arranged in advance, and are praised by guests for ample portions of straightforward home cooking. Of the 4 double/twin bedrooms, 2 are en suite, the others share a bathroom. Children over 10 welcome, restricted smoking, no dogs in the house. B&B £18.

What Else to Enjoy

This is a short selection of the many good things recommended in the area by owners of places to stay. Your hosts will certainly be able to provide additional information.

Other Places to Stay

At **Hillside House**, the garden leads seamlessly via a lawn, borders, trees and shrubs to wonderful open Peak District countryside. There are 3 double/ twin rooms, 1 en suite and the others sharing a bathroom. In the evenings, you can eat at good pubs not far away. Children welcome, no smoking, no dogs. B&B £18–£20. It lies just N of the visit, on the E side. Address: Jayne Webster, Hillside House, Pindale Road, **Castleton**, Derbyshire S30 2WU. Tel 01463 620312.

If It's Wet

The great stately homes at **Chatsworth** (Garden 2), **Haddon Hall** (Garden 3), **Hardwick Hall** (Garden 8) and **Renishaw Hall** (Garden 9) are all major tourist attractions, and are open at approximately the same times as given for the gardens.

You probably sense from what I have written that if you have time for only one, Haddon Hall would be my choice. Not so well known, but truly fascinating, is the flour mill at **Stainsby Mill** in the grounds of Hardwick Hall, and open on the same days. The magnificent wooden machinery and water-wheel are in working order.

At **Darley Dale**, on the A6 2m NW of Matlock, you will find **Red House Stables**, probably the best working carriage museum in the country, with hansom cabs, a stage coach, a Royal Mail coach and many elegant carriages (when they're not out on hire for films and TV). Tel 01629 733583 to check visiting times, and to book yourself on a sight-seeing tour in one of the carriages, if that takes your fancy.

Eating Out

For a meal to remember in surroundings to remember, everyone recommends **Riber Hall.** This superbly converted Elizabethan manor, with a wonderful garden, has everything you could ever expect in a house of this period – masses of beams, stone fireplaces, oak floors and antiques – the food matches up to the surroundings. A set dinner menu has lots of choice, and costs £25 per person. With wine and service, expect to spend about £35–£40 each. You can stay here too. There are 9 rooms with four-posters with a B&B price of £50 per person. You find it at **Tansley**, 1m E of Matlock off the A615. Tel 01629 58279.

From Harrogate to the Dales

Harrogate is an elegant Georgian town, with a pump room and spa, on the southern edge of the Yorkshire Dales. As well as its famed municipal gardens, the RHS's northern centre, Harlow Carr, is here, and is full of interesting trial grounds. What surprised me about the Yorkshire gardens was how cleverly gardeners had used shelter and warm south walls to coax quite tender plants into bloom. Ripley Castle was a great day out. I found myself humming Gilbert and Sullivan's *Yeomen of the Guard* which seemed to suit this jolly place.

OS maps: Landrangers **99, 104**

Gardens

Opening times: in larger gardens, and in NT properties, last admissions are usually 30–45 minutes before the garden closes. Admission charges are a guide to what one adult can expect to pay to go round the garden. It sometimes varies with the season or days of the week. When the house is also open to the public, there is usually an additional charge.

I HARLOW CARR Harrogate   Tel 01423 565418
Daily, all year, 9.30–6 or dusk. £3.20
From centre of Harrogate go SW on B6162 for 1½ m. Garden well signed on R in Cray Lane.

Gardeners who know Wisley and Kew will be interested to compare those gardens with the Northern Horticultural Society's garden at Harlow Carr where you can see just what will grow in the north of England – and how to grow it. Set in a pretty valley with streams and woodland, there are many different display areas for plants – winter gardens, rose garden, bulb garden, an arboretum – lots of veggies and fruit, and a marvellous alpine house. The plant centre is excellent, with a wide variety of the more unusual shrubs and plants. There is a coffee shop, a restaurant, a museum of gardening, a model village and a children's play area.

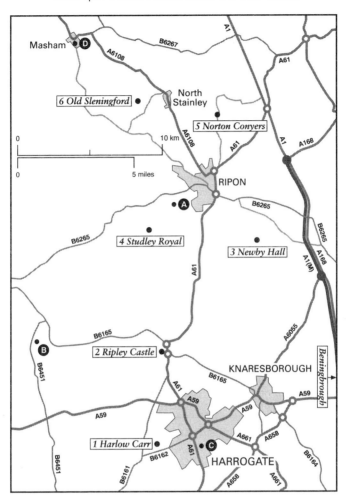

2 RIPLEY CASTLE   nr Harrogate   Tel 01423 770152

Daily, April to Oct, 11–5. In other months, telephone for times of opening. £3.
From Harrogate go N on A61 for 3m. Castle is in centre of Ripley.

Ripley Castle has been the home of the Ingilby family for nearly 700 years.
It is intriguing and full of history, and the gardens are fabulous. There is a
5-acre walled garden, a landscape designed by Capability Brown, a marvellous Regency conservatory, hundreds of thousands of spring bulbs including a special planting of hyacinths in formal beds (the National Collection
of hyacinths is here), and a tropical house with bananas, pineapples, coffee,

sugar cane, ginger, citrus and ferns thriving in it. The herbaceous borders are 20 ft wide and 180 ft long, crammed with colour and interest from agapanthus, delphiniums, phlox, lupins, dahlias and asters. In contrast to these are the white and silver beds, designed in 1992 by Lady Ingilby. The terrace has tender climbers and wisteria up the south wall, and a fuchsia hedge. I particularly like the Bell Gate, an entrance to the bottom gardens. The bell was rung by the cook to let the head gardener know that she wanted something from the garden. The kitchen garden now grows old and rare varieties of fruit and veggies. The National Collection of hyacinths is here. Each Sunday, a children's farmyard is open.

3 NEWBY HALL nr Ripon   Tel 01423 322583

Tues–Sun and BH Mons, April to Sept, 11–5.30. £3.50
From Ripon go E on B6265 for 2m. Turn R onto minor road for 2m to Skelton-on-Ure and follow signs to garden on R.

This lovely house is late 17th-century, with additions, and is the family home of the Comptons. The 25 acres of award-winning garden were the inspired creation of the present owner's father, and he in turn was influenced by Lawrence Johnston's Hidcote. A great central axis of double herbaceous borders, flanked by yew hedges, runs from the south front of the house to the River Ure. Off these borders are several formal compartmented gardens designed to be at their best in different seasons. Sylvia's garden is a haven of herbs, aromatic plants and grey-leaved foliage. An excellent collection of old roses waft their perfume and loll about in a blowsy way. There is a sheltered tropical garden, an autumn garden, a water garden and a long statuary walk. The rock garden is attributed to Ellen Wilmott, and there is a fine woodland garden. Robin and Jane Compton have made this one of the finest and most fascinating gardens in Britain – absolutely not to be missed. Children have an adventure garden to play in, and there is a miniature railway. You can very happily spend all day here. The restaurant is licensed.

4 STUDLEY ROYAL with FOUNTAINS ABBEY (NT)
nr Ripon   Tel 01765 608888

Daily, all year (except Christmas and Fri in winter), 10–7 or dusk. £4.
From Ripon go W on B6265 for 4m. Garden well signed on L.

This superb 150-acre water garden was created by John Aislabie in the 18th century, and is linked to Fountains Abbey, an eye-catching, romantic and amazing monastic ruin. There are grottoes, water features, cascades and a long, mirror-like canal. The buildings are architecturally stunning, and include an octagon tower, a Temple of Filial Piety and a banqueting house. A gazebo known as Anne Boleyn's Seat gives a superb surprise vista. The best view of many here is from the top of the tower. Paths lead you around this garden, and dogs are allowed to enjoy it too.

5   NORTON CONYERS   nr Ripon   Tel 01765 640333

Many charity days, March to Sept, 2–5, and by written appointment. Free, but donation to charity welcomed.
From Ripon go NE on A61 for ½m. Turn L on minor rd signed to Wath. The garden is 3m on L.

This old house has been the home of the Graham family since 1624. They are still hard at work in the garden here. It is thought that Norton Conyers was the house described by Charlotte Brontë as Thornfield Hall in *Jane Eyre*. In 18th-century fashion, the garden lies away from the house, and is entirely enclosed by a long wall. Double herbaceous borders, backed by an old yew hedge, lead from the garden gate to the central feature, a late 18th-century orangery, standing behind a small pool and flanked by contemporary greenhouses. The rest of the garden is much less formal, and includes a pick-your-own fruit area. Sir James and Lady Graham have started a programme of garden renovation, and have a small nursery garden specialising in unusual and old-fashioned hardy plants.

6   OLD SLENINGFORD   Mickley, nr Ripon   Tel 01765 635229

Charity weekend in May, and by appointment. £2.
From Ripon go NW on A6108 for 5m. Just after North Stainley, turn L to Mickley; garden signed on R after 1m.

What a peaceful garden you find here, with wide lawns and old trees lounging around the house. The garden is full of variety, with a long herbaceous border backed by immaculate beech and yew hedges. In the walled kitchen garden there are box hedges, lots of veggies and fruit trained up the wall, and colourful flowers and grasses grown for picking and drying. A walk through the wood leads to a water garden with a lovely lake and islands, where you can watch swans, duck and koi carp. Mr and Mrs Ramsden keep this large garden looking great with only a little part-time help.

Where to Stay

All B&B prices are approximate per person, sharing a double/twin room usually with private or en suite facilities. It is a good idea to ask for any special requirements when booking.

A LAWRENCE HOUSE   Tel 01765 600947

John & Harriet Highley, Lawrence House, Studley Roger, nr Ripon, North Yorkshire HG4 3AY.

Lovely 2-acre gardens, with wide lawns, borders and walks, surround this immaculate Georgian house whose grounds border the historic Studley Royal deer park and Fountains Abbey (*see* Garden 4). Inside the house are antiques and paintings, and log fires if it gets chilly. The 2 double/twin bedrooms are spacious and beautifully furnished, and have luxurious bathrooms. John has been in the wine trade for many years, and Harriet, an interior decorator, loves cooking (4-course dinners £18.50, ask about wine). Dogs by arrangement, children should be over 10, restricted smoking. B&B £35.

B LOW HALL   Tel 01423 780230

Patricia Holliday, Low Hall, Dacre, nr Harrogate, North Yorkshire HG33 4AA.

Returning to her childhood home twelve years ago, Mrs Holliday set to work restoring and improving what is now a stunning garden, filled with colour and architectural form that perfectly set off the wonderful stone of her farmhouse dating from 1635. Everywhere, you can see the results of her loving care – and this extends to the interior of the house, with its treasured pieces of oak furniture, and its beams, mullioned windows and open fireplaces. You feel pampered here. The 3 bedrooms, including 1 single, are luxurious, with bathrooms to lounge in. Dinners are what she calls 'country-house cooking' (£17, bring your own wine). No smoking, no dogs, no children. B&B £29–£31.

C GRANBY HOUSE   Tel 01423 884829

Norma Renny, Granby House, 11 Granby Road, Harrogate, North Yorkshire HG1 4ST.

On the edge of Harrogate, with a garden at the back of the house over-looking tranquil parkland, this handsome Georgian house is a good place to enjoy Harrogate and its surroundings. Norma, a keen bridge player, has a fund of local knowledge, and as a workaholic gardener can point you in the direction of good nurseries nearby. Evening meals (£17, bring your own wine) are excellent. There are 3 well-furnished and spacious double/twin bedrooms. No smoking, no dogs, no children. B&B £29.

D BANK VILLA   Tel 01765 689605

Philip Gill & Anton van der Horst, Bank Villa, Masham, North Yorkshire HG4 4DB.

The garden behind this pretty, friendly house slopes steeply upwards on terraces which, in spring, are full of bulbs and fruit blossom. Philip and Anton have a gift for making you feel at home here. Their dinners (£16, bring your own wine) have imaginative menus, and are served with flair. The house, charmingly decorated, is full of books and antiques. No smoking, no dogs, children by arrangement. B&B £18.

What Else to Enjoy

This is a short selection of the many good things recommended in the area by owners of places to stay. Your hosts will certainly be able to provide additional information.

Other Gardens

To the E of the visit map (Yorkshire is a large county, as you will no doubt discover) is a major garden which you should consider visiting.

Beningbrough Hall, a NT property, has a garden which covers 7 acres and the park more than 300 acres. There are two formal gardens each side of the house, enclosed with yew hedges. One is planted up with hot colours of reds, oranges and yellows, the other with cooler pastel shades. There is also an American shrub garden. The old walled kitchen garden has fruit trained up the walls, and there is a spectacular double herbaceous border. The conservatory, vine house and an old-fashioned potting shed are all worth visiting. There are plant sales, a tea shop and gift shop. To find it from the visit map, go E on A59 for 9m. Turn L on the A1237 by-pass for 1m. At second roundabout, turn L on A19 for 3m. The garden is signed on L at Shipton-by-Beningborough. Open Sat–Wed, April to Oct (and Fri in July/Aug), 11–5. Admission £3. Tel 01904 470666. The interior of this elegant Georgian house is hung with magnificent paintings on loan from the National Portrait Gallery.

Other Places to Stay

Follow the B6161 for 3m to the S of the visit and you come to the little village of Leathley. Here **Leathley Cottage** is a lovely place to stay for anyone who enjoys gardens. Home of the Ryott family for 70 years, it is in fact a substantial stone house rather than a cottage, and the garden is Georgina's pride. Covering 3 acres in all, it is superbly planned, with long vistas which link the walled garden with a peaceful yew garden. Inside the house, antique furniture and pictures fill comfortable sunny rooms. Evening meals by arrangement (£17.50, bring your own wine). The two double/twin rooms are of a high standard. No smoking, no dogs, children should be over 10. B&B £30–£32. Address: Georgina & David Ryott, Leathley Cottage, Leathley, nr **Otley**, North Yorkshire LS21 2JY. Tel 01132 843406

If It's Wet

Newby Hall (*see* Garden 3) is a beautifully restored Adam house with a magnificent tapestry room, library, statue gallery and some of Chippendale's finest furniture. **Norton Conyers** (Garden 5) has family pictures, furniture and costumes, and is of interest to anyone who has read Charlotte Brontë. Opening times are as for gardens.

On the E edge of the visit map, adjoining the A1 just N of its junction with the A59, is **Allerton Park**, once owned by Prince Frederick, brother to King George IV. It is extraordinarily grand and ornate, with huge rooms, extensive panelling and much intricate carving. All the main rooms can be seen, including the great hall, drawing-room, morning-room, library and dining-room. (If you want to celebrate with, say, 50 friends you can hire the place for your personal enjoyment.) Open Suns and BH Mons, Easter to Sept, 1–6. Tel 01423 330927.

Harrogate has plenty to offer. The Royal Pump Room Museum certainly shouldn't be missed. Housed in the town's foremost spa building, and site of Europe's strongest sulphur well, displays show why visitors from all over the world made Harrogate the place to be at the turn of the century. Two famous and traditional tea rooms are still in their prime: Betty's Café, and the Pump Hall where music is played in the best Palm Court tradition.

Ripon has an altogether different sort of character. The city dates from the 7th century, and has a cathedral not to be missed, approached through old cobbled streets. You will find plenty of good shops here, but true shopaholics ought to go to the more modern **Lightwater Village**. It is signed on the L of the A6108, 2½ m NW of Ripon, and has a courtyard of buildings devoted to 'factory shopping' where you can find extraordinary discounts, as well as traditional butchers, bakers and delicatessen and Yorkshire's biggest cheese shop.

Eating Out

Within the grounds of **Ripley Castle** (*see* Garden 2) is a 19th-century coaching inn, the **Bull's Head**, adorned with paintings and furnishings from the castle. Lady Ingilby oversees things here, and the atmosphere and food are outstanding. You will probably spend about £35 per head, particularly if you dip into Sir Thomas Ingilby's wine list, which has more than 200 wines from which to choose. You can stay here too, in luxury bedrooms with wonderful bathrooms where Lady Ingilby provides little wooden catamarans for you to play with – 'so that you can push the boat out' she says. B&B £45–£55. Tel 01423 771888.

The Lake District

The mountains and lakes in this spectacular part of England have inspired many writers and painters. Wordsworth lived and wrote much of his poetry here. Ruskin lived here, too. Turner painted here. There are some great gardens to visit, all of them designed to make the most of the scenery. A very English, grave and beautiful piece of music to listen to in these surroundings is Elgar's 'The Music Makers', with words by Arthur O'Shaugnessy. This work has always been very popular with choirs in the north of England. The best version I know has the voice of Dame Janet Baker, with Sir Adrian Boult conducting.

OS maps: Landrangers 90, **97**

Gardens

Opening times: in larger gardens, and in NT properties, last admissions are usually 30–45 minutes before the garden closes. Admission charges are a guide to what one adult can expect to pay to go round the garden. It sometimes varies with the season or days of the week. When the house is also open to the public, there is usually an additional charge.

I   HOLKER HALL   nr Grange-over-Sands   Tel 01539 558328

Daily except Sat, end March to Oct, 10–6 (last admission 4.30). £3.15
From Grange-over-Sands go W on B5277 for 3m. In Flookburgh turn R onto B5278 for 1½m. Garden signed on L.

Lord Cavendish and his ancestors have developed this garden over two centuries. Lord George Cavendish, godson of George II, planted many of the trees including the Cedar of Lebanon grown from seed brought back from the Middle East. Joseph Paxton gave advice on enlarging the gardens and added the extensive walled garden, hot-houses, an arboretum and a fountain. Recently, a new cascade has been created, the rose garden enlarged and a rhododendron and azalea walk planted. Many rare and ancient trees

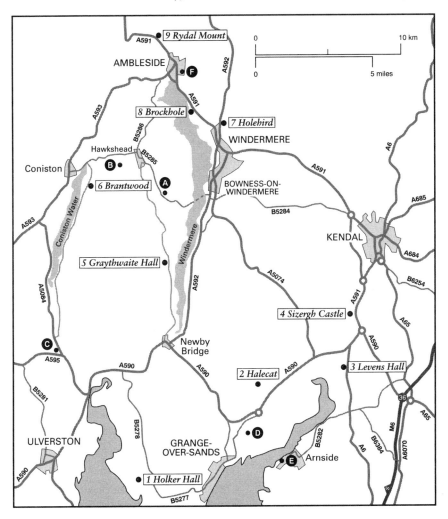

grace the garden, and in spring great drifts of daffodils light up the wood-land. Wildflowers and martagon lilies thrive here. The summer garden is always full of colour to delight the visitors. The prestigious 'Great Garden and Countryside Festival' is held at Holker, usually on the last weekend in May.

2 HALECAT

Witherslack, nr Grange-over-Sands   Tel 01539 552229

Mon–Fri, April to Sept, 9–4.30. Garden free.
From Kendal go S on A591 for 3½ m. At roundabout junction go SW on A590
for 6m. Turn R for ½ m to Witherslack; garden signed on L near centre of the
village.

Mrs Stanley came here nearly 45 years ago, and immediately started work on the garden at the head of a small valley, looking across to Arnside Knott. It is divided in sections, each with a different character. Colour is achieved over a long period of the year, with interesting hedges of potentilla, philadelphus, prunus and whitebeam, under-planted with blue and pink hardy geraniums and masses of daffodils. The sunken garden has a very pretty gazebo, designed by F.F. Johnson in the Gothic style. He also designed four obelisks in the upper garden, and a lovely flight of steps. Azaleas grow well here, and Mrs Stanley has more than 70 varieties of hydrangeas. There is an excellent nursery attached, with plants for sale particularly of interest to flower arrangers.

Nearby is **Holme Cragg** where Jack Watson has made a natural garden of great interest to botanists and bird watchers. It has rockeries, shrubberies, a large pond, and a woodland area with wildflowers. It is open by appointment all year (Tel 01539 552366). From Witherslack, follow signs towards High Newton for 1½ m. There is a garden open sign on the gate on R.

3 LEVENS HALL   nr Kendal   Tel 01539 560321

Sun–Thurs, April to Sept, 11–5. £3.50
From Kendal go S on A591 for 3½ m. At roundabout junction go SW on A590
for ½ m and then turn L onto A6 for 1½ m. Garden signed on R.

This is one of Britain's most renowned gardens, famous for the topiary designed by Guillaume Beaumont in 1694, since when it has grown mightily. Most gardens of this time were ripped out later, when the natural landscape look advocated by Capability Brown became so popular. Luckily, Levens decided not to be fashionable. The topiary is of yew and box. There are chess pieces, a judge's wig, four peacocks, Queen Elizabeth I and her maids and a great umbrella. Some of the topiary is bejewelled with scarlet *Tropæolum speciosum*. The box parterre is bedded out twice a year, using more than 15,000 plants, and every year the topiary takes 6 weeks to trim.

Other delights are the rose garden, with David Austin's English roses under-planted with aquilegia, polyanthus, campanulas and alliums, plus many varieties of foxgloves. The principal herbaceous borders are on the main axial pathway either side of a great beech circle. Large shrub roses are used to give height, with cardoons, fennel and billowing clouds of *Crambe cordifolia*. You can enjoy an ornamental vegetable garden, the orchard and the nuttery. In the herb garden, the central bed is of lavender, with a huge stone urn in the middle full of *Pelargonium tomentosum*. Wigwams of golden hop give height, and the Apothecary's rose flanks the path. The Bagot family still live here, and the famous Bagot goats with their long curved horns roam in the old deer park, along with black fallow deer. You need a whole day to explore all the delights here. Lunches and teas are made in the hall kitchen. Home-propagated plants are for sale, and the children can let off steam in a play area. There is a steam engine collection: steaming-up day is Sunday.

4   SIZERGH CASTLE (NT)   nr Kendal   Tel 01539 560070

Sun–Thurs, April to Oct, 12.30–5.30. £2
From Kendal go S on A 591 for 3m. At roundabout junction with A590, double-back to the R and follow signs to garden, 1m N.

This great fortified mansion has been the home of the Strickland family for more than 750 years, and the house is steeped in history. The garden, made in the 1920s, is renowned for one of the best limestone rock gardens in England. Japanese maples have matured into magnificent gnarled specimens. A stream splashes through the garden, and there is a large collection of hardy ferns. The rose garden has my favourite moss and musk roses, there are fat herbaceous borders and a terrace wall with tender climbers ramping up it. Steps lead down to a lake, where wildflowers, including orchids, grow on its banks. The castle is wreathed in Virginia creeper, spectacular to see when the leaves turn russet.

5   GRAYTHWAITE HALL

nr Newby Bridge   Tel 01539 531248

Daily, April to mid July, 10–6. £2.50
From Newby Bridge go briefly NW on A590, crossing to W side of Windermere. Go N on minor road along lakeside. After 4m, garden signed on L.

This is a lovely creation by Thomas Mawson. The formal gardens around the house include a rose garden, a Dutch garden and some spectacular topiary in the form of battlemented yew hedges. The lawns drop down to a stream and woodlands, crammed with azaleas, rhododendrons and spring-flowering shrubs. It's best in May and early June. Dogs can visit on leads.

6 BRANTWOOD nr Hawkshead Tel 01539 441396

Daily, mid March to mid Nov, 11–5.30. Sun–Wed rest of year closing at dusk.
£1
From Hawkshead go S along Coniston Water for 1½ m. Garden well signed on
L. Or you can take a boat from Coniston Pier.

This is quite the most beautifully situated house in the Lake District, enjoying the finest lake and mountain views. Its cultural associations are profound. Ruskin, whose philosophy influenced Gandhi, Proust, Tolstoy and Frank Lloyd Wright, lived here from 1872 until his death in 1900. Little paths zig-zag up and down the slope. The old kitchen garden and the harbour walk provide stunning displays of daffodils, old azaleas and cottage garden flowers. Ferns and bluebells grow in the upper oak woods, and there are masses of rhododendrons in the woodland garden.

7 HOLEHIRD Troutbeck, nr Windermere Tel 01539 446008

Daily, all year, sunrise to sunset. Entrance by donation.
From Windermere town go NW for ½ m on A591. Turn R on A592. Garden
signed ½ m on R.

The Lakeland Horticultural Society's garden covers 4 acres, and is looked after by members who maintain it to a very high standard. On a marvellous site, with rocks, streams and grand views, it contains splendid trees, a rock garden, heathers, a winter garden, two alpine houses, masses of roses, dwarf conifers and the National Collection of astilbes and hydrangeas. The walled garden has a huge variety of herbaceous perennials and herbs, everything well labelled. It is very much a place for garden-lovers, and those who will appreciate the quiet tranquillity here.

8 BROCKHOLE nr Windermere Tel 01539 446601

Daily, end March to early Nov, 10–dusk. Free to pedestrians. Car park £2.50
From Windermere town go NW for 1½ m on A591. Garden signed on L.

These popular gardens cover 10 acres and were designed by Thomas Mawson. With a mild westerly aspect and acid soil, many rare and usually tender shrubs thrive here. At the top of the garden are formal terraces with burgeoning roses, herbaceous borders, shrubs and a scented garden. The view from here is across to the Langdale Pikes. Lower down the hill is woodland, a wildflower meadow which is simply glorious in early summer, and another 20 acres of informal pleasure gardens which include an adventure playground and picnic spots.

9   RYDAL MOUNT   Ambleside   Tel 01539 433002

Daily, March to Oct, 9.30–5; Daily except Tues, Nov to Feb, 10–4. £3
From Ambleside go NW on A591 for 1m. Garden signed on R.

Rydal Mount was the home of William Wordsworth from 1813 until his death in 1850. All the Wordsworths were keen gardeners, and William designed the garden here. He wanted it to harmonise with the countryside, and thought it should consist of 'lawns and trees carefully planted so as not to obscure the view'. He built three terraces and a summer-house, and set out a curving path leading to the fell above. It is lovely here in spring and autumn, with colour from a collection of acers and rare shrubs. There are tens of thousands of bluebells and daffodils, good herbaceous borders and an ancient mound to climb to view Windermere the lake.

Where to Stay

All B&B prices are approximate per person, sharing a double/twin room usually with private or en suite facilities. It is a good idea to ask for any special requirements when booking.

A   EES WYKE   Tel 01539 436393

John & Margaret Williams, Ees Wyke, Sawrey, nr Hawkshead, Cumbria LA22 0JZ.

Beatrix Potter used to spend holidays in this handsome Georgian house, and loved the outlook so much that she made the village of Sawrey her home. Staying here is a real treat, with Margaret pampering guests and creating a house-party atmosphere in her beautifully furnished small hotel. John cooks the evening meals, which are amazingly good value (5 courses, licensed, £12, with a good choice on the menu). His breakfasts are banquets. There are two sitting-rooms to relax in, and the views from the dining-room are stunning. Of the 8 double/twin bedrooms, 3 have an en suite bathroom and the remainder have showers or share a bathroom. No smoking in dining-room, no dogs in public rooms, children should be over 8. B&B £38.

B   HIGHFIELD HOUSE   Tel 01539 436344

Pauline & Jim Bennett, Highfield House, Hawkshead Hill, nr Ambleside, Cumbria LA22 0PN.

This country hotel has a large terraced garden, set on a hillside with panoramic views. Pauline and Jim are great at making you feel at home here. The furnishings are comfortable and mainly modern, and there is a cosy bar as well as a large sitting-room for guests. Dinners (£16, licensed) are notable for their generosity and for sweet and sticky puddings. The 11 bedrooms include 2 singles, and are all en suite. Children welcome, no dogs in public rooms, and no smoking in the dining-room. B&B £31–£35.

C   LOWICK HOUSE   Tel 01229 885227

Dorothy Sutcliffe, Lowick House, Lowick Green, nr Ulverston, Cumbria LA12 8DX.

The gardens around this substantial white-painted house, dating from the early 18th century, are marvellous. Surrounded by farmland with a back-cloth of fells, they are landscaped and planted over a total of 2 acres, with a trout stream and lawns where ducks waddle. Dorothy is an enthusiastic hostess whose candle-lit dinners (£20, bring your own wine) are memorable. The house is full of antiques, and the 2 double/twin bedrooms very comfortable. Children and dogs welcome, restricted smoking. B&B £30–£33.

D   GREENACRES   Tel 01539 534578

Joe & Anne Danson, Greenacres, Lindale, nr Grange-over-Sands, Cumbria LA11 6LP.

Since this charming 19th-century cottage was lavishly refurbished a few years ago, it has won a number of awards and recommendations not just for its comfort but for the warmth of welcome you receive from Anne and Joe. Dinner (£13.50, licensed) is served in a pretty dining-room, with a conservatory and sitting-room alongside. Packed lunches to take with you on your garden visits are a speciality. The 5 double/twin bedrooms are all en suite. Strictly no smoking, no dogs, and children (over 12) are by arrangement. B&B £26.

E 4 REDHILLS ROAD Tel 01524 761778

Dan & Margaret Bateman, 4 Redhills Rd, Arnside, Cumbria LA5 0AR.

Margaret is a garden lover and, being on the committee of the local horticultural society, can point you towards many gardens open by appointment only. Her own cottage garden around the gabled house is informal and full of interesting plants which give something to enjoy all year round, with many varieties of fuchsias, clematis and hardy geraniums, a small pond and alpines and heathers. Arnside is a peaceful place, so far not over-run by tourists, and only a minute away from the shore of the Kent estuary. You will find it very peaceful here. There are 2 double/twin bedrooms, sharing a bathroom. Eat out locally at many pubs and restaurants in the area. No smoking, dogs and children by arrangement. B&B £18.

F KENT HOUSE Tel 01539 433279

Margaret & Richard Lee, Kent House, Lake Road, Ambleside, Cumbria LA22 0AD.

This lakeland house is like so many you see around here – solid, stone-built, warm and comfortable. The garden and views are lovely for a wander before dinner, and you can play tennis if you're feeling energetic. Dinners (£14, licensed) are substantial and much praised. Of the 6 bedrooms, 3 are en suite, the others sharing a bathroom. No smoking, dogs and children welcome. B&B £14–£20.

What Else to Enjoy

This is a short selection of the many good things recommended in the area by owners of places to stay. Your hosts will certainly be able to provide additional information.

Other Gardens / Nurseries

On the edge of visit map, 3m S of Arnside, is the little sea-side town of **Ilverdale.** Here Reginald Kaye runs **Wathmans Nurseries**, specialising in rock and alpine plants, with particularly good examples of campanulas and saxifrages. Open daily, March to Oct, 8–5.30 (closed lunchtime 12.30–2). He is hard to find, so telephone for final directions. Tel 01524 710252.

If It's Wet

In **Hawkshead**, the **Beatrix Potter Gallery** is housed in the building where her husband, William Heelis, worked as a solicitor, its interior almost unaltered since his time. The NT's exhibition changes somewhat every year, but always has selections of the original drawings and illustrations for her children's story books. Open daily, April to Oct, 10.30–4.30 (Fri 2–4.30). To prevent overcrowding, a timed ticket system is used. Tel 01539 436355.

The small cottage where Beatrix Potter wrote many of her books is the NT-owned **Hill Top**. It contains many of her belongings and has a charming old-fashioned garden. It is in the hamlet of **Near Sawrey**, 2m S of Hawkshead on the B5285. Open Sat–Wed (and Good Fri), April to Oct, 11–5. Tel 01539 436269. Be warned: the NT allows a maximum of 800 visitors a day, and there are often long queues. The adjoining **Tower Bank Arms**, also NT-owned, has good bar lunches.

The late medieval **Sizergh Castle** (*see* Garden 4) has been occupied by the Strickland family for more than 750 years. Much of the interior dates from Elizabethan times; you find magnificent plasterwork, carved stone and intricate over-mantels as well as fine furniture and furnishings. Open as for garden.

Nearby, there is excellent local produce to be bought at **The Barn Shop**, at Low Sizergh Farm, **Sizergh**. The cheeses, made by traditional methods, are particularly good. There is a large range of other foods, including home-cured bacon and black pudding, and a craft gallery. Find it by going E from Sizergh Castle for ½ m under the A591. The shop is signed immediately on L. Tel 01539 560426.

Eating Out

The Nixon family has been running **Rothay Manor** as a country house hotel for 30 years, and Jane Binns has been chef for nearly 20 years. The Regency building is set back from Lake Windermere and has landscaped gardens. Local produce lies at the heart of the imaginative cooking. Set dinner menus are from £23–£29 per person. Find it at Rothay Bridge, **Ambleside**. Tel 01539 433605.

Northumbria

Castles and fortresses, built to keep out marauding Scots, abound in this visit. To the south-west is Hadrian's Wall, to the north and north-west are the Cheviot Hills and to the east are great cliffs and long beaches. Hexham is a charming old market town, and you should try to visit Hexham Herb garden there. As you must have guessed by now, I am very keen on English composers, and their music suits this landscape perfectly. Drive along listening to William Walton's Viola Concerto, played by Nigel Kennedy with André Previn conducting the Royal Philharmonic Orchestra.

OS maps: Landrangers **81**, 87, **88**

Gardens

Opening times: in larger gardens, and in NT properties, last admissions are usually 30–45 minutes before the garden closes. Admission charges are a guide to what one adult can expect to pay to go round the garden. It sometimes varies with the season or days of the week. When the house is also open to the public, there is usually an additional charge.

1 KIRKLEY HALL COLLEGE nr Ponteland Tel 01661 860808

Mon—Fri all year, 10—4, and by appointment. £1.50
From centre of Ponteland go N on minor road N signed Kirkley. On outskirts of town fork L and continue for 2½ m. Horticultural centre signed immediately ahead at T-junction.

Kirkley Hall is an agricultural college, where plenty of students keep the garden amazingly tidy and full of healthy plants. Mown paths meander around the 12-acre site, with many island beds. There is a strong emphasis on contrasting foliage, form and colours. More traditional herbaceous borders are in the Victorian walled garden where you find lovely big clumps of astrantias, hostas, euphorbias and phlox. The salad potager is highly ornamental, and fruit trees are trained against what would once have been

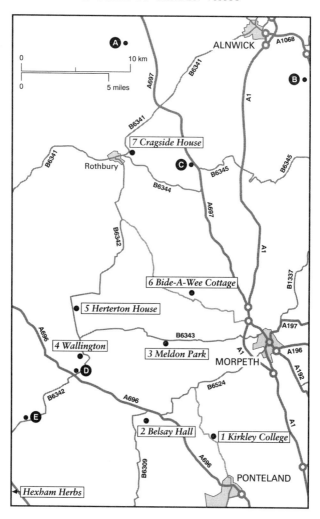

heated walls. The terraces have many large containers, creatively planted, leading down to a sunken garden planted with dwarf conifers; there is also a wildlife pond. The work of local sculptors is displayed in the garden. It's great to find everything so clearly labelled.

2 BELSAY HALL   nr Ponteland   Tel 01661 881636

Daily, April to Oct, 10–6; rest of year 10–4. £3
From Ponteland go NW for on A696 for 8m. Garden signed on L.

Belsay is remarkable for its quarry garden. Stone for building the house in 1795 was taken from here, leaving a rugged and dramatic backdrop for the informal planting. Banks of native and exotic ferns, rogersias, ligularia and huge gunneras are planted in boggy areas created by underground streams. The rhododendrons in early summer make a splendid display. Near the house are terraces with deep mixed borders, a magnolia terrace and a winter garden with heathers and a giant Douglas fir. The sunken lawns are used for croquet tournaments – fun to watch. There is a tea-room, a picnic area, and dogs are allowed on leads.

3 MELDON PARK   nr Morpeth   Tel 01670 772661

Daily late May to late June, 2–5; also August BH, some charity Suns, and by appointment. £3
From Morpeth go W on B6343 for 6m. About ½m after Dyke Neuk Inn, garden signed on L.

This fine house, built by John Dobson in 1832, is now home to Mr and Mrs Cookson. It is framed by a magnificent old cedar which gives an air of calm serenity. There is a charming Edwardian rose garden, and an old conservatory (now a painter's studio). A splendid herbaceous border is stuffed with peonies, and leading away from the house is a woodland walk with many rare rhododendrons and unusual varieties of daffodils. The walled garden is lovely, with espaliered apples running down the centre as a backdrop to two beautiful double herbaceous borders. Old greenhouses are charming, and along the warm walls grow figs, nectarines and grapes. Mrs Cookson is an enthusiastic and knowledgeable gardener and fearlessly re-plants any area she is not happy with.

4 WALLINGTON (NT)
Cambo, nr Morpeth   Tel 01670 774283

Daily, April to Oct, 10–7. Rest of year 10–4. £2.30
From Morpeth go W on B6343 for 12m. At T-junction in Cambo turn L on B6342 for 1m. In Wallington, garden signed on R.

It's marvellous that this garden can be viewed all the year round, because it can be magical on a frosty morning. The garden is a good walk from the house, through the beautiful East Wood. On the way, you pass ponds, follies and fragments of stone statuary. The walled garden contains a conservatory on the upper terrace, with clouds of plumbago, jasmine, abutilons and an ancient fuchsia thought to be nearly 100 years old. Clematis covers an arch over the steep path which is bordered by brilliant flower beds. For a longer, circular walk, you can take the path to the West Wood. This area is left fairly wild, and the path runs beside a shaded river you can cross via stepping stones. You can then approach the walled kitchen garden through an avenue of gnarled old apple trees. Sir George Trevelyan designed the arrangement of terraces, walks, borders and lawns when he inherited Wallington in 1886, and his ideas still form the bones of this lovely garden. When Capability Brown was a boy, he lived locally, and would often have walked this way; I like to think this landscape had a strong influence on him. Wallington holds the National Collection of sambucus.

5   HERTERTON HOUSE

Hartington, nr Morpeth   Tel 01670 774278

Daily except Tues and Thurs, April to Sept, 1.30–5.30. £2
From centre of Morpeth go briefly N on A192. Turn L on B6343 for 12m. At T-junction in Cambo, turn R on B6342 for 2m. Turn R into lane signed Hartington. Garden is 100 yards on L.

Frank and Marjorie Lawley came to Herterton House in 1975. They found a wilderness and three derelict stone buildings – hard to believe now when you see this lovely Elizabethan house and ravishing garden which is divided into five distinct areas. The formal garden in front of the house has immaculate clipped yews and box, with holly and ivy. The physic garden is in a simple knot, around a clipped silver pear. Beds are edged with thrift and dwarf London Pride. The flower garden is full of their favourites – veronicas, valerian, campanulas and poppies. The nursery garden is divided into narrow beds, with stock raised here to sell. The soil is wonderfully prepared, looking like rich Christmas pudding, and plants for sale are dug straight out of the beds and wrapped in paper. Nothing is under-nourished or pot-bound here. A fifth part of the garden, under development, has an ornate summerhouse and two parterres filled with unusual annuals. The Lawleys are fanatical plantsmen, and their garden should not be missed.

6   BIDE-A-WEE COTTAGE

Stanton, nr Morpeth   Tel 01670 772262

Sats, May to Aug, 1.30–5, and groups by appointment. £1.75
From centre of Morpeth go NW on A192 for 1m. Turn L onto minor rd signed
to Netherwitton. After 6m turn R into Stanton village. Garden is immediately
on L.

This fascinating garden has been developed over the past fifteen years by
Mark Robson, and now incorporates an adjacent field and a disused sandstone quarry. Dense shelterbelts have been planted, and in summer the
quarry is so thick with colour and plants that the little winding paths are
almost obscured. A large pool is fringed with bog-loving plants – gunneras,
rogersias, ligularias and primulas. Planting around the cottage is more
formal where Mark's skill as a stonemason and plantsman is very evident.
The garden has been featured on TV and in leading horticultural magazines.
A neighbouring meadow has had no artificial fertilizer for three years, and
an amazing array of wildflowers is becoming established there. This garden
is the perfect antidote to Cragside.

7   CRAGSIDE HOUSE (NT)

nr Rothbury   Tel 01669 620333

Daily except Mons (open BH Mons), April to Oct, 10.30–6. £3.60
From Rothbury go NE on B6341 for ½m. Garden signed on R.

Cragside was built for Lord Armstrong, the Victorian engineer, and was the
first house to be lit by hydro-electricity. The garden is solidly Victorian. A
3-acre rock garden surrounds the house, with heathers, alpines, small shrubs
and bulbs, and is particularly fine in spring when the landscaped grounds
have hundreds of rhododendrons amid fine conifers. The formal gardens are
set apart from the house, and there are fabulous views from the terrace.
An orchard-house with revolving pots of vines, figs, peaches and cherries is
fascinating. Below it is an Italian terrace with a rose loggia at its centre: this
originally had glass panels for tender perennials which are still a speciality
of this garden. There is a display of Victorian summer bedding plants, and
that Victorian favourite, a fernery.

Where to Stay

All B&B prices are approximate per person, sharing a double/twin room usually with private or en suite facilities. It is a good idea to ask for any special requirements when booking.

A CALLALY MAINS   Tel 01665 574665

Anne Fisher, Callaly Mains, Whittingham, Northumberland NE66 4SZ.

Anne is a passionate Northumbrian whose family has been in the county for more than 700 years. Callaly Mains is a handsome grey stone house, gloriously set in the Cheviot foothills with wonderful views from a large, well-kept garden. Anne sets herself very high standards. The rooms are beautifully furnished, with lovely touches such as hand-embroidered sheets in the 3 bedrooms, of which 1 is a single. Evening meals (£22.50, bring your own wine) are based on fresh local produce. Restricted smoking, dogs welcome by arrangement, children should be over 8. B&B £38.

B HIGH BUSTON HALL   Tel 01665 830341

John & Alison Edwards, High Buston Hall, nr Alnwick, Northumberland NE66 3QH.

There are fine views, with the sea in the distance, from the landscaped garden of this award-winning place to stay. The Georgian house has beautifully proportioned rooms, with period furnishings and decor. John and Alison give you a great welcome, with a lavish tea in front of the sitting-room fire. The 3 double/twin bedrooms are exceptionally comfortable; one has a sea view. Evening meals (£22, wine to be discussed) should be arranged in advance. No smoking, no dogs, children welcome. B&B £28–£30.

C RIMSIDE HOUSE   Tel 01665 570259

Derek & Norma Sadler, Rimside House, Longframlington, Northumberland NE65 8DR.

Three acres of garden, pasture and woodland surround this square-built early 19th-century house. There is a relaxed and informal feel to your stay here – it's very much a come-and-go-as-you-please sort of place. The 3 spacious double/twin are en suite. You can arrange in advance for evening meals (£14, bring your own wine), where the vegetables are usually from

Derek and Norma's garden. No smoking, no dogs, children to be discussed. B&B £26–£28.

D SHIELDHALL   Tel 01830 540387

Stephen & Celia Robinson-Gaye, Shieldhall, Wallington, nr Morpeth, Northumberland NE61 4AQ.

Stephen and Celia's 18th-century farmhouse nestles into the rolling Northumbrian landscape and overlooks the NT's Wallington estate (*see* Garden 4). The gardens, with fine old trees and a croquet lawn, make much use of local stone. Stephen is a cabinet-maker (you can watch him in his workshop) who restores and copies antique furniture. His workmanship is displayed in the superb conversions of the outbuildings which now provide 7 ground-floor double/twin bedrooms, one with a four-poster. Inside the main house, there is a lovely library leading to a small bar. Dinner menus (£15, bring your own wine) should be discussed in advance. No smoking, children welcome, dogs by arrangement. B&B £20–£26.

E OLD POST OFFICE COTTAGE   Tel 01830 530331

John & Christine Rodger, Old Post Office Cottage, Little Bavington, nr Ponteland, Northumberland NE 19 2BB.

Roses and climbers ramble over this pretty cottage, its garden surrounded by peaceful countryside. Inside, the house is warm and comfortable, heavily beamed and with a large log fire in the sitting-room. There are 2 double/twin bedrooms, sharing a bathroom. Christine enjoys cooking, often using French-based recipes for seasonal dishes with local produce. Evening meals (from £12, bring your own wine) should be arranged in advance. Children welcome, no smoking, dogs by arrangement. B&B £15–£18.

What Else to Enjoy

This is a short selection of the many good things recommended in the area by owners of places to stay. Your hosts will certainly be able to provide additional information.

Other Gardens/Nurseries

Even though it is off our map to the SW, I urge you to visit **Hexham Herbs**. It is as much a garden as a nursery, with dense planting inside box-edged beds set in a 2-acre walled garden. Herbaceous and wildflower plants are for sale, but the speciality here – and the National Collection – is thyme, with more than 120 varieties. Open daily, Easter to Oct, 1–6, or by appointment. Find it by going N from Hexham for 3m on A6079. Turn L briefly on B6318 to cross river and go round Chesters Fort in **Chollerford**. Garden signed on L. Tel 01434 681483.

If It's Wet

English Heritage have mounted an excellent exhibition at **Belsay Hall** (*see* Garden 2) showing how the house evolved from a fortified dwelling to a neo-classical mansion over the course of 600 years. Open as garden.

Wallington Hall (Garden 4) is a gracious country house largely lacking the formality of so many of the NT's stately homes. Built in 1688, it has exceptional plasterwork, fine collections of porcelain and dolls' houses and a Museum of Curiosities. Opening hours as garden, but only from April to Oct.

Cragside (Garden 7) is an extraordinary, vast Victorian house built by the first Lord Armstrong, notable in its time as being the only house to be lit by hydro-electricity. Today, the interior is a showpiece for Victorian art, architecture and technology. Open as garden.

Alnwick is a lovely old town in which to potter about, with history seeping out of every street. The helpful Tourist Information Centre in the Shambles (Tel 01665 510665) will guide you through a circular walk. The crowning glory is, of course, Alnwick Castle, which Victorians used to describe as the 'Windsor of the North'. Home of the Dukes of Northumberland, it is open daily all year, 10–5. Tel 01665 510777.

Eating Out

Alnwick also has the most-recommended place to enjoy a rich meal. At **Sim's**, Wyn Coltman, with her son-in-law Richard as chef, runs a charming and intimate restaurant with delicious food. They specialise in local game and fish and have two dining-rooms, each seating about 20 people, in their 18th-century house at 22 Narrowgate, close to the castle in Alnwick. Main courses cost £8–£15. With wine, expect to spend £25 per head. Tel 01665 602050.

Indexes

Gardens and Nurseries

Places to Stay

Restaurants and Pubs